ORATIONS

JOSEPH CHOATE

Orations—Volume twenty-one

ORATIONS

FROM HOMER TO
WILLIAM MCKINLEY

EDITED BY

MAYO W. HAZELTINE, A.M

ILLUSTRATED
IN TWENTY-FIVE VOLUMES
VOL. XXI

NEW YORK
P. F. COLLIER AND SON
MCMII

CONTENTS

VOLUME TWENTY-ONE

ORATIONS

CARPENTER

MATTHEW HALE CARPENTER, an American statesman, was born at Moretown, Vermont, December 22, 1824, and educated at the United States Military Institute. He then studied law in Waterbury, Vermont, being admitted to the bar in 1847 and removing the next year to Beloit, Wisconsin, where he soon rose to prominence in his profession. In 1856 he made Milwaukee his home and when the civil war broke out he travelled extensively in the west, making many speeches in behalf of the Union cause. He received the appointment of judge advocate general of Wisconsin and in 1868 was engaged as government counsel in the famous McArdle case, which involved the legality of the Reconstruction Act of 1867. His success in this instance brought him into such prominence that he was soon after elected to the United States Senate, serving there 1869-75. After practising his profession for a few years he was in 1879 again returned to the Senate, but did not live to complete his term of office, dying in Washington February 25, 1881. Carpenter was known politically as "a war Democrat," opposing the Fugitive Slave law in his earlier career, advocating emancipation of the slaves as early as 1864, and in 1864 declaring that they must be enfranchised. Among his more noted efforts in the Senate were his speeches on Johnson's Amnesty Proclamation, on the bill to restore Fitz John Porter, and his defence of President Grant against the attack of Sumner. His name was originally Decatur Merritt Hammond Carpenter, but about the time of his removal to Wisconsin he adopted the signature by which he was afterwards known.

MISSION AND FUTURE POLICY OF THE UNITED STATES

DELIVERED AT THE DEDICATION OF MEMORIAL HALL, BELOIT
COLLEGE, JULY, 1869

MR. PRESIDENT, LADIES AND GENTLEMEN,— The American people have just emerged from the thick darkness of national distresses: emerged, as no other nation could reasonably have expected to from such dangers, triumphant, though bleeding at every pore. The first impulse of a great people on being delivered from eminent perils is that of joy and thanksgiving; then comes gratitude for those by whose guidance, under God, safety

(8767)

has been attained; then a sad reflection upon the fearf
sacrifices by which success has been purchased and a tend
recollection of those who have fallen in the strife; and finall
the composed mind gathers up the teachings of such a fea
ful experience,—wisdom for the guidance of future year
On the surrender of Lee and Johnston in 1865 our peop
gave themselves up to the wildest rejoicings; for a time th
toils, the trials, the sufferings of four dreadful years were a
forgotten; business places were closed, our people rushe
out of doors, impromptu processions filled the streets, musi
led our exultant emotions as far as musical sounds could con
duct them; and then the roar of cannon and the shoutings o
the multitude took up the joyful strain and bore it in tumul
to the skies. Our people are fond of excitement and may be
aroused to enthusiasm upon slight provocation. But ther
the grounds for national rejoicing were adequate and philosophical. Such dangers as had never threatened any government had been averted; such a rebellion as the world had
never seen had been suppressed; such results as had never
before been accomplished by war had been achieved. We
plunged into the war cursed with the institution of slavery,—
three millions of our fellow creatures held in bitter bondage;
we came forth a nation of free men, equal in civil rights, no
longer recognizing any distinctions of caste or color. Our
young Republic had successfully ended the experiment of its
existence and for the first time took its place—a full, round,
high place—among the powers of the earth. We had to
thank God, after the storms of war had passed, that we at
last possessed what our fathers had hoped and prayed for, " a
country, and that a free country."

Our people had shown their gratitude to their leaders in
works more substantial than words. They have raised Grant

ove the army to the chair of Washington. Sherman they
ve made their chief captain; an appointment for life with
nual salary second only to that of the president. Sheridan
ey have made the worthy lieutenant of such a captain; and
hers have been rewarded, and are still to be honored ac-
ording to their great merits. The widows and orphans of
ie war have been generously provided for. Everything
iat could be has been done to smooth the scars of a fright-
ul struggle. We have demonstrated that a great people
now how to be both just and generous.

And now, four years after the war and after the imme-
iate and pressing demands upon us have been fully satis-
ied toward those who survived and came back to us from the
attle-field, we have come in the midst of profound peace
and general prosperity, on this beautiful day of teeming sumner, to show our reverence for those who came not back
from the war; and to dedicate to their memory the beautiful
hall which you have erected, monumental in form, and useful in fact; thus uniting the memory of the departed with
one of the great facilities for acquiring knowledge, a college
library.

Pericles delivered his great oration, which Thucydides has
preserved for us,—one of the grandest specimens of ancient
art,—standing by the unburied remains of those who had
fallen on the field and surrounded by weeping mourners
whose anguish had not yet been soothed by the healing power
of time. Nevertheless, by far the greater part of that oration is devoted to an examination of the character of Athenian institutions; to show that those who had fallen for
Athens had not died for a vain or useless thing.

We stand here to-day not in the freshness of individual
grief; not to pay the last sad offices of respect to the out-

ward material forms of those we have loved. Over their graves the green grass is waving and tropical flowers are cheerfully blossoming. Time has dried our tears and composed our emotions. The sister comes not to weep for the brother; the father comes not to bend over the ghastly remains of his first born, not yet committed to sepulture. But we come as American citizens to thank God that in our deepest need the patriotism of our people was equal to the hour; we come to reflect rather than to weep; we come to gather up the lessons taught by their example; to consider the fruits of the victory they have secured for us, and hence to deduce our duty as a nation in the great future which opens before us with immortal splendor.

You have just been addressed by Professor Emerson, specially upon the character and services of those whose names are to be engraved upon the tablet of honor in this memorial hall. He knew them personally, loved them well, and has spoken of them with the tenderness befitting his theme, and an earnest eloquence becoming to himself. I shall therefore devote the short time allotted to me to a consideration of the character of our government and its duty in the immediate future.

God never made a man for the sake of making him; nor that he might amass wealth and corrupt himself with its enjoyment. Every man is sent into the world with certain qualities to be cultivated and developed; charged with duties to be performed, and clothed with responsibilities commensurate with his power; sent into the world that some other may be better for his having lived. So with nations; they grow up not for themselves alone; they are ordained of God; they are the instrumentalities by which God accomplishes his purposes towards the human race. They who study

human history, they who believe in the Gospels of Christ—
believe that the very hairs of our head are numbered and
that not a sparrow falls without his notice—cannot doubt
that empires come and go, and states are born and perish, in
obedience to his sovereign will. . . .

A little band of patriots, of God-fearing men, lovers of
liberty because lovers of God, too few to stand upright in
England, too resolute of purpose to submit to tyranny,
turned their steps, still westward, and in mid-winter planted
the empire of freedom upon this then unpromising continent.
It is quite unnecessary, for you are as familiar with it as I
am, and time would fail me to dwell upon the details of that
settlement, and the settlement of other colonies upon these
shores. I only refer to it to ask you, who protected them
from famine, from dissensions internal, from dangers external, from the inclemency of the elements, and the hostility of savages? Who gave them the courage and inspired
them with the faith equal to their great task? Turn over
in your own minds, for I have no time even to refer to the
strange incidents in their wonderful history, verifying our
belief that God superintends the founding of States; follow
the colonies through their infancy, down to the commencement of the revolution which ultimately separated them
from the parent State and made us an independent nation,
and then say, do you believe God had no part, no design in
all those wonderful events? He saw the end from the beginning; and the beginning would not have been if the end had
not been intended.

It is true that the love of liberty in their hearts, the
tyranny of their king, their fleeing to these shores, their
founding of a free commonwealth, their growth to power as
a people, were all natural events. No supernatural inter-

vention attests God's purpose in their case. No thunder rolled down the mountains, no summer led them over the wintry sea, no law of nature was reversed for their aid or protection. If we were about to send a colony to take possession of a distant continent, we should make great display about it; have long processions and longer orations. When we send an envoy extraordinary to a foreign power, we send him in a government vessel, we land him from beneath the star spangled flag and amid the roar of cannon to notify our foreign neighbor that the United States has sent him to her shores. But God's " ways are not as our ways, nor his thoughts our thoughts." He " speaks in his work." Jesus came an envoy from heaven to earth, not in the glory which he had with his father before the world was; not by angels attended through the opening heavens; but he came not the less directly from the Father. . . .

On the 4th of July, 1776, our fathers met in solemn council and promulgated to the world the principles which were to be our chart as a nation and assumed a place among the nations of the earth. To that event and that day we refer our birth as a nation. Let us consider for a moment the great distinguishing principle upon which our institutions were based. We boast that that was the commencement of a new order of political things. Let us see for a moment in what that declaration differed from prior fundamental articles of political and governmental faith.

The brotherhood of man, the absolutely equal rights of all men, the right of all to participate in the privileges and benefits of civil government, as they share its burdens, although to our minds familiar and self-evident truths, have dawned gradually upon the world and made their way slowly into creeds of men. The Jew denied to every one not a Jew not only the rights of citizenship in temporalities, but all hope of enjoying the blessings of heaven.

The Gentile might indeed be adopted into the Jewish commonwealth, but as a Gentile he was nobody. When Pericles boasted that in Athens all men enjoyed equal privileges and were preferred for their merits and not for their birth, he spoke in a city of which no inconsiderable portion of its inhabitants were slaves. By all men he meant all Athenians; he did not recognize that any but Athenians were men. Jesus first burst the bonds of national selfishness. He came to establish a kingdom that should know no end, be united with the destinies of no nation, which should survive all and supersede all; and its foundations were laid broadly accordingly.

The Jew, the Gentile, the Scythian, the Barbarian, the bond, the free, the black, and the white, were invited to equal benefits in his kingdom. He first taught principles broad enough to include all nations, races, and colors in a common benefit. The Declaration of our Independence, the cornerstone of our nationality, was man's first attempt to introduce the liberality of Christian principle into the framework of civil government; it was a declaration—not that all Americans, all Englishmen, all Frenchmen were equal—but that all men were equal; no matter where born, no matter whether learned or ignorant, rich or poor, black or white.

It deduced the right to equality before the law, the right to participate in civil government, not from the accident of birth or condition, nor yet from race or color, but from the fact of manhood alone.

Upon this principle, as the one great faith of our people, the ideal we intended to realize, the consummation we pledged ourselves to the accomplishment of, our fathers appealed to the God of battles, and succeeded. A more solemn covenant was never entered into between a nation and the God of nations. Upon that principle we stood through eight years of bloody war against one of the most powerful nations on the earth. Without an army, without a navy, without an exchequer, we stood, and withstood all the power of England, because truth will always stand, and right triumph over wrong, while God sits on the throne of the universe.

But after war had established our right to self-government, and we came to fashion a government, this principle was not fully carried out. Slavery existed as a fact, and our fathers temporized with the condition of things. In the constitution they virtually secured the slave-trade until 1808 and substantially guaranteed slavery in the States until the States should abolish it. It is due to our fathers, however, to say that they expected slavery would soon be abolished by the States. No man who signed the constitution expected slavery would survive thirty years. But—and perhaps to show the sad consequence of ever compromising with evil—the event did not realize the expectation.

The introduction of the cotton plant made slavery profitable; and gilded vice too often finds favor. The South first excused, then justified, then clamored for the extension of slavery; and down to the commencement of the rebellion of 1861 no man could see how the nation could purge itself of this monstrous sin. By civil means it could not. The constitution had put it out of the power of the nation by committing it to the States where slavery existed; and those States would not abolish it. Our statesmen in 1850 resolved to cure the evil by wholly ignoring its existence. They solemnly resolved that the subject should never again be alluded to in or out of Congress. That all agitation should cease. This was securing to the country peace according to the wisdom of time-serving politicians; but their wisdom was quite different from "the wisdom that is from above (which) is first pure, then peaceable."

The so-called "compromise measures" of 1850 were designed to secure peace; but they were a solemn prediction of war. From that moment it was evident that no peaceful measures would be adopted to redress the great wrong of three millions of our people; and then it became evident also that the whole country must soon become slave country or free country. And after ten years of preparation on the part of the South and of criminal inactivity on the part of the North, the two sections drew the sword to determine the question of liberty or slavery for all the States; and during four bloody, dismal years "hope and fear did arbitrate the event."

Grievously had we sinned and grievously did we answer it. Army after army rushed to the conflict; hundreds after hundreds were laid in their graves; the land was baptized with blood. It was in this strife that your companions, whom to-day you honor, went forth with faith in their hearts, prayers on their lips, and the sword in their hand to stand and to fall for truth, for justice, for liberty, and for God. Often in the darkness of those fearful years our sight failed us; we could see no light; but our people stood up strong in faith that God ruled the universe and that our cause was safe.

This faith carried us through the gloom. And finally in God's good time we emerged into the light of a triumphant and honorable peace. In this war our people expiated the sin of slavery and then the curse was withdrawn. And our nation stands to-day regenerated and renewed; won by fearful evidences back to its first love,—universal liberty. Now for the first time in the history of our nation it is true as a fact, what our fathers announced as a theory, that all men are created equal.

Now our reconstructed Union takes its place among the nations, the standard-bearer and the champion of the rights of man. Our infancy is over, our pupilage past, our manhood attained. We are no longer to flee from city to city to escape observation, no longer to bid men not to mention our works, no longer to feed on the wild figs of Bethany; we have come into our own kingdom, and are ready to make up our jewels.

Let me pause in thought one moment at the close of the late war, and asking you to recall your emotions as the war progressed, your doubts, your fears, the magnitude of the conflict, the bitterness of our enemies, the unfriendly attitude of foreign nations, all the obstacles overcome, the dangers past; then let me ask if you do not believe that the hand of God in an especial manner led us through this sea of troubles to the dry land of peace? If you believe your Bible you do believe that God interfered by special providences to secure the deliverance of the children of Israel from the land of Egypt.

Turn to that history once more and read again of the successive plagues that fell like so many blows upon the heart of Egypt before she would consent that her slaves might go forth. Then consider the similar conduct of the South; how without war, slavery would have been continued; how long after the war had begun the South might have laid down their arms and kept the slaves; how after the war was ended the South might have determined the question of negro suffrage; and how by repeated obduracy, amounting to absolute stupidity, the South has forced the government to free the slaves and finally raise them to the full enjoyment of legal and political rights; then let me ask, do you see no parallel?

Another coincidence and I will leave this part of the subject. It would be interesting to consider, but time forbids, the analogies that run through the universe, moral and material; and to point out how strangely, if it is mere accident, similar things, though ages distant in point of time, are similarly surrounded.

Jesus was " a man of sorrows and acquainted with grief." His public ministry was one of toil and trial. He was bearing the world's burdens, touched at its sorrows, and suffering for its sins. We read of him walking up the mountain, walking on the waters, agonizing in prayer, and weeping at the grave of him whom he loved.

On one occasion, and on one only, he employed the semblance of a triumph. Once he rode into Jerusalem; rode over a way sprinkled with the garmerts of his disciples and the green branches of Judean palms; rode in triumph, amid the shoutings of the multitude, " Hosanna to the son of David." The day upon which this event transpired is celebrated by the church, and for designation it is styled " Palm Sunday." On the next Friday—" Good Friday "—Jesus gave up his life and was laid in the tomb.

I am not appealing to any superstitious feeling, nor drawing any irreverent comparison; merely noting a remarkable coincidence. President Lincoln took the helm of state amid the storms of war. For four years he suffered the anguish his situation imposed, he mourned with the mourners, he wept and prayed for the deliverance of his people. But finally, on a bright Sabbath morning in April, 1865, Lee surrendered the rebel hosts to Lincoln's captain and the war was ended. The news flew on the wires all over the land. That was a day of national rejoicing. None of us will ever forget it.

On that day the clergy ministered in the usual way at the

altar. And old deacons, accustomed by life-long discipline never to turn their backs upon the " illuminated temple of the Lord," remained to attend the morning and evening sacrifices as usual. But where were the people? In the streets, wild with excitement of joy. There are times when the Christian heart is too full for mere utterance; times when the roar of cannon and the shoutings of the multitude are as genuine—may they not be as acceptable—praise as the chanted psalm or the whispered prayer. So Miriam went forth, celebrating the deliverance from the Red Sea, and led the women of Israel with timbrels and dances, chanting that immortal song of human exultation, " Sing ye to the Lord, for he hath triumphed gloriously; the horse and his rider hath he thrown into the sea."

This first happy day of President Lincoln's official life, the first happy day of our people for four long years, chanced to fall on the " Palm Sunday " of 1865. The next Friday— " Good Friday "—Lincoln was shot. Mere coincident; mere accident; yes, but human history is full of such suggestive accidents.

In passing from our first proposition, that God has established this nation, watched over it in an especial manner, and protected it by special providences; it is encouraging to think that such is the belief of our people. It crops out everywhere; from the pulpit, in the press, in the speeches of our public men, in the conversation of our people. All speak the language of hope, of young, ardent hope, and faith in God's superintending providence. In no other nation is this so eminently true.

Look at the condition of old England to-day and read the suggestive debates in the House of Lords on the Irish Church bill. The lords speak as though they were oppressed with the belief that there is no future for the monarchy. England stands to-day in the decrepitude of age, folding about her the shabby robes of worn-out custom; "perplexed with the fear of change;" unable to advance; unable to suppress the influences which are advancing step by step to throw open the temple of exclusive and hereditary privilege to the admission of the profane populace. "The voice of the people," when it utters the settled faith of a nation, "is the voice of God." . . .

And now, in the firm belief that God in his providence established this nation for a purpose,—to stand as a bulwark among the nations for the protection of the rights of man,—that it will prosper in proportion as it is true to the purpose of its institution, and will cease to be, whenever it no longer performs its duty; that its manhood is attained, and its time for action arrived, it remains to inquire what can we do in the interest of universal liberty? . . .

The brave young men who went forth from this college to suppress the slaveholders' attempt to reverse the decree of God and exalt slavery above liberty, sleep in bloody graves, yet live in our tender and our grateful remembrance. Their example appeals to our manhood and our conscience. They helped to carry our government through a crisis in its existence; to establish it firmly upon immutable truth; and give it the grandest opportunity a nation ever had to benefit mankind. It now devolves upon us who survive to determine whether their lives were laid down in vain. And in no way, I conceive, can we so truly honor them as in studying well and performing faithfully the duty they have helped to cast upon us. If we prove equal to our opportunity, if we stand firmly for justice and for equality among men, if we keep the lamp of liberty trimmed and burning, and allow its light to shine from our altitude throughout the world, we honor them;

they have not died in vain; therefore it seems to be appropr ate to this occasion to inquire into our new duties and gir ourselves for their performance.

They died for others, not for themselves; and let us so liv as to exert the influence of the exalted position they hav conferred upon us for the welfare of mankind and not for th attainment of selfish ends.

McGEE

THOMAS D'ARCY McGEE, an eloquent Irish-Canadian statesman and orator, was born at Carlingford, County Louth, Ireland, April 13, 1825. He was the second son of Mr. James McGee, then in the coastguard service, and Dorcas Catherine Morgan, the highly educated daughter of a Dublin bookseller. About the age of seventeen, seeing little chance of advancement at home, he emigrated to America with one of his sisters, and arrived in Boston in June, 1842. On the 4th of July he addressed the people and astonished them by his eloquence. Two years later he became chief editor of the Boston " Pilot." He rendered such good service to his countrymen that O'Connell at a public meeting referred to his editorials as " the inspired writings of a young exiled boy in America." He was invited by the proprietor of the Dublin " Freeman's Journal " to become its editor. But the paper was too moderate and cautious for him and he accepted the offer of Charles Gavan Duffy to help edit the " Nation," which soon became the mouthpiece of what was called " Young Ireland," and its fiery poetry, even more than its prose, was quoted everywhere. When the "Young Irelanders" tried to stir the famine-stricken and desperate people to rebellion some of the leaders were arrested, and a reward was offered for the arrest of McGee. He found a friend and host in Dr. Maginn, the bishop of Derry, and in the disguise of a priest sailed for America. On October 10, 1848, he reached Philadelphia, and on the 26th of that month the New York " Nation " issued its first number under the editorship of the exile. In 1850 McGee removed with his wife and infant daughter to Boston, where he began the publication of the "American Celt," which, until 1857, when it ceased to exist, was regarded by friend and foe as the best advocate of the Irish race in America; but it lost ground with the " politicians " as it took no side with any political party, and at length languished for want of support. During these years McGee had lectured in many Canadian cities and had made warm friends in Montreal. He now sold his interest in the "American Celt," and removed with his family to Montreal, where he at once established " The New Era." Before the end of his first year in Montreal he was returned to the Canadian Parliament as one of the three members for Montreal, and became one of the most popular men in Canada, being elected by acclamation and without any opposition in his second, third, and fourth elections. At times he was spoken of by his enemies as an " Irish Adventurer," "A Stranger From Abroad," and was twitted with having been a " rebel " in former years. To this charge he replied calmly and candidly: " It is true, I was a rebel in Ireland in '48. I rebelled against the misgovernment of my country by Russell and his school. I rebelled because I saw my countrymen starving before my eyes, while my country had her trade and commerce stolen from her. I rebelled against the church establishment in Ireland; and there is not a liberal man in this community who would not have done as I did if he had been placed in my position, and followed the dictates of humanity."

(8781)

About 1865 Mr. McGee's countrymen in Montreal and elsewhere presented him with a handsome residence, suitably furnished, in a pleasant part of the city which he so ably represented. In 1862 he had accepted the office of president of the executive council, and, while discharging these onerous duties, acted for a time as provincial secretary. In 1865 he visited Ireland, and, during his stay with his father in Wexford, offended his countrymen in the United States by a speech in which he contrasted the States unfavorably with Canada as a home for Irishmen. In 1867 he was sent to Paris by the government as one of the Canadian commissioners to the first exposition. In London he met by appointment some of his Canadian colleagues, who had gone to lay before the imperial government the plan for the proposed union of the British provinces, a project which was in a great measure his and had long been the object of his earnest endeavors. He was then minister of agriculture and emigration, which office he held till in the summer of 1867. The confederation was at last effected, and he took his seat as member for Montreal West in the first Parliament of the Dominion on November 6, 1867. On St. Patrick's day, 1868, he was entertained at a public banquet in Ottawa city and his speech on that occasion was one of the noblest efforts of his eloquence. It was on the general interests of the Irish race, and affirmed in the clearest language his all-enduring love for his race and country, joined with the fervent hope that he might yet do Ireland signal service in years to come. On the 6th of April he delivered one of the most striking speeches ever heard in the Canadian Parliament. The subject was the cementing of the lately-formed union of the provinces by mutual kindness and good will. Shortly after midnight he left the House and was shot from behind through the head. He is still regarded as the truest counsellor and guide of the Irish race in North America.

"THE LAND WE LIVE IN"

[Delivered before the "New England Society of Montreal, on the Anniversary of the Landing of the Pilgrims," December 22, 1860.]

M R. PRESIDENT, LADIES, AND GENTLEMEN,— As one of the representatives of the city of Montreal, I feel it to be an act of duty, and a most agreeable duty it is, to attend the reunions of our various national societies, and to contribute anything in my power to their gratification. My respect for all these societies, and my own sense of what is decorous and fit to be said, have, I hope, always confined me to the proprieties of such occasions; but still, if I speak at all, I must speak with freedom, and free speech, I trust, will never be asserted in vain among a society composed of the men of New England and their descendants.

I congratulate you and the society over which you preside, Mr. President, on the recurrence of your favorite anniversary, and not only for your own gratification as our fellow citizens of Montreal, but in the best interests of all humanity in the New World, let us join in hope that not only the sons of New England, but Americans from all other States settled amongst us, will long be able to join harmoniously in the celebration of the arrival of the first shipload of emigrants in Massachusetts Bay on this day, 240 years ago,— a ship which wafted over the sea as large a cargo of the seeds of the new civilization as any ship ever did since the famous voyage recorded in the legends of the Greeks.

It is rather a hard task, this you have set me, Mr. President, of extolling the excellencies of " the land we live in,"— that is, praising ourselves,— especially at this particular season of the year. If it were midsummer instead of midwinter, when our rapids are flashing, and our glorious river sings its triumphal song from Ontario to the ocean; when the northern summer, like the resurrection of the just, clothes every lineament of the landscape in beauty and serenity; it might be easy to say fine things for ourselves, without conflicting with the evidence of our senses.

But to eulogize Canada about Christmas time requires a patriotism akin to the Laplander, when, luxuriating in his train oil, he declares that " there is no land like Lapland under the sun." Our consolation, however, is that all the snows of the season fall upon our soil for wise and providential purposes. The great workman, Jack Frost, wraps the ploughed land in a warm covering, preserving the late-sown wheat for the first ripening influence of the spring. He macadamizes roads and bridges, brooks and rivers, better than could the manual labor of 100,000 workmen. He forms and lubricates the track through the wilderness by which those sailors of the forest—lumbermen—are enabled to draw down the annual supply of one of our chief staples to the margins of frozen rivers, which are to bear their rafts to Quebec at the first opening of the navigation.

This climate of ours though rigorous, is not unhealthful, since the average of human life in this Province is seven per cent higher than in any other portion of North America; and if the lowness of the glass does sometimes inconvenience individuals, we ought to be compensated and consoled by remembering of how much benefit these annual falls of snow are to the country at large. So much for our climatic difficulties. Let me say a word or two on our geographical position.

Whoever looks at the map — a good map is an invaluable public instructor — not such maps as we used to have, in which Canada was stuck away up at the North Pole, but such maps as have lately appeared in this country — will be tempted to regard the Gulf of St. Lawrence as the first of the Canadian lakes, and our magnificent river as only a longer Niagara or Detroit. His eye will follow up through the greater tidal volume of that river the same parallel of latitude — the 46°—which intersects Germany and cuts through the British Channel; if he pursues that parallel, it will lead him to the valley of the Saskatchewan, and through the Rocky Mountain passes, to the rising settlements of our fellow subjects on the Pacific. It will lead him through that most interesting country — the Red River territory, 500,000 square miles in extent, with a white population of less than 10,000 souls; a territory which ought to be " the Out-West " of our youth — where American enterprise has lately taught us a salutary, though a rebuking lesson, for while we were debating about its true limits and the title by which it is held, they were steaming down to Fort Garry with mails and merchandise from St. Paul's.

The position of Canada is not only important in itself, but it is important as a " *via media* " to the Pacific; from a given point on our side of Lake Superior to navigable water on the Fraser River has been shown to be not more than 2,000 miles — about double the distance from Boston to Chicago. A railway route with gradients not much, if at all, exceeding those of the Vermont Central, or the Philadelphia and Pittsburg, has been traced throughout by Mr. Fleming, Mr. Hind, Mr. Dawson, Captain Synge and Colonel Pailisser; and though neither Canada nor Columbia are able of themselves to undertake the connection, we cannot believe that British and American enterprise, which risked so many precious lives to find a practicable passage nearer to the Pole, will long leave untried this safest, shortest and most expeditious overland Northwest passage. We cannot despair that the dream of Jacques Cartier may yet be fulfilled, and the shortest route from Europe to China be found through the valley of the St. Lawrence. Straight on to the west lies Vancouver's Island, the Cuba of the Pacific; a little to the north, the Amur, which may be called the Amazon of the Arctic; farther off, but in a right line, the rich and populous Japanese group, which for wealth and enterprise have not been inaptly called the British Isles of Asia. These, Mr. President, are some of our geographical advantages. There are others which I might refer to, but on an occasion of this kind I know the fewer details the better.

Now, one word more as to our people; the decennial census to be taken next month will probably show us to be nearly equal in numbers to the six States of New England, or the great State of New York, deducting New York City. An element, over a third, but less than one half of that total, will be found to be of French-Canadian origin; the remainder is made up, as the population of New York and New England has been, by British, Irish, German, and other immigrants and their descendants. Have we advanced materially in the ratio of our American neighbors? I cannot say that we have. Montreal is an older city than Boston, and Kingston an older town than Oswego or Buffalo. Let us confess frankly that in many material things we are half a century behind the Americans, while at the same time — not to give way altogether too much — let us modestly assert that we possess some social advantages which they, perhaps, do not. For example we believed until lately — we still believe — that such a fiction as a slave, as one man being another man's chattel, was wholly unknown in Canada. And we still hope that may ever continue to be our boast. In material progress we have something to show, and we trust to have more.

All we need, Mr. President, mixed up and divided as we naturally are, is, in my humble opinion, the cultivation of a tolerant spirit on all the delicate controversies of race and religion, the maintenance of an upright public opinion in our politics and commerce, the cordial encouragement of every talent and every charity which reveals itself among us, the expansion of those narrow views and small ambitions which are apt to attend upon provincialism, and with these amendments, I do think we might make for Christian men, desirous to bring up their posterity in the love and fear of God and the law, one of the most desirable residences in the world, of this " land we live in."

THE POLICY OF CONCILIATION

REMARKS MADE AT A DINNER GIVEN HIM BY HIS CONSTITUENTS
AT MONTREAL, MARCH, 1861

THE career I have had in Canada led me chiefly into those parts of the country inhabited by men who speak the English language, and using the opportunities I have had between the time when I ceased to be a newspaper publisher to that of my admission as a member of the Lower Canada bar, I trust I have learned something which may be profitable to me in the position to which you elevated me on trust and in advance.

The result of my observations thus made, is, that there is nothing to be more dreaded in this country than feuds arising from exaggerated feelings of religion and nationality. On the other hand, the one thing needed for making Canada the happiest of homes is to rub down all sharp angles, and to remove those asperities which divide our people on questions of origin and religious profession. The man who says this cannot be done consistently with any set of principles founded on the charity of the Gospel or on the right use of human reason is a blockhead, as every bigot is, while under the influence of his bigotry he sees no further than his nose. For a man who has grown to years of discretion —though some never do come to those years — who has not become wedded to one idea, who, like Coleridge, is as ready to regulate his conduct as to set his watch when the parish clock declares it wrong; who is ready to be taught by high as well as by low, and to receive any stamp of truth — I may say that such a man will come to this conclusion: that there are in all origins men good, bad and indifferent; yet for my own part, my experience is that in all classes the good predominate. I believe that there have come out of Ireland, noble as she is, those whom she would not recognize as her children; and so with other countries celebrated for the noble characteristics of their population as a whole.

In Canada, with men of all origins and all kinds of culture, if we do not bear and forbear; if we do not get rid of old quarrels, but on the contrary make fresh ones, whereas we ought to have lost sight of the old when we lost sight of the capes and headlands of the old country; if we will carefully convey across the Atlantic half-extinguished embers of strife in order that we may by them light up the flames of our inflammable forests; if each neighbor will try not only to nurse up old animosities, but to invent new grounds of hostility to his neighbor, then, gentlemen, we shall return to what Hobbes considered the state of nature — I mean a state of war. In society we must sacrifice something, as we do when we go through a crowd, and not only must we yield to old age, to the fairer and better sex, and to that youth, which, in its weakness, is entitled to some of the respect which we accord to age; but we must sometimes make way for men like ourselves, though we could prove by the most faultless syllogism our right to push them from the path.

In his great speech respecting the Unitarians, Edmund Burke declared that he did not govern himself by abstractions or universals, and he maintained in that same argument (I think) that what is not possible is not desirable — that the possible best is the absolute best — the best for the generation, the best for the man, since the shortness of life makes it impossible for him to achieve all that he could wish.

I believe the possible best for us is peace and good will. With this belief I did my part to heal up those feuds which

THE POLICY OF CONCILIATION 8789

prevailed in Montreal and westward before and at the election of 1857; I felt that someone must condone the past, and I determined, so far as I could be supposed to represent your principles, to lead the way. I tried to allay irritated feeling, and I hope not altogether without success.

We have a country, which, being the land of our choice, should also have our first consideration. I know, and you know, that I can never cease to regard with an affection which amounts almost to idolatry the land where I spent my best, my first years, where I obtained the partner of my life, and where my first-born saw the light. I cannot but regard that land even with increased love because she has not been prosperous.

Yet I hold we have no right to intrude our Irish patriotism on this soil; for our first duty is to the land where we live and have fixed our homes, and where, while we live, we must find the true sphere of our duties. While always ready therefore to say the right word, and to do the right act for the land of my forefathers, I am bound above all to the land where I reside; and especially am I bound to put down, so far as one humble layman can, the insensate spread of a strife which can only tend to prolong our period of provincialism and make the country an undesirable home for those who would otherwise willingly cast in their lot among us. We have acres enough; powers mechanical and powers natural; and sources of credit enough to make out of this Province a great nation, and though I wish to commit no one to my opinion, I trust that it will not only be so in itself, but will one day form part of a greater British North American State, existing under the sanction and in perpetual alliance with the empire, under which it has its rise and growth.

PENDLETON

GEORGE HUNT PENDLETON, an American congressman, was born at Cincinnati, Ohio, July 25, 1825, and educated at the University of Heidelberg. On his return to the United States he studied law and was admitted to the Cincinnati bar. In 1854 he made his entrance into public life as State senator, and in 1856 was sent to Congress as Democratic representative. While in Congress he served on a number of important committees, and in 1864 was candidate for vice-president on the Democratic ticket with McClellan. In 1866 he was a member of the Philadelphia loyalist convention and three years later was an unsuccessful candidate for the governorship of Ohio. About this time he was somewhat prominent as an advocate of the scheme for payment of bonds in greenbacks. He was elected United States senator in 1878, and while in the Senate procured the passage of the civil service law, but his warm support of this reform prevented his re-election to Congress. In 1885 he was appointed minister to Belgium and died at Brussels while serving in this capacity, November 24, 1889. Pendleton was a man of the most courteous bearing and among his friends was frequently styled " Gentleman George."

ON RECONSTRUCTION; THE DEMOCRATIC THEORY

HOUSE OF REPRESENTATIVES, MAY 4, 1864

THE gentleman [Mr. Davis of Maryland] maintains two propositions, which lie at the very basis of his views on this subject. He has explained them to the House, and enforced them on other occasions. He maintains that, by reason of their secession, the seceded States and their citizens " have not ceased to be citizens and States of the United States, though incapable of exercising political privileges under the constitution, but that Congress is charged with a high political power by the constitution to guarantee republican government in the States, and that this is the proper time and the proper mode of exercising it." This act of revolution on the part of the seceding States has evoked the most extraordinary theories upon the relations of the

(8790)

States to the Federal government. This theory of the gentleman is one of them.

The ratification of the constitution by Virginia established the relations between herself and the Federal government; it created the link between her and all the States; it announced her assumption of the duties, her title to the rights, of the confederating States; it proclaimed her interest in, her power over, her obedience to, the common agent of all the States. If Virginia had never ordained that ratification, she would have been an independent State; the constitution would have been as perfect and the union between the ratifying States would have been as complete as they now are.

Virginia repeals that ordinance, annuls that bond of union, breaks that link of confederation. She repeals but a single law, repeals it by the action of a sovereign convention, leaves her constitution, her laws, her political and social polity untouched. And the gentleman from Maryland tells us that the effect of this repeal is not to destroy the vigor of that law, but to subvert the State government, and to render the citizens "incapable of exercising political privileges;" that the Union remains, but that one party to it has thereby lost its corporate existence, and the other has advanced to the control and government of it.

Sir, this cannot be. Gentlemen must not palter in a double sense.

These acts of secession are either valid or invalid. If they are valid, they separated the State from the Union. If they are invalid, they are void; they have no effect; the State officers who act upon them are rebels to the Federal government; the States are not destroyed; their constitutions are not abrogated; their officers are committing illegal acts, for which they are liable to punishment; the States have never left the Union, but, as soon as their officers shall perform their duties or other officers shall assume their places, will again perform the duties imposed and enjoy the privileges conferred by the Federal compact, and this not by virtue of a new ratification of the constitution, nor a new admission by the Federal government, but by virtue of the original ratification, and the constant, uninterrupted maintenance of position in the Federal Union since that date.

Acts of secession are not invalid to destroy the Union, and valid to destroy the State governments and the political privileges of their citizens. We have heard much of the twofold relations which citizens of the seceded States may hold to the Federal government — that they may be at once belligerents and rebellious citizens. I believe there are some judicial decisions to that effect. Sir, it is impossible. The Federal government may possibly have the right to elect in which relation it will deal with them; it cannot deal at one and the same time in inconsistent relations.

Belligerents, being captured, are entitled to be treated as prisoners of war; rebellious citizens are liable to be hanged. The private property of belligerents, according to the rules of modern war, shall not be taken without compensation; the property of rebellious citizens is liable to confiscation. Belligerents are not amenable to the local criminal law, nor to the jurisdiction of the courts which administer it; rebellious citizens are, and the officers are bound to enforce the law and exact the penalty of its infraction. The seceded States are either in the Union or out of it. If in the Union, their constitutions are untouched, their State governments are maintained, their citizens are entitled to all political rights, except so far as they may be deprived of them by the criminal law which they have infracted.

This seems incomprehensible to the gentleman from Mary-
nd. In his view, the whole State government centres in
e men who administer it, so that, when they administer it
nwisely, or put it in antagonism to the Federal government,
he State government is dissolved, the State constitution is
brogated, and the State is left, in fact and in form, *de jure*
nd *de facto*, in anarchy, except so far as the Federal government may rightfully intervene. This seems to be substantially the view of the gentleman from Massachusetts [Mr.
Boutwell]. He enforces the same position, but he does not
use the same language. I submit that these gentlemen do
not see with their usual clearness of vision. If, by a plague
or other visitation of God, every officer of a State government should at the same moment die, so that not a single
person clothed with official power should remain, would the
State government be destroyed? Not at all. For the moment it would not be administered; but as soon as officers
were elected and assumed their respective duties it would
be instantly in full force and vigor.

If these States are out of the Union, their State governments are still in force, unless otherwise changed; their citizens are to the Federal government as foreigners, and it has
in relation to them the same rights, and none other, as it had
in relation to British subjects in the war of 1812, or to the
Mexicans in 1846. Whatever may be the true relation of
the seceding States, the Federal government derives no power
in relation to them or their citizens from the provision of the
constitution now under consideration, but, in the one case,
derives all its power from the duty of enforcing the " supreme
law of the land," and in the other, from the power " to declare war."

The second proposition of the gentleman from Maryland

is this — I use his language : " That clause vests in the Con gress of the United States a plenary, supreme, unlimited political jurisdiction, paramount over courts, subject only to the judgment of the people of the United States, embracing within its scope every legislative measure necessary and proper to make it effectual; and what is necessary and proper the constitution refers in the first place to our judgment, sub- ject to no revision but that of the people."

The gentleman states his case too strongly. The duty im- posed on Congress is doubtless important, but Congress has no right to use a means of performing it forbidden by the constitution, no matter how necessary or proper it might be thought to be. But, sir, this doctrine is monstrous. It has no foundation in the constitution. It subjects all the States to the will of Congress; it places their institutions at the feet of Congress. It creates in Congress an absolute, unqualified despotism. It asserts the power of Congress in changing the State governments to be " plenary, supreme, unlimited," " subject only to revision by the people of the United States." The rights of the people of the State are nothing; their will is nothing. Congress first decides; the people of the whole Union revise. My own State of Ohio is liable at any moment to be called in question for her constitution. She does not permit negroes to vote. If this doctrine be true, Congress may decide that this exclusion is anti-republican, and by force of arms abrogate that constitution and set up another, per- mitting negroes to vote. From that decision of Congress there is no appeal to the people of Ohio, but only to the people of New York and Massachusetts and Wisconsin, at the elec- tion of representatives, and, if a majority cannot be elected to reverse the decision, the people of Ohio must submit. Woe be to the day when that doctrine shall be established, for from its centralized despotism we will appeal to the sword!

Sir, the rights of the States were the foundation corners of the confederation. The constitution recognized them, maintained them, provided for their perpetuation. Our fathers thought them the safeguard of our liberties. They have proved so. They have reconciled liberty with empire; they have reconciled the freedom of the individual with the increase of our magnificent domain. They are the test, the touchstone, the security of our liberties. This bill, and the avowed doctrine of its supporters, sweeps them all instantly away. It substitutes despotism for self-government—despotism the more severe because vested in a numerous Congress elected by a people who may not feel the exercise of its power. It subverts the government, destroys the confederation, and erects a tyranny on the ruins of republican governments. It creates unity — it destroys liberty; it maintains integrity of territory, but destroys the rights of the citizen.

Sir, if this be the alternative of secession I prefer that secession should succeed. I should prefer to have the Union dissolved, the Confederate States recognized; nay, more, I should prefer that secession should go on, if need be, until each State resumes its complete independence. I should prefer thirty-four republics to one despotism. From such republics, while I might fear discord and wars, I would enjoy individual liberty, and hope for a reunion on the true principles of confederation.

LAMAR

LUCIUS QUINTUS CURTIUS LAMAR, an American jurist, the son of a Georgia jurist of the same name, was born in Jasper county, Georgia, September 1, 1825. He was educated at Emory College in his native State, studied law and was admitted to the bar in 1847. For a short time he taught mathematics in the University of Mississippi, and then settling in Covington, Georgia, practised his profession there for a few years. He sat in the Georgia legislature in 1853 and then returned to Mississippi and entered Congress as representative from that State in 1857. Resigning his seat after the ordinance of secession was passed by Mississippi, he entered the Confederate army as colonel of a Mississippi regiment, and soon after the close of the war he became a professor of political economy in the State University. After a few years he resigned this post, and in 1872 was elected to Congress, serving as representative till 1877, when he entered the Senate. He was not a frequent speaker in Congress, but always eloquent and effective. In March, 1885, he was appointed secretary of the interior in President Cleveland's cabinet, resigning in 1888 in order to become an associate justice of the Supreme Court of the United States. He died at Macon, Georgia, January 23, 1893. Lamar was a man of independent action, and his uncompromising stand against inflation of the national currency gave great offence in his State, the legislature of which instructed him to use his influence and vote against the principles he had hitherto held or resign his seat. Lamar refused to do either, and, defending his position in an eloquent speech before the Senate, received the approbation of men of both parties for his independent attitude. Among other noted oratorical efforts of his may be mentioned the eulogy which he delivered upon Charles Sumner April 27, 1874.

EULOGY OF CHARLES SUMNER

DELIVERED IN THE UNITED STATES HOUSE OF REPRESENTATIVES, APRIL 27, 1874

MR. SPEAKER,—In rising to second the resolutions just offered, I desire to add a few remarks which have occurred to me as appropriate to the occasion. I believe that they express a sentiment which pervades the hearts of all the people whose representatives are here assembled. Strange as in looking back upon the past the assertion may seem, impossible as it would have been ten

years ago to make it, it is not the less true that to-day Mississippi regrets the death of Charles Sumner and sincerely
unites in paying honors to his memory.

Not because of the splendor of his intellect, though in him
was extinguished one of the brightest of the lights which have
illustrated the councils of the government for nearly a quarter of a century; not because of the high culture, the elegant
scholarship, and the varied learning which revealed themselves so clearly in all his public efforts as to justify the application to him of Johnson's felicitous expression, " he
touched nothing which he did not adorn;" not this, though
these are qualities by no means, it is to be feared, so common
in public places as to make their disappearance, in even a
single instance, a matter of indifference; but because of those
peculiar and strongly marked moral traits of his character
which gave the coloring to the whole tenor of his singularly
dramatic public career; traits which made him for a long
period to a large portion of his countrymen the object of as
deep and passionate a hostility as to another he was one of
enthusiastic admiration, and which are not the less the cause
that now unites all these parties, ever so widely differing, in
a common sorrow to-day over his lifeless remains.

It is of these high moral qualities which I wish to speak;
for these have been the traits which in after years, as I have
considered the successive acts and utterances of this remarkable man, fastened most strongly my attention, and impressed
themselves most forcibly upon my imagination, my sensibilities, my heart.   I leave to others to speak of his intellectual
superiority, of those rare gifts with which nature had so
lavishly endowed him, and of the power to use them which
he had acquired by education.   I say nothing of his vast and
varied stores of historical knowledge, or of the wide extent

of his reading in the elegant literature of ancient and modern times, or of his wonderful power of retaining what he had read, or of his readiness in drawing upon these fertile resources to illustrate his own arguments. I say nothing of his eloquence as an orator, of his skill as a logician, or of his powers of fascination in the unrestrained freedom of the social circle, which last it was my misfortune not to have experienced. These, indeed, were the qualities which gave him eminence not only in our country but throughout the world; and which have made the name of Charles Sumner an integral part of our nation's glory. They were the qualities which gave to those moral traits of which I have spoken the power to impress themselves upon the history of the age and of civilization itself; and without which those traits, however intensely developed, would have exerted no influence beyond the personal circle immediately surrounding their possessor. More eloquent tongues than mine will do them justice. Let me speak of the characteristics which brought the illustrious senator who has just passed away into direct and bitter antagonism for years with my own State and her sister States of the South.

Charles Sumner was born with an instinctive love of freedom, and was educated from his earliest infancy to the belief that freedom is the natural and indefeasible right of every intelligent being having the outward form of man. In him in fact this creed seems to have been something more than a doctrine imbibed from teachers, or a result of education. To him it was a grand intuitive truth inscribed in blazing letters upon the tablet of his inner consciousness, to deny which would have been for him to deny that he himself existed. And along with this all-controlling love of freedom, he possessed a moral sensibility keenly intense and vivid, a conscientiousness which would never permit him to swerve by the breadth of a hair from what he pictured to himself as the path of duty. Thus were combined in him the characteristics which have in all ages given to religion her martyrs and to patriotism her self-sacrificing heroes.

To a man thoroughly permeated and imbued with such a creed, and animated and constantly actuated by such a spirit of devotion, to behold a human being or a race of human beings restrained of their natural rights to liberty, for no crime by him or them committed, was to feel all the belligerent instincts of his nature roused to combat. The fact was to him a wrong which no logic could justify. It mattered not how humble in the scale of rational existence the subject of this restraint might be, how dark his skin, or how dense his ignorance. Behind all that lay for him the great principle that liberty is the birthright of all humanity, and that every individual of every race who has a soul to save is entitled to the freedom which may enable him to work out his salvation.

It matters not that the slave might be contented with his lot; that his actual condition might be immeasurably more desirable than that from which it had transplanted him; that it gave him physical comfort, mental and moral elevation and religious culture not possessed by his race in any other condition; that his bonds had not been placed upon his hands by the living generation; that the mixed social system of which he formed an element had been regarded by the fathers of the Republic, and by the ablest statesmen who had risen up after them, as too complicated to be broken up without danger to society itself, or even to civilization; or finally, that the actual state of things had been recognized and explicitly sanctioned by the very organic law of the Republic.

Weighty as these considerations might be, formidable a
were the difficulties in the way of the practical enforcemen
of his great principle, he held none the less that it mus
sooner or later be enforced, though institutions and constitu
tions should have to give way alike before it. But here let
me do this great man the justice which amid the excitements
of the struggle between the sections, now past, I may have
been disposed to deny him. In this fiery zeal and this earnest
warfare against the wrong, as he viewed it, there entered no
enduring personal animosity toward the men whose lot it
was to be born to the system which he denounced.

It has been the kindness of the sympathy which in these
later years he has displayed toward the impoverished and suffering people of the southern States that has unveiled to me
the generous and tender heart which beat beneath the bosom
of the zealot, and has forced me to yield him the tribute of
my respect, I might even say of my admiration. Nor in the
manifestation of this has there been anything which a proud
and sensitive people, smarting under a sense of recent dis-
comfiture and present suffering, might not frankly accept,
or which would give them just cause to suspect its sincerity.
For though he raised his voice as soon as he believed the
momentous issues of this great military conflict were decided
in behalf of amnesty to the vanquished, and though he stood
forward ready to welcome back as brothers and to re-establish in their rights as citizens those whose valor had so nearly
riven asunder the Union which he loved, yet he always insisted that the most ample protection and the largest safeguards should be thrown around the liberties of the newly
enfranchised African race. Though he knew very well
that of his conquered fellow citizens of the South by far the
larger portion, even those who most heartily acquiesced in

and desired the abolition of slavery, seriously questioned the expediency of investing in a single day and without any preliminary tutelage so vast a body of inexperienced and uninstructed men with the full rights of freemen and voters, he would tolerate no half-way measures upon a point to him so vital.

Indeed, immediately after the war, while other minds were occupying themselves with different theories of reconstruction, he did not hesitate to impress most emphatically upon the administration, not only in public, but in the confidence of private intercourse, his uncompromising resolution to oppose to the last any and every scheme which should fail to provide the surest guarantees for the personal freedom and political rights of the race which he had undertaken to protect. Whether his measures to secure this result showed him to be a practical statesman or the theoretical enthusiast is a question on which any decision we may pronounce to-day must await the inevitable revision of posterity. The spirit of magnanimity, therefore, which breathes in his utterances and manifests itself in all his acts affecting the South during the last two years of his life, was as evidently honest as it was grateful to the feelings to those to whom it was displayed.

It was certainly a gracious act toward the South—though unhappily it jarred upon the sensibilities of the people at the other extreme of the Union and estranged from him the great body of his political friends—to propose to erase from the banners of the national army the mementoes of the bloody internecine struggle, which might be regarded as assailing the pride or wounding the sensibilities of the southern people. That proposal will never be forgotten by that people so long as the name of Charles Sumner lives in the memory of man.   But while it touched the heart of the South and elicited her profound gratitude, her people would not have asked of the North such an act of self-renunciation.

Conscious that they themselves were animated by devotion to constitutional liberty, and that the brightest pages of history are replete with evidences of the depth and sincerity of that devotion, they can but cherish the recollections of sacrifices endured, the battles fought, and the victories won in defense of their hapless cause.   And respecting, as all true and brave men must respect, the martial spirit with which the men of the North vindicated the integrity of the Union and their devotion to the principles of human freedom, they do not ask, they do not wish, the North to strike the mementoes of her heroism and victory from either records or monuments or battle flags.   They would rather that both sections should gather up the glories won by each section, not envious, but proud of each other, and regard them a common heritage of American valor.

Let us hope that future generations, when they remember the deeds of heroism and devotion done on both sides, will speak not of northern prowess or southern courage, but of the heroism, fortitude, and courage of Americans in a war of ideas—a war in which each section signalized its consecration to the principles, as each understood them, of American liberty and of the constitution received from their fathers.

It was my misfortune, perhaps my fault, personally never to have known this eminent philanthropist and statesman. The impulse was often strong upon me to go to him and offer him my hand and my heart with it, and to express to him my thanks for his kind and considerate course toward the people with whom I am identified.   If I did not yield to that impulse it was because the thought occurred that other days were

coming in which such a demonstration might be more opportune and less liable to misconstruction. Suddenly, and without premonition, a day has come at last to which, for such
a purpose, there is no to-morrow.

My regret is therefore intensified by the thought that I
failed to speak to him out of the fulness of my heart while
there was yet time.

How often is it that death thus brings unavailingly back
to our remembrance opportunities unimproved; in which generous overtures, prompted by the heart, remain unoffered;
frank avowals which rose to the lips remain unspoken; and
the injustice and wrong of bitter resentments remain unre-
paired! Charles Sumner in life believed that all occasion for
strife and distrust between the North and South had passed
away, and there no longer remained any cause for continued
estrangement between these two sections of our common
country. Are there not many of us who believe the same
thing? Is not that the common sentiment, or if it is not
ought it not to be, of the great mass of our people North and
South? Bound to each other by a common constitution, destined to live together under a common government, forming
unitedly but a single member of the great family of nations,
shall we not now at last endeavor to grow toward each other
once more in heart as we are already indissolubly linked
to each other in fortunes? Shall we not, over the honored
remains of this great champion of human liberty, this feeling
sympathizer with human sorrow, this earnest pleader for the
exercise of human tenderness and charity, lay aside the concealments which serve only to perpetuate misunderstandings
and distrust, and frankly confess that on both sides we most
earnestly desire to be one; one not merely in political
organization; one not merely in identity of institutions; one

not merely in community of language and literature and traditions and country; but, more and better than all that, one also in feeling and in heart. Am I mistaken in this?

Do the concealments of which I speak still cover animosities which neither time nor reflection nor the march of events have yet sufficed to subdue? I cannot believe it. Since I have been here I have watched with anxious scrutiny your sentiments as expressed not merely in public debate, but in the abandon of personal confidence. I know well the sentiments of these my southern brothers, whose hearts are so infolded that the feeling of each is the feeling of all; and I see on both sides only the seeming of a constraint which each apparently hesitates to dismiss. The South—prostrate, exhausted, drained of her life-blood as well as of her material resources, yet still honorable and true—accepts the bitter award of the bloody arbitrament without reservation, resolutely determined to abide the result with chivalrous fidelity; yet, as if struck dumb by the magnitude of her reverses, she suffers on in silence.

The North, exultant in her triumph and elated by success, still cherishes, as we are assured, a heart full of magnanimous emotions toward her disarmed and discomfited antagonist; and yet, as if mastered by some mysterious spell, silencing her better impulses, her words and acts are the words and acts of suspicion and distrust.

Would that the spirit of the illustrious dead whom we lament to-day could speak from the grave to both parties to this deplorable discord in tones which should reach each and every heart throughout this broad territory, "My countrymen, know one another, and you will love one another."

CASTILLO

ANTONIO CANOVAS DEL CASTILLO, like many other Spanish statesmen, was a man of letters. He was born in Málaga on February 8, 1826. He was first known as a poet, but his historical work gave him eminence. His achievements in this and other literary fields gained him an election to the Spanish Academy. At the age of twenty-five he was made editor of the Conservative newspaper, "La Patria," and in 1854, at the age of twenty-seven, he was elected to the Córtes, beginning the political activity that ended only with his tragic death shortly before the culmination of the trouble with the United States. In 1858-59 he was business representative of the Spanish government at Rome. From 1860 to 1864 he was repeatedly a member of the ministry under the Liberal Union. In 1864 he received a cabinet position as minister of the interior and in 1865 was minister of finance, at which period he drew up the law for the abolition of slavery. He had been nominally a Liberal for a number of years, but in 1868 became the leader of the Liberal-Conservatives. In the revolutionary period of 1868 he steadfastly maintained the principle of constitutional monarchy in the Constituent Assembly and refused to accept the republic. On the abdication of Queen Isabella II in 1870, he headed the party that desired to call Prince Alfonso of Asturias to the throne. When in 1874 this aim became successful the king made Cánovas the president of the ministry. On June 30, 1876, Cánovas brought about the adoption of the new constitution which, in a degree, satisfied the clergy without being false to Liberal principles. His efforts to restore peace and order to the long disturbed country were successful. From that time on till the day of his death he was the chief of the Conservative elements in the Córtes and stood at the head of the ministry whenever his party was in power. His first retirement from that post was due to the desire of the king not to estrange the Liberals, and his second retirement came from his refusal to make the king's daughter the Princess of Asturias. On the death of the king in November, 1885, public affairs seemed so critical that Cánovas resigned and helped Sagasta form a Liberal ministry, deeming that statesman better qualified to unite the elements of order against the intrigues of the Carlists. At the end of 1888 he again returned to power and in February, 1890, with characteristic courage caused the adoption into the Conservative program of a demand for universal manhood suffrage. From this reform he looked for a strengthening of the Conservative and clerical elements. Returning to power as prime minister in July of that year he carried this program into effect and also took up a protective tariff system. His own party, however, became increasingly discordant, breaking up into various groups, and in December, 1892, he resigned and was succeeded for the third time by Sagasta. Returning to power in March, 1895, he was confronted by the second great revolt in Cuba. Continued discords in his party caused him to dissolve the Córtes in February, 1896. He was assassinated by an Italian anarchist on August 8, 1897.

Notable among the writings of Cánovas are the following: "Estudios Literarios" (1868); "Historia del dominio austriaco en España" (1869); a biography of his uncle the poet Serafino Estébanez Calderon (1883); "Problemas contemporaneos" (1884); and "Estudios del Reinado de Felipe IV" (1888-90); his poetical works appeared in 1887.

It is noteworthy that Cánovas and Castelar were lifelong personal friends. The conservatism of Cánovas had a fundamentally liberal quality, as indicated by the accompanying example from one of his addresses in which he lays stress on the inevitable tendency of society toward democracy. Juan Rico y Amat says of him:

"Cánovas is the fervent believer of a school, but neither its representative nor its apostle; he is a notable parliamentary orator, but not one of the foremost. His talent, his special merit, consists in having comprehended better than others the true temper of representative government, the policy of which may not ever be radical, absolute, and fixed, but must vary in its application according to the circumstances that give it life, adaptable and accommodating in its form as the interest and convenience of the nation may demand. This policy of circumstance, sold and indispensable base of representative government, the just medium between radical parties, and the symbol of the Liberal Union which was created as a moderate party between those that stand extreme—has always been Cánovas del Castillo's policy."

ON CONSTITUTIONAL REFORM

PERORATION OF ADDRESS DELIVERED APRIL 11, 1864

B UT, gentlemen, is it not true, passing to a plane a little more elevated and even repeating certain ideas of Señor Barzanallana (for I say frankly that what has most surprised me in the speech of the gentleman is that side by side with conclusions which in my judgment are inexact, dialectically false, it was accented and filled throughout with genuine estimations of politics, of economy, and of history), is it not true, gentlemen, that if we review history at any one of its grand moments,—be it in the Middle Ages, in the epoch of feudalism and of the birth of municipalities or town councils; be it later, at the period of the exaggeration of Catholic influence and the beginning of heretical resistance; be it when absolutism was predominant and aristocracy humiliated; be it in the epoch of the French Revolution, at the instant when all the combustible deadwood of the centuries took fire—is it not true that in all the institutions of

Europe we encounter a singular, an intimate, an indisputable analogy?

Is it by chance that all serious historians have been surprised to find how the organization of the municipality in the twelfth and thirteenth centuries, in the heart of the Middle Ages, was identical among all the peoples of Europe? Is it by chance that the terrible unity of the Gothic cathedrals is written upon pages of stone? Have you not remarked how here and there the same ideas are realized, how identical institutions arise and pass from one country to another?

It is because the spirit of humanity is one, and all that opposes this unity must fall irremediably to destruction, whatever its strength, whatever its potency?

Such is the truth. And vainly we oppose the operation of the universal spirit; even though a nation by exceptional circumstances may have separated from the general current of civilization as Spain had the misfortune of doing in the sixteenth century, as had England the fortune of doing in that very same epoch; there comes a day when at last it must join it again.

Therefore we ourselves, since the days of theocratic despotism, are incontestably going the road to liberty, and let Señor Barzanallana not doubt it. And England, by another path, in a different manner, is marching to merge herself in continental democracy. No, it cannot be impeded; it is vain to attempt it, for could it be impeded it would give the lie to the unity of the human spirit. The way leads toward democracy, toward a certain democracy in all parts of the world, toward the fall of social inequalities; the way leads toward a common right in all parts of the world, the same in England as in all other nations; a little sooner, a little later, the way will be trod; there is no doubt of it whatever.

Considered in this aspect, not political but social, democracy is inevitable.

Do you believe that perhaps England may with its aristocratic spirit oppose with better resistance the modern spirit, the universal spirit of human kind, than did ancient Spain, the Spain of Philip II, with her inquisition, with her convents, with her little primogenitures, with all her antiquated organization? And you that tremble because that society with those conditions and with that form must be lost, how can you claim that it is a phenomenon peculiar to this country of ours; that it is not an inevitable condition of the march of humanity; that what has already occurred in Spain is not to be reckoned with at last, and in its own time, in England, though in a contrary sense; that what must occur must occur everywhere.

Therefore, gentlemen, because this is true, because it is the certain lesson of history, I defend, I proclaim with intimate and profound conviction, the politics of circumstances and of transactions. Yes; because circumstances are reality itself, circumstances are life itself; to fly from them is to travel toward the impossible, toward the absurd. If you study all the periods of decadence, that same decadence of which Señor Barzanallana has spoken to us this very day, the grand decadence of the Spanish monarchy—in my opinion the greatest that history has to register—you will find at the bottom as its original and fundamental cause not the natural exaggeration of all things proper to the Spaniards,—for this, as I regard it, would be a trivial cause,—but institutions, social conditions battling against inexorably opposing circumstances.

Does Señor Barzanallana know wherein lies the secret of the decadence of Spain from the Emperor Cárlos V to King

Cárlos II? It is because the spirit, the institutions, the politics, the diplomacy, the military pretensions of the time of Cárlos II were the same, identically the same, as those of the time of Cárlos V; were the same without the occasion, without the circumstances, without the force that the circumstances gave of themselves; and because of this there was a descent from tragedy to farce, from the heroic epic to the burlesque. What was grand when it might have been done, when it had to be done, at the time of Cárlos V, was petty, was even a subject for ridicule at the time of Cárlos II. This is the inexorable judgment of history, which is not poesy, which is not pure idealism, but which above all is reason, reality, human.

And in respect to transactions, there is in all societies, in all parties, in all governments, something in which change is not permissible, in regard to which any transaction would be a crime. These are the minority. There are other things, and these are the majority, in which change according to circumstance may take place, must take place, and where it is legitimate. The conservative schools may not, the conservative schools must not, attempt to change any of the fundamental principles of the society in which they live, the society which they are called to conserve. But when they encounter, for example, in our present conditions an artificial institution like the hereditary senatorship; when they encounter an idea its own authors would not venture to put into practice, as in the same instant when they presented hereditary senatorship they proposed also a system of entails; when they encounter a reform in a method of regulations which may in two senses be diametrically opposed, interpreted by two ministers of the same cabinet—it is clear that we treat of matters in relation to which changes may be, must be, admitted; in relation to which, in my judgment, a crime would be committed if at times and with discretion they might not be changed.

I shall be told, perhaps: It is a concession to radical parties, to revolutionary parties; that those revolutionary parties are thirsty and insatiable, and the more is conceded to them the more they will demand, and in the end they will demand that which cannot be given to them, and then you cannot avoid that which you would avoid through the concessions that you are making. Very well; I say to the Congress with profound conviction: I shall see with more or less feeling, certainly with much feeling, the radical tendencies that certain parties n Spain may take; I shall deplore them and shall ever deplore hem; but however I deplore such tendencies the more they are exaggerated, the more they depart from the path of constitutional legality, the more inexorable will be shown my will and my spirit toward them.

No, not with parties, whatever they may be (I will not characterize them or even mention them at this moment), may we transcend the legal limitations of what may legitimately be subject to change, and to whom it is legitimate to give this manner of satisfaction.

But Señor Aparisi told us the other day: "Effect the reunion of the conservative elements, for a great and uncommon battle is in prospect in which it will be necessary for all the defenders of these ideas more or less advanced, more or less liberal, to be at their posts and under their common flags."

And I ask Señor Aparisi and those who think with him: Where will you fix the point of reunion? Where will you have us make the convocation of the conservative forces? Have you ever seen an able general who awaits the enemy on the extreme frontier in order to defend some ancient oak or some isolated hut? Have you ever seen him go to seek his adversary in the positions convenient to the latter? No; an able general retires to the point where he may summon all his forces, to the point where he may oppose the most vigorous resistance, to the strategic point where he may count upon the greatest support in the country that he is defending. This point which we have to seek is that of the constitution of 1845.

Gentlemen, that constitution which was accepted by so many illustrious persons of the old progressive party, that constitution which to-day is accepted by so many others of the same party, that constitution which at divers times has been accepted by all the conservative factions of the country, that constitution is the sole rallying point and centre for the conservative hosts.

If it is true, therefore, that the battle is coming, that the combat is at hand, you that most claim to be friends of order will not refuse your consent to the point of reunion where is to be found the honor, the interest, the banner, of all true conservatives. Rally there and defend it; and do not attempt more, whatever may be the conviction—which I respect most profoundly — of those who at another time have sought to defend in more advanced positions the conservative interests of the country; do not drag forward to those positions where you will be few and isolated, so many other sincere convictions as have been raised up here from the same bosom of the conservative party to protest against reforms projected or carried into effect. Do not seek to do that, for you will never be able to do it, and even if you were you would do a fatal thing for the very same interests that you claim to defend.

I have nearly finished, gentlemen, and I will conclude with

a few words regarding the melancholy divinations and auguries of Señor Barzanallana in respect to the Spanish nationality.

The gentleman sat down pursuing his system — in my opinion a mistaken one—of picking out small and trifling causes for grand and notorious effects; attributing, I say, following our this system, to this and that French thing that we had introduced—not recollecting at the time that they were not French things but English things that we introduced —a great influence upon the moral decadence of Spanish society.

Señor Barzanallana declared that he could not be a materialist in politics, that he could not agree with the economic school that looked upon everything from the point of view of the interests concerned; that he belongs with those who, on the contrary, behold everything in the light of sentiment, and of those who prefer above all things the grandeur of their country.

I am with the gentleman in such sentiments; but I do not participate—and I am not so familiar with economic studies as the gentleman; they have never constituted my immediate profession—I do not participate, I say, in the error that the material development we are undergoing, that the augmentation of purely material prosperity that now distinguishes us, contributes either little or much to the moral decadence of Spanish society.

On the contrary it is my opinion—and an opinion confirmed in all the events and crises of history; an opinion that, confronted by the poetical exclamations of Señor Barzanallana I hesitate to expose to the consideration of the Chamber—that on the field of reality and in the corridor of history there is no glory whatever for the poverty-stricken nations.

No; individual heroism suffices not; a great self-consciousness in the individual suffices not; the peculiar genius of a nation for figuring grandly in history, and above all in modern history, suffices not. In all those nations where lack of work, industry, conditions of wealth, have brought great poverty upon them, as by a melancholy fatality, this has been followed by a genuine decadence of all their glories, literary and military alike.

You will not maintain, you cannot prove, that there was less moral spirit, less moral consciousness, in the Spanish of the times of Cárlos II than in those of his grand predecessors. You cannot prove that the victors of Rocroy were less valorous than the comrades of Gonzalo de Córdoba.

That would not be true. If you will examine the duel to the death, that lasted for twenty-seven years between the Spanish monarchy and the French monarchy for the first position in the world, you will see that great deeds divide themselves almost equally between the two nations; but after these valorous deeds, after these military actions, France was nevertheless left in the first place and Spain in the last. This was brought about by the diversity of social conditions in which we existed; and of them many examples might be cited, now just as in the old times. And why should we not be able to cite them if this is the inexorable law of history?

The truth must be told the country; it must be told that it is not the remembrance of Lepanto or the remembrance of San Quintin which they lack, but it is examples of patience, of industry, of progress, and of civil virtues that produce the development of public prosperity by means of which the Spanish people can attain the grandeur for which it hungers, and it still has too little thereof.

Such is the existence, such is the reality of history, and

neither Señor Barzanallana nor I, nor any poet greater than he and than I (and I mention myself here because I find myself a term of comparison with the gentleman) can vary even if he would the natural and inevitable course of things. Give us the agricultural prosperity, give us the industrial prosperity and the mercantile prosperity of England and I will have no fear that our navies shall be fugitive from theirs; I will not fear that their flag shall float in any part of our territory for any considerable time; I will fear nothing that may permanently wound the heart of a Spaniard who feels his worth.

For my part, therefore, when I see that the conditions of work, of labor, and of industry are developing in my country; when I see that the breeze from abroad—unfortunately the breeze from abroad, but that is whence it comes to us—is awakening among us all the germs of prosperity; when I see that we are progressing, I am tranquil and I do not fear the moral decadence with which we are menaced. Like the vanquished Roman, I do not despair of my country.

[Special translation by Sylvester Baxter.]

LOGAN

JOHN ALEXANDER LOGAN, an American soldier and politician, was born in Jackson County, Illinois, February 9, 1826, and educated in the common schools and at Shiloh College. During the Mexican War he served as lieutenant in an Illinois regiment and at its close studied law and was elected clerk of Jackson County in 1849. Still continuing the study of law he entered Louisville University and was admitted to the bar in 1851. He sat in the State legislature, 1852-57, and entered Congress in 1858. In 1861 he resigned his seat in order to join the Federal army, where he served with distinction until the end of the conflict, and attained the rank of major-general. He returned to Congress in 1866 and was active soon after in the impeachment proceedings against President Johnson. In 1871 he was elected to the United States Senate and re-elected in 1878 and 1885. In 1884 he was the Republican candidate for the vice-presidency. He died in Washington, December 26, 1886. He was a brilliant though florid speaker and made many important addresses in Congress, including a vindication of President Grant from the attack of Sumner in 1872, on the power of government to enforce the United States laws, in 1879, and in the FitzJohn Porter case in 1880. Logan's personal appearance was striking, his complexion being very swarthy, and his hair and moustache, which were jet black, being worn very long. His published works comprise " The Great Conspiracy " (1886); " The Volunteer Soldier of America " (1887).

ON THE INDEPENDENCE OF CUBA

SPEECH DELIVERED IN THE HOUSE OF REPRESENTATIVES,
JUNE 15, 1870

CUBA, with its broad acres, its beautiful vales, its rich soil, its countless resources, is expected to pass into the hands of a few men, to whom it will be a mine of wealth.

Let me appeal to this House not to allow this scheme to be carried out. While this brave band of patriots are wrestling for the dearest rights known to man, the right of self-government, should we hesitate to make the simple and single declaration which will save them from being robbed and

(8815)

murdered day after day? Can we, with all our boasted principles of liberty, justice, and equality to all men, stand tamely by and witness these people, within sight of our own shores, following the example which we have furnished, hanged, drawn, and quartered, with most atrocious brutality, without the protection of any flag on God's earth, and not raise our voice against the inhumanity so much as to declare that there is a contest — a war? This poor boon is all they ask, and in my judgment it can be denied to them by none but heartless men.

In what I am saying I have no contest with the President. I am his friend as I ever have been. I have no contest with Mr. Fish or with anybody else. I have no warfare with those who differ from me; they have their opinions, and I am entitled to mine. I look upon General Grant as a good man, but I think that on this question he is deceived. I think if he had not been fishing up in Pennsylvania when this message was written he would not have signed it so readily as he did. I do not think it was necessary to go to Pennsylvania for more fish. We have all we need here. I think it is a message not well considered, and I do not believe he examined it well before signing it. It does not state the case correctly; and I am sorry to see him put upon the record as misstating the law.

I entertain the highest respect for the President and his administration, and I do not purpose that any man shall put me in a false position. I do not intend to allow myself to be placed in antagonism with the administration, nor do I intend to allow any man or set of men to howl upon my heels that I do not support the administration and am therefore to be denounced.

No, sir, I am supporting the administration; I am maintaining the former views of the President, and I think his former views on this question are better than his later ones. Once we held like opinions on this question of Cuban belligerency, and I see no reason on my part to change those opinions. If he has changed his I find no fault with him. But I prefer to stand by his former judgment, formed when he was cool, when he deliberated for himself, when he had not men around him to bother and annoy him with their peculiar and interested notions; when he thought for himself and wrote for himself. I believed then as he believed. I believe now as I believed then, and I do not propose to change.

Now, Mr. Speaker, I think the Republicans on this side of the House owe it to themselves to take the side of the oppressed. I wish to say to the Republican party as the friend of this administration, that the most friendly act toward this present administration is to let this message go before the country, so far as the opinion of the President is concerned. Do not let us make any war upon it. Let it appear to the country that we differ from the President in this matter honestly. Let us as Republicans, notwithstanding the message, declare that we will accord to these people all the rights of civilized warfare. Let us do this, and I have no doubt the country will say, " Well done, good and faithful servants."

If your action be taken in the interest of freedom, if you shall help the oppressed and act on the side of liberty and humanity, if in a contest between despotism and a people struggling bravely for independence you give the preference to the latter, if in doing this you should happen to commit error, and that error should happen to be on the side of humanity and liberty, there is no country in the world which can or ought to find fault with you. In questions tried be-

fore our juries they are always instructed to give the benefit
of the doubt in favor of the prisoner.

In this case, if there be any doubt, I implore the House
let it be in favor of Cuba. By taking the side of Cuba
against Spain we are true to the instincts of our organization
in sympathizing with a people suffering under oppression.
It will show that you do not sympathize with despotism. It
will show that now, as heretofore, the Republican party
sympathize with struggling humanity seeking freedom and
independence.

Your record is clear in the past. We have had too much
sympathy of late years for great monarchies. Indeed there
seems to be too great a disposition in some quarters to
sympathize too much with monarchy, and to sympathize too
much with the exercise of arbitrary power in oppression to
justice and liberty. And why is this? Because these are
great governments and controlled by the great ones. These
monarchical governments have mighty fleets floating upon
the high seas. They have ministers residing in our midst.
They have pleasant men who can afford to give splendid
entertainments. They are genial men at the dinner table,
and facile in the artful manœuvres of diplomacy. They are
what was known in the time of Louis XIV and the " Fronde,"
as *honnéte* men. They have all the appliances for making
good their cause when they wish to crush out people who are
struggling for independence. They are heard, and they have
official access to our government, which is denied to all
others.

But never let it be said that the Republican party sympa-
thizes with the oppressors against the oppressed. I warn you
that no statesman and no political party ever had a long life
in this country which did not love liberty, no matter from

where the cry came, whether from South America, or from Mexico, or from our own slaves when they were held in bondage. When the South American States raised the standard of rebellion against Spain we sympathized with them; when Mexico did the same thing, she also had our sympathy; and gentlemen should not forget that it was the Republican party that gave freedom and franchise to four million slaves in our own midst. Let gentlemen carefully examine the history of this country before they cast these people off and consign them to the merciless horrors of a Spanish inquisition. Read and mark well that no party ever succeeded which refused justice or sympathized with the oppressor against the oppressed.

If the party which abolished slavery; the party which, in the spirit of justice, gave citizenship to those who were freed by it; the party which has always held itself to be the great exponent of free principles and justice to all, of liberty and humanity — if that party shall now turn its back upon its former glorious record and lend moral support and material aid to Spain in its cruel crusade against the revolutionists of Cuba it must inevitably go down under the indignation of the people who now make up its formidable numbers. If, however, we shall give the aid which is asked to encourage and sustain struggling humanity; if we shall help these Cubans fighting for independence; if we shall do that which every dictate of justice demands of us in the emergency; in a word, if we are true to the doctrines and principles we have enunciated, then the Republican party will live to ride safely for many years to come through the boisterous storms of politics, and will override in the future, as it has done in the past, all such theories as secession and rebellion in our government, and all that is antagonistic to the universal liberty of man. It will overcome every obstacle that stands in the way of the great advance, the great civilization, the great enlightenment, the great Christianity of this age. And whenever you fail to allow it to march onward in the path in which it has started, and undertake to impede it in its efforts to press onward, you strike a blow at your own party, your own interests and safety.

For I tell you that whenever you halt, or shirk the responsibilities of the hour as Republicans the Democrats will overtake you.

The Democrats were once formidable so far as the questions of the day were concerned. They are far behind you now; and I say to you, Republicans, do not let the Democrats beat you to-day as regards the position they take in favor of liberty. If you do, the country will perhaps give you reason to learn after awhile that you have forgotten the trust that was reposed in you, and have failed to perform the duty with which it has honored you, but allowed it to slip from your hands to be discharged by others.

For these things you must answer before the great forum of the people; and if they adjudge you recreant in the support of the principles reposed in you, and false to the requirements of the present, they will not find you worthy of confidence in the future.

VINDICATION OF PRESIDENT GRANT

[Delivered in the Senate of the United States, June 3, 1872, in reply to Senator Sumner's attack on President Grant's administration.]

MR. PRESIDENT,—At the close of the war in 1865, on the 22d day of May, when the armies were marshalled here in the streets of Washington, as we passed by this Senate Chamber and marched down Pennsylvania Avenue, with the officers at the head of their columns, I remember to have read on the outer walls this motto: "There is one debt this country can never repay, and that is the debt of gratitude it owes to the soldiers who have preserved the Union."

Little did I think, then, sir, that within seven years afterward I should hear an assault like this upon the leader of that army within these very walls.

Mr. President, is that debt of gratitude so soon forgotten? Shall the fair fame and reputation of the man who led those armies be trampled in the dust by one man, who claims so egotistically here that he organized the party which made the war against the oligarchy of slavery?

But, sir, that attempt has been witnessed here, to our great sorrow. The eloquence, the power, the education, all that belong to the senator from Massachusetts has been brought to bear, not in consonance with that motto, not in keeping alive in the bosoms of the people of the United States that feeling of gratitude to the men who saved the country, but of ingratitude; and worse, of want of decent respect which should be shown either for the memory of the dead or for the character of the living.

The next division of the speech of the senator from Massachusetts is in reference to " presidential pretension," and in discussing presidential pretensions he draws himself to his full height and exclaims, " Upon what meat doth our Cæsar feed that he assumes so much ? "   That is the language of the senator from Massachusetts.   I might reply to the Senator and ask:

> " Upon what meat doth this our Cæsar feed,
> That he is grown so great? "

Where did he acquire the charter or the right to stand in this Senate Chamber and perpetrate slander upon slander, vile and malignant, against the best men of our land?   I ask the senator from Massachusetts, where does he acquire that title; where does he obtain that right belonging to himself alone?   A right, however, that no one will covet.

The senator says the President of the United States violates the constitution, violates law, violates every principle that ought to govern the chief magistrate of a great nation. I should like to ask a question of the senator if he were here, and I am sorry that he is not.   " The wicked flee when no man pursueth."   It certainly is not that he is in terror of anything that may be said; but why is it?   Is he afraid that the ghost of his own slanders will come back to haunt him even here as well as in his chamber at night? Will it haunt him as the ghost of San Domingo haunts him every day?   And this seems to follow him like the ghost of Banquo, making its appearance when he leasts expects it.

Now, sir, in what has the President of the United States violated the constitution?   If the President has violated the constitution, it is the duty of the House of Representatives to prefer charges against him, and of the Senate to try him

for that offense. In what has the President violated the law?
I ask the senator from Massachusetts to tell this country in
what has he violated the constitution, in what particular?
It may be that all of us have not construed the law alike. It
is possible to construe the constitution differently in certain
respects. The President may have differed from us at times
in reference to a construction of the law or of the constitution, but if he has I have no knowledge of it. But even if
that were the case it would be no violation of the constitution
or of the law in the sense in which the word " violation " is
used by the senator.

But the senator says the presidency is made " a plaything
and a perquisite." I read from his printed speech:

" To appreciate his peculiar character as a civilian it is
important to know his triumphs as a soldier, for the one is
the natural complement of the other. The successful soldier
is rarely changed to the successful civilian. There seems an
incompatibility between the two, modified by the extent to
which one has been allowed to exclude the other. One
always a soldier cannot late in life become a statesman;
one always a civilian cannot late in life become a soldier.
Education and experience are needed for each."

This I read from page 6 of the pamphlet which was published prior to the publication of the speech in the " Globe."
The senator says that the camp is not the training school for
a statesman, that a different training must be given a man
for the purpose of making him a statesman from that which
is required to make him a soldier. I shall not appeal to the
senator from Massachusetts on that point; but I do appeal
to the people of this country. I appeal to the million and a
half of soldiers who are living, and if I could reach the ears
of the dead I would appeal to the three hundred thousand

that lie beneath the sod who fell fighting, that their country might live, to know why a soldier cannot be a statesman and why a statesman cannot be a soldier.

I am in favor of education; but I am in favor of that education which is compatible with common sense, which gives judgment to deal with men and things.

Now I want to compare the statesman of Massachusetts with the poor little dwarfed soldier of Illinois who is now President of the United States. According to the senator from Massachusetts he is ignorant; according to the senator from Massachusetts he is a mere soldier. Before the war he followed the occupation of a tanner and received but a small pittance for his labor, and during the war he served his country in the camp and in the field and did not have the opportunity to fit himself for President of the United States. That was the language of the senator. In other words no man who has ever worked at the tanner's trade should be President; no man who was ever a shoemaker should be a senator; no man who was ever a carpenter should be a legislator; no man who was ever a farmer should aspire to position or honors from the people.

In other words, the laboring classes are, according to his theory, the " mudsills of society," but if those like the senator himself are permitted to occupy positions in this land, or can be President or Vice-President, how will it be with the poor tanners, the poor carpenters, the poor farmers, the poor printers, the poor everybodies? None of these are fit to be President or Vice-President, or senators, or members of Congress, or governors; but they are, according to the theory of the senator from Massachusetts, only fit to make food for gunpowder as mere soldiers.

Now let us see what has been accomplished by this educated, crammed senator from Massachusetts, who has been in the Senate Chamber I believe for nearly twenty-four years.

I believe I state a fact when I say that the records of Congress will not show a measure that was ever originated by himself which passed without amendment. I believe I state a fact when I say that the records and the history of this country show fewer acts of Congress on the statute-book to-day originated by him than by any other man who ever claimed to be a statesman.

His statesmanship has consisted for twenty-four years in high-sounding phrases, in long-drawn-out sentences, in paragraphs taken from books of an ancient character, as an instance of which we find in his speech pages on "nepotism" taken almost bodily from a biographical dictionary of the popes and rulers of Rome. There is wherein his greatness consists. It consists in paragraphing, in plagiarism, in declamation, and in egotism.

He has accomplished much in his own estimation. He is writing a history, or some one is for him, of himself. I have been reading it latterly. I find in it many of his speeches. If he were here now I would, as one who has been his steadfast friend, beg of him to exclude from that history of himself this last speech. It is a pleasant history to read so far as it has been written, but I say to him its pages will be marred by this malignant philippic against President Grant, filled as it is with venom and gall from one end to the other.

Let us compare the tanner President with the magnificently educated senator from Massachusetts, who has accomplished so much, and see how he will stand the comparison. The senator from Massachusetts has lived his life without putting upon the records of his country a solitary act of his own origination without amendment by other men having more understanding than himself in reference to men and things.

General Grant, the President of the United States, a tanner from Galena, has done what? He has written his history in deeds which will live. So long as pens are dipped in ink, so long as men read, and so long as history is written, the history of that man is worth something. It is valuable; it is not a history of glittering generalities and declamation in speeches, but it is a history of great deeds and great things accomplished for his country.

In 1861, soon after the breaking out of the war, we found this President of the United States the commander of a small force on the banks of the Mississippi River. On the banks of the Potomac was a large and well-organized army and the sounds were heard throughout the land of battle from day to day. When the battle was over there was but one thing that trembled along the wires and that was the army of the United States had again been defeated. Defeat upon defeat followed; and never did you find your armies successful until the fame of this little man was heralded from one end of the land to the other. Every battle that he engaged in he won.

I was with him in his first battle on the banks of the Mississippi River, the battle of Belmont, and travelled through with the western armies in the western campaign. If you will allow me—and I refer to myself only to show the facts within my knowledge—I hesitate not to say that the man who says he is ungenerous does not know him. The man who says he is not a man of ability does not know him. The man who says he ever depreciated the character or reputation of another does not know him. In all his acts he was generous to a fault with his comrades and no report did he ever make n which he did not give full credit to every man in the army who had done his duty, as can be testified to by every man who served under him.

I have seen him time and again in the hottest and thickest of battle, sitting coolly and calmly, without parting his lips or lisping a word, watching the different manœuvers of the troops and the management on either side to see how the battle was going. He was not a man of many words. He gave his orders quietly and saw that they were executed.

He was brought to the Army of the Potomac. He made a success; he won the battle; victory perched upon our banners; we succeeded; slavery was abolished and our country saved. After four years passed the people of the United States made him President. He is now assaulted because of his ignorance, because he was a soldier, and charged with having done nothing during his life to be remembered. Look at his administration and see if he shows no ability. How does it compare with others? I have not indorsed everything he has done nor do I believe a friend is required to indorse everything that another does in order to be his friend; but take his administration generally so far as the material part is concerned and so far as that which does substantial good to the country and I say it has been a great success.

[After submitting a tabular statement of the expenses of this administration, as compared with preceding ones, the senator continued:]

Now, Mr. President, I desire to draw the attention of the Senate but a short time to some of the specific charges that have been made by the senator from Massachusetts. He says the President is guilty of nepotism, and, as I said, several pages of his speech are copied for the purpose of showing first the origin of the word. It is necessary for a learned man when he discourses upon a word to show its origin. We then find the origin of the word "nepotism." He shows that it i of Italian origin and then goes on through the history o the popes, the history of those who once ruled Rome, to show how many nephews and kinsfolk they appointed to office.

Then he comes down to President Grant and he charges the President of the United States with having usurped the power of the presidential office and made it a mere perquisite and appointed to office his kinsfolk and for that reason he ought not to be recognized as a suitable candidate for President again.

Now, I want to put this question to the country. I admit that he has appointed some of his relatives to office; but I want the senator from Massachusetts to point his finger to the law that forbids that being done. If it is not in violation of law is there anything that shows that it is in violation of good morals? It seems to me for a man to take care of his own household is not in violation of good morals. It certainly is in violation of no law; and I believe we are told that "he who provideth not for his own household hath denied the faith and is worse than an infidel."

The senator does not believe there is anything like wit or genius or common sense in the President. I will repeat a remark that I heard that he had made once, that perhaps has aroused the anger of the senator to some extent. A gentleman once said to the President that the senator from Massachusetts did not altogether believe the Bible. The President quietly said there was a reason for that, and that was that he did not write it himself.

Now, if it is not any violation of the law to appoint your relatives to office, if it is not in violation of any moral prin-

ples, then I ask the senator from Massachusetts why this
raignment?

President Grant has a few relatives in office, but I never
eard their honesty or ability questioned.   I have a personal
nowledge of some of these appointments.   One is a mail
gent on a railroad, at a thousand or twelve hundred dollars a
ear.   One, Captain Ross, is a clerk in the third auditor's
ffice.   Captain Ross was the bearer of letters as mail mes-
enger to my headquarters frequently during the war.   He is
cousin of President Grant.

I went myself to the third auditor and asked that appoint-
nent, and he was appointed on my recommendation.   It is
harged that he was appointed because he is a relative of
President Grant.   The President knew nothing of it.   I ob-
ained the appointment myself.

Another one of his relatives was appointed to an office in a
Territory.   That has been paraded, too, all over the coun-
try that he was appointed, being a relative of President
Grant.

I say to the Senate to-day that that man was appointed on
the recommendation of gentlemen in Chicago, unknown to
President Grant, and I went myself to the secretary of the
interior and obtained the appointment for them.   These things
I state so far as they go because they are within my own
knowledge and I am responsible for a portion of them myself;
and the portion that I am responsible for it is my duty to
state here and I do so state it.

This is paraded as almost a crime and therefore a man is
not qualified to be President if he happens to have a father
or relatives of any kind or if he happens to appoint a few of
his relatives to office.   These are a portion of the disqualifica-
tions of a President of the United States as prescribed by the

senator from Massachusetts! On this theory he might stand a better chance for President than on some other for aught I know. But if we only elect those who have no relatives I fear we would all claim to be poor orphans picked up on the street and thereby fitted for the office of President.

The next proposition of the senator is " gift-taking recompensed by official positions." I understand that in slander there is such a thing as innuendo and the senator from Massachusetts, by the innuendoes in his speech, would leave the impression on the country that President Grant has appointed men to office who made him gifts because of the fact that they did make gifts; in other words that the gift was the consideration for the office; therefore it was a corrupt bargain between the President and the office-taker.

So far as this intimation, insinuation, or innuendo is concerned, as any one may please to term it, I say, and take the responsibility, for the President of the United States, of denouncing it as false, and basely false. I do so for the reason that men who have been appointed to office were appointed to the two offices he mentioned because of their friendship to the President and their ability for the duties of the office and their fealty to the Republican party.

Let us see for a moment what this gift-taking is. Is it a crime for a man to receive gifts who has accomplished great deeds for his country? If it is let us examine the history of the country for a moment.

President Grant was a great chieftain. He had achieved great things for this government. He was a great commander of armies and forces. He was victorious in all his battles. When he came home from a victorious war, when States had been joined together that had before been severed and people were united that had been divided by war, the people of the country felt grateful to him for his achievements and what he had done for them.

There was no way in which some of the wealthy men of this country believed they could show their gratitude to this great chieftain more appropriately, inasmuch as he was a man of small means, than by presenting him with that which would make him a comfortable income the rest of his life. They did it because they were actuated by generous feelings toward him, because they were loyal men, because they loved their country. Their country had been saved, their property had been saved, and they were willing to contribute to the benefit of this man. They did so.

In contributing to him they contributed to many others, as was said by the senator from Wisconsin. General Sherman and other generals that I could mention they contributed to because of their gratefulness to them for the service they had rendered the country. These contributions were made to him when he was a soldier; they were made to him when he was not President; they were given to him and given to him with good feeling, a generous feeling, a feeling of kindness, without any hesitancy on the part of the people who gave them, without the expectation of any remuneration or any reward that would be given to them by the President of the United States.

When General Sherman and General Grant received presents, men, women, and children all over the land thanked God that some persons were able to make them presents, because of the fact that they deserved it, the people being a grateful people.

I might go on and enumerate quite a number of men who have received gifts because of the gratitude of the people of their country for that which they had done. In fact if we were to search the pages of ancient history for the purpose of finding something objectionable to apply to General Grant we would find that those who came home victorious received triumphs. It has been from time immemorial the case that men who achieved great things in war were received triumphantly by their people, some with gifts and presents, some in one way and some in another; and yet because the custom of the ancient world is followed down to the present day in the instance of President Grant it is brought against him here as a charge to show that he has used it as a consideration by giving office to persons not entitled thereto and therefore should not be again elected. Sir, you must show something more than the acquiescence in customs to turn this country against its greatest preserver among men.

Let me call the attention of the senator from Massachusetts to the fact that on our statute-books to-day we find the law that where naval officers capture prizes they are entitled to a division of the prizes. Why? To encourage the navy to capture prizes and be vigilant. Even here you make presents to naval officers by statute law for doing what? Just for performing their duty and nothing more.

But inasmuch as President Grant performed his duty without prize money, when he came home and the people bestowed upon him that which you bestow by law on naval officers the eloquent senator from Massachusetts arises in his place and charges corruption. How easy it is, sir, for us to find fault with others whom the people honor, lest we may never be placed in a position to be so highly favored ourselves.

After discussing the question of gift-taking he says that Mr. Stewart of New York was appointed secretary of the treasury, and he uses that for the purpose of showing the ignorance of President Grant. He says that President Grant appointed Mr. Stewart; he does not say it was because Mr. Stewart had made him a present but that is the inference from his language, and at the same time he intimates the ignorance of the President to be so great that he did not know that an importing merchant could not be collector of the port of New York or secretary of the treasury. Now, I venture the assertion, and I think I can prove it from the record, that the senator's ignorance was so great at the same time that he did not know it was the law.

Mr. Lincoln, without a knowledge of the law, once tendered to an importing merchant an appointment to the office of collector of New York, and the merchant declined. It was an old statute, unknown to any one almost, unthought of for years. Mr. Stewart's name was sent to the Senate Chamber; in the message withdrawing the name of Mr. Stewart the President said, after mentioning the statute:

" In view of these provisions and the fact that Mr. Stewart has been unanimously confirmed by the Senate, I withdraw his name."

In view of what? In view of the fact that this statute exists and what other fact? The fact that he has been unanimously confirmed! Tell me how could he be unanimously confirmed in this Senate if there was a man in the Senate who knew that law existed at that time. It was not ignorance on the part of President Grant any more than it was on the part of the senator from Massachusetts, who voted for his confirmation with that statute on our books.

Yet he brings this forward as a fact to prove the ignorance of President Grant that he did not know that the law existed. We are all very wise after finding out something. If we only find out that which others did not know before we are very anxious to tell the world of our great discovery and when it was ascertained. The senator did not tell the Senate that he found and discovered this statute. It is a wonder he did not say, " I arose and objected at the time, because it was in violation of law." He did not say that; but the statute was discovered by a clerk in the treasury department and not by the senator from Massachusetts or any other senator. Yet the senator from Massachusetts has achieved a great victory over President Grant in proving him to be ignorant of a statute that he knew nothing about himself.

The next suggestion of the senator is that President Grant quarrels with every one.

I know that President Grant is not a quarrelsome man. If he dislikes you he has nothing to do with you, but he does not quarrel.

In the army if an officer did not perform his duty he merely sent him a little order relieving him from duty and you have never heard General Grant lisp the reason up to this day why he relieved an officer in the army, and if you will go and ask him now why he relieved many officers during the war he will not tell you. He did it because he thought they had failed to perform their duty, but the reason he did not give, because perhaps he thought others might not see the fault as he did, and if he was mistaken he would let it work itself out without trying to injure the party any worse than by simply relieving him.

This was his mode of doing business in the army. I believe it is his manner to-day. If you dislike him and let him know it, that is enough; you hear nothing from him. If he dislikes you it is the same thing precisely, but he quarrels with no one.

Mr. President, the speech of the senator from Massachusetts, presented to the country at this particular time, is a very significant fact. I wish to call his attention to one point in it, but this suggestion I wish to make in order to show him how fatal to himself this speech may be.

He says that at the time he approached Secretary Stanton on his dying bed and the secretary repeated to him the reasons why he had no faith in General Grant's ability to administer the government, he said to the secretary, " It is too late; why did you not say this sooner ? "

I repeat the same thing to Senator Sumner. Your speech, to perform the office you intended it, came too late. Hence I am led to the conclusion that it was not intended to perform the office which he says it was intended but it was to perform a very different office from that which he intimates he intended it should perform; that is to say, to advise the American people that President Grant was not qualified to exercise the functions of that office, and hence ought to be supplanted by some one else at Philadelphia. No, sir; if that was the object it comes too late. That being so, I have come to the conclusion that a man of so much wisdom and of so many pretensions as the senator from Massachusetts had a very different intention.

Sir, his intention was to strangle and destroy the Republican party, that party which he says he created. If he did, I say to him he performed a great work. If he was the architect and builder of the Republican party he is a great master-workman—its dome so beautifully rounded, its columns so admirably chiselled, and all its parts so admirably prepared and builded together so smoothly and so perfectly that the mechanism charms the eye of every one who has ever seen it. Since the senator has performed such a great work, I appeal to him to know why it is that he attempts to destroy the workmanship of his own hands.

But let me give him one word of advice. While he may think, Samson-like, that he has the strength to carry off the gates and the pillars of the temple, let me tell him when he stretches forth his arm to cause the pillars to reel and totter beneath this fabric, there are thousands and thousands of true-hearted Republicans who will come up to the work and stretching forth their strong right arms, say, " Stay thou there; these pillars stand beneath this mighty fabric of ours, within which we all dwell; it is the ark of our safety and shall not be destroyed." . . .

The history of the world would write the American people down as a people not worthy of trust, as a people without gratitude, as a people who had seen a man hew his way to fame by his own strong arm, and then allowed an ambitious politician to strike him down with a merciless blow and no one to stand by and to say, " The blow is too severe;" and I say to the senator from Massachusetts that while he has struck this blow, as he believes a heavy one, on the head of the political prospects of General Grant he has made him friends by the thousand, strong ones, too, that were merely lukewarm yesterday.

He has aroused the spirit of this land that cannot be quelled. He has in fact inflamed the old war spirit in the soldiery of the country. He has aroused the feeling of indignation in every man that warmed his feet by a campfire during the war. He has sent through this land a thrill which will return to him in such a manner and with such force as will make him feel it.

For myself I will say that I have sat quietly here for months and had not intended to say anything; I had no argument to make, intending to await the nomination of the Philadelphia convention, be it Grant or be it whom it might, believing, however, it would be Grant; but when I heard these vile slanders hurled like javelins against the President of the United States it aroused a feeling in my breast which has been aroused many times before. I am now ready to buckle on my armor and am ready for the fray and from now until November next to fight this battle in behalf of an honest man, a good soldier, and a faithful servant.

You will hear a response to this everywhere. As I said the other day it will be heard from one end of this land to the other. The lines of blue coats that were arrayed upon the hill-tops and along the valleys, with burnished bayonets, ready for the fight, the same men, although they have divested themselves of their battle array, yet retain their warlike spirit burning in their bosoms.

They will respond to this challenge; they will say to the eloquent senator from Massachusetts, "You have thrown down the glove and we will take it up."

I tell the senator he will find a response in his own State that will not give his slumberings much quiet. He will find a response everywhere. The people of this country will not see a man sacrificed to vile calumny. I would be willing, and I believe every one else would, to allow the contest to be settled fairly and justly.

Let the people select whom they desire to have for their President or for any other position. And when the senator from Massachusetts, with his thundering voice echoing in this chamber, proposes to exclude every man who fought for his country, every man that has been a soldier, from civil office, and claiming that the right to hold office belongs alone to men like himself, I say he will find even poor but honest, hard-working men saying to him the time has not come in this free republic of America for such doctrine to be tolerated on the floor of the Senate or on the floor of the lower House of Congress, and if so, it will not be taken and relished as a sweet morsel by the people of this land.

No, Mr. President, when we are challenged to the contest and when we are told that soldiers are only made to be soldiers and educated civilians only should hold high positions of trust in this country, I am sorry to say to the senator: Unfortunate man, you were never born to be President of the United States; you will never be the President of that grand party which you claim to have originated and organized. No man with such aspirations and such views and such feelings for the common people of this country can ever succeed as a politician or statesman in the midst of a people devoted to republican institutions.

President Grant has made an honest President. He has been faithful. The affairs of the nation are in good condition. We are at peace with the civilized world. Notwithstanding the senator said we were in a muddle with every nation, we are at war with none.

Every State in this Union is quiet; the laws have been faithfully executed and administered; we have quiet and peace throughout our land. Such blessings we have not had since the war until recently. But the senator from Massachusetts would turn the government of the United States over to the hands of our enemies.

That is what we do not desire. If he desires not to accomplish that let him be faithful and stand by the old Republican ship in which there is life and outside of which there is death. But whether he does or not success will be ours; this government will be peaceful, the people happy and prosperous, harmony and unity will prevail, to the great advancement of the material interests of this great nation.

Mr. President, let me ask senators here who stood anxiously waiting at the close of this war to see the very state of things brought about that we see to-day, peace, comfort, quiet, and prosperity, as they looked out upon the boisterous ocean of secession and saw the raging and fierce billows of angry strife, if it was not the prayer then of every patriotic man, woman, and child in this land that the angry billows should cease and that we should once more have placid seas; and as we looked out upon these angry waves of rebellion and strife and saw the old ship of state struggling to make her way to a harbor of safety and saw this man, now President, then guiding and commanding the crew that managed this craft, when at his command our guns ceased their thunder and everything was still and quiet, the old ship, manned by her devoted crew, came safely into the harbor of safety, freighted with the hopes of mankind, where she is moored quiet and peaceful to-day? Who is there that can describe the outbreak of overjoyous hearts in strains of praise for the safety of our republic that went forth on that day of triumph? Sir, that feeling still is in the bosom of patriots and though slumbering will break forth again, having been aroused by the blast of the enemy's bugle.

Who is there among the Republicans that desires to set the old craft adrift again into the boisterous seas of tumult and confusion? I presume there is not one. Then let us as quiet, law-abiding, peaceable citizens, desirous of doing the best we can for our country, go straight forward in the execution of the proper plans and designs for the accomplishment of the objects for which republican institutions are established and are maintained.

Let us, then, proceed with our business; let us go home an
present to the people of this country the indictment with i
malignant charges, and ask them if they will submit to hav
a man so worthy as the President of the United States receiv
such calumny at the hands of any one without a proper re
buke, and I pledge you that you will have a response indi
cating no uncertain sound coming from the lips and heart o
every true patriot in the land.

Mr. President, I have detained the Senate much longer
than I intended, but I deemed it just to myself and to my
constituents that that document should not go before them
without my raising my voice at least in protest against it. I
have done so in my feeble manner, not ably, but the best that
I could do; having done that, I have performed what I consider my duty and will now give way for the business of the
Senate to proceed.

SELF-GOVERNMENT IN LOUISIANA

DELIVERED JANUARY 8, 1875

MR. PRESIDENT,—I believe it is considered the duty
of a good sailor to stand by his ship in the midst of a
great storm. We have been told in this chamber
that a great storm of indignation is sweeping over this land
which will rend asunder and sink the old Republican craft.
We have listened to denunciations of the President, of the
Republicans in this chamber, of the Republican party as an
organization, their acts heretofore and their purposes in reference to acts hereafter, of such a character as has seldom been
listened to in this or any other legislative hall.

Every fact on the side of the Republican party has been perverted, every falsehood on the part of the opposition has been exaggerated, arguments have been made here calculated to inflame and arouse a certain class of the people of this country against the authorities of the government, based not upon truth but upon manufactured statements which were utterly false.

The Republican party has been characterized as despotic, as tyrannical, as oppressive. The course of the administration and the party toward the Southern people has been denounced as of the most tyrannical character by men who have received clemency at the hands of this same party.

Now, sir, what is the cause of all this vain declamation? What is the cause of all this studied denunciation? What is the reason for all these accusations made against a party or an administration? I may be mistaken, but if I am not, this is the commencement of the campaign of 1876. It has been thought necessary on the part of the opposition senators here to commence, if I may use a homely phrase, a raid upon the Republican party and upon this administration, and to base that upon false statements in reference to the conduct of affairs in the State of Louisiana.

It does not belong to my feeble powers to do justice to this question, to this outrage that has been perpetrated upon the people of this country by falsifying the facts with reference to the conduct of these people within the State of Louisiana.

Some remarks have been made upon this floor peculiar in their strength and strained I must say in the manner of their utterance. Our amiable friend from Delaware [Mr. Bayard] who seldom so far forgets himself as to use harsh language toward any one, in his calm and deliberate speech the other day made use of language that I must say aroused somewhat in me a feeling different from that which I desire to have in reference to that senator, for I have always had great respect for him. He said, in speaking of General Sheridan's despatch, "Let us see if that man Sheridan is fit to breathe the free air of a republic."

He then said his acts were those of cruelty and disgraceful to the American nation. If Sheridan is not fit to breathe the free air of the republic I appeal to heaven to name the man in this land who is. If Sheridan, after having done as much perhaps as almost any man beneath the shining sun to preserve this republic, is not fit to breathe its free air, tell me the name of that living man who is?

What are we to infer from such language as this? If a man is not fit to breathe the free air of a republic he is not fit to hold office under it. If his acts are disgraceful to this country he is unfit to wear the badge of official position. All this being the case in the estimation of the senator from Delaware, we have plainly depicted on the canvas that is now moving before us that which will be done when they succeed to power. What is it? When the Democrats shall have control with their allies what shall we expect? Sheridan is not fit to breathe the free air of a republic; he is a disgrace to the nation; he must go out. Sherman, too, indorsing Sheridan, must go out. Grant must pass away. All the men that helped save the republic are now a disgrace to the republic. They must bow themselves out and you must bow yourselves in.

Who bow in? Your Earlys, your Davises, and others of like ilk, your men that tried to destroy the government by thundering at its gates for four years, trampling the constitution and laws under foot, violating their oaths as citizens, are to take their places. Is that what you mean? I want to know it now if that is the meaning of the remarks of the senator from Delaware.

Sir, it will be a good while in this country before a little indiscreet remark in a despatch that has no force in it, that cannot be executed in any way whatever, will cause the American people to forget the gallantry of a man like Phil. Sheridan. This country will have to be subsoiled and plowed over and the bones of every soldier in this land buried so deep that you cannot touch them before such a man will stand in disgrace for an indiscreet remark in a despatch. The gentleman who undertook to bury his patriotism, to destroy his fair fame and his fair name by such remarks in this chamber did not well understand the hearts of the American people.

But we are told that the people of the South are loyal and true to the government. We are told by our friend from North Carolina [Mr. Merrimon] that peace reigns in that State, peace reigns in Georgia, in Alabama, in every State in the South. When you mention here the fact that disorders are existing in Southern States you find senators jumping up at every corner and saying, " There is no trouble in my State." Our friend from North Carolina says there is no trouble in his State. They did elect a Ku-Klux judge down there, but still they have no trouble. It was necessary probably to protect the rest of the Ku-Klux and therefore it gave peace!

My friend from Maryland says, " Give the Democrats control of the Southern States and you will have peace, but you cannot have it unless they have control! " I do not doubt that this is true, but what a peace that would be! I have heard that remark before. Do you not remember—sir, I know you do—that some fourteen years ago the only remark was " Let us alone," " Let us alone? "

The only remark was, " Do not interfere with us and you will have peace; if you do not make war we will not."

This remark of " Let us have the States and we will give you peace " is the cry of men seeking to destroy the government by insinuating themselves into power, and if they cannot insinuate themselves into power they will use terror, threat, murder, and everything else for that purpose. Give the Democracy control and you will have peace, but if they cannot have control they will not let us have peace!

I only give the facts as they are of record, and of course there may be an exception which I know nothing about. I only take that from the record as I find it. I am always ready to be corrected if I am wrong in reference to anything, and I am glad to give the senator the benefit of his correction, and that part of the statement was made under a misapprehension of the facts.

Now, Mr. President, I want to ask candid, honest, fairminded men, after reading this report of General Sheridan showing the murder, not for gain, not for plunder, but for political opinions in the last few years of thirty-five hundred persons in the State of Louisiana, all of them Republicans, not one of them a Democrat—I want to ask if they can stand here before this country and defend the Democratic party of Louisiana? I put this question to them, for they have been here for days crying against the wrongs upon the Democracy of Louisiana. I want any one of them to tell me if he is prepared to defend the Democracy of Louisiana. What is your Democracy of Louisiana?

You are excited, your extreme wrath is aroused at General Sheridan because he called your White Leagues down there " banditti." I ask you if the murder of thirty-five hundred men in a short time for political purposes by a band of men banded together for the purpose of murder does not make them banditti, what it does make them? Does it make them Democrats? It certainly does not make them Republicans. Does it make them honest men? It certainly does not. Does it make them law-abiding men? It certainly does not. Does it make them peaceable citizens? It certainly does not.

But what does it make? A band of men banded together and perpetrating murder in their own State? Webster says a bandit is " a lawless or desperate fellow; a robber; a brigand," and " banditti " are men banded together for plunder and murder; and what are your White Leagues banded together for if the result proves that they are banded together for murder for political purposes?

O, what a crime it was in Sheridan to say that these men were banditti! He is a wretch. From the papers he ought to be hanged to a lamp-post; from the senators he is not fit to breathe the free air of heaven or of this free republic; but your murderers of thirty-five hundred people for political offences are fit to breathe the air of this country and are defended on this floor to-day, and they are defended here by the Democratic party, and you cannot avoid or escape the proposition. You have denounced Republicans for trying to keep the peace in Louisiana; you have denounced the administration for trying to suppress bloodshed in Louisiana; you have denounced all for the same purpose; but not one word has fallen from the lips of a solitary Democratic senator denouncing these wholesale murders in Louisiana. You have said, " I am sorry these things are done," but you have defended the White Leagues; you have defended Penn; you have defended rebellion; and you stand here to-day the apologists of murder, of rebellion, and of treason in that State.

I want to ask the judgment of an honest country, I want to ask the judgment of the moral sentiments of the law-abiding people of this grand and glorious republic to tell me whether men shall murder by the score, whether men shall trample the law under foot, whether men shall force judges to resign, whether men shall force prosecuting attorneys to resign, whether men shall take five officers of a State out and hang or shoot them if they attempt to exercise the functions of their office, whether men shall terrify the voters and office-holders of a State, whether men shall undertake in viola-tion of law to organize a legislature for revolutionary pur-poses, for the purpose of putting a governor in possession and taking possession of the State and then ask the Democ-racy to stand by them—I appeal to the honest judgment of the people of this land and ask them to respond whether this was not an excusable case when this man used the army to protect the life of that State and to preserve the peace of that people?

Sir, the man who will not use all the means in his power to preserve the nationality, the integrity of this government, the integrity of a State, or the peace and happiness of a people, is not fit to govern, he is not fit to hold position in this or any other civilized age.

Does liberty mean wholesale slaughter? Does republican government mean tyranny and oppression of its citizens? Does an intelligent and enlightened age of civilization mean murder and pillage, bloodshed at the hands of Ku-Klux or White Leagues or anybody else, and if any one attempts to put it down, attempts to reorganize and produce order where chaos and confusion have reigned, they are to be denounced as tyrants, as oppressors, and as acting against republican institutions? I say then the happy days of this republic are gone. When we fail to see that republicanism means nothing, that liberty means nothing but the unrestrained license of the mobs to do as they please, then republican government is a failure.

Liberty of the citizen means the right to exercise such rights as are prescribed within the limits of the law so that he does not in the exercise of these rights infringe the rights of other citizens. But the definition is not well made by our friends on the opposite side of this chamber.

Their idea of liberty is license; it is not liberty but it is license. License to do what? License to violate law, to trample constitutions under foot, to take life, to take property, to use the bludgeon and the gun or anything else for the purpose of giving themselves power. What statesman ever heard of that as a definition of liberty? What man in a civilized age has ever heard of liberty being the unrestrained license of the people to do as they please without any restraint of law or of authority? No man, no not one until we found the Democratic party, would advocate this proposition and indorse and encourage this kind of license in a free country.

Mr. President, I have perhaps said more on this question of Louisiana than might have been well for me to say on account of my strength, but what I have said about it I have said because I honestly believed it. What I have said in reference to it comes from an honest conviction in my mind and in my heart of what has been done to suppress violence and wrong. But I have a few remarks in conclusion to submit now to my friends on the other side in answer to what they have said not by way of argument but by way of accusation. You say to us—I had it repeated to me this morning in private conversation—" Withdraw your troops from Louisiana and you will have peace."

Ah, I heard it said on this floor once, " Withdraw your troops from Louisiana and your State government will not last a minute." I heard that said from the opposite side of the chamber, and now you say, " Withdraw your troops from Louisiana and you will have peace."

Mr. President, I dislike to refer to things that are past and gone; I dislike to have my mind called back to things of the past; but I well remember the voice in this chamber once that rang out and was heard throughout this land, " Withdraw your troops from Fort Sumter if you want peace." I heard that said. Now it is, " Withdraw your troops from Louisiana if you want peace."

Yes, I say, withdraw your troops from Louisiana if you want a revolution, and that is what is meant.

But, sir, we are told, and doubtless it is believed by the senators who tell us so, who denounce the Republican party, that it is tyrannical, oppressive, and outrageous. They have argued themselves into the idea that they are patriots, pure and undefiled. They have argued themselves into the idea that the Democratic party never did any wrong. They have been out of power so long that they have convinced themselves that if they only had control of this country for a short time, what a glorious country they would make it.

They had control for nearly forty long years, and while they were the agents of this country—I appeal to history to bear me out—they made the government a bankrupt, with rebellion and treason in the land, and were then sympathizing with it wherever it existed. That is the condition in which

hey left the country when they had it in their possession
nd within their control.

But they say the Republican party is a tyrant; that it is
ppressive. As I have said, I wish to make a few sugges-
ions to my friends in answer to this accusation—oppressive
o whom? They say to the South, that the Republican party
as tyrannized over the South. Let me ask you how has it
yrannized over the South?

Without speaking of our troubles and trials through which
we passed, I will say this: at the end of a rebellion that
scourged this land, that drenched it with blood, that devas-
tated a portion of it, left us in debt and almost bankrupt,
what did the Republican party do? Instead of leaving these
our friends and citizens to-day in a territorial condition,
where we might exercise jurisdiction over them for the next
coming twenty years, where we might have deprived them
of the rights of members on this floor, what did we do? We
reorganized them into States, admitted them back into the
Union, and through the clemency of the Republican party
we admitted representatives on this floor who had thundered
against the gates of liberty for four bloody years. Is that
the tyranny and oppression of which you complain at the
hands of the Republican party? Is that a part of our oppression against you Southern people?

Let us go a little further. When the armed Democracy,
for that is what they were, laid down their arms in the
Southern States, after disputing the right of freedom and
liberty in this land for four years, how did the Republican
party show itself in its acts of tyranny and oppression toward
you? You appealed to them for clemency. Did you get
it? Not a man was punished for his treason. Not a man
ever knocked at the doors of a Republican Congress for a

pardon who did not get it   Not a man ever petitioned the
generosity of the Republican party to be excused for his
crimes who was not excused.   Was that oppression upon
the part of Republicans in this land?   Is that a part of the
oppression of which you accuse us?

Let us look a little further.   We find to-day twenty-seven
Democratic representatives in the other branch of Congress
who took arms in their hands and tried to destroy this government, holding commissions there by the clemency of the
Republican party.   We find in this chamber by the clemency of the Republican party three senators who held
such commissions.   Is that tyranny; is that oppression; is
that the outrage of this Republican party on you Southern
people?

Sir, when Jeff Davis, the head of the great rebellion, who
roams the land free as air, north, south, east, and west, makes
Democratic speeches wherever invited, and the vice-president
of the Southern rebellion holds his seat in the other House
of Congress, are we to be told that we are tyrants and oppressing the Southern people?

These things may sound a little harsh, but it is time to tell
the truth in this country.   The time has come to talk facts.
The time has come when cowards should hide and honest
men should come to the front and tell you plain, honest
truths.   You of the South talk to us about oppressing you.
You drenched your land in blood, caused weeping throughout this vast domain, covered the land in weeds of mourning
both north and south, widowed thousands and orphaned
many, made the pension-roll as long as an army-list, made
the debt that grinds the poor of this land—for all these
things you have been pardoned, and yet you talk to us about
oppression.

So much for the oppression of the Republican party of your patriotic souls and selves. Next comes the President of the United States. He is a tyrant, too. He is an oppressor still, in conjunction with the Republican party. Oppressor of what? Who has he oppressed of your Southern people, and when, and where? When your Ku-Klux, banded together for murder and plunder in the Southern States, were convicted by their own confession, your own representatives pleaded to the President and said, " Give them pardon and it will reconcile many of the Southern people." The President pardoned them; pardoned them of their murder, of their plunder, of their piracy on land; and for this I suppose he is a tyrant.

More than that, sir, this tyrant in the White House has done more for you Southern people than you ought to have asked him to do. He has had confidence in you until you betrayed that confidence. He has not only pardoned the offenses of the South, pardoned the criminals of the Democratic party, but he has placed in high official position in this Union some of the leading men who fought in the rebellion He has put in his cabinet one of your men; he has made governors of Territories of some of your leading men who fought in the rebellion; he has sent on foreign missions abroad some of your men who warred against this country; he has placed others in the departments; and has tried to reconcile you in every way on earth, by appealing to your people, by recognizing them and forgiving them for their offences; and for these acts of generosity, for these acts of kindness, he is arraigned to-day as a Cæsar, as a tyrant, as an oppressor.

Such kindness in return as the President has received from these people will mark itself in the history of generosity.

O, but say they, Grant wants to oppress the White Leagues
in Louisiana; therefore he is an oppressor.

Yes, Mr. President, Grant does desire that these men
should quit their every-day chivalric sports of gunning upon
negroes and Republicans. He asks kindly that you stop it.
He says to you, "That is all I want you to do;" and you say
that you are desirous that they shall quit it. You have but
to say it and they will quit it. It is because you have never
said it that they have not quit it. It is in the power of the
Democratic party to-day but to speak in tones of majesty,
of honor, and justice in favor of human life, and your Ku-
Klux and murderers will stop. But you do not do it; and
that is the reason they do not stop. In States where it has
been done they have stopped.

But it will not do to oppress those people; it will not do
to make them submit and subject them to the law; it will
not do to stop these gentlemen in their daily sports and in
their lively recreations. They are White Leagues; they are
banded together as gentlemen; they are of Southern blood;
they are of old Southern stock; they are the chivalry of days
gone by; they are knights of the bloody shield; and the shield
must not be taken from them. Sirs, their shield will be
taken from them; this country will be aroused to its danger;
this country will be aroused to do justice to its citizens; and
when it does the perpetrators of crime may fear and tremble.
Tyranny and oppression! A people who without one word
of opposition allows men who have been the enemies of a
government to come into these legislative halls and make
laws for that government to be told that they are oppressors
is a monstrosity in declamation and assertion. Whoever
heard of such a thing before? Whoever believed that such
men could make such charges? Yet we are tyrants!

[Mr. Logan here gave way to allow a message to be received from the House of Representatives, which announced the passage of a bill removing the political disabilities of John Withers, Joseph F. Minter, and William Kearney.]

Mr. President, the reading of the title of that bill from the House only reminds me of more acts of tyranny and oppression of the Republican party, and there is a continuation of the same great offences constantly going on in this chamber. But some may say, " It is strange to see Logan defending the President of the United States." It is not strange to me. I can disagree with the President when I think he is wrong; and I do not blame him for disagreeing with me; but when these attacks are made, coming from where they do, I am ready to stand from the rising sun in the morning to the setting sun at evening to defend every act of his in connection with this matter before us.

I may have disagreed with President Grant in many things; but I was calling attention to the men who have been accusing him here, on this floor, on the stump, and in the other House; the kind of men who do it, the manner of its doing, the sharpness of the shafts that are sent at him, the poisonous barbs that they bear with them, and from these men who at his hands have received more clemency than any men ever received at the hands of any President or any man who governed a country.

Why, sir, I will appeal to the soldiers of the rebel army to testify in behalf of what I say in defence of President Grant—the honorable men who fought against the country, if there was honor in doing it. What will be their testimony? It will be that he captured your armed Democracy of the South, he treated them kindly, turned them loose, with their horses, with their wagons, with their provisions; treated

them as men, and not as pirates. Grant built no prison-pens
for the Southern soldiers; Grant provided no starvation for
Southern men; Grant provided no " dead-lines " upon which
to shoot Southern soldiers if they crossed them; Grant provided no outrageous punishment against these people that
now call him a tyrant. Generous to a fault in all his actions
toward the men who were fighting his country and destroying the constitution, that man to-day is denounced as a very
Cæsar!

Sherman has not been denounced, but the only reason is
that he was not one of the actors in this transaction; but I
want now to say to my friends on the other side, especially
to my friend from Delaware, who repeated his bitter denunciation against Sheridan yesterday—and I say this in all kindness, because I am speaking what future history will bear me
out in—when Sheridan and Grant and Sherman, and others
like them, are forgotten in this country you will have no
country. When the Democratic party is rotten for centuries
in its grave, the life, the course, the conduct of these men
will live as bright as the noonday sun in the heart of every
patriot of a republic like the American Union. Sirs, you
may talk about tyranny, you may talk about oppression, you
may denounce these men; their glory may fade into the darkness of night; but that darkness will be a brilliant light compared with the darkness of the Democratic party. Their
pathway is illuminated by glory; yours by dark deeds against
the government. That is a difference which the country will
bear witness to in future history when speaking of this country and the actors on its stage.

Now, Mr. President, I have a word to say about our duty.
A great many people are asking, what shall we do? Plain
and simple in my judgment is the proposition. I say to

Republicans, do not be scared. No man is ever hurt by doing an honest act and performing a patriotic duty. If we are to have a war of words outside or inside, let us have them in truth and soberness, but in earnest. What then is our duty? I did not believe that in 1872 there were official data upon which we could decide who was elected governor in Louisiana. But this is not the point of my argument. It is that the President has recognized Kellogg as governor of that State, and he has acted for two years. The legislature of the State has recognized him; the supreme court of the State has recognized him; one branch of Congress has recognized him. The duty is plain, and that is for this, the other branch of Congress, to do it, and that settles the question. Then, when it does it, your duty is plain and simple, and as the President has told you, he will perform his without fear, favor, or affection. Recognize the government that revolution has been against and intended to overthrow, and leave the President to his duty and he will do it. That is what to do.

Sir, we have been told that this old craft is rapidly going to pieces; that the angry waves of dissension in the land are lashing against her sides. We are told that she is sinking, sinking, sinking to the bottom of the political ocean. Is that true? Is it true that this gallant old party, that this gallant old ship that has sailed through troubled seas before is going to be stranded now upon the rock of fury that has been set up by a clamor in this chamber and a few newspapers in the country? Is it true that the party that saved this country in all its great crises, in all its great trials, is sinking to-day on account of its fear and trembling before an inferior enemy? I hope not. I remember, sir, once I was told that the old Republican ship was gone; but when I steadied myself on the shores bounding the political ocean of strife and commotion, I looked afar off and there I could see a vessel bounding the boisterous billows with white sail unfurled, marked on her sides " Freighted with the hopes of mankind," while the great Mariner above, as her helmsman, steered her, navigated her to a haven of rest, of peace, and of safety. You have but to look again upon that broad ocean of political commotion to-day, and the time will soon come when the same old craft, provided with the same cargo, will be seen, flying the same flag, passing through these tempestuous waves, anchoring herself at the shores of honesty and justice, and there she will lie undisturbed by strife and tumult, again in peace and safety.

ROSS

JONATHAN ROSS, a noted American jurist, was born at Waterford, Vermont, April 30, 1826, and educated at Dartmouth College. He taught school in his native State for a time, subsequently studied law, and was admitted to the bar in 1856. He then began the practice of his profession in St. Johnsbury, Vermont, which continued to be his home from that time. After serving three terms in the Vermont house of representatives he entered the State Senate in 1870, and in the same year was elected one of the judges of the Vermont supreme court. He became chief judge in 1890 and in January, 1899, soon after the death of the senior senator from Vermont, Justin Morrill, was chosen to fill out the latter's unexpired term in the Senate of the United States.

THE NATION'S RELATION TO ITS ISLAND POSSESSIONS

FROM SPEECH DELIVERED IN THE UNITED STATES SENATE,
JANUARY 23, 1900

IN REGARD to Cuba the duty is particular. It is so constituted by the resolutions antedating the war and by the provisions of the treaty. The preamble of the joint resolution of Congress approved April 20, 1898, counts upon the abhorrent conditions which have existed in that island for more than three years, shocking to the moral sense of the people of the United States, a disgrace to Christian civilization, culminating in the destruction of the "Maine" with two hundred and sixty-six of its officers and crew, and thereupon it is solemnly resolved: (1) That the people of the island are, and of right ought to be free and independent; (2) That it is the duty of this government to demand, and it does demand, that Spain at once relinquish its authority and government of the island; (3) Authorizes the President to use the entire land and naval forces and to call out the militia to enforce the demand; (4) The United States disclaims any disposition or intention to exercise sovereignty, jurisdiction, or control over the island except for the pacification thereof, and then asserts its determination to leave the government and control of the island to its people.

These were followed by the act approved April 25th, declaring that a state of war had existed between the United States and Spain since April 21st, and directing and empowering the President to use the entire land and naval forces and to call into the service the militia of the United States in the prosecution of the war. The President exercised the power conferred, obeyed the direction, prosecuted the war to a successful termination, resulting first in the protocol and then in the treaty ratified by the Senate, by which Spain relinquishes her sovereignty over Cuba, and the United States announces to the world that she is about to occupy and while the occupation continues she—

will assume and discharge the obligations that may, under international law, result from the fact of its occupation for the protection of life and property.

The United States is now in the exercise of such occupation. It has been claimed that she did not take sovereignty over the island; that on the relinquishment by Spain it vanished into thin air to some place unknown, or, as one eminent writer on international law has said, was in abeyance until the inhabitants of the island should be in condition to receive and exercise it. Sovereignty is supreme or paramount control in the government of a country. The United States is now and has been since the signing of the protocol in the exercise of this control in the government of the island. It has not been a divided control, as sometimes happens in the

onflict of arms. Her control has been unquestioned and
ındisputed. I think the United States, upon the surrender
)f sovereignty over the island by Spain, immediately follow-
ng the signing of the protocol, took sovereignty over the
sland, not as her own, nor for her benefit, nor for the people
)f the United States, but for the inhabitants of the island,
for the specified and particular purpose of pacification of the
ısland. What is meant by the pacification of the island? It
may be difficult to determine.

Persons and nations may differ in regard to the state of
things which must exist to have this accomplished. The
Cubans may say that they are pacified, in a state of peace
now, and therefore it is our duty to withdraw and allow them
to set up such a government as they may choose. We may
say that pacification means more than absence of a state of
war; that, considering the state of things that had existed for
three or more years, it means until the inhabitants shall have
acquired a reliable, stable government. Are the Cubans
capable of establishing and maintaining a stable government?
Who shall decide? If that be the meaning, what kind of
a government? A monarchy, a despotism abhorrent to the
fundamental principles that have ruled and inspired this
nation from its origin? Who can tell? Then the announcement makes no provision for any return by such government
when established for the expenditures and obligations incurred in prosecuting the war and administering the sovereignty. Is the United States to receive such compensation?
She became a volunteer in the war, and announced herself
such volunteer in taking the sovereignty until pacification is
accomplished. As such the United States stands to-day before the civilized nations of the world. The inhabitants of
Cuba are the beneficiaries of this voluntarily assumed duty,

and when a difference arises between this government a[n]
them, whether the duty has been performed and whether t[h]
nation is to be compensated for the expense of its administr[a]
tion, have a right to arraign this nation at the bar of natio[n]
and demand that it give account of the stewardship which
voluntarily assumed. The determination of the rights of th
nation and of the Cubans under this assumed duty may i[n]
volve many nice questions and many difficulties.

Yet there are those who earnestly urge that Congre[ss]
should make a declaration that the nation holds Puerto Ric[o]
and the Philippine Islands under the same undefined, ye[t]
in a sense particular, duty. In my judgment, such a cours[e]
is beset with complications and difficulties. By adopting i[t]
the nation would court these and invite the inhabitants o[f]
the islands to engender perplexing questions and entangle[-]
ments. Under the treaty the nation takes the sovereignt[y]
of Puerto Rico and of the Philippine Islands, under the ge[n]
eral duty to use it in such a manner as Congress may judg[e]
will best subserve the highest interests of their inhabitant[s]
and the inhabitants of this nation. I would announce n[o]
other duty in regard to them. Many more complication[s]
and entanglements may arise in the discharge of the par[-]
ticular duty to Cuba than are likely to arise in the discharge
of the general duty to Puerto Rico and the Philippine
Islands.

It is urged that this nation should announce the policy of
its purpose in the administration of the sovereignty. The
flag of the nation has been planted on those islands. That
is the emblem of its policy and ever has been, even when
at half-mast, mourning the loss of her sons slain in its defence. The flag never did, and I hope never may, represent
but one policy. That policy is individual manhood; the right

enjoy religious and civil liberty; the right of every man
believe in and worship God according to the dictates of
s own conscience; the right to stand protected equally with
ery other man before the law in the enjoyment of freedom,
personal rights, and of property. Let the flag, as the
presentative of these principles, be planted and become
ominant on and over every island and every inhabitant. No
her, no better, policy can be proclaimed. In no other
ay can this Congress and nation discharge its duty to the
eople of the United States and to the people of the islands.
ongress should proclaim this policy by its acts and make
o attempt to do what it has no power to do—to pledge or
mit the action of future Congresses. What future Con-
resses shall do is for them to determine and proclaim. It
annot be assumed that wisdom will die with the present
Congress, nor that it is any part of its duty to proclaim what
uture Congresses shall do. Sufficient unto the day is the
duty thereof.

If these principles are enforced as far as applicable to the
government of these islands, the inhabitants will be blessed,
whether they consent thereto in advance or not. In a representative government the right to govern is not derived from
the consent of the governed until they arrive at a stage of
advancement which will render them capable of giving an
intelligent consent. Four fifths of the inhabitants of this
country have given no consent except representatively. The
consent of women, as a rule, and of minors is never required
nor allowed to be taken. Wives and children are assumed
to be represented by husbands and fathers. Boys are to be
educated, trained, and ripened into manhood before they are
capable of giving consent. Doubtless the boys of fifteen in
this country are better prepared to give an intelligent con-

sent than are the inhabitants of those islands. This is n
their fault. After having lived for more than three hu
dred years under a government of oppression and practic
denial of all rights it is not wonderful that they are n
capable of judging how they should be governed. They a
to be trained in these principles: first, by being allowe
under experienced leaders, to put them in practice in th
simpler forms of government, and then be gradually ad
vanced in their exercise as their knowledge increases.

All accounts agree that the administration of justice i
the islands through the courts has been a farce; that no nativ
could establish his rights or gain his cause, however righteous,
against the Spaniards and priests; that therein bribery and
every form of favoritism and oppression prevailed. Under
such training and abuse falsehood and deceit have become
prevalent. These most discouraging traits of character cannot be changed in a generation, and never except by pure,
impartial administration of justice through the courts, regardless of who may be the parties to the controversies. In
my judgment, the people of this nation obtain more and
clearer knowledge of their personal and property rights
through the administration of justice in the courts than from
all other sources.

All experience teaches that the requirements and impartial practice of the principles of civil and religious liberty
cannot speedily be acquired by the inhabitants, left to their
own way, under a protectorate by this nation. The experience of this nation in governing and endeavoring to civilize
the Indians teaches this. For about a century this nation
exercised in fact a protectorate over the tribes and allowed
the natives of the country to manage their tribal and other
relations in their own way. The advancement in civiliza-

tion was very slow and hardly perceptible. During the comparatively few years that Congress has by direct legislation controlled their relations to each other and to the reservations the advancement in civilization has been tenfold more rapid. This is in accord with all experience. The untaught cannot become acquainted with the difficult problems of government and of individual rights and their due enforcement without skilful guides.

No practical educator would think of creating a body of skilled mechanics by turning the unskilled loose in a machine shop. He would place there trained superintendents and guides to impart information to their untaught brains and to guide their unskilled hands. It is equally true that they would never become skilled without using their brains and hands in operating the machines. So, too, if this nation would successfully bring the inhabitants of these islands into the practice of the principles of religious and civil liberty it must both give them the opportunity to be taught in and to practice them, first in their simpler forms and then in their higher application, but under competent and trained teachers and guides placed over them by this nation. It is equally true that the laws and customs now prevailing must neither be pushed one side nor changed too suddenly. They must be permeated gradually by the leaven of civil and religious liberty until the entire population is leavened. To accomplish this without mistake in the interest of the people of this nation and of the inhabitants of the islands is a most difficult task, demanding honesty, intelligence, and the greatest care and good judgment. The task is rendered much more difficult because the people of the islands have hitherto been governed by the application of the direct opposite of these principles, and are composed of great numbers of tribes,

speaking different dialects and languages and governed by
different customs and laws.

The successful solution of this problem demands accurate
knowledge of the present conditions of the entire population
and of the different classes, of their respective habits, customs, and laws. As the principles of civil and religious liberty are gradually intermingled with their present customs,
habits, and laws, changes will be constantly going forward.
An intimate knowledge of these changes will also be necessary for their successful government. Hence, as a first step
to a successful discharge of this duty, Congress should create a department of government charged with the sole duty
to become accurately acquainted with and to take charge of
their affairs and place exact knowledge of them before Congress for its guidance. They should not, as now, be left in
charge of departments overloaded and overworked.

The second step to be taken is to remove all civil appointments in the islands from the realm of politics. The nation
will utterly fail in the discharge of its duty if the islands
are made political footballs subject to change in government
with every political change in the administration. The administration of the sovereignty must be intelligent, honest,
and uninterrupted. A faithful, intelligent man with a full
knowledge of the situation must not be displaced to give
place to one ignorant of the conditions, however capable
otherwise. The duty rests upon the entire nation. It must
be discharged for the interest of the whole nation. There
are honest, capable men in every political party. These
should be sought out and given place in the administration
of this sovereignty, as nearly as may be in proportion to the
strength of the several political parties in the nation. Then
when there is a political change in the administration there

will be no inducement to make extensive changes in the administrative appointees of the sovereignty.

Difficult as is the administration of this sovereignty, if honestly and intelligently undertaken such administration, I believe, will be beneficial both to the people of this nation and to the inhabitants of the islands. Difficulties which have come as these have come—unsought—honestly and faithfully encountered, bring wisdom and strength. The struggle for nearly a century in this nation over slavery gave wonderful wisdom, strength, and clearness of insight into the great principles which the nation is now called upon to apply to these oppressed islands. Stagnation is decay and ultimate death. Honest struggle, endeavor, and discussion bring light, growth, development, and strength. The primary object to be attained by the discharge of this duty is the elevation of the inhabitants of the islands physically, mentally, and morally; to make them industrious, honest, intelligent, liberty-loving, and law-abiding. This end attained, the secondary object—commercial and material growth among them and among the surrounding millions—will surely follow. The first unattained, the second, at best, will be spasmodic and of little worth.

The intelligent, thoughtful observer sees more in nature and in the ordering of the affairs of this world than the unguided plans and devices of men and nations. For him the wisdom of the Eternal shapes the affairs of men and of nations, sometimes even against their selfish plans and desires. For such, his hand planted the seed of individual manhood and for centuries watched over and cared for it in its slow growth amidst infinite sufferings, struggles, and conflicts, until at length planted on these shores, not entirely in its purity, but at last brought to full fruitage in the terrible struggles and conflicts which ended with the Civil War. Under him no man, no nation, lives to itself alone. If it has received much, much must it give to the less favored. Under his guidance, I believe, the discharge of this great and difficult duty has fallen, unsought, to the lot of this nation. Then let the nation take up the duty which the Ruler of men and nations has placed upon it; go forward in an honest, unselfish, intelligent, earnest endeavor to discharge it for the highest interest of the nation and of the islands in the fear and under the direction of the Supreme Ruler, who guided the fathers and founders; and the nation will not, cannot, encounter failure.

BROWN

BENJAMIN GRATZ BROWN, an American politician, was born in Lexington, Kentucky, May 28, 1826, the son of Mason Brown, a Kentucky
jurist. He was educated at Transylvania and Yale Universities, and
studied law in Louisville, where he was admitted to the bar. He soon
removed to St. Louis and in 1852 entered the Missouri legislature of
which he continued a member for fourteen years. During these years
he was a very conspicuous opponent of slavery, delivering in 1857 a
memorable anti-slavery speech. As the editor of the "Missouri Democrat,"
a radical Republican journal, he was the mouthpiece of the Free-Soil
movement in Missouri, and in 1857, as the Free-Soil candidate for governor,
was defeated by only five hundred majority. At the outset of the Civil
War he threw all his influence into the Union cause, raising a regiment,
and afterward leading a brigade of militia against Price and Van Dorn
when these Confederate generals invaded Missouri. From 1863 to 1867 he
sat in the United States Senate and in 1871, as a Liberal Republican nominee, was elected governor of Missouri by a large majority. In 1872 he was
nominated for vice-president by the Democratic party on the ticket with
Horace Greeley. The canvass was conducted with extraordinary bitterness
and the Democratic party suffered defeat at the polls. Brown subsequently
practised his profession at St. Louis, dying there on December 13, 1885.

ON SLAVERY IN ITS NATIONAL ASPECTS AS RELATED TO PEACE AND WAR

FROM ADDRESS DELIVERED AT ST. LOUIS, SEPTEMBER 17, 1862

THE lover of his country is not apt to be discouraged
as to the eventual triumph of its arms. The lost
battle, the miasmatic campaign, abandoned lines and
blown-up magazines are regarded as incidents of war. They
are deplored but not held as conclusive or even significant
of the ending. There are " signs of the times," however, in
our horizon that have a gloomier look than lost battles. And
darkest and strangest of all the discouragements that have
of late befallen must be considered the spectacle presented
by the government in its dealings with this terrible crisis—

reposing itself altogether upon the mere barbarism of force.

One would think when reading the call for six hundred thousand men to recruit our armies, and seeing there no appeal to or recognition of the ideas that rule this century, not less than this hour, that as a government ours was intent on suicide—as a nation we had abandoned our progression. Can it be that those who have been advanced for their wisdom and worth to such high places of rulership do not understand that since this world began the victories of mere brute force have been as inconsequent as the ravages of pestilence and as evanescent as the generations of men. Or can it be that, understanding, they care only for tiding over the present contest to bequeath revolt and internecine war as the inheritance of those who are to come after them. That would be virtual disintegration—national death.

If the government undertakes to abandon the revolution in its very birth-pains—if it intends to have no reference to the ideas of which it is the representative—if it contemplates a disregard of the progressing thought that not only installed it, but has carried it so far forward since installation—if it is determined to found its dominion over subjugated States not in the name of a principle that shall assimilate its conquests and assure their liberties, but of simple power—then will it place itself by its own action in the attitude of other and equally gigantic powers that have attempted the same work and have failed. It may have its day of seeming successes, but even that will entail an age of complications.

Does not Poland, as fully alive to-day, after ninety years of forcible suppression, as on that morning of the first partition, convince us that this thing of the dominion of power without the assimilation of nations can only continue upon condition of an ever-recurring application of those forces that achieved the first reduction? Does not the uprising and the cry for a united Italy, after five hundred years of fitful effort, continuous conflict, and successive disintegration under the tramp of a multitudinous soldiery, tell how fixed are social laws, how faithful to freedom are peoples, and how certain the retribution following upon those policies of government that sacrifice the future to the present, the moral to the mere material, the consolidating the foundations of a great commonwealth to the hollow conquest, the mock settlement, the outward uniformity. History is full of such illustrations, because history repeats itself.

But I need not go with you further in citing its judgments in condemnation of that reliance upon physical force which deems itself able to dispense with any appeal to principle. We cannot if we would cast behind us the experience of eighteen centuries of Christian amelioration, in which mankind have been learning to rely upon moral and intellectual forces rather than simple violence in their dealings with each other as nations. Not that civilization has surrendered its rights of war, but that it insists that ideas shall march at the head of armies. Napoleon III, when he announced that the French nation alone in Europe made war for an idea, intended to represent it as leading, not relapsing from the civilization of the age. And therein he both uttered a philosophic truth and penetrated the secret of success.

Strip the choicest legions of the inspiration they derive from a controlling, elevating cause—especially that cause whose magic watchword cheers to victory in every land—and in vain will you expect the heroic in action or the miracle in conquest. It is a coward thought that God is on the side of the strongest battalions. The battles that live in memory —that have seemed to turn the world's equanimity upside down—have been won by the few fighting for a principle as against the multitude enrolled in the name of power. When therefore it is conceded that the mere announcement of a policy of freedom as the policy of this war would paralyze the hostility of all the sovereigns of Europe and wed to us the encouragement of their peoples, why is it that so little faith obtains among our rulers that it would equally strengthen the government here amid the millions of our own land? Have the populations of our States fallen so low —become so irresponsive to the watchwords of liberty that it is not fit to make such an appeal to them? Is there no significance in the fact that amid the five thousand stanzas that have vainly attempted to exalt the unities of the past into a nation's anthem—a song of war kindling the uncontrollable ardors of the soul—one alone, proscribed like the " Marseillaise," has been adopted at the camp fire—

> " John Brown's body lies a moldering in the grave,
> His soul is marching on."

Six hundred thousand soldiers summoned to the field, and for what? The nation asks of the President, for what? Is it that the government may wring a submission from the possible exhaustion on the part of the seceding States, that shall be a postponement, not a settlement, of this great crisis, and that shall be unrelated to the causes that have produced it or the progression on our part that has put on the armor of revolution? If so, the government will find when perhaps it is too late that in addition to the rebellion it will have to confront a public opinion that has no sympathies with reaction and that will withdraw, as unitedly as it has hitherto given all its trust, from those in power. Or is it that grounding this great struggle upon its true basis, upholding the national honor whilst battling for the national thought, our armies are to be marshalled under the flag of freedom, and the peace achieved is to be one that shall assure personal and political liberty to every dweller in the land? If that be so let the fact be proclaimed, not hidden from the people, and there will need no call from President, no conscription from Congress, to recruit the ranks of the soldiers of the republic.

The two great revolutions of modern time which mark the most signal advance in political freedom, that of England during the Commonwealth and that of France in 1789, have this among many other striking features of similarity—that in each case a large part of the empire resisting the advent of free principles took up arms again the government to contest the issue. In the *Vendée*, as in Ireland, it became necessary to establish by force the supremacy of the new order. It was antagonism by the population of whole sections, and in both instances, courses of conciliation having proved worthless, a stern and vigorous policy of subjugation was required. That even the success which crowned such measures was only partial and transient, demanding a supplemental work of assimilation, is also well worthy of attention. But in subduing the resistance now presented this nation has that to contend with, not less than that to assist it, which was not present in either of the parallels cited. I allude to slavery, the strength and the weakness of the South.

Look steadily at the prospect. Nine millions of people in all—five millions and a half of whites addressing themselves exclusively to warfare, sustained by three millions and

a half of blacks drilled as slaves to the work of agricultur
Such are the official statistics of the seceding States.

With the whites the conscription for military purpos
reaches to every man capable of bearing arms; with tl
blacks the conscription for labor recognizes neither weaknes
nor age, nor sex. Solitary drivers ply the lash over tl
whole manual force to transform plantations into granarie
This allotment necessarily gives to war the largest possib
number of soldiers and extracts from labor the greatest po
sible production of food. Combined, protected, undisturbe
the relation so developed presents a front that may we
shake our faith in any speedy subjugation.

Of these five and a half millions white population, the rat
over the age of twenty-one which, according to statistical ave
ages, is one in six, will give a fraction over 900,000 men, fro
which deduct as exempts or incapables twenty per cent, lea-
ing 720,000, and add on the score of minor enlistments on
half of those between the ages of sixteen and twenty-one, c
55,000, and there existed 775,000, as the total possible Co
federate force in the outset. If from this number 100,00
be stricken off as the aggregate of the killed, disabled, im
prisoned, and paroled since the outbreak of the war, an
70,000 be added as the probable number of recruits fro
Kentucky, Missouri, and Maryland, there will result 745,00
as the effective force. From these are to be taken the me
needed for the civil service, for provost and police duties, an
for regulating the transmission or exchange of productions—
certainly not less than 90,000, and there remains an aggre
gate of 655,000 as the fruit of thorough conscription.

Perhaps, however, it is right to make from such rigid pos
sible military array a deduction in favor of the populatio
which abandoned the seceding States since the war began an

aat which, intrinsically loyal, has evaded enrollment. In
default of any certain information this may be placed at
5,000 men, thus leaving 600,000 soldiers fit for service and
ready to be concentrated and marched as the skill of their
commanders may determine.

Such is the strength of the array that now contests and re-
sists the cause of advancing freedom in the nation. That the
strength is not overestimated; that the conscription has been
remorseless is proven by every critical battle-field where our
armies have been outnumbered, and is to-day doubly attested
by our beleaguered capital and widely menaced frontiers.
There then is the rebellion stripped to the skin. Look at it
squarely. Those 600,000 soldiers stand between us and any
future of honor, liberty, or peace. How are they to be disposed of, defeated, suppressed?

It is an imposing column of attack, but it has also its
element of weakness and dispersion. Remember that in
making such an estimate it has been predicted upon the fact
that the whole available white population was devoted to the
formation of armies. No part was assigned to the labor of
the field or workshop, to production or manufacture; but all
this vast organization reposes for sustenance—not to speak of
efficiency, on the hard-wrung toil of slaves.

Reflect, furthermore, that this whole foundation is mined,
eruptive, ready to shift the burden now resting on it so
heavily. The three and a half millions of black population
engaged in supplying the very necessaries of life and movement to the Confederate armies are all loyal in their hearts
to our cause and require only the electric shock of proclaimed
freedom to disrupt the relation that gives such erectness and
impulsion to our adversaries and such peril to ourselves.
Years of bondage have only sharpened their sensibilities

toward liberty, and the word spoken that causes such a hope will penetrate every quarter of the South most speedily and most surely.

Emancipate the industry that upholds the war power of the South; destroy the repose of that system which has made possible a levy " *en masse* " of every white male able to bear arms; recall to the tillage of the field; to the care of the plantation; to the home supports of the community a corresponding number of the five and a half millions whites, and there will be put another face to this war.

Compel the rebels to do their own work, hand for hand, planting, harvesting, victualling, transporting—to the full substitution of the three and a half millions blacks, now held for that purpose, and where now they advance with armies they will fall back with detachments; where abundance now reigns in their camps, hunger will hurry them to other avocations. It needs only that the word be spoken.

A national declaration of freedom can no more be hidden from the remotest sections of the slave States than the uprisen sun in a cloudless sky. The falsehoods, the doubts, the repulsions that have heretofore driven them from us will give place to the kindling, mesmeric realization of protection and deliverance. In the very outset their forces, which now march to the attack, will be compelled to fall back upon the interior to maintain authority and prevent escapades " *en masse.*" Insurrection will not so much be apprehended, for where armies are marshalled and surveillance withdrawn, the slave is wise enough to know that a plot with a centre—an uprising would be sure to meet with annihilation, whilst desertion from the plantations is only checked by the repressive rules of our own lines.

The right to do these things needs not to be argued; it is

of the muniments of freedom, of the resorts of self-preservation, of the investure that charges the government with the defence of the national life. And in this hour can be effected that which hereafter may not be practicable. Occupancy of the entire coast with many lodgments made by our navy, a penetration of the valley of the lower Mississippi, giving access to all its tributary streams, and the exposed front of Virginia, Tennessee, and Arkansas, give ample basis for extending such a proclamation. Resuming the advance ourselves, with augmented forces, we shall find the 600,000 Confederates compelled to detach one half their force for garrisoning the cotton States, whilst of the remaining 300,000, large numbers will necessarily fall out to replace the industrial support of their families along the border. State by State, as it is occupied and liberated, will recall for substitution those spared to offensive war in reliance upon slave production. The 300,000 will speedily become 100,000, and instead of concentrating back upon their reserves, massed in imposing column, as has heretofore been their policy when temporarily checked, the very condition of the South will require a wide dispersion of their forces Conquest and suppression will thus be rendered matters of absolute certainty. The double result of immensely diminished numbers in the Confederate armies and of its separation into broken columns for local surveillance over all threatened slave territory is thus seen to flow from emancipation as a war measure.

In the grave contest on which we have entered for life and for death no appreciative judgment can be formed of the absolute necessity of writing freedom on the flag that leaves out of view the organization of the labor and the valor for military purposes of the population thereby liberated. The substitution of freed blacks, whenever they can relieve for other

duties the enlisted soldier, has already so far commended itself
in defiance of slave codes and equality fears as to have been
adopted in some divisions of our armies. The wisdom that
should have foreseen in such a policy extended as far as practicable the addition to-day of 50,000 soldiers to the effective
fighting force of the government, perhaps changing the fate
of critical campaigns, has been unfortunately wanting. And
yet the army regulations as applied to the muster-rolls of our
forces will show that nearly twice that number of disciplined
troops could have been relieved of ditching, teaming, serving
or other occupation, and sent to the front. Moreover, any
policy which looks distinctly to the subjugating and occupying, militarily, until the national authority shall be sufficiently respected to work through civil processes the States
now in rebellion, must embrace within its scope the employment of acclimated troops for garrison and other duties during those seasons fatal to the health of our present levies.

The diseases of a warm climate have already been far more
destructive to the lives of our soldiers, as shown by aggre-
gated hospital reports at Washington, than all other battle-
fields, and hereafter in the prevalence of those epidemics so
common in the Gulf States our battalions, if subjected to
Southern service, would melt away disastrously. It is not
possible, therefore, to separate the holding of the rebel States
from the employ of acclimated troops. And for that purpose
but one resource exists—the liberated blacks, whose veins
course with the blood of the tropics. Arm them, drill them,
discipline them, and of one fact we may be sure—they will
not surrender.

I take it that a race liberated by the operation of hostilities
is entitled by every usage of warfare to be armed in defence
of those who liberated them, and furthermore I take it that a

people made free in accordance with the humanities of this
century is entitled by every right, human and divine, to be
armed as an assurance of its own recovered freedom.

This step will be at once the guarantee against future attempt at re-enslavement and the bond that no further revolt
on the part of the States occupied shall be meditated. Above
all else it will be assurance unmistakable that no disgraceful
peace, no dismembered country, no foresworn liberties, will
end this war. What, shall we stand halting before a senti-
mentality, blinking at shades of color, tracing genealogies up
to sons of Noah, when our brothers in arms are being weighed
in the scales of life and death! Go, ye men of little faith;
resign your high charges, if it be you cannot face a coward
clamor in the throes of a nation's great deliverance.

Go and look yonder upon the pale mother in the far north-
land, weary with watching by her lonely hearth for the bright-
faced boy's return. Her hope had nerved itself to trust his
life to the chances of the battlefield; but the trundling wheels
bear back to her door a stricken form, in coarse pine box,
with the dear name chalked straggling across, indorsed
"fever." Listen then to the wail of crushing woe sobbed
out by a broken heart, and say to her if you can, general,
statesman or president, that you refused the aid that would
have saved that double life of mother and son. Verily the
graves of the northmen have their equities equally with those
of the rebellion.

There are those strange to say who, in addition to the war
now waged by us against five and a half millions of whites,
would add to the task of reduction thus imposed upon our
government the further work of taking possession of and de-
porting to other lands the three millions and a half of blacks.
Disregarding the assistance that might be derived from the

co-operation and enfranchisement of the slave labor of the seceding States, they would not only strip the slaves of the present uncertain hope of personal freedom which may be found within our lines, but, still viewing them as " chattels," to be dealt with as fancy may dictate, would serve a notice on the world that the best usage they can hope for from risking life to render us aid will be transportation to climes and countries beyond the reach of their knowledge, and that only inspire ignorance with terror.   According to such, the practical solution of the present crisis consists :

First. In conquering the rebellion by making its cause a common cause, as against us, by both master and slave.

Second. In holding the conquered territory and superinducing a state of peace, plenty, and obedience by the deportation of all who are loyal and of all who labor.

With such the magnitude, not to say impracticability, of migrations that would require—even if all were favoring—transport fleets larger and costlier than those employed for the war, is not less scouted at as an obstacle, than the resistance to be foreseen from the unwilling and the depopulation that may be objected by the interested is treated as a fanaticism.   Without challenging the sincerity of those who advocate such views, it will be sufficient to say that I differ from them altogether.   I do not believe the government has " chattel rights " in the slave emancipated by act of war any more than the rebellion had; and I do believe that the doctrine of personal liberty, if it be worth anything — if it be not a sham and a delusion — if it is to have any application in this conflict — must be applied to them.

It is not in behalf of the noble and the refined, the generous and the cultivated, that the evangels of freedom have been heretofore borne by enthused armies in the deliverances history so much loves to delineate and extoll, but to the down-trodden — to the ignorant from servitude — to the enfeebled in spirit from long years of oppression. Why, then, shall those liberated in this country be bereft of the rights of domicile and employ? Because they are black, forsooth!

That answer will scarcely stand scrutiny by the God who made us all. It would moreover justify slavery as fully as extradition. Deportation, if forcible, is in principle but a change of masters, and in practice will never solve the problem of the negro question as growing out of this war. If voluntary, it needs not to be discussed in advance of emancipation. The lot of the freed race will be to labor — in the future as in the past — but to labor for the wage and not for the lash. That there must be colonization as a resultant of the complete triumph of the national arms, and the complete restoration of the national authority, no one can reasonably doubt.

But it will be a colonization of loyal men into and not out of the rebel States. The great forces of immigration, fostered and directed, will work out the new destiny that awaits the seceded States — the assimilation that must precede a perfect union. What it has done for the Lake shore, for the Pacific coast, for the Centre and the West, that will it do for the South also, when no blight of slavery lingers there to repel its coming or divert its industrial armies. And if in the development caused by its vast agencies, those natural affinities, so much insisted on by many, shall lead the African race toward the tropics, to plant there a new Carthage, it will be one of these dispensations of Providence that will meet with support and co-operation, not hindrance and antagonism from the friends of freedom on this continent.

The half-way house where halt the timid, the doubtful, the

reactionary in this conflict, hangs out a sign: " The Union
as it was." Within its inclosure will be found jostling side
by side the good man who is afraid to think, the politician
who has a record to preserve, the spy who needs a cloak to
conceal him, and behind all these the fluctuating camp fol
lowers of the army of freedom. Not that there are no wise
and brave men who phrase their speech by the attachments of
the past; but that such have another and purer significance
in their language than the received meaning on " the Union
as it was." All who look at events which have come upon
us see that " the Union as it was " contained the seeds of
death — elements of aggression against liberty and reaction
through civil war. Its very life-scenes, as time progressed,
were ever and anon startled by the bodeful note of coming
catastrophe, to be lulled again into false security by pæan
songs to its excellence — like some old Greek tragedy with
its inexorable fate and its recurring chorus. And tragic
enough it would seem has been its outcome to dissipate any
illusion.

Is it believed that the same causes would not produce the
same results to the very ending of time? Is it wished to
repeat the miserable years of truckling and subserviency on
the part of the natural guardians of free institutions to the
exaction, arrogance and dominion of the slave power through
fear of breaking the thin ice of a hollow tranquillity? Is
it longed to undergo new experiences of Sumner assaults,
Kansas outrages, Pierce administrations, Buchanan profli-
gacies, knaveries and treasons, with spirited interludes of
negro-catching at the North, and abolition hanging at the
South? Is it desired to recall the time when the man of
Massachusetts dared not name his residence to the people of
Carolina; when free speech was a half-forgotten legend in

the slave States, when the breeding of human beings to sell into distant bondage was the occupation of many of the élite of the borderland; and when demoralization, that came from sacrificing so much self-respect to mere dread of any crisis or mere hope of political advancement, had dwarfed our statesmen, corrupted our journalism, and made office-holding disreputable as a vocation?

For one, I take witness here before you all, that I want no such Union, and do not want it, because it contained that which made those things not only possible, but probable. I trust that I value as much as another the purities of a Union, the excellencies of a constitution, the veracities and accomplishments of a former generation, but who would be the blind worshipper of form rather than substance — of a name, rather than a reality — of a bond that did not bind, and a federation that has resulted only in disjunction? There are those I know who regard " the Union as it was " as a sentiment significant of material prosperity — unrelated to rights or wrongs, and as such they worship it, just as they would a State bank corporation with large dividends, or any named machine that would enable them to buy cotton, sell goods, or trade negroes. But such should be content to pass their ignoble lives on the accumulation of other days, and not dare to dictate to others a return to such debasing thraldom.

Of one thing they may be sure — that the great Democracy of this nation will insist that the Union of the future shall be predicated upon a principle uniting the social, moral, and political life of a progressive people — and purged of the poison of the past. When asked, therefore, as the charlatans of the hour often do ask, would you not wish the " Union as it was " restored, even if slavery were to remain intact and protected — say, emphatically, No! say No! for such an admission would be a self-contradiction — a yielding of all the longings of the spirit to an empty husk whose only possible outcome we see to-day in the shape of civil war.

It is, perhaps, the fate of all revolutions involving social changes, to be officered at the outset by the inherited reputations, great and small, of the foregoing time, and so far as this fate has fallen on our nation it is less to be wondered at than deplored. But soon there comes the time for change, when the Fairfaxes, the Dumouriers, the Arnolds, must give place to soldiers of the faith. And hopeful to say, it has ever happened that conjointly with the public assumption of the principle of the Revolution, mediocrity, routine, half-heartedness have passed from command, and victory has replaced disaster. So much is historic. We may take comfort then; for the uses of adversity are ours.

Pro-slavery generals at the heard of our armies are the result of pro-slavery influence in our national councils, and the hesitanoy of the government to proclaim officially any distinct policy of freedom has kept them there. By no possibility, however, can such, even if the chance victors of to-day, remain possessed of the future.

I do not underrate the prestige of military success — but military prestige is as naught before the march of revolution; and it is only when revolutions are accomplished, that the reputations of great captains become great dangers. Pro-slavery generals, therefore, are only dangerous now from the disasters that accompany their administration. Their appeciation of the present being at fault, their methods, their reliances, their results will be inconsequent, and without force. Witness the miserable months of projected concili-ations, of harmless captures, of violated oath taking, of border State imbecilities, of Order No. Threes, of paroling guer-

rillas, of halting advances and wasted opportunities. Could
these things have been possible to commanders comprehend-
ing either the magnitude, the characteristics, or the consequences of the war that slavery has inaugurated, and that must
end in slavery extinction or the abandonment of our development as a free people? Or can it be possible that the same
series of incompetencies and sham energies shall be prolonged
indefinitely? No! It needs not that I should insist how
surely all such must give way before the force of a public
sentiment which, when once on the march, speedily refuses
to trust any with responsibility who are not born of the age.

It was just such a common thought of the Long Parliament
that gave a " new model " to their army and a " self-denying
ordinance " to themselves, extirpating insincerity from the
former and imposing stoicism and self-sacrifice on each other.
It was a similar growth of public opinion in France that set
the guillotine at work to keep account of lost battles with
unsympathizing generals. The pregnant question then, of
this crisis, is, how long, my countrymen, shall we wait for
the " new model " and the " self-denying ordinance " and the
swift punishment in this day of calamitous command and disgraceful surrenders.

No one has ever read of a more touching spectacle in the
life of nations, than that now presented by this people.
Beyond any parallel it has made sacrifice of those things dear
to its affection — I might almost say traditionally sacred from
violation. All its rights of person and of property have been
placed unmurmuringly at the disposal of the government,
asking only in return a speedy, vigorous, uncompromising
conduct of the war upon a true principle to an honorable
ending. The habeas corpus has been suspended, not only
in the revolted territory, but likewise in many of the loyal

States. A passport system, limiting and embarrassing both travel and traffic, has been enforced with rigor. The censorship of the press not only controls the transmission of news but curtails even the expression of opinion within restrictions heretofore unimaginable.

Arbitrary imprisonment by premiers of the cabinet, banishments summarily notified, exactions levied at discretion, fines assessed by military commissions, trials postponed indefinitely — in short, all the panoply of the most rigid European absolutism has been imported into our midst. It is not to complain that these things are recited; for, so far as necessary, they will be, as they have been, cheerfully borne with; but to show how tragic is the attitude of this nation and yet how brave.

The President of the United States, to-day, holds a civil and military power more untrammelled than ever did Cromwell; and, in addition thereto, has enrolled by the volunteer agencies of the people themselves, a million of armed men, obedient to his command. Nay, did I say the President was absolute as Cromwell? In truth I might add that of his officials intrusted with administering military instead of civil law — every deputy provost marshal seems to be feeling his face to see if he too has not the warts of the Great Protector.

If this were the occasion for stale flatteries of the constitution and the Union, it might well be asked just here, where in that much lauded parchment and league is the warrant for these things specifically? But I carp not at such technicalities. Give him rather more power if necessary — give him any trust and every appliance, only let it be not without avail.

And yet with all this sacrifice, with all this effort, with quick response to every demand for men and money, what o we see? A beleaguered capital, only saved by abandoning year of conquest and long lines of occupation; the confidence of the whole nation shaken to its very foundations by ccumulated disasters and halting policies; and the grave inquiry, mooted in no whispered voice by men who have never nown fear in any peril, can this country survive its rulers? do not say the doubt is justified; but I do say that it exists n many minds that have been prone heretofore to confidence. We have seen fifty thousand soldiers, the élite of the nation, acrificed, and six hundred millions of treasure, the coin vealth of the people, expended. We have reached the stage f assignats and conscriptions, and are now summoning the nilitia of the loyal States to repel invasion. And can any ne cognizant of our actual condition, and not misled by alse bulletins, or varnished glories, stand forth and say with ruth and honor, we are any nearer a solution in this hour f the great crisis in which we are involved than we were a ear ago? I challenge a response. Or will any delude you ong with the belief that a great victory will accomplish the nding? I do not believe it.

In the presence, therefore, of such thick coming danger, nd having borne itself so continently and so well, has not this nation now the right to demand of President and of cabinet, nd generals, that there shall be an end of policies that have nly multiplied disasters and disrupted armies, and a substiution of civil policies that shall recognize liberty as the orner-stone of our Republic, and write " Freedom " on the lag.

In conclusion let me say, that the time has passed when such a demand could be denounced, even by the most servile follower of administrations, as a fanaticism, for the chief of the Republic has himself recognized his right to do so, if the occasion shall require, in virtue of being charged with the preservation of the government. He has furthermore become so far impressed with the urgency that manifests itself that he has ordered immediate execution to be given to the act of the last Congress, prescribing a measure of confiscation and emancipation.

This day, too, is the anniversary of its enforcement, as it is the anniversary of the adoption of the original constitution of the United States. Let us, then, in parting, take hope from the cheering coincidence. The act of Congress, it is true, is but an initial measure, embarrassed by many clauses, and may be much limited by hostile interpretation. Still it can be made an avatar of liberty to thousands who shall invoke its protection, and the instrument of condign punishment to those who have sought the destruction of all free government. And more than all else, its rigid enforcement and true interpretation will give earnest to the nation of that which must speedily ensue — direct and immediate emancipation by the military arm, as a measure of safety, a measure of justice, and a measure of peace.

HOAR

GEORGE FRISBIE HOAR, United States senator from Massachusetts, was born at Concord, Massachusetts, August 29, 1826. He was educated at Concord Academy and at Harvard University, where he was graduated in 1846. He studied law, and upon graduating from the Harvard Law School began practice in Worcester, Massachusetts. During twenty years at the bar he won high position in the legal profession. Senator Hoar's first appearance in the political field was as chairman of the committee of the Free-Soil party in 1849. In 1852 he became a member of the Massachusetts House of Representatives, and of the State Senate in 1857. He was an early advocate of woman suffrage, making his first address on that subject in 1868. His service in the legislature of his native State was followed by his election, as a Republican, to four successive Congresses, serving from March, 1869, to March, 1877. In 1877 he became a United States senator. He is still in the Senate, being the senior member from Massachusetts. The senator was a delegate to the Republican national conventions of 1876, 1880, and 1884, and he was chairman of the convention which nominated James A. Garfield for the presidency. He was one of the managers, on the part of the House of Representatives, of the Belknap impeachment trial in 1876, and in the same year was a member of the electoral commission. In the administration of President Hayes he was offered the post of ambassador to Great Britain, but declined it. From 1874 to 1880 Senator Hoar was an overseer of Harvard University and in 1880 he became a regent of the Smithsonian Institution. In 1887 he was elected president of the American Antiquarian Society. He was one of the corporators of Clark University, is a trustee of the Peabody Museum of Archæology and a member of the Massachusetts Historical Society. He has received the degree of LL. D. from William and Mary, Harvard, Yale, and Amherst. Senator Hoar is a humanitarian as well as a statesman and a scholar. In 1897 he wrote and placed on file at the Massachusetts State House a petition against the use of birds and feathers as ornaments for hats, which purported to be signed by thirty-five undomesticated song birds. The senator is a supporter of bimetallism and an ardent anti-expansionist. In his long career he has frequently been in opposition to public sentiment, and the South was particularly indignant at his action in the matter of the Force Bill. While Senator Hoar is independent in thought and action, the purity and honesty of his motives have never been doubted. His keen wit, scholarship, and great readiness in extempore debate have made him one of the most prominent figures in national politics. His success in securing the return of the Governor Bradford manuscript to this country was not the least of his services.

(8887)

ADDRESS AT THE BANQUET OF THE NEW ENGLAND
SOCIETY

DELIVERED DECEMBER 22, 1898, AT CHARLESTON, SOUTH CAROLINA

I NEED not assure this brilliant company how deeply I
am impressed by the significance of this occasion. I
am not vain enough to find in it anything of personal
compliment. I like better to believe that the ties of common history, of common faith, of common citizenship, and in-
separable destiny, are drawing our two sister States together
again. If cordial friendship, if warm affection (to use no
stronger term), can ever exist between two communities they
should exist between Massachusetts and South Carolina.
They were both of the " Old Thirteen." They were alike in
the circumstances of their origin. Both were settled by those
noble fugitives who brought the torch of liberty across the
sea, when liberty was without other refuge on the face of the
earth. The English Pilgrims and Puritans founded Massachusetts, to be followed soon after by the Huguenot exiles
who fled from the tyranny of King Louis XIV, after the revocation of the edict of Nantes. Scotch Presbyterianism
founded Carolina, to be followed soon after by the French
exiles fleeing from the same oppression. Everywhere in
New England are traces of the footsteps of this gentle, delightful, and chivalrous race. All over our six States to-day
many an honored grave, many a stirring tradition bear witness to the kinship between our early settlers and the settlers
of South Carolina. Faneuil Hall, in Boston, which we love
to call the " Cradle of Liberty," attests the munificence and
bears the name of an illustrious Huguenot.

These French exiles lent their grace and romance to our history also. Their settlements were like clusters of magnolias in some warm valley in our bleak New England.

We are, all of us, in Massachusetts, reading again the story of the voyage of the "Mayflower," written by William Bradford. As you have heard, that precious manuscript has lately been restored to us by the kindness of His Grace the Lord Bishop of London. It is in the eyes of the children of the Pilgrims the most precious manuscript on earth. If there be anything to match the pathos of that terrible voyage it is found in the story of Judith Manigault, the French Huguenot exile, of her nine months' voyage from England to South Carolina. Her name, I am told, has been honored here in every generation since.

If there be a single lesson which the people of this country have learned from their wonderful and crowded history it is that the North and South are indispensable to each other. They are the blades of mighty shears, worthless apart, but when bound by an indissoluble union, powerful, irresistible, and terrible as the shears of fate; like the shears of Atropos, severing every thread and tangled web of evil, cutting out for humanity its beautiful garments of liberty and light from the cloth her dread sisters spin and weave.

I always delight to think, as I know the people of South Carolina delight to think, of these States of ours, not as mere aggregations of individuals, but as beautiful personalities, moral beings, endowed with moral characters, capable of faith, of hope, of memory, of pride, of sorrow, and of joy, of courage, of heroism, of honor, and of shame. Certainly this is true of them. Their power and glory, their rightful place in history, depended on these things, and not on numbers or extent of territory.

It is this that justifies the arrangement of the constitution of the United States for equal representation of States in the upper legislative chamber and explains its admirable success.

The separate entity and the absolute freedom, except for the necessary restraints of the constitution of our different States, is the cause alike of the greatness and the security of the country.

The words Switzerland, France, England, Rome, Athens, Massachusetts, South Carolina, Virginia, America, convey to your mind a distinct and individual meaning and suggest an image of distinct moral quality and moral being as clearly as do the words Washington, Wellington, or Napoleon. I believe it is, and I thank God that I believe it is, something much higher than the average of the qualities of the men who make it up. We think of Switzerland as something better than the individual Swiss, and of France as something better than the individual Frenchman, and of America as something better than the individual American. In great and heroic individual actions we often seem to feel that it is the country, of which the man is but the instrument that gives expression to its quality in doing the deed.

It was Switzerland who gathered into her breast at Sempach the sheaf of fatal Austrian spears. It was the hereditary spirit of New England that gave the word of command by the voice of Buttrick, at Concord, and was in the bosom of Parker at Lexington. It was South Carolina whose lightning stroke smote the invader by the arm of Marion and whose wisdom guided the framers of the constitution through the lips of Rutledge and Gadsden and Pinckney.

The citizen on great occasions knows and obeys the voice of his country as he knows and obeys an individual voice, whether it appeal to a base or ignoble or to a generous or noble passion. "Sons of France, awake to glory," told the French youth what was the dominant passion in the bosom of France and it awoke a corresponding sentiment in his own. Under its spell he marched through Europe and overthrew her kingdoms and empires and felt in Egypt that forty centuries were looking down on him from the Pyramids. But at last, one June morning in Trafalgar Bay, there was another utterance, more quiet in its tone, but speaking also with a personal and individual voice, "England expects every man to do his duty."

At the sight of Nelson's immortal signal duty-loving England and glory-loving France met as they have met on many an historic battle-field before and since, and the lover of duty proved the stronger. The England that expected every man to do his duty was as real a being to the humblest sailor in Nelson's fleet as the mother that bore him.

The title of our American States to their equality under this admirable arrangement depends not on area or upon numbers but upon character and upon personality. Fancy a league or a confederacy in which Athens or Sparta were united with Persia or Babylon or Nineveh and their political power were to be reckoned in proportion to their numbers or their size.

I have sometimes fancied South Carolina and Massachusetts, those two illustrious and heroic sisters, instead of sitting apart, one under her palm trees and the other under her pines, one with the hot gales from the tropics fanning her brow and the other on the granite rocks by her ice-bound shores, meeting together and comparing notes and stories as sisters born of the same mother compare notes and stories after a long separation. How the old estrangements, born of ignorance of each other, would have melted away.

Does it ever occur to you that the greatest single tribute ever paid to Daniel Webster was paid by Mr. Calhoun? And the greatest single tribute ever paid to Mr. Calhoun was paid by Mr. Webster?

I do not believe that among the compliments or marks of honor which attended the illustrious career of Daniel Webster there is one that he would have valued so much as that which his great friend, his great rival and antagonist, paid him from his dying bed.

" Mr. Webster," said Mr. Calhoun, " has as high a standard of truth as any statesman whom I have met in debate. Convince him and he cannot reply; he is silent; he cannot look truth in the face and oppose it by argument."

There was never, I suppose, paid to John C. Calhoun during his illustrious life any other tribute of honor he would have valued so highly as that which was paid him after his death by his friend, his rival, and antagonist, Daniel Webster.

" Mr. Calhoun," said Mr. Webster, " had the basis, the indispensable basis, of all high character; and that was unspotted integrity—unimpeached honor and character. If he had aspirations they were high and honorable and noble. There was nothing grovelling or low or meanly selfish that came near the head or the heart of Mr. Calhoun. Firm in his purpose, perfectly patriotic and honest, as I was sure he was, in the principles he espoused and in the measures he defended, aside from that large regard for that species of distinction that conducted him to eminent stations for the benefit of the republic, I do not believe he had a selfish motive or a selfish feeling. However he may have differed from others of us in his political opinions or his political principles, those opinions and those principles will now descend to posterity and under the sanction of a great name. He has lived long enough, he has done enough, and he has done it so well, so successfully, so honorably, as to connect himself for all time with the records of the country. He is now an historical character. Those of us who have known him here will find that he has left upon our minds, and upon our hearts, a strong and lasting impression of his person, his character, and his public performances, which, while we live, will never be obliterated. We shall hereafter, I am sure, indulge in it as a grateful recollection that we have lived in his age, that we have been his contemporaries, that we have seen him and known him. We shall delight to speak of him to those who are rising up to fill our places. And when the time shall come that we ourselves shall go, one after another, in succession, to our graves, we shall carry with us a deep sense of his genius and character, his honor and integrity, his amiable deportment in private life, and the purity of his exalted patriotism."

Just think for a moment what this means. If any man ever lived who was not merely the representative but the embodiment of the thought, opinion, principles, character, quality, intellectual and moral, of the people of South Carolina for the forty years from 1810 until his death, it was John C. Calhoun. If any man ever lived who not merely was the representative, but the embodiment of the thought, opinion, principles, character, quality, intellectual and moral, of the people of Massachusetts, it was Daniel Webster. Now if, after forty years of rivalry, of conflict, of antagonism, these two statesmen of ours, most widely differing in opinions on public questions, who never met but to exchange a blow, the sparks from the encounter of whose mighty swords kindled the fires which spread over the continent, thought thus of one another, is it not likely that if the States they represented

could have met with the same intimacy, with the same knowledge and companionship during all these years, they, too,
would have understood, and understanding would have loved
each other?

I should like to have had a chance to hearken to their talk.
Why, their gossip would almost make up the history of liberty! How they would boast to each other, as sisters do, of
their children, their beautiful and brave! How many memories they would find in common! How the warm Scotch-Irish
blood would stir in their veins! How the Puritan and the
Presbyterian blood would quicken their pulses as they re-
counted the old struggles for freedom to worship God! What
stories they would have to tell each other of the day of the
terrible knell from the bell of the old tower of St. Germain de
L'Auxerrois, when the edict of Nantes was revoked and
sounded its alarm to the Huguenot exiles who found refuge,
some in South Carolina and some in Massachusetts! You
have heard of James Bowdoin, of Paul Revere, and Peter
Faneuil, and Andrew Sigourney. These men brought to
the darkened and gloomy mind of the Puritan the sunshine
of beautiful France, which South Carolina did not need.
They taught our Puritans the much needed lesson that there
was something other than the snare of Satan in the song of a
bird or the fragrance of a flower.

The boys and girls of South Carolina and the boys and girls
of Massachusetts went to the same school in the old days.
Their schoolmasters were tyranny and poverty and exile and
starvation. They heard the wild music of the wolves' howl
and the savages' war-cry. They crossed the Atlantic in mid-
winter, when

" Winds blew and waters rolled,
　Strength to the brave, and power, and Deity."

They learned in that school little of the grace or the luxury of life. But they learned how to build States and how to fight tyrants.

They would have found much, these two sisters, to talk about of a later time. South Carolina would have talked of her boy Christopher Gadsden, who George Bancroft said was like a mountain torrent dashing on an overshot wheel. And Massachusetts would try to trump the trick with James Otis, that flame of fire, who said he seemed to hear the prophetic song of the Sybil chanting the springtime of the new empire.

They might dispute a little as to which of these two sons of theirs was the greater. I do not know how that dispute could be settled unless by Otis's own opinion. He said that "Massachusetts sounded the trumpet. But it was owing to South Carolina that it was assented to. Had it not been for South Carolina no Congress would have been appointed. She was all alive and felt at every pore." So perhaps we will accept the verdict of the Massachusetts historian, George Bancroft. He said that "When we count those who above all others contributed to the great result of the Union, we are to name the inspired madman, James Otis, and the unwavering lover of his country, Christopher Gadsden."

It is the same Massachusetts historian, George Bancroft, who says that "the public men of South Carolina were ever ruled by their sense of honor, and felt a stain upon it as a wound."

"Did you ever hear how those wicked boys of mine threw the tea into the harbor," Massachusetts would say; "Oh, yes," South Carolina would answer, "but not one of mine was willing to touch it. So we let it all perish in a cellar."

Certainly these two States liked each other pretty well when Josiah Quincy came down here in 1773 to see Rutledge and Pinckney and Gadsden to concert plans for the coming rebellion. King George never interfered very much with you. But you could not stand the Boston port bill any more than we could.

There is one thing in which Massachusetts must yield the palm, and that is the courage to face an earthquake, that terrible ordeal in the face of which the bravest manhood goes to pieces, and which your people met a few years ago with a courage and steadfastness which commanded the admiration of all mankind.

If this company had gathered on this spot one hundred and twenty years ago to-night the toast would have been that which no gathering at Charleston in those days failed to drink — "The Unanimous Twenty-six, who would not rescind the Massachusetts circular."

"The royal governor of South Carolina had invited its assembly to treat the letters of the Massachusetts 'with the contempt they deserved;' a committee, composed of Parsons, Gadsden, Pinckney, Lloyd, Lynch, Laurens, Rutledge, Elliot, and Dart, reported them to be 'founded upon undeniable constitutional principles;' and the house, sitting with its doors locked, unanimously directed its speaker to signify to that province its entire approbation. The governor, that same evening, dissolved the assembly by beat of drums."

Mr. Winthrop compared the death of Calhoun to the blotting out of the constellation of the Southern Cross from the sky.

Mr. Calhoun was educated at Yale College, in New England, where President Dwight predicted his future greatness in his boyhood. It is one of the pleasant traditions of my own family that he was a constant and favorite guest in the house of my grandmother, in my mother's childhood, and formed a friendship with her family which he never forgot.

It is delightful also to remember on this occasion that Mr. Lamar, that most Southern man of Southern men, whose tribute to Mr. Calhoun in this city is among the masterpieces of historical literature, paid a discriminating and most affectionate tribute also to Charles Sumner at the time of his death.

In this matchless eulogy Mr. Lamar disclaims any purpose to honor Mr. Sumner because of his high culture, his eminent scholarship, or varied learning, but he declares his admiration for him because of his high moral qualities and his unquenchable love of liberty. Mr. Lamar adds: " My regret is that I did not obey the impulse often found upon me to go to him and offer him my hand and my heart with it."

Mr. Lamar closes this masterpiece of eulogistic oratory with this significant sentence: " Would that the spirit of the illustrious dead whom we honor to-day could speak to both parties in tones that would reach every home throughout this broad territory,—' My countrymen, know one another, and you will love one another.' "

There is another memorable declaration of Mr. Lamar, whom I am proud to have counted among my friends. In his oration at the unveiling of the statue of Calhoun, at Charleston, he said that the appeal to arms had " led to the indissolubility of the American Union and the universality of American freedom."

Now, can we not learn a lesson also from this most significant fact that this great Southern statesman and orator was alike the eulogist of Calhoun and the eulogist of Sumner?

For myself I believe that whatever estrangements may have existed in the past, or may linger among us now, are born of ignorance and will be dispelled by knowledge. I believe that of our forty-five States there are no two who, if they could meet in the familiarity of personal intercourse, in the fulness of personal knowledge, would not only cease to entertain any bitterness, or alienation, or distrust, but each would utter to the other the words of the Jewish daughter, in that most exquisite of idylls which has come down to us almost from the beginning of time:

" Entreat me not to leave thee, or to return from following after thee; for whither thou goest, I will go; and where thou lodgest, I will lodge; thy people shall be my people, and thy God my God.

" Where thou diest, will I die, and there will I be buried; the Lord do so to me, and more also, if aught but death part me and thee."

Mr. President, I repeat to-night on Southern soil what I said first in my place in the Senate, and what I repeated in Faneuil Hall, with the full approbation of an enthusiastic and crowded audience, representing the culture and the Puritanism of Massachusetts.

The American people have learned to know as never before the quality of the Southern stock, and to value its noble contribution to the American character; its courage in war, its attachment to home and State, its love of rural life, its capacity for great affection and generous emotion, its aptness for command; above all, its constancy, that virtue above all virtues, without which no people can long be either great or free. After all, the fruit of this vine has a flavor not to be found in other gardens. In the great and magnificent future which is before our country, you are to contribute a large share both of strength and beauty.

The best evidence of our complete reconciliation is that there is no subject that we need to hurry by with our fingers on our lips. The time has come when Americans, north,

south, east, and west, may discuss any question of public
interest in a friendly and quiet spirit, without recrimination
and without heat, each understanding the other, each striving
to help the other, as men who are bearing a common burden
and looking forward with a common hope. I know that this
is the feeling of the people of the North. I think I know
that it is the feeling of the people of the South. In our part
of the country we have to deal with the great problems of
the strife between labor and capital, and of the government
of cities where vast masses of men born on foreign soil, of
different nationalities and of different races, strangers to
American principles, to American ideas, to American history,
are gathered together to exercise the unaccustomed functions
of self-government in an almost unrestricted liberty. You
have to deal with a race problem rendered more difficult still
by a still larger difference in the physical and intellectual
qualities of the two races whom Providence has brought
together.

I should be false to my own manhood if I failed to express
my profound regret and sorrow for some occurrences which
have taken place recently, both in the North and in the South.
I am bound to say that, considering all the circumstances,
the Northern community has been the worse offender.

It is well known (or if it be not well known I am willing
to make it known) that I look with inexpressible alarm and
dread upon the prospect of adding to our population millions
of persons dwelling in tropical climes, aliens in race and in
religion, either to share in our self-government, or, what is
worse still, to set an example to mankind of the subjection of
one people to another. We have not yet solved the problem how men of different races can dwell together in
the same land in accordance with our principles of

republican rule and republican liberty. I am not one
of those who despair of the solution of that problem
in justice and in freedom. I do not look upon the dark
side when I think of the future of our beloved land. I
count it the one chief good fortune of my own life that,
as I grow older, I look out on the world with hope and
not despair. We have made wonderful advances within the
lifetime of the youngest of us. While we hear from time to
time of occurrences much to be deplored and utterly to be
condemned, yet, on the whole, we are advancing quite as
rapidly as could be expected to the time when these races will
live together on American soil in freedom, in honor, and in
peace, every man enjoying his just right wherever the American constitution reigns and wherever the American flag floats
—when the influence of intelligence, of courage, of energy, inspired by a lofty patriotism and by a Christian love will have
its full and legitimate effect, not through disorder, or force,
or lawlessness, but under the silent and sure law by which
always the superior leads and the inferior follows. The time
has already come when throughout large spaces in our country both races are dwelling together in peace and harmony.
I believe that condition of things to be the rule in the South
and not to be the exception. We have a right to claim that
the country and the South shall be judged by the rule and
not the exception.

But we want you to stand by us in our troubles as brethren
and as countrymen. We shall have to look, in many perils
that are before us in the near future, to the conservatism
and wisdom of the South. And if the time shall come when
you think we can help you your draft shall be fully honored.

But to-night belongs to the memory of the Pilgrims. The
Pilgrim of Plymouth has a character in history distinct from

any other.   He differed from the Puritan of Salem or Boston in everything but the formula in which his religious faith was expressed.   He was gentle, peaceful, tolerant, gracious. There was no intolerance or hatred or bigotry in his little commonwealth.   He hanged no witches, he whipped no Quakers, he banished no heretic.   His little State existed for seventy-two years, when it was blended with the Puritan Commonwealth of Massachusetts.   He enacted the mildest code of laws on the face of the earth.   There were but eight capital offences in Plymouth.   Sir James Mackintosh held in his hand a list of two hundred and twenty-three when he addressed the House of Commons at the beginning of the present century.   He held no foot of land not fairly obtained by honest purchase.   He treated the Indian with justice and good faith, setting an example which Vattel, the foremost writer on the law of nations, commends to mankind.   In his earliest days his tolerance was an example to Roger Williams himself, who has left on record his gratitude for the generous friendship of Winslow.   Governor Bradford's courtesy entertained the Catholic priest, who was his guest, with a fish dinner on Friday.   John Robinson, the great leader of the Pilgrims, uttered the world's declaration of religious independence when he told his little flock on the wharf at Delft Haven, as reported by Winslow:

" We are ere long to part asunder and the Lord knoweth whether he should live to see our face again.   But, whether the Lord hath appointed it or not, he charged us before God and his blessed angels to follow him no further than he followed Christ; and, if God should reveal anything to us by any other instrument of his, to be as ready to receive it as we were to receive any truth by his ministry, for he was very confident the Lord had more truth and light yet to break out of his Holy Word."

The Pilgrim was a model and an example of a beautiful, simple, and stately courtesy. John Robinson, and Bradford, and Brewster, and Carver, and Winslow differ as much from the dark and haughty Endicott, or the bigoted Cotton Mather as, in the English church, Jeremy Taylor, and George Herbert, and Donne, and Vaughn differ from Laud, or Bonner, or Bancroft.

Let us not be misunderstood. I am not myself a descendant from the Pilgrims. Every drop of my blood through every line of descent for three centuries has come from a Puritan ancestor. I am ready to do battle for the name and fame of the Massachusetts Puritan in any field and against any antagonist. Let others, if they like, trace their lineage to Norman pirate or to robber baron. The children of the Puritan are not ashamed of him. The Puritan, as a distinct, vital, and predominant power, lived less than a century in England. He appeared early in the reign of Elizabeth, who came to the throne in 1558, and departed at the restoration of Charles II, in 1660. But in that brief period he was the preserver, aye, the creator of English freedom. By the confession of the historians who most dislike him, it is due to him that there is an English constitution. He created the modern House of Commons. That House, when he took his seat in it, was the feeble and timid instrument of despotism. When he left it, it was what it has ever since been —the strongest, freest, most venerable legislative body the world has ever seen. When he took his seat in it, it was little more than the register of the king's command. When he left it, it was the main depository of the national dignity and the national will. King and minister and prelate who stood in his way he brought to the bar and to the block. In the brief but crowded century he made the name of Englishman

the highest title of honor upon the earth.   A great historian
has said: " The dread of his invincible army was on all the
inhabitants of the island.   He placed the name of John
Milton high on the illustrious roll of the great poets of the
world, and the name of Oliver Cromwell highest on the roll
of English sovereigns."   The historian might have added
that the dread of this invincible leader was on all the inhabitants of Europe.

And so, when a son of the Puritans comes to the South,
when he visits the home of the Rutledges and the Pinckneys
and of John C. Calhoun, if there be any relationship in
heroism or among the lovers of constitutional liberty, he feels
that he can

> " Claim kindred there and have the claim allowed."

The Puritan differs from the Pilgrim as the Hebrew
prophet from St. John.   Abraham, ready to sacrific Isaac at
the command of God; Jeremiah, uttering his terrible prophecy of the downfall of Judea; Brutus, condemning his son
to death; Brutus, slaying his friend for the liberty of Rome;
Aristides, going into exile, are his spiritual progenitors, as
Stonewall Jackson was of his spiritual kindred.   You will find
him wherever men are sacrificing life or the delights of life
on the altar of duty.

But the Pilgrim is of a gentler and a lovelier nature.   He,
too, if duty or honor call, is ready for the sacrifice.   But
his weapon is love and not hate.   His spirit is the spirit of
John, the Beloved Disciple, the spirit of grace, mercy, and
peace.   His memory is as sweet and fragrant as the perfume
of the little flower which gave its name to the ship which
brought him over.

So, Mr. President, responding to your sentiment, I give you mine:

South Carolina and Massachusetts, the Presbyterian and the Puritan, the Huguenot and the Pilgrim; however separated by distance or by difference, they will at last surely be drawn together by a common love of liberty and a common faith in God.

FAVORING McKINLEY'S RE-ELECTION

SPEECH DELIVERED AT CONCORD, MASSACHUSETTS, OCTOBER 12, 1900

IT is more than fifty years since I ceased to be a dweller in Concord. A few old men are all there are left of the companions of my boyhood. And yet I cannot overcome the feeling that it is strange that I should come here to speak and not to hear—to give instruction and not to get it. Certainly no Concord man, however long he may live, wherever on the face of the earth he may wander, can fail to carry with him the inspiration of the spot. The great generations of the Puritan and the Revolution and the war for the Union seem ever standing upon these plains, clasping hands in an eternal companionship. For myself, the influence of Concord through my whole life has been around me and over me like a sky.

From the beginning, since Peter Bulkeley came here in 1635, this town has been consecrated to righteousness and liberty. There have been great men here whose fame, like the shot our ancestors fired at the bridge, has been heard round the world. Concord has owed much to them. But I think they would all be glad to say they have owed quite as much to Concord.

Governor Banks said at Cambridge, in his somewhat gran-
diloquent way, speaking of old Josiah Quincy, that he would
be reckoned among honorable men if their number were reduced to that of the mouths of the Nile or the gates of
Thebes. I suppose of the number of the men who have been
great inspirers of mankind, either of the intellect or the spirit,
for a thousand years were to be counted upon the fingers of
the two hands, however otherwise the list might be made up,
it would still contain the name of Waldo Emerson.

I remember also the gracious and beautiful woman whose
presence gave a new charm to the historic old manse whose
genius explored almost the whole range of literature and
science; of whom Edward Everett said she could fill every
professor's chair in Harvard College and who, while she discharged every household duty, read Æschylus or Tacitus or
the "Mécanique Céleste" in the interval of rocking the
cradle.

I will not speak of men of my own blood and kindred. But
I recall also, what a few only of you will recall with me, the
name of another Emerson, also a dweller in Concord, whom
I think with good reason to have been the brightest genius
ever born on New England soil. His brother Waldo, who was
eight years his senior, said of him that all the years to come
of his life leaned upon him; that he deferred to him on so
many questions and trusted him more than himself; that he
never should hear again such speaking as his; that his genius
and the weight of his thoughts made Shakespeare seem more
conceivable to him. This estimate of Charles Emerson was
not born of a brother's fondness. Daniel Webster, with
whom he studied law, when he was asked where Charles Emerson should settle, answered: "Let him settle anywhere.
Let him settle in the midst of the backwoods in Maine. The

clients will throng after him." Dr. Channing said when he
died that all New England mourned his loss; and Edward
Everett spoke his eulogy at Harvard. Wendell Holmes said
of him: "A beautiful, high-souled, pure spirit, he was the
very ideal of an embodied celestial intelligence; a soul glowing
like the rose of morning with enthusiasm; a character white
as the lily in purity." Charles Emerson died in early youth.
But he was already preparing himself to deal with the great
question which then lowered like a dark cloud over the public
life of this country and looked forward with good reason to the
debates in the Senate as to his natural and proper sphere. He
was alive with the spirit of liberty. Miss Martineau records
that when, after the murder of Lovejoy, the mob in Boston
threatened the persons who met in Faneuil Hall to express
their sympathy that the adored Charles Emerson, as she calls
him, said that it was better that Boston be laid in ashes than
that free speech should be suppressed.

So I hope you will believe that I could not come to Concord to bring base and ignoble counsel. Four years ago this
town gave President McKinley 517 votes, against 105 for Mr.
Bryan. The State gave him 175,000 majority. I suppose
but for one question that majority would be largely increased
this year. But for one question our Republican meetings in
Massachusetts would be not to debate public policies, but only
to sing pæans of triumph. We have the same old Democratic party; we have the same old Mr. Bryan; we have, with
this one exception, the same old declaration of purpose in the
same old platform. Every Republican promise, every Republican prophecy has been fulfilled. We touched the high-
water mark of prosperity so far under the McKinley bill four
years before. We had touched the low-water mark of adversity in the four years' nightmare of Democratic administra-

tion. We have waked from that hideous dream and the prosperity of the American people has risen higher yet.

We had a great debate in 1896. We made up the issue and the Democratic party was defeated. We have had four years' experience. The Democratic party comes back, I say, for a new trial with the same old candidate, the same old leaders, and, with one, or perhaps I ought properly to say, two exceptions, the same old doctrines. They mean to elect Mr. Bryan if they can; they mean to get the free coinage of silver at 16 to 1 if they can; they mean to overthrow the protective system, if they can; they mean to adopt Mr. Bryan's remedy for what they call "trusts" or great and overgrown aggregations of capital, if they can; they mean to impose an income tax by national authority, if they can, and they mean to reconstruct the Supreme Court of the United States, if they can. Two other questions have assumed prominence at the present time not discussed in the last election, but practical questions now. In five States at the South the Democratic party has succeeded by ingenious processes in taking away from the colored men the right to vote. Other States are following their examples, so that before long if they do not stop there are to be ten million colored peons in the United States deprived of the rights of American citizenship, and the question is upon us whether we shall execute the constitutional mandate that the Southern Democratic States which have done this thing shall have their representation in Congress proportionately reduced, or whether you and I also are to be disfranchised and have fifty or sixty men make laws for us who represent nothing but usurpation. That question demands our attention now.

Another question has come up for our consideration. That

question is how we are to deal with the people of the Philippine Islands. And in speaking of it, as I shall do before I get through, I purpose to take the bull squarely by the horns. I stated in my place in the Senate, as I have stated in many appeals to the public while the question was going on, my total dissent from the policy which was adopted in the Spanish treaty of 1899. I declared at the same time with equal emphasis that my hope for the ultimate triumph of justice and righteousness and liberty, as I understood them in this matter, was in the Republican party and nowhere else. I have never said one thing without saying the other. Both those propositions I stand by to-day. If there has been any mistake or wrong in the past, Mr. William J. Bryan is as responsible for it as any man, as any ten men in the United States, since the treaty left the hands of the President. It was he who stabbed the cause of anti-imperialism in the back in the hour of its assured victory. He says that he wanted to get the question out of the way and to restore peace, and that he trusted to a resolution of the Senate to prevent the mischief which the treaty would accomplish. I shall deal with this pretext a little later. I will say one thing about it at this moment. The Senate was the stronghold, the citadel, the West Point of the opposition to what is called imperialism. It was agreed by everybody, it was distinctly asserted by the President, that we had no title whatever to any part of the Philippine Islands save only the city of Manila. We could get no title to any part of the Philippine Islands except by a treaty with Spain, which could be accomplished only by a two thirds vote of the Senate. The defeat of the treaty was as sure, as it seemed, as the rising of to-morrow's sun, with many votes to spare, when Mr. Bryan came in person to Washington to secure its adoption.

He was the acknowledged leader of the Democratic party; he had been its candidate at the last election; he was sure to be at the next election. He put forth all his authority to induce his unwilling followers to change their attitude and to vote for the treaty, in spite of the remonstrances of the wisest and most experienced leaders of the Democracy. It was as if some great military and political leader of the Revolutionary war had surrendered West Point to the enemy in the midst of the struggle, had got the Continental Congress to declare that we were the lawful subjects of Great Britain and that King George was our rightful sovereign, and said that he did it because he wanted peace; that he hoped later to get through a resolution somewhere which would declare our independence.

But I wish to speak for a moment of the other issues of the campaign. I speak of them because I believe that Mr. Bryan does not mean business in this matter of imperialism, or if he does mean business, he means nothing that will not be better and more safely accomplished by the Republican party, and that he does mean business in the matter of the free coinage of silver and the attack on the supreme court and the establishment of free trade and his reckless and destructive plans of dealing with the matter of trusts.

Nobody is talking much about the tariff just now. We have debated that question in this country for a hundred years. I am not going to debate it now. We have the theorist on one side and the practical man and the statesman on the other. All the time experience has given the lie to theory. Nearly every statesman whose name has survived the falling of the gravel on his coffin has come to adopt the doctrine of protection. The men who are charged with the administration of great industries, who must pay good wages if they are to be paid, are on that side. The two great men, Jefferson and Jackson, to whom Democracy likes to trace its lineage, were extreme protectionists. So were the fathers of the republic. So were Washington, Lincoln, Grant, Webster, and Clay. So were the two Adamses. So, in his earlier and better days, was Calhoun.

We were told that this policy would increase the cost of living and would not raise wages. Yet under it the cost of living steadily goes down and wages steadily go up.

We were told that the rich would get richer and the poor would get poorer. But under it the rich get richer and the poor get richer too, as is shown by the $550,000,000 of deposits in the savings banks of Massachusetts, and the $1,623,000,000 of deposits in the savings banks of the country. They told us it would isolate the country and cut us off from other markets; that we must buy of other countries or we could not sell to them. They are answered by foreign exports of $1,370,000,000; by exports of manufactures alone of $432,000,000, and a balance of trade in our favor during the present administration greater than all such balances in our previous history added together. We shall not get our Democratic friends to talk free trade this year to the workingmen of the country. They remember too well the two terrible nightmares of Mr. Cleveland's two administrations. Under the McKinley bill the prosperity of the workingmen of this country reached the high-water mark of the world's history. Under Mr. Cleveland it went down to the worst condition we have known in our own history, while under the Dingley bill the tide has come back again and risen higher than ever before.

During Cleveland's two administrations the most sanguine prayer either workman or employer dared to breathe was,

" God grant I may be no worse off to-morrow than I was yesterday." Under President McKinley the employer gets rich and the workman every Saturday night lays up a half or a third of his wages.

What does that one thing mean? We hear with a glow of pride that the balance of trade is in our favor and that England is coming to New York to borrow money; of the swelling tide of our exports; of the supremacy of the United States in agriculture and in manufacture; of an internal commerce that thrusts into insignificance all the foreign commerce of the earth.

But, after all, what is that compared with the thought of five million American homes where there has been employment, and a half or a third of the earnings are laid up at the week's end? Comfort for the wife, education for the children, a quiet Sabbath for the family, lectures and books and music and good clothes.

I speak of this matter now only because Mr. Bryan makes it a very practical question again when he proposes his remedy for the evil of trusts.

The American people are becoming alarmed by great aggregations of wealth and by great business monopolies and combinations which we call trusts. They can, in general, be reached only by State authority. Congress has no power unless the trust be engaged in foreign commerce or in commerce between the States. If a trust carry on a manufactory and sell and deliver its product at its own factory, even if the article be afterward transported to another State, the State legislature and not Congress must deal with it. I do not find that in any Democratic State, so far, any efficient remedy has been adopted or proposed.

If there be a comedy in political history it is the Democratic attitude toward the question of these large concentrations of capital. Take them east, west, north or south—wherever you find a great trust you will find a great Democratic leader in the midst of it. Just as the Democratic campaign begun came the disclosures of the Ice Trust with the great Democratic king of New York, where Democracy itself is nothing but a great trust, among its largest owners. The Senate committee, of which I was a member, spent a large part of last winter in investigating the contest between the two Democratic leaders of Montana over a seat in the Senate. They were two of the richest men in the world. One of them was said, I don't know how truly, to be the richest man in the world. His son testified that he himself had an income of $250,000 a year. The other contestant charged him with having bought up an entire legislature by wholesale. The Senate committee—Republicans and Democrats alike—were unanimous in finding the case made out. But Mr. Clark resigned his seat without bringing it to a vote in the Senate. The Democrats on the committee agreed with us, but they thought our report was defective because we didn't report that the other Democrat was just as bad. Clark went home, was put on the Democratic National Committee, made an enormous contribution to the campaign fund, and now is one of the pillars of the Democratic platform. He stands immediately under that plank which sets forth the danger to the Republic of large aggregations of capital.

They talk about silver and imperialism and trusts. I do not include the whole Democratic party in what I say. But there are large communities in this country where the Democratic party is nothing but an aggregation of trusts. It is like an artichoke. If you peel off one layer you come to another, and so on down to the core. There are States where the real Democratic platform is a bank account. The Democratic leaders confront each other like knights of old, but with this difference: The knights of old laid their hands on the hilts of their swords. The Democratic champion confronts his antagonist each with a pen in one hand and a check book in the other, and shouts his angry defiance, "Draw, villain, draw!"

But we are told that these great trusts are a great public danger. We are told that they are likely to become a cancer on the body of the State. I hope they are not quite so bad as that. But I agree that they are in danger of becoming a great evil. Mr. Bryan is not the first cancer doctor who has sought to induce a confiding patient to trust his remedy. In general in such cases the doctor has been more dangerous than the disorder. If the patient gets cured of his disease he is pretty sure to die of his physician. If the trust be as bad as Mr. Bryan represents it, it is not, in my judgment, as great a danger as Bryanism. I do not believe either in his diagnosis or his prescription.

It is barely possible that among Mr. Bryan's numerous speeches there may have been one or two that you and I have not read. But the only practical remedy that he suggests is that if any protected article be manufactured by a trust, that article shall at once be put upon the free list. They tell us the tariff is not an issue in this campaign; but when Mr. Bryan comes to talk of trusts he makes the tariff a very real and vital issue. His remedy is, in substance, to put the whole protective policy of the country in the power of any corrupt trust, great or small, that may choose to assail it. Let a half dozen men get together and form a trust to manufacture woollen machinery or to manufacture woollen cloth, and at once every machine shop in the country or every woollen cloth factory in the country loses its protection. The trust may be formed for that very purpose. It makes no difference to this sage philosopher. If the patient get a pimple on his nose, it is a sign the blood is disordered, and Dr. Bryan proposes to cut the nose off; if he get a tumor in his arm his only remedy is amputation.

I have never heard of a single practical suggestion to prevent these great monopolies from any Democratic quarter. The Republicans in Congress passed a measure under which the Supreme Court of the United States has declared illegal a large railroad combination, which in my opinion will have a great influence in breaking up large combinations of manufacturing monopolies. I think also that the laws of trade will overthrow them sooner or later. They have, so far, in general proved unprofitable to the men who have engaged in them. They have enabled men who wish to sell out to get a large price for their plants, and they have enabled watered stocks to be put upon the market. They have in many cases cheapened prices and raised wages. In some cases they have inflated prices and reduced wages. They are not going to ruin this country. The American people will outgrow them and will find the way to deal with them.

The trust is not a cancer. It is only a boil. They do not threaten the life, they do not seriously impair the health of the industries of this country. They will hurt the employer and the capitalist in the end more than they will hurt the workman. The great law of the human progress, of which our own country is the great example, will still prevail.

Among the best political teachers of the English-speaking race, both here and in the Old World, have been the poets.

Milton and Wordsworth and Tennyson, Emerson, and Whittier have been among the wisest and the surest of political guides to the thought of the youth of America and England. Tennyson truly says of England that her freedom slowly broadens down from precedent to precedent. And, gentlemen, I think we can affirm truthfully and without boasting that many of the great precedents that have broadened English liberty have been precedents set to her by America and have been precedents set to America by Massachusetts. But the same process is going on surely and not too slowly with us at home. Ever the poor are becoming richer; ever the ignorant are learning; ever the wretched are becoming happier. There is little danger from aristocracy or from armies or navies. There is little permanent danger from wealthy classes. There is little danger where every child has an equal share of the father's estate. Gathered wealth scatters again. The army disperses. The soldier becomes the citizen. Seventy million freemen will never be enslaved by their own armies. Seventy million Americans, educated in common schools, will never be corrupted by their own wealth. There is but one danger. That comes from agitators like Mr. Bryan, who would destroy alike the security of property, the protection of courts, and the sanctity of laws. That danger also will pass by and disappear. There is evil enough in this world. But of one thing I am sure—that from year to year and from generation to generation the lot of mankind is growing better. This life of ours is sometimes compared to a vast staircase, of which the top and the foot are alike shrouded in darkness, but from which is heard the sound of ascending and descending humanity. And one thing is certain, that the sound most clearly to be distinguished is the sound of the footstep of the rich man descending and of the poor man ascending. As has been well said, the polished boot comes down and the wooden shoe goes up.

Four years ago the people of Massachusetts rejected Mr. Bryan by an overwhelming vote largely because of his proposal to degrade the currency. He proposed to make a silver dollar coined at the ratio of sixteen to one legal tender for all debts and lawful payment of all wages. He tried to get favor for this plan by a passionate attack on wealth, by undertaking to set class against class, to set the farmer against the manufacturer, to set the poor against the rich, and to destroy respect for the courts. The people of Massachusetts rejected him and his schemes. They said he was inviting them to a passionate crusade of dishonor. They said that to pay the foreign creditor that way would be a breach of national faith, would disgrace the flag, would destroy the credit of the republic. They said that to pay wages in that way would cut down the three quarter value of the workman's wage more than one half. They thought that to pay debts at home in that way would diminish by one half the value of every deposit in a savings bank, of every policy of insurance, of every note, and every mortgage. Nothing has happened to change our mind since, except that Mr. Bryan's prophecies and Mr. Bryan's arguments have all been proved worthless by the four years' experience. He told you you would have a time of extreme depression and poverty if you did not take his advice, and you had a time of unexampled prosperity. He told the farmers of the country that the price of silver and the price of wheat always remained the same. And the farmer's wheat went up to a dollar a bushel and silver went down to thirty-seven cents.

Mr. Bryan and his party in their platform—all his parties in their platforms—stand for the same doctrine now. But we are told he cannot do anything about it. The matter is settled and silver is not an issue. Mr. Schurz, of whom I would speak with entire respect, says in the first place that Mr. Bryan cannot do it while there is a Republican Senate, and in the next place, that Congress next winter can pass a law to tie his hands. On the other hand, Mr. Gage, the secretary of the treasury, tells you that Mr. Bryan can do it by executive power alone; that he can pay the interest on the debt and all the current expenses of the government in silver dollars, and that will bring the country on to a silver basis.

Now, I will not undertake to say whether Mr. Gage or Mr. Schurz be wrong as to the interpretation of existing laws. But I think I can speak with some authority, from a pretty long experience, as to the possibility of getting new legislation next winter. And I say, with whatever title I may have to respect, that with thirteen great appropriation bills to be passed in thirteen weeks, besides the other great questions that must be dealt with, it would be absolutely impossible to get through such a law as Mr. Schurz proposes, even if a majority of the House and Senate should attempt it. And in the next place, I say that no Congress ever would dare to pass such a bill after the American people at a presidential election had elected a President in favor of the free coinage of silver. It would be a gross and wanton defiance of public sentiment, upon which no party and no Congress would ever venture.

So it seems to me that Mr. Bryan will have no difficulty in doing this thing if he wants to. It is not a question whether Mr. Schurz be right or whether Mr. Gage be right in his idea of the extent of executive authority under existing law. The question is, what the President thinks he has the lawful right to do. There can be no remedy but impeachment—impeachment by a House of Representatives elected at the same time he was elected—and conviction by the Senate by a two thirds vote. Now, what does Mr. Bryan himself mean to do and think he has the right to do? He said four years ago, in a speech at Knoxville, Tenn.:

" If there is any one who believes the gold standard is a good thing, or that it must be maintained, I warn him not to cast his vote for me, because I promise him it will not be maintained in this country longer than I am able to get rid of it."

And at Topeka, August 13, 1900, when he accepted the Populists' nomination, speaking of monetary reform, he said:

" If a bad monetary system drags down the price of the farmer's products, while monopolies raise the price of what he buys, he burns the candle at both ends and must expect to suffer in comparison with those who belong to the classes more favored by legislation.

" No Populist, however sanguine, believes it possible to elect a Populist President at this time, but the Populist party may be able to determine whether a Democrat or a Republican will be elected.

" If the fusion forces win a victory this fall, we shall see the reform accomplished before the next presidential election, and with its accomplishment the people will find it easier to secure any remedial legislation which they may desire."

He was not speaking then of legislation, or of calling Congress together to propose something. He says, if you carry the election this thing shall be done, and then, after it is done, we will have our remedial legislation. He is thinking of the use of executive power and not trusting it to anybody else. He is proposing to act in that matter on our friend Edward Everett Hale's celebrated maxim, "If you want a thing done, do it yourself." He does not tell his followers, I will call Congress together and see what they will do; he says this thing shall be done.

He says the thing will be done. He means business. It will be in Mr. Bryan's power to do it. He can do it without the help of Congress. That man deceives himself, that man lulls himself into false security, who believes that these things mean dishonor and ruin and proposes to vote for Mr. Bryan because he thinks there is no danger that it will be done.

Mr. Gage has told us that Mr. Bryan could break down the gold standard. He could order his secretary of the treasury to pay in silver all the public debt payable in coin, principal and interest, and all the current disbursements of the government, amounting from $1,000,000 to $1,750,000 a day. Mr. Gage tells us that while there would be a little difficulty in getting silver enough to do it in the beginning from the silver certificates and the silver coin, it would stop the inflow of gold and that the time would not be distant when all the revenues of the government and the disbursements of the government would be paid in silver.

That would excite alarm. It would excite alarm the whole world over. The greenback and the treasury certificates would come for redemption. We should have a deficiency instead of a surplus and we should have the industrial paralysis of 1893 and 1896, when the question what was to be the standard agitated the public mind.

No, fellow citizens, President Bryan, if there be a President Bryan, will do in this matter exactly what candidate Bryan thinks he could do and what he has declared his purpose to do. He will not leave that responsibility to an unwilling Congress. I think I make no mistake when I impress upon the men who believe as I do and as you do that the free coinage of silver means national dishonor and the ruin of business, the message of Mr. Bryan himself: "If any man believes the gold standard is a good thing, I warn him not to vote for me."

How can you put confidence in Mr. Bryan or in the men who are to be his counsellors and advisers in the Solid South, in Mr. Croker, in Mr. David B. Hill, in the men who are governing our great cities? This is not political or partisan prejudice. It is the judgment which the sober sense of the American people formed four years ago. Nothing has happened since to change it. I wish to read a sentence from Mr. Carl Schurz, whom no one will charge with being a partisan. I would not speak unkindly or disrespectfully of Mr. Schurz. I have differed from him many times. I think he has erred in undervaluing the importance of party organization, without which all government in a republic must be chaos, and whether it be a chaos of fallible men or of archangels, the difference in the result will not be very great. But Mr. Schurz has rendered some notable service to the republic. He was a soldier in the war for the Union. Before the war he made a powerful contribution to the great debate for liberty and was of inestimable service in bringing his German fellow countrymen into the Republican party. Since the war he has argued with great power and effect the questions of honest money and sound finance many times when honest money and sound finance were in peril. Let us not forget these things.

But here is what Mr. Schurz said—if he be correctly reported—at Peoria, Ill., in 1896:

"Abraham Lincoln and Bryan! Abraham Lincoln and Altgeld! To associate these names together as allies in a common cause—aye, to pronounce them together in the same breath—is not only a fraud, it is a sacrilege."

Has anything happened since to change that estimate of Mr. Bryan? He has made a few vague promises, which in my judgment it will be impossible for him to carry out. He has made a most impracticable suggestion as to what he will do in regard to imperialism—vague, indefinite, and, in my judgment, absolutely worthless.

We are to judge of men, especially candidates for office, by acts, not by promises; by what they do, not by what they say. The one thing that Mr. William J. Bryan has done since Mr. Schurz said that of him was to stab the opposition in the back in the hour of its assured victory and procure the passage of the Spanish treaty, which purchased sovereignty over ten million people for a price; pledged the faith of the United States to pay for it; promised that Congress, and not the people, should hereafter determine their fate; and made it the constitutional duty of the President of the United States to reduce them to subjection until Congress should act. Since Mr. Schurz uttered that opinion of Mr. Bryan, Mr. Bryan has by his conduct piled mountain high the reasons which justify that estimate.

Abraham Lincoln told his countrymen in 1864 that it was not a good time to swap horses when they were crossing a stream. It does not seem to me to be a very good time to swap horses now, while we are crossing the tempestuous Chinese Sea in a typhoon. I like the way President McKinley and the department of state are handling this great and difficult Chinese question. They will go through with it to the satisfaction of the American people.

But they tell you that a great mistake has been made in
the matter of the Philippine Islands. I think so, too. My
opinion is well known, or if it be not well known, I am willing to make it known, that I thought we should have done
in the Philippine Islands exactly what we have done and
mean to do in Cuba. I think that in that way we should
have saved the war, we should have had the love of that
people instead of their hatred, we should have had everything heart could desire in the way of glory, in the way of
trade, aye, and in the American sense of the word, in the
way of empire. The policy which seemed to me best for
the country seemed to me also best for the Republican party.
If that course had been pursued, we should, in my opinion,
have had the presidential election almost without a struggle.
I met the other day in New York the man whom I regard
as the ablest and wisest Democratic leader in the country—
the man to whom more than to any ten others President
Cleveland owed his victory in two elections. I asked him
what he thought of the prospect of the campaign. He said
he was not yet well enough informed to make a prediction,
but all the Democrats he talked with felt very confident.
I said: "Suppose we had taken toward the Philippine
Islands the same course that we took in regard to Cuba;
what sort of a campaign should we have had?" He replied:
"We could hardly have made a fight with you." I believed
that if that course had been taken we should have had, with
perhaps the exception of a single State, a solid North and
should have carried quite a number of States at the South
besides those we carried four years ago. But thinking so,
I never doubted the integrity and the patriotic purpose of
the large majority of the Republican party in both Houses
of Congress. They were misled, in my opinion, as to the

facts. They were misled as to the character and capacity of the people of the Philippine Islands. They were misled, some of them, by a dream of empire and by what I deem a false conception of glory. But it never occurred to me to doubt their sincerity and their love of liberty. It never occurred to me to withdraw my confidence from them, whom I have known through and through, in and out, for more than thirty years, and transfer it to Mr. Bryan and Mr. Croker and the leaders of the white Democracy of the South.

My relations with President McKinley have remained unchanged and unbroken. I have watched the career of that brave soldier, of that eloquent orator, of that able statesman, from the time when he offered his life for his country in earliest youth, a life spent in the face of day, until the time when his countrymen who knew him elevated him to the foremost place on the face of the earth. The feeling on my part, in spite of this one difference of opinion, has been a feeling of unbroken confidence and respect, and on his part, if I may trust the assurances of those who are nearest to him, of unbroken kindness.

Men differ in opinion as to great concerns of public policy. Men differ in opinion as to great questions, righteousness, justice, and liberty, when they are involved in the affairs of state. Our history has been full of the dissensions of great men and the bitter divisions of good men whom their countrymen to-day, looking back, regard with equal honor and reverence. I held an opinion upon this question which I stated then as became a Massachusetts senator, and which I am ready to state now as becomes a son of Massachusetts and a son of Concord. But I cannot impute to the men who differ from me—men like my colleagues in both Houses of

HOAR

Congress, men like Andrew White and James B. Angell and
President Schurman among our instructors of youth; men
like Edward Everett Hale and Lyman Abbott and the editors
of the "Congregationalist" and the "Independent" among
our religious teachers—that they are actuated by any less
patriotic motives than I am, or that they are less deserving of
confidence than Mr. Bryan or Mr. Tillman or Mr. Richard
Croker.

What has been done has been done. What has been has
been.

> "Not fate itself can o'er the past have power."

Our question now is for the future.

We cannot forget that for everything that has happened
Mr. Bryan is more responsible than any other man, than
any other twenty men, since the Spanish treaty left the hands
of the President. That treaty involved this whole question.
It affirmed the constitutional power of the United States to
acquire foreign territory; it pledged the faith of the people
that the Congress of the United States and not the people of
the Philippine Islands should determine their future fate. It
purchased sovereignty over an unwilling people and pledged
the faith of the United States to a foreign Power to pay for
it. And when the defeat of that treaty seemed assured,
with many votes to spare, Mr. Bryan, the great leader of the
Democratic party, its last candidate for the Presidency, certain to be its next candidate for the Presidency, came to
Washington in person, disregarding the remonstrances of his
wisest supporters, and stabbed the Opposition in the back in
the hour of its assured victory. I cannot doubt that he did
that because he wished to keep this question open as a political issue for the campaign. He knew that the issues he
had lost in a time of adversity he could not maintain in a

time of prosperity. He knew that his case was hopelessly lost, as we all knew it, unless he could keep alive this question for this election. The pretexts which he puts forth and which satisfy some of his supporters now did not satisfy them then. Mr. Mason of Illinois, who had opposed the acquisition of the Philippine Islands, had been invited to deliver an address by the anti-imperialists of Boston. He voted for the treaty, and they at once cancelled the invitation. They did not think a man worthy to be heard in Boston who had voted for that treaty. And now they claim that the man who procured its passage is worthy to be trusted with the destiny of the American people.

The excuses Mr. Bryan gives for this course seem to me infinitely frivolous and pitiful. He says that he expected that the Senate would pass a resolution declaring our purpose not to retain sovereignty over these islands, and that he wanted to stop the war with Spain, and thought it better to trust the question to our own friends than to the foreign enemy. He knew perfectly well, as every man knows, that the war with Spain was over. The commissioners of Spain had said formally that the United States must dictate its own terms, and that they were helpless to make further resistance. That communication of the Spanish commissioners had been communicated to Congress and made public. He knew perfectly well that there was not the slightest validity to such a resolution unless it passed both houses and was approved by the President. It was as I have said elsewhere, as if in the middle of the Revolutionary war some great general and political leader had surrendered West Point to the enemy and got the Continental Congress to declare that King George was our lawful sovereign, and that Parliament was our lawful legislature, and then said that after peace on those terms he hoped to get a resolution declaring that we should some time have our independence. That treaty made it the constitutional duty of Congress to exercise sovereignty over the Philippine Islands, and according to the decision of the supreme court made it the constitutional duty of the President to reduce them to order and submission until Congress should act. It has been said by a New York newspaper that such a power has not been conferred on Congress by the constitution. It is not in the least inconsistent with it. When the faith of the American people has been pledged to a foreign government by a treaty, the treaty-making power must of necessity decide the constitutional question, just as the supreme court decides it in domestic questions. But if that be not so the question of constitutionality is practically settled for the executive of the next four years by the opinion of Mr. McKinley who negotiated the treaty and the opinion of Mr. Bryan who procured its adoption. Mr. Bryan thinks that treaty constitutional or he would not have secured the ratification. So our anti-imperialistic friends propose to-day to support a President who believes it within the constitutional power of Congress to govern the Philippine people, who advised and secured the adoption of a treaty pledging them to do it, and who must believe also that it is the constitutional duty of the President to reduce them to order and submission until Congress acts.

No, fellow citizens. If this Spanish treaty be right, President McKinley and Mr. Bryan were both right. If this Spanish treaty be wrong, President McKinley and Mr. Bryan were equally wrong. Now, what are we to do for the future? I can find no substantial difference when we come to any practical declaration of purpose between the two candidates or the two parties on that question. There are men in both parties who say that we ought to hold on forever to this conquest. Some of them think it our interest to do it, regardless either of the desire or the character of the Philippine people. I suppose Mr. Morgan of Alabama, who, if the Democrats come into power, will have charge in the Senate of the great committee on foreign relations, is of that way of thinking. And he has the Democratic State of Alabama at his back. But in general both parties say they mean to give to the Philippine Islands self-government as soon as they are ready for it, and I do not see that one party goes any further than the other party in this respect. I do not myself like this phrase, " give self-government " or " give good government." I think the right to self-government, as the fathers said in the Declaration of Independence, is a thing that they are entitled to by the laws of nature and of nature's God. But the phrase is Mr. Bryan's and the phrase is the phrase of the Democratic platform, and not mine.

The Democratic platform gives no assurance of immediate independence. It is to come after, according to their promise, a stable form of government established by us. Now, Mr. Bryan in his speech of acceptance says not even that he will do that. He makes no suggestion of recalling our troops by executive power, or of letting the Filipinos alone, or of making them any promise by executive authority. He says he will call Congress together to do the things set forth in the Democratic platform. Now, he knows perfectly well, if he knows anything, that the Congress he will call together will do nothing beyond what the President has declared his purpose to have done. He knows very well the vast strength of imperialism among his Democratic supporters which will render the hope of accomplishing any such purpose utterly idle and delusive. Why, the Democrats in New York have nominated for governor this very autumn Mr. Stanchfield, one of the most zealous and extreme imperialists in the country. He, perhaps, will not outact Governor Roosevelt; but so far in the matter of imperialism he has outtalked him. Mr. Morgan of Alabama, who will be chairman of the committee on foreign relations if the Democrats get the Senate, his colleague, Senator Pettus, who will be chairman of the judiciary if the Democrats get the Senate, are among the most zealous and thorough-going supporters of the purpose to maintain our authority over the people of the Philippine Islands. Of the nineteen followers of Mr. Bryan who voted for the ratification of the treaty about half were imperialists upon conviction.

So when Mr. Bryan says he is going to call Congress together and recommend them to carry out the Democratic platform he may as well call spirits from the vast deep. He may be more fortunate than Glendower, and the spirits may come when he doth call them. But the spirits will not do the bidding of the magician. The magician will have to do the bidding of the spirits.

There are undoubtedly many persons in the Republican party who have been carried away by the dream of empire. They mean, I have no doubt, to hold on to the Philippine Islands forever. But they do not constitute the strength of the party. They do not, in my judgment, express its purpose, and they do not constitute the strength of the American people. The Republican party in its platform, State and national, promises to give these people self-government when they are ready for it and as fast as they are ready for it.

I have an abiding confidence that these pledges are to be kept. The Republican party has kept its pledge as to Cuba,

and it will do sooner or later to the Filipinos what it has done
to the Cubans.   We have been in the dark as to the facts
regarding this distant and strange Oriental people.   But we
shall know them after peace has been declared.   Their
leaders will come over here to tell their story to the American
people, and they can go from one end of the country to the
other and no man will hurt a hair of their heads, unless it
be such ruffians as those who attacked Governor Roosevelt.
If it prove to be true, as I think it will, that they are a civilized people, able to live, governing themselves in orderly
village communities, capable of self-defence, seeking a
national life like Japan, better than many countries south
of us on the American continent, and they then desire their
independence, do you suppose any man or any party could
put forth the power of this republic to interfere with it and
live? Great Britain, with all her power, all her aristocracy,
and all her traditions of empire, would not venture for an
hour to deny independence to Canada or Australia if they
wanted it.   She would not deny it in Ireland if Ireland were
not at her door.   And the people of the United States will
never repeat the experiment of Ireland anywhere.

Which party can you trust in this matter—the party that
has done everything that has been accomplished for liberty
in the past, or the party which has resisted everything that
has been accomplished for liberty; the party that sustained
slavery, or the party that abolished it; the party that made
war upon the Union, or the party that put down the Rebellion; the party that adopted the three great amendments
which made every slave a free man and every free man a
citizen and every citizen a voter, or the party that filibustered
for days and nights against the adoption of the thirteenth
amendment, which was carried by a single vote?   Will you

trust the party that governs Massachusetts, or the party that governs New York City and Mississippi?

The author of the Democratic platform of Kansas City, or at any rate the gentleman by whose lips it was reported to the convention, uttered in my hearing these sentences last winter on the floor of the Senate. Let me read them:

"We took the government away. We stuffed ballot-boxes. We shot them. We are not ashamed of it. The senator from Wisconsin would have done the same thing. I see it in his right eye now. He would have done it. With that system—force, tissue ballots, etc.—we got tired ourselves. So we called a constitutional convention, and we eliminated, as I said, all of the colored people whom we could under the fourteenth and fifteenth amendments."

When the anti-imperialist sees the smiling countenance of my honorable friend, Governor Boutwell, at one end of the Democratic line and hears this thing from Mr. Tillman at the other, I should think he would find himself something in the condition of the two tramps I once heard of who approached a farm-house in the country, and were encountered by a large bulldog. "Come on, Jim," says one of them, "don't you see he is wagging his tail?" "Yes," says the other, "but don't you hear him growl? I don't know which end of him to trust."

Mr. Tillman, of South Carolina, is a brave and outspoken gentleman. He is the rising leader of the Democracy of the Solid South. If Mr. Bryan be elected there will be no man in the country, save perhaps Mr. Croker, of New York, who will be more powerful in the councils of the administration. Five Democratic States with marvellous ingenuity have just disfranchised their colored voters. Others are preparing to follow. If the thing goes on, before the end of the next presidential term ten million American citizens, to become within half a century thirty-five million American citizens, will be disfranchised by these Democratic frauds. Not only will they be disfranchised, but you are to play the game of politics hereafter with the Democratic party which will use these loaded dice. Fifty or sixty Democratic representatives will vote on every question in which you have an interest—free silver, socialism, free trade—representing not numbers, but only fraud and usurpation.

We have two defences under the constitution. One is that if people of any race or class are deprived of the right to vote in any State, it becomes the duty of Congress to diminish the representation of that State in that proportion —a duty which every man knows will never be performed if Mr. Bryan and the Democratic party come into power. Why, he was asked the other day what he thought of North Carolina. And he answered that if you would read the Sulu treaty you would be so ashamed that you could not think about North Carolina.

The other defence is in the supreme court of the United States, the majority of whom are old men. Against that court, the great bulwark and safety of our rights, Mr. Bryan and the Democratic party have already declared war. But if there be no war, the majority of that court are old men, and it is not unlikely that its complexion may be changed within the coming four years.

The Republican party in its long and splendid history has made one mistake. That mistake, so far as it affects the past, cannot be remedied. It would have done no harm but for Mr. Bryan. So far as it affects the future, it will be remedied by the Republican party, or it will not be remedied at all. I believe that the Philippine Islands belong of right to the Philippine people; that they have a right, having thrown off their old government, to institute for themselves a new government, laying its foundation on such principles and organizing its powers in such form as to them and not to us shall seem most likely to effect their safety and happiness. But I do not believe it wise, while claiming this right, for that Oriental people of eight or ten millions to stand with a party or with a candidate who denies the same right to ten million Americans at home. I do not propose to enfranchise ten million Filipinos while I disfranchise ten million Americans.

I believe Aguinaldo and Mabini entitled to self-government. I believe also that Booker Washington and Robert Small are entitled to self-government. I have little respect for the declaration of love of liberty of the men who stand with one heel on the forehead of Booker Washington of Alabama, and the other on the forehead of Robert Small of South Carolina, and wave the American flag over Aguinaldo and Mabini.

Now, fellow citizens, I do not know whether these things seem important to our friends who think of leaving the Republican party. This is no waving of the bloody shirt. It is no tale of individual outrage caused by what is left of the spirit of slavery or the passion of the Civil War. It is a deliberate attempt, avowed, undisguised, to overthrow the American constitution so far as it secures to ten million Americans on our own soil political equality. It is an attempt to overthrow the principle that government at home rests on the consent of the governed. For myself, I distrust such statesmanship. I abhor such political morality, and I decline to follow such leadership.

You are not helping the cause of anti-imperialism by going into partnership with Bryanism. You cannot mix tyranny, dishonor, broken faith, anarchy, license in one cup, and have constitutional liberty the result of the mixture. If the firm of Bryan, Croker, Altgeld, Boutwell, Tillman, and Schurz do business at the old Democratic stand, they will transact the old Democratic business. The new partners are not to have a controlling interest. They will not contribute much of the capital. They will not be authorized to sign the name of the firm.

When the new administration comes in, to whom, do you think, it will listen? Will it listen to Mr. Morgan and Mr. Pettus, with Alabama behind them? Will it listen to Mr. McEnery, with Louisiana behind him? Will it listen to Mr. McLaurin? All these men are imperialists. They are as thoroughly intrenched in the political leadership of their States as ever was Daniel Webster in Massachusetts. Or will it listen to Mr. Schurz or Mr. Boutwell, with nothing behind him? Democratic South Carolina will speak with a divided voice as to liberty in the Philippine Islands. It will speak with a united voice as to the disfranchisement of ten million Americans at home. Mississippi will speak with a divided voice about Aguinaldo or Mabini; but there will be no difference of opinion as to Booker Washington or Robert Small. There will be behind that administration a Solid South, intent on disfranchising the negro, in earnest and meaning business. There will be behind it the Populist, the Anarchist, and Socialist of the great cities, in earnest and meaning business. There will be behind it Richard Croker and Tammany Hall, intent on spoils and jobs and patronage, in earnest and meaning business. All these must be listened to, and will be. Mr. Boutwell and Mr. Schurz and the anti-imperialists will have served their purpose. They will have nothing more to do. They have made good bait. The Democratic fisherman will have done with them and will throw them back, stiff and half dead, into the sea.

I have little disposition to submit to lectures, public or private, from gentlemen who, whatever they profess, are practical allies of the great movement to establish a peonage on American soil of which ten million American citizens are to be the victims.

We cannot shut our eyes to the changes that have been wrought in our time. Until lately this country stood to Asia and Africa as the earth to the other planets in the solar system. We knew they were there. But we exerted and desired no influence upon them. They had little influence upon us. We sent them a few missionaries. But they concerned themselves with their relations to the next world and not to this. To-day the whole earth is but a neighborhood. The events that happen in Asia, half way around the earth, are printed in the Boston papers twelve hours before they happen. Now these new relations are to be hereafter constant, intimate, supreme. I for one prefer to trust the important questions they are bringing upon us to the men who have so far dealt with the Chinese problem rather than to Mr. Bryan. Do not misunderstand me. Let us not in our new relations abandon our old principles. Conditions on this planet may have changed. But the stars have not changed their places in the heavens. The Declaration of Independence must still be our guide. The eternal laws of justice and righteousness and liberty are still to govern the relations of citizens to one another, and the relations of nations to one another. The eternal law of righteousness which we learned in the beginning from Asia must still guide us in dealing with the east, from which it came.

DOUGHERTY

D ANIEL DOUGHERTY, an American orator, was born in Philadelphia, Pennsylvania, October 15, 1826, and educated at private schools. After studying law he was admitted to the bar in 1849, and soon became one of the most prominent advocates in his native city. He was a well-known and popular speaker on the Democratic side, but being a strong Unionist he left the Democratic party in 1861 and in 1864 worked with the Republicans in order to secure the re-election of President Lincoln. In 1876 he returned to the Democratic party and in 1880 nominated Hancock for the presidency in a noted speech. Other much admired oratorical efforts of his were, an address before the literary societies of Lafayette College in 1859, a speech of welcome to Lincoln in Philadelphia in 1864, and an oration at Baltimore, November 11, 1889, before the Roman Catholic lay congress. Dougherty's orations display both power and finish, and he was nearly if not quite as popular on the lecture platform as when making political speeches. He never held office and his latest years were passed in New York City, where he gave himself almost entirely to his profession. His death occurred in New York City September 5, 1891.

ORATION ON DEMOCRACY

DELIVERED IN PHILADELPHIA, JULY 4, 1856

T HERE are a few spots about the earth, some separated by seas and distant thousands of leagues from others, which the voice of the world has proclaimed holy and around which the memories of mankind will cling with everlasting reverence.

Such is Sinai, where God proclaimed to man the rules of human action.

Such, too, is Calvary, where, amid the darkness of the sun, the rocking of the earth, and the rising of the dead, the Saviour died, even as the portals of heaven opened.

After these, sanctified by the Divine Presence, may be mentioned Marathon, where the dauntless soldiers of glorious Greece achieved the liberty of Athens and won imperishable renown.

Runnymede, where the English barons wrung from a tyrant king the Magna Charta. The Pilgrim's Rock, where the founders of New England sought a shelter from the religious persecutions of the Old World. The quiet town of St. Mary's, where religious freedom first found a foothold in the new.

And that other spot—the spot that made this day immortal, where, Pallas-like, a new-born nation sprung into giant life—where man reclaimed his long-lost prerogatives and asserted the justice of heaven in his own equality—where freedom made her last and noblest stand against the encroachments of time-covered and world-cursed tyranny— where the great work was begun in which Americans will ever toil and never tire until wrong is righted, every throne levelled with the dust, oppression swept from the earth, the world regenerated, and mankind free.

Upon this hallowed spot, this heaven-smiling morn, we meet to bow our heads and hearts in humble adoration to the Almighty Power, on whom we relied in the hour of our extremest need and whose protecting care we implore now in the day of our abundance—to reaffirm our never-dying gratitude to our departed fathers—to renew the holy vows of political equality and declare our fixed resolve to transmit unimpaired to posterity the inestimable heritage bequeathed to us.

When first through chaos rolled the voice of God, " Let there be light, and there was light;" when the Omnipotent spoke, and this beautiful world, obedient, sprung into its fixed existence—then in the image of his Maker—with a soul that shall never die,

> " In beauty clad,
> With health in every vein,
> And reason throned upon his brow,
> Stepped forth immortal man."

Yes; for man God called forth the new created world and gave to him and his posterity perpetual " dominion over the fishes of the sea and the fowls of the air and the beasts and the whole earth and every creeping creature that moveth upon the earth."

Thus, to the morning of creation, to the threshold of time, to God himself, can man trace back the title of his nobility.

It was the divine economy that all men should stand forth erect and free, bound as one people in the ties of endless brotherhood, each striving for the general good, the earth bountifully yielding her luscious fruits, all created things subject to their control, and they to God alone.

But man, though clothed with an eternity of bliss, listened to the voice of the tempter, yielded and fell from his high estate,

> " Brought death into the world and all our woe."

The designs of heaven were thwarted—fierce contention and inveterate hate usurped the seat of love—justice affrighted, fled—crime mocked at mercy—might triumphed over right—custom sanctioned wrong, and man became a slave to do the bidding of his master. And thus through thousands of years the innumerable hosts that spread themselves over the world, formed in the same mold with us, of the same majestic presence, with minds to ponder, and hearts to feel, and arms to strike, bowed their heads in abject submission to succeeding tyrants, and made their existence but to live, labor, and die.

Open the pages of history, trace back the course of empire

even to Egypt, Assyria, and Babylon, whence it is lost in the twilight of fable, and what is it but a story of uncounted and never-ending wrongs?

Does history describe in glowing language the pursuits of prosperous people? How governments spoke by the voice of the governed? How justice and equality reigned supreme in council? How virtue was respected—the domestic ties regarded—merit and mind the only steps to distinction, while peace, with its attendant blessings, crowned a happy world?

Ah, no! It tells how nations rose by conquest to renown and sunk by servility to oblivion. How oppression, despotism, and cruelty covered the earth. How generation after generation, century after century, mankind was stripped of every prerogative and robbed of every right, while wars, waged for mad ambition, shook the earth and sent their shrieks along the sky.

History, with minutest skill, describes a man miscalled monarch. The millions are forgotten. It fills chapters in narrating the prowess of the victor. The people are never named save to tell the number of the slain, or captives chained to the chariot wheels to grace the triumph of the conqueror.

Liberty became a homeless wanderer through the world. True, for a time, she flashed her glories over Greece. In after years she dimly shone along the plains of Italy and over the waters of the Adriatic. She sought the Alpine hills of Switzerland, and where'er she rested for a day her presence shed joy and gladness, but never found a fast and fitting home.

Thus oppression spread its iron sway over a prostrate world. Each century served but to rivet the tighter and shackle the stronger the will and might of enslaved man.

His mind, his very soul, was not his own. If he but breathed
the name of country the tyrant called it treason and struck
his head from off his body. To worship his God was to mount
from the funeral pile through the flames of martyrdom to
heaven.

But even then, in the darkest hour, the high court of
eternal justice decreed the liberation of mankind and the
doom of its oppressors.

The curtain of the deep was drawn aside, and beyond the
blue waves that dashed their white spray upon Europe's
shore, far away toward the setting sun, lo! a continent appears! where nature herself assumes a grander air, and speaks
in sublimer tones the wonders of the Deity.

Here, on the unpolluted soil of America, a bright existence
was to dawn upon down-trodden man — here should he
assume the authority delegated to him in Paradise—here
should the big waters of a people's might be let loose, and
in the great flood of freedom perish the last vestige of governmental wrong.

From the sixteenth to the eighteenth century, the religious
strifes, the civil broils, and bloody wars that made Europe
one Golgotha served to scatter along these eastern shores a
brave and hardy people, who, in a common hatred of oppression, forgot the differences of country, race, and religion, to
rejoice in the native liberty of the new-found land.

Such was the people appointed to carry out the great work
of man's political regeneration — such the people whom
heaven decreed should fight the great battle on which was
staked the freedom or slavery of the world. And, to make
the victory grander, they were matched against the mighty
power that claimed jurisdiction over earth and sea — who
boasted her banner played in every breeze — that the sun

never sunk on her possessions — that her arms were invincible, and her name the synonym of victory.

The people of the American colonies accepted the high trust delegated to them. It was not for themselves they fought — it was for their children's children to the remotest posterity; it was for the cause of freedom all over the world.

Everything considered, they were as favorably circumstanced as any people. They groaned under no galling yoke of oppression — no wail of woe sent a shudder through the land — they were not compelled to stand abashed beneath the gaze of a superior, or brook the presence of a master. They were the favorites of the mother country, had their colonial assemblies, and made their local laws. They enjoyed personal security and private property.

But the hour had arrived when a pernicious principle was to be crushed, lest it might enslave their children. They denied the right of a distant Parliament to legislate for them. They refused to compromise an eternal truth. They were willing to spend " millions for defence, but not one cent for tribute." Rather than submit to the Stamp Act, they were ready to bleed. Sooner than yield to the encroachments of a king, they were prepared to die.

In yonder venerated Hall they deliberated and decided. Upon this immortal spot they startled the tyrants of the earth from their long sleep of security by the declaration of a principle never before successfully asserted since the fall of Adam, that liberty and equality were the birthright of all men and linked inseparably to their nature. They declared that these were colonies no longer, but sovereign States, and, with the approving smiles of God, should continue so forever.

How they met the shock of arms history delights to tell;

what they suffered will ever be the theme of speech and story.

Through five long and dreary years, enduring hardships of the severest kind, frequently without the necessaries of life, they bore themselves as freedom's soldiers alone could do. Though many were the acts of cruelty which disgraced the British arms and cried aloud for vengeance, yet they chained their just resentments and no cruel or ignoble act stained the pure record. But one traitor dimmed the glory of their arms. Even when defeat followed defeat and despair seemed to cover their cause, confiding alone in heaven, they clung as brothers to each other until the tyrant's hordes shrunk from our shores to leave the land forever free.

Oh, Americans! my countrymen! how deep and profound is the debt of gratitude we owe the men of '76. How our hearts should swell with emotion at the bare mention of their honored names and our lives be devoted to the preservation of their priceless boon.

Yet even now, when the last of that noble race still lingers in our midst; when the forms of many still live in our recollection; when that Hall stands untouched by time, there are Americans — degenerate sons — cursed with ingratitude; " the marble-hearted fiend," who would desecrate the memories of the dead, destroy the happiness of the living, and wither the hopes of the future by dashing aside as a worthless toy that which was achieved at the price of rivers of blood and mountains of slain.

To have stopped with the Revolution would have been to risk if not to have lost all. Perhaps for a time we might have been spared a foreign yoke, but internal differences and domestic jealousies would have engendered conflicts that might end again in monarchy. The struggle had been severe

— the victory grand; to have risked the prize would have been an insult to heaven, a crime against humanity.

Therefore the American fathers met in council to establish a lasting peace where they had met to wage a glorious war. Even in Independence Hall the representatives of the old thirteen States, headed by Washington, in a spirit of mutual concession and lofty patriotism, dictated the sacred instrument that makes us one people, enabling us to guard with jealous care the rights of the humblest citizen at home and maintain the nation's honor against an embattled world.

Mark its language and contrast it with the documents of kings:

" We, the people of the United States, in order to form a more perfect Union, establish justice, ensure domestic tranquillity, provide for the common defence, promote the general welfare, and secure the blessings of liberty to ourselves and our posterity, do ordain and establish this constitution for the United States of America."

And may that constitution, and every letter and line, be preserved unaltered and untouched, and the blessings of liberty shall endure until the earth shall crumble and the stars be plucked forever from the sky.

Then for the first time a government was formed that derived its just powers from the consent of the governed.

Liberty achieved, independence acknowledged, the constitution adopted, the United States took her place in the Olympian race, to contend with the nations for the prize of pre-eminence.

The titled minions of the earth scoffed aloud at what they conceived to be a chimera of democracy, but soon a look of dread came o'er them as they beheld rising the magnificent reality.

In the short space of time spanned by a single life, as if by " the touch of the enchanter's wand," the people have built a government before which the mightiest realms of the earth pale their splendors as do the stars of night before the refulgent glory of the coming day. Population has in- creased from three to thirty millions. Instead of thirteen, thirty-one stars now shine in the clear blue of this glorious flag. The multitudinous pursuits of enlightened life are cultivated to their highest pitch. The press is mighty and free. Peace and contentment smile alike around the poor man's hearth and the rich man's hall. Education scatters its priceless gift to every home in the land. Religion gathers around its altars the faithful of every creed. Statesmen have arisen " fit to govern all the world and rule it when 'tis wildest." Orators have appeared who have rivalled the great masters of antiquity. The doors of the American Par- thenon are ever open to invite the humble but aspiring youth to enter and fill the loftiest niche. The highest dignity is within the grasp of all; for the lowly boy born and reared in our own sweet valley of Cumberland shall when the spring comes round again be clothed by the people with the first of mortal honors—that of guiding for a time the American republic upon her highway of glory.

The European emigrants leave their native fields for the American forests, and soon become life-long devoted to the country that adopts them as her own. Commerce with its golden chains links our shores with the farthest corners of the earth. The Alleghenies are climbed by the steam-car, or dashed aside to make way for the channel upon which trade floats her inland argosies.

The American advances westward and the wilderness falls, and on its ruins rise splendid cities and cultivated fields. He reaches the broad river, and soon its glassy surface is cleft by a thousand keels. He strikes the quarry and the white marble comes forth to beautify cities and to be chiselled into monuments to commemorate the mighty deeds of the nation and to transmit to posterity the features of the great. He perforates the mountain and drags to the sunlight the inexhaustible treasures of its mines. He searches the stream, and behold! its waters run bright with shining gold. The metallic rod is raised aloft, and the storm is robbed of its terrors; the wires are thrown about the land, and the lightning leaps to do our bidding.

Our statesmen dictate new rules for the peace of nations and freedom of the seas. Our soldiers—may they never fight but in a righteous cause—have planted our banner in triumph upon foreign strands. Our sailors land upon the shores of Japan, and its gates are open the first time for centuries.

The sun of American republicanism looms proudly up in the western sky, and shedding back its rays over the darkened plains of the Old World, beholds the millions rising and preparing to demand a restoration of their natal rights. Europe already quakes to its centre with the throes of a gigantic revolution. It may be stifled for years, perhaps for generations, but it will come as sure as the day follows the night.

The people are thinking. Education is being diffused among the masses. Intolerance is departing; the Irish Catholic is emancipated; and the Protestant worships in his chapel beneath the shadow of the Vatican.

Ireland, Poland, Hungary, and Italy have raised aloft the angry arm of rebellion. It has been stricken to their side by treachery, but the life-blood still warms its veins and feeds it with strength for another and successful blow. France has twice burst into a flame; the flame again is smothered but the fire still burns. In England the Chartists gather a hundred thousand strong on Kennington Common to petition Parliament for universal suffrage and the press thunders at the throne the demand that England's councils and England's arms shall be led by men of mind, not those whose only merit is titled blood.

These, these are the fruits of the seed sown in the soil beneath our feet. These are the achievements wrought by the people—they alone who really rule by " divine right," and are the " Lord's anointed."

Our past is but a life—a day in history. Our future—when all over this broad continent our institutions shall have peacefully extended—each year new States rising and rushing to join the happy throng—sister republics seeking the shelter of our flag—a hundred millions of freemen speaking the same language and obeying the same laws! O! to sketch the future of our beloved country would require the pen of an angel dipped in ethereal fire!

Should not a contemplation of these things make our hearts leap beyond the barriers of party, to link in love all who claim America as their home and acknowledge allegiance to the constitution?

But how intense our delight, how unbounded our joy, who can this day proudly boast that we are a part and portion of the democracy of America, the instruments with which heaven has worked these blessed changes in the past and to whom alone is entrusted our country's mission in the future.

Let our aim be to smooth down the asperities of party feeling—to frown upon the turbulent spirits who seek to widen the political differences of the people. Let our hearts expand with an enlarged patriotism. Let us respect the opinions of others and seek to win them to our side by the dear memories which cluster around this holy spot.

As each grave political question presents itself for our consideration let us weigh it in the scales with democracy and the constitution; if it balance with these let our every effort be devoted to its triumph; if not, let us wage honorable war against it until we have accomplished its destruction. Let the " Farewell Address " be reverenced by us and our children be taught to obey its sacred injunctions. Let us not be tempted to our fall by the demon of discord who seeks, Lucifer-like, to have us driven from this political paradise—or if you do

> " Let me prophesy,
> The blood of Americans shall manure the ground,
> And future ages groan for this foul act;
> Peace shall go sleep with Turks and infidels,
> And in this seat of peace, tumultuous wars
> Shall kin with kin, and kind with kind confound;
> Disorder, horror, fear and mutiny,
> Shall here inhabit, and this land be call'd
> The field of Golgotha, and dead men's sculls;
> O! if you rear this house against this house,
> It will the wofullest division prove
> That ever fell upon this cursed earth;
> Prevent, resist it, let it not be so,
> Lest child, child's children cry against you—woe! "

But confiding in the principles of democracy, cherishing as holy the constitution of our common country—like to the Pontic Sea—no—rather let me say like our own Mississippi, whose waters indissolubly link the North and the South together—the American Union, unchecked by a returning flood, shall flow forever on through the countless ages of the future until it, with all, is lost in the great gulf of eternity.

ADDRESS ON THE PERILS OF THE REPUBLIC

AMID all these events and scenes which foretell our swift and sure destruction and which, as if an angel spoke, should recall us to our allegiance to the republic, the people, like a sleeping drunkard, will not awake and avert the impending doom.

The politicians, the evil spirits of the nation, with whom fair is foul and foul is fair,—these close contrivers of all harms, these juggling fiends who trade and traffic in affairs of death, who met the people in the days of success and with prophetic speeches that did sound so fair solicited them to the sacrilegious murder of their country,—are now with wild glee dancing around the boiling cauldron of partisan hate, pouring in every envenomed lie and poisoned argument to make the hell-broth boil and bubble, telling the spell-bound people they bear a charmed life, can never vanquished be, urging them to still further step in blood,

> " To spurn fate, scorn death, and bear
> Hopes 'bove wisdom, grace, and fear; "

despairing of the charm only when brought to a dismal and fatal end, their liberties and rights are struck down and forever destroyed by the swords they thought could only fall on vulnerable crests.

We of the North, with interests identical, knowing that in this dread crisis whatever our fate, all must share it alike, instead of standing united, firm as a mountain in support of our government, are divided against ourselves; our differences exhibiting themselves fiercely and distinctly in social clubs, family circles, public charities, and religious denominations. Part of our people, with hearts devoted to the precious cause, yet stand paralyzed like passengers on a ship struggling amid a stormy sea, forgetting that in this hurricane we are all of the crew and belong to the ship itself. Tens of thousands there are who care not whether the nation is saved or lost. Thousands on thousands in private conversations openly oppose their country and declare their sympathies are with the traitors. Some admit the army needs soldiers, but, even to violence and murder, will oppose conscription! They say the war is for the black man, yet will not agree to the black man fighting! Carry on the war, say they, but inflict on the rebels as little harm as possible! Shoot them, but don't exasperate them! Kill them in battle, but don't confiscate their property! it is true they are resolved to destroy the nation, but give them their constitutional rights!

With others, slur the flag with impunity, but, on peril of your life, utter no free speech against a favorite general! These leave the house of God when prayers are said for the government; curse the President as a tyrant who should die, and in our very presence praise the arch-traitor Davis!

With them to defend slavery is patriotism! to advocate freedom is treason! They say a secessionist must be conciliated, an abolitionist hung! South Carolina should be coaxed back into the Union, Massachusetts must be "left out in the cold !" They are against war, but will organize to assassinate soldiers sent to arrest deserters! They prate of peace and call the foe, reeking with the hot blood of our slaughtered patriots, their brothers; yet are eager to clutch their weapons and kill their own kinsmen who dare to be true when they are false!

Treason, the bloodiest and blackest of crimes, has from the

beginning been unchecked, and aids the enemy in the very capital of the nation! All the roads leading to the armies, our cities and towns, swarm with conspirators ready to seize on our mishaps to raise the banner of revolt. Yet no death-warrant has been signed. When, at last, in loyal Kentucky, a traitor was arrested, tried, found guilty, and sentenced to die, the President of the United States pardoned the culprit.

Every lover of the Union, whatever may be his partisan proclivities, remembering that Douglas is dead and the other two candidates are arrant traitors, must rejoice that Mr. Lincoln was elected to the presidency. No fair man can question his personal integrity and patriotic motives, and it is proper to bear in mind that he is contending with trials and difficulties the like of which never before fell to the lot of a chief magistrate or ruler. Yet had the President been entirely incompetent to discharge his high responsibilities the people could have no right to complain. They did not choose to meddle in the selection of a President.

For the last quarter of a century the people have exercised no authority in the nominations of the candidates for the presidency. The first officer of the republic—the executive of the nation—has been chosen by a national convention, a body not recognized by the constitution, and far removed from the people—" a scheme," said a great statesman, " perfectly calculated to annihilate the control of the people over the presidential election and vest it in those who make politics a trade and who live or expect to live on the government."

A system so base that an experienced and distinguished statesman of the Democratic party declared it to be an " Evil that must be corrected, or the elective franchise abandoned."

Was the selection of Mr. Lincoln advocated for the reason that he was a tried statesman, able to steer the nation through the coming storm? No such argument was urged. The two principal appeals were that he was the nominee of his party and had been a " rail-splitter! "

The partisan organizations are now bending every energy to grasp the presidency in 1864.

This is the mainspring of all their actions; it is to achieve this the leaders are goading the people to madness against each other. A rebellion is ripening in the North. State authorities may at any moment clash with the national sovereignty. Probably each party, to deceive the people, will dazzle their eyes with the glare of military glory, and one failing to elect its favorite may seize on the excitement and attempt to overturn the government.

Let any thoughtful American who loves his race survey the present and tell his reasonable fears for the future. Either one of four fatal consequences seems likely to be near at hand.

If the armies of the foe once gain a firm foothold in the North they will lay waste our fertile fields, sack our cities, seize the capital, and dictate terms of peace that will make us, freemen, slaves.

If the Southern Confederacy be acknowledged, then we surrender to an implacable foe three fourths of the national domain, the greater part of our ocean boundaries, the mouths of most of our large rivers, all the gulf shore, forts necessary to the protection of our commerce, public property, victorious battle-fields, graves of the immortal dead, the capital, the archives of the nation, the statues of our ancestors, the untold treasures, the prestige and power of the republic, our rank among the nations, and purchase a short-lived peace, to be fol-

lowed by a protracted war, only ending in a military despotism or a part or all the North seeking the shelter of a throne.

If the war be prolonged on Southern soil, partisan malignity, growing in fury as approaches the presidential election,
may burst into internecine war and all the horrors of the
French Revolution make red with blood the streets of Northern cities.

Even if we conquer the South, as conquer we must, unless
chastened by visible misfortunes in the North, our triumph
breeding unbounded conceit, we will plunge the deeper in the
vortex of voluptuous prosperity, our country forgotten by the
people, its honors and dignities the sport and plunder of every
knave and fool that can court or bribe the mob, the national
debt repudiated, justice purchased in her temples as laws now
are in the legislature, the life and property of no man safe,
the last relics of public virtue destroyed, anarchy will reign
amid universal ruin.

Thus night thickens around the republic, and in all the sky
there is not a star.

I am not unconscious of the thousand blessings we yet
enjoy, nor indifferent to the succession of splendid victories
this month has given to the national cause. But who can forget—can it ever be forgotten—that since these victories were
announced an organized mob, instigated by partisan leaders,
was for three days master of the commercial metropolis of the
Union, and did deeds of fiend-like cruelty unmatched in the
annals of crime? that this same mob was harangued, amid
great cheering, by the governor of the State and two judicial
dignitaries, one of whom, in a public speech two months before, cried out " be not afraid," and counselled resistance to
the government to the death? and that the board of aldermen,
without one dissenting vote, appropriated out of the public

funds $2,500,000 to deprive our army of reinforcements and pander to ruffians, each one of whom should feel the halter?

I have uttered sentiments that clash with the opinions and prejudices of all classes of my countrymen, but have not spoken to wound the sensibilities of any one. I know it is easy to state the wrong and hard to find the remedy, but from my soul I believe the only way this nation can be saved, except by the hand of God, which we have no right to expect, is to know at once the depths of the disease that radical remedies may be applied.

Think not I counsel that we sit and despairingly contemplate our downfallen fortunes until we float to either of the sad alternatives; that we allow the glories of the republic to wither in our keeping; that we, like cravens, should seek to survive our country. God of our fathers forbid.

As a last resort let the true men come forth from their seclusion and, in the name of liberty and our country, appeal to the majesty of the people. They have deceived themselves and been deceived. Incompetent officials, a venal press, aspirants for office, and partisan leaders have flattered their follies, praised their weaknesses, applauded their crimes, and made them believe even defeats in the field were strategic triumphs.

Come forth, virtuous citizens, from the workshop and the factory, from the store, the study, and the forum, from the closet, the college, and the altar, and by the historic memories of the revolution, by the victories won in foreign wars, by the blood of our countrymen—our dear brothers—shed in this sublime struggle for the life of the nation, by the boundless prosperity that three generations enjoyed, by the love we bear our children, by our hereditary hatred of royalty and despotism, by our sympathies with oppressed humanity, by our hopes for the triumph of right, justice, and liberty all over the world, let us call on the people to rise, as their fathers did, and dedicate life, fortune, and honor to the restoration of the republic. Let each citizen conquer his prejudices. Let us shiver to atoms the vile organizations of the day; let us cease to be New Yorkers or Pennsylvanians, Republicans or Democrats, and remember only we are Americans; by enactments destroy the whole breed of those who barter and sell their country's offices for gold to undeservers, and let competent and honest officials, like employees in private life, be retained during good behavior—punish public defaulters with the heaviest penalties—purify the ballot-box, and make sacred the privilege of suffrage—let elections be rare except for representatives—render the judiciary independent of popular clamor and fearless and inexorable in its administration, decrees, and sentences—reform your constitutions in every particular where experience has proved the necessity— teach in schools and colleges the science of government— give genius and integrity once again a chance in public life —let him who faithfully serves his country in the prime of manhood enjoy its rewards in his old age—inspire all with a love of the Union and fixed resolve to crush with mighty blows, like those of Gettysburg and Vicksburg, this accursed rebellion—let every leading traitor die a traitor's death—be not elated by victory or dejected by defeat—keep buoyant and brave—bury all dissensions in the graves of our dead heroes—cheer our gallant brothers in the field with the heartiest sympathies, arriving at the just conception of the duties of American citizenship and of what should be the full measure of our country's future—pray God we may yet see floating over a once more united people our dear old flag, the terror of tyrants, the hope of the oppressed, and emblem of the free.

At this appalling crisis, when the life of the republic, the destinies of a hundred millions immediate and remote are staked on the actions of the hour, you, gentlemen of the Senate, "the latest seed of time," appear upon the scene. Gifted with education, unspotted in morals, untrammelled with the chains of party and fired with patriotism, as are all fresh hearts, I call on you to dedicate your ambition, your future, and your fame to rescue the republic. Be firm when tempted, fearless in danger, ready like the Roman to leap into the gulf to save your country. If needs be, sacrifice ease, fortune, home, love, and life.

HAWLEY

JOSEPH ROSWELL HAWLEY, a noted American congressman and journalist, was born at Stewartsville, North Carolina, October 31, 1826, and
educated at Hamilton College, New York. After studying law he began
practice at Hartford, Connecticut, in 1850. Early in his career he entered
actively into politics, and, being strongly opposed to slavery and slavery
extension, he was among the founders of the Republican party in Connecticut. Retiring from the law in 1857 he engaged in journalism, becoming the editor of the Hartford "Evening Press." He was the first man in
Connecticut to enroll his name in the volunteer service at the opening of
the civil war, and he remained in the federal army throughout the war
period, being commissioned brigadier-general in 1864 and brevetted major-
general in 1865. In 1866 he was elected governor of Connecticut and served
as such one term, after which he began editing the "Hartford Courant,"
with which the "Press" had been consolidated. He entered the national
House of Representatives in 1872 and sat there three terms, though not
consecutively, and since 1881 has been a member of the United States Senate. He was president of the Centennial Commission through the entire
period of its existence, 1875-76.

ON THE FLAG AND THE EAGLE

FROM SPEECH ON THE CENTENNIAL CELEBRATION DELIVERED IN
THE HOUSE OF REPRESENTATIVES, MAY 7, 1874

SOME gentlemen tell us that we may have a national
celebration but not in connection with an international exhibition; that there is some incongruity
between the two; and as the celebration is national, the exhibition must be only and strictly national. I would like to
be heard a few moments on that point.

I believe in the Fourth of July in the popular acceptation
of that term. I believe in the Fourth of July all over, from
the crown of my head to the sole of my feet. As a boy and
young man I fired my guns and had my good time. I like
to see the boys do the same now. You may belong to a city
council, and may pass volumes of ordinances against guns

and fire-crackers; you may send platoons of policemen to
arrest the boys who violate your ordinances, but you still
have within you a secret sympathy with the young rascals
and you like to be awakened on the morning of the Fourth
by great bells and guns, even if you do swear a little about it
I believe in the Fourth of July; I believe in " sentiment; "
I believe in the Flag; and I honor the memory of Daniel
Webster when I remember how he pointed up through yonder rotunda at the " gorgeous ensign of the Republic," and
trampled with magnificent scorn upon the poor, puny, con
temptible spirit that dared to ask " How much is all this
worth ? "

God bless Daniel Webster for that one paragraph.

I was grieved, not angry — grieved in my very soul —
when I heard men on this floor, of wealth and culture and
honor and ability, sneering at what they called "sentiment,"
and laughing at " tears," and when I heard a Massachusetts
man from the very hills of Berkshire ridiculing the " eagle "
and all that " cheap clap-trap." God grant that the day may
be far distant when what you call " Fourth of July talk "
shall be out of fashion. Let it always be in fashion. Our
millions of " Boys in Blue " talked it from the cradle; and
while perhaps infidels to free government sneered at them,
and ridiculed the " cross-roads talk about the Fourth of
July " and " the eagle," those boys believed in it; five hundred thousand graves bear witness to their belief. God help
the poor, narrow soul whose eyes never moisten at the sight
of the Flag.

Shall this exhibition be national alone, and not international also? First, we are thoroughly committed to the
international idea by the act itself, by the proclamation of
the President, by the circular of the secretary of state com-

nunicating it to the diplomatic representatives, by his cir-
ular to our ministers abroad, and by the acceptances of
nany nations. Secondly, it is interwoven with the whole
cheme — the classification, the policy, and the pledges.

We are committed to it by personal presentation to foreign
xhibitors, commissioners, jurors on the international jury,
nd others at the Vienna exposition; by the publication of
his proclamation and of this scheme in three foreign lan-
uages in the pages of the Vienna catalogue. The Vienna
eople asked us to do it. They offered us pages for advertis-
ng our international exhibition. We observed the words of
our act, and thus advertised all over Europe. We are com-
nitted to the international idea by the acceptance of dona-
ions from foreign commissions. Goods that were offered to
s at Vienna by commissioners from foreign states are
lready on the way or in store. We told them we would take
he articles gladly. From various foreign citizens we have
ccepted such contributions. Why, sir, the Marquis of Bute,
he descendant of the Bute who was in the famous Lord
North ministry that urged on George III to the long seven
ears' war, proposes to furnish largely a room in that exhi-
ition displaying the wonderful resources of his estate in
Wales. Being instructed to conduct an international exhi-
ition we have felt at liberty to accept these offers.

International equity requires that our exhibition should
ave this character. We have as a nation taken part in three
reat exhibitions, while our citizens have participated in
thers. . . .

International exhibitions advance the common sciences,
he common arts, the common progress of modern civiliza-
ion. Common courtesy and good feeling require reciproca-
on. Reciprocation of effort for the advancement of civili-

zation and human welfare is the graceful adjunct of the national festival, especially as we have drawn benefit from other exhibitions, and are, as a people, made up of all peoples. Their usefulness is in geometrical proportion to their universality. A well-balanced exhibition of the industries of the world commands the attention of the world. It makes exhibitors willing to come and spend money to extend the field of their enterprises. It draws more exhibitors and more visitors. Many important industries — mark this, if you please — many important industries cannot be shown independently of foreign products, the basis of their manufacture. You cannot have a purely national exhibition of really great value. The men who have studied this subject of exhibitions will tell you so. To exhibit industries without bringing in materials produced abroad is impossible. For example, tin-ware, dye-woods, precious stones, coffee, tea, foreign woods, foreign hides, furs, irons, steels, and partly manufactured articles of many kinds.

Are you going to make a " know-nothing " exhibition of it, that you refuse to extend invitations to other peoples — we all the time professing above all other peoples to a generous and cosmopolitan spirit, willing to accept and embrace all peoples ? Do you wish to make a little " know-nothing " exhibition of the affair ?

An abandonment of the international feature would operate to exclude very large classes of our own people — all who import and deal in articles of foreign production; would exclude all pictures, statues, and works of art, whenever or however they may have come into possession of Americans — all beautiful and useful machinery, furniture, woven goods, etc.; a multitude of articles just such as we wish to learn to produce.

You say that it is a Fourth of July celebration. While I tell you I believe in cannon and trumpets, thunder and glory, orations, bonfires, and bell-ringing, still I wish something more, further and higher — an exhibition which will mark our progress for one hundred years and exhibit the modern spirit of advancement and civilization characterizing the nineteenth century. Are not gentlemen aware that this exhibition is a bazaar at which for six months all the nations will assemble to shake hands as brethren and as friends? You say they will not feel at home here. I tell you, men of Massachusetts, and Ohio, and Maine, who tell us to-day the people of other nations would not be welcomed here, that strangers would not feel at home here during this exhibition, you may learn a lesson from that " old tyrant," as boys were taught to style him, George III. He had the manhood and the kingly courtesy, despot as he was, to rise before his Parliament and acknowledge our independence and say what I will read :

" I lost no time in giving the necessary orders to prohibit the further prosecution of offensive war upon the continent of North America. Adopting, as my inclination will always lead me to do, with decision and effect whatever I collect to be the sense of my Parliament and my people, I have pointed all my views and measures in Europe, as in North America, to an entire and cordial reconciliation with the colonies. Finding it indispensable to the attainment of the object, I did not hesitate to go to the full length of the powers vested in me, and offer to declare them "—[here he paused, and was in evident agitation; either embarrassed in reading his speech by the darkness of the room or affected by a very natural emotion. In a moment he resumed]—" and offer to declare them free and independent States. In thus admitting their separation from the crown of these kingdoms I have sacrificed every consideration of my own to the wishes and opinions of my people. I make it my humble and ardent prayer to Almighty God that Great Britain may not feel the evils which might result from so great a dismemberment of the empire, and that America may be free from the calamities which have formerly proved in the mother country how ..ential monarchy is to the enjoyment of constitutional liberty. Religion, language, interests, and affections may, and I hope will, yet prove a bond of permanent union between the two countries."

And whenever the English flag and American flag meet in foreign waters, there the Englishman salutes the Stars and Stripes on the Fourth of July. And when the Queen's birthday comes around, the American salutes the Cross of Saint George. They exchange the salutes of guns and dipping of colors, as becomes gentlemen among the nations of the earth. And while I would fight John Bull to-morrow, and so would you, John Bull and we are friends to-day; we are blood relations, welcome here and welcome there.

And in the great struggle which makes the glory of the nineteenth century, for pre-eminence in the application of science, to lift up the weak and lowly and lighten the sorrows of labor, we are generous rivals, standing on a common platform. We welcome here the Englishman, the German, the Frenchman — all of them! While the kings of those European monarchies may not love the Declaration of Independence their people love it, and we want to invite their people here. We want their people to know the character and boundless magnitude of our resources, that they may come here in still greater numbers. Human ingenuity cannot devise a fairer way — to use the commercial expression — to advertise the American continent than by this exhibition. . . .

I have a right to be proud of American industry, of American art and science. In nine tenths of the fields embraced in these exhibitions we may boldly challenge the competition of the world. I say that deliberately, and thereon put my all at stake. You will have no reason to be ashamed of this exhibition. True, we cannot produce a Titian, or a Raphael, or a Rubens, or a Praxiteles; but it took thousands of years to produce them, and we have done very well in one hundred.

But that is not all. We have had a people to make in a hundred years; and, the Lord be praised, we have made a people. Bitterly as we fought among ourselves, I think we have got to be one nation now and shall remain so. We have done a great work in one hundred years. Why should we not let the world see what it is? Why should not we stop to examine it ourselves? You do not know your country. You do not know what an exhibition we can make. Let us put in one hall the progress of education and its present condition; in another the progress of religious denominations — and several of them are already making their arrangements. In another, the varied and innumerable soils and their capacity; elsewhere the treasures of the mine. Why, the gentleman from Alabama [Mr. White] told you last night that you could ride in his State, which we think of as a "cotton State," one hundred miles over the very best iron ore, the bed fifteen feet deep and forty wide, and with the mountains full of it besides; and engineers say that there is coal enough in that State to supply the world for two thousand years. How many of you knew the resources of Alabama? We can beat Great Britain in coal and iron in that one State. We can produce iron there at fourteen dollars per ton, the gentleman says; and others have told me the same. And my friend before me from Chattanooga [Mr. Crutchfield] can give a similar account of the region around him.

Look at your wheatfields. We can furnish bread to the whole world and not miss it. Look at the wheat growth on the Pacific coast. Ten years ago we did not know that wheat could be produced there, and now California is feeding nations. There are fields ready for wheat over which you cannot ride in a week; where not only no plow has ever passed, but where the white man's foot has hardly yet trod, in the boundless Saskatchewan Valley, yet to be brought under cultivation.

You have not tickled the surface of the great Mississippi Valley. You have gold and silver enough to keep your miners at work for centuries; your coal, your iron; your soil, black and rich, fifteen feet deep, the deposit of centuries. Spread this information on maps, charts, and tabulated statements, on the walls of your exposition building. You wish the world to know it.

There are men now making ready specimens of the root, the bark, the wood, the leaf, flower, and fruit of every tree from Maine to California — a collection such as no other country in the world can make. There will be an exhibition of the fishes to be gathered from Maine to Galveston, on the Pacific coast, and in our inland seas, such as will be of interest to all the naturalists of the world. Then there are our firearms, in which we beat the world; our clocks which we export everywhere; our edge tools, in which we now beat Sheffield in her own markets, because the Yankee brain works through the machine that makes the tool, and we are quicker in that than John Bull. We have been building locomotives and passenger cars for Europe. John Bull did not know how to go comfortably from London to Edinburgh till we sent him the other day some trains of Pullman cars. Then there are the cold fields of Maine, where they raise two hundred bushels of potatoes to the acre; and all the various soils and climates between that State and the sunny fields of San Diego, in

California, rich in oranges, limes, lemons, almonds, all fruits of all climates, the sugar cane of Louisiana, the matchless cotton of the Sea Islands, the grape culture, destined to an infinite development — everywhere productive capability immeasurable.

Let us devote a few weeks to arranging all these things in rooms and cases, and then ask the world to come and see them. In both aspects, that of fraternity and that of profit also, I believe this enterprise is legitimate and lawful. We will have scientific men and commissioners, who will come here and make their reports, published at home, and read and talked over by their people. The press of the world will sketch in words and pictures the wonders and uses we shall have, and the year after your immigration will be increased by thousands upon thousands. Your trade will be increased. New ships and flags will come to sell and buy.

How grand the opportunity to promote fraternity among the nations, whose representatives will there meet in the friendly competitions of a Christian civilization!

One consideration more that lies near my heart. In that summer of 1876 we of these States will meet under one flag and one name, avowing one purpose and one destiny, looking back far beyond the fierce and bloody quarrels that have tortured our hearts and reddened our fields. Pass our amnesty bills, secure the civil rights of all, clear the ground, and shake hands. I look around and see men who would have shot each other at sight a few years ago. I have learned something in this hall, gained somewhat, I hope, of a kindlier feeling, just through these daily friendly greetings. We need such opportunity for all, as you, Mississippi [looking at Mr. Lamar] have said, that we may " know one another better, and love one another better."

ON THE PRESS

SPEECH AT THE BANQUET OF THE NEW ENGLAND SOCIETY, DECEMBER 22, 1875

GENTLEMEN,—Our distinguished president paid the very highest compliment to the press to-night; for, while he has given at least a fortnight's notice to every other gentleman, he only told me to-night that I had to respond to the toast of "The Press." But as I have attended a good many dinners of the New England Society, and never knew "The Press" to be called upon before midnight, I felt entirely safe.

Now, sir, I have spent an evening — some six hours — here, enjoying all the festivities and hospitalities of this occasion to the utmost, and at last I am called upon, at an hour when we are all full of jollity and mirth, to respond to a toast that in reality calls upon me for my most serious effort.

I assure you that, had I known that I was to speak upon this subject to-night, I would, contrary to my usual custom, have been deliberately prepared; for I, in reality, have a great deal to say upon that matter; and permit me to add that I have a somewhat peculiar qualification, for I have been a man within the press, "a chiel amang ye takin' notes, an' prentin' them;" and I have been again a man altogether outside of the press, not writing for months to his own people, and subject to receive all the jibes and criticisms and attacks of the press. "I know how it is myself."

The "Press of the Republic" is a text worthy of the noblest oration. It has a great, a high, and a holy duty. It is at once the leader and educator, and, on the other hand, the representative of the people. I can only touch on some points that I have in my mind, upon this occasion. It seems to me that we are passing through a period of peculiar importance regarding the value and influence of the press of the American Republic. There are times when I join with them in the most indignant denunciation, in the warmest appeal. There are times when I feel the cutting, cruel, stinging injustice of the American press.

It is the duty of an editor, sitting, as he does, as a judge — and I mean all that the word implies — upon all that goes on about him in public life — it is his duty to hear both sides, and all sides, as deliberately and calmly as he may, and to pronounce a judgment that, so far as he knows, may be the judgment of posterity.

It is true that he has two duties. We know that it is his duty to condemn the bad. When it be made perfectly clear that the bad man is really a bad man, a corrupter of youth, make him drink the hemlock, expel him, punish him, crush him.

But there is another duty imposed upon the American press, quite as great. If there be a man who loves the Republic, who would work for it, who would talk for it, who would fight for it, who would die for it — there are millions of them, thank God! — it is the duty of the American press to uphold him, and to praise him when the time comes, in the proper place, on the proper occasion.

The press is to deal not alone in censure of the bad, but in praise of the good. I like the phrase, "The independent press." I am an editor myself. I love my calling. I think it is growing to be one of the great professions of the day. I claim, as an editor (and that is my chief pursuit in life), to be a gentleman also. If I see or know anything to be wrong in the land, high or low, I will say so. If it be in my own party, I will take special pains to say so; for I suppose it to be true of both parties that we have a very high, a very glorious, a very beautiful, a very lovable idea of the future American Republic. So I will condemn, I say, whatever may be wrong. I hold myself to be an independent journalist.

But, my friends, I hope you will excuse the phrase — I am going to follow it by another — at the same time I do freely avow that I am a partisan; for I never knew anything good, from Moses down to John Brown, that was not carried through by partisanship. If you believe in anything, say so; work for it, fight for it.

There are always two sides in the world. The good fight is always going on. The bad men are always working; the devil is always busy. And again, on the other side you have your high idea of whatever is beautiful and good and true in the world; and God is always working also. The man who stands between them — who says, "This is somewhat good, and that is somewhat good; I stand between them"— permit me to say, is a man for whom I have very little respect.

Some men say there is a God; some men say there is no God. Some of the independents say that the truth lies between them. I cannot find it between them. Every man has a God. If you believe in your God, he may be another God from mine; but if you are a man, I want you to fight for him, and I may have to fight against you, but do you fight for the God that you believe in.

I do sincerely think (and I wish that this was a congregation of my fellow editors of the whole land, for my heart is in reality full of this thing) — I do sincerely think that there is something of a danger that our eloquent, ready, powerful, versatile, indefatigable, vigorous, omnipresent, omniscient men of the press may drive out of public life — and they will ridicule that phrase — may drive out of public life, not all, but a very considerable class of sensitive, high-minded, honorable, ambitious gentlemen.

Now, I do not say anything about the future for myself. I have got a "free lance," I have got a newspaper, and I can fight with the rest of them; but I will give you a bit of my experience in public life. I tell you, my friends of the New England Society, that one of the sorest things that a man in public life has to bear is the reckless, unreasonable censure of members of the press whom individually he respects.

That large-hearted man, whom personally I love, with whom I could shake hands, with whom I did shake hands, with whom I sat at the social board time and again, grossly misinterprets my public actions; intimates all manner of dishonorable things, which I would fight at two paces rather than be guilty of; and it would be useless for me to write a public letter to explain or contradict.

Now, I am only one of hundreds. I can stand still and wait the result, in the confidence that, if not all, yet some men believe me to be honorable and true; if they do not, God and I know it, and would "fight it out on that line."

Gentlemen, it is rather my habit to talk in earnest. Next to the evil of having all public men in this land corrupt; next to the evil of having all our governmental affairs in the hands of men venal and weak and narrow, debauching public life and carrying it down to destruction, is the calamity of having all the young men believe it is so, whether it be so or not.

Teach all the boys to believe that every man who goes into public life has his price; teach all the boys to believe that there is no man who enters public life anywhere that does not look out for his own, and is not always scheming to do something for himself or his friends, and seeking to prolong his power; teach every young man who has a desire to go into political life to think — because you have told him so — that the way to succeed is to follow such arts, and by that kind of talk you may ruin your country.

Now, gentlemen, as I have said, this is a matter for an evening oration. I have barely touched some of the points. I have said the press has a twofold duty and fortune: it is the leader, the educator, the director of the people. It is, at the same time, the reflector of the people. I could spend an hour upon the theme. . . .

I cannot cease, however, without thanking the president of the St. Patrick's Society, the only gentleman who has mentioned the word "centennial." When I was leaving Philadelphia, my wife warned me not to use that word, knowing to what it might lead me; and so I shall simply ask you all to come to Philadelphia next year, and join in the great national exhibition, where you will have an opportunity of seeing the progress which this nation has made under the ideas of liberty, government, industry, and thrift which were instilled by the Pilgrim Fathers.

SAGASTA

PRAXETES MATEO SAGASTA was born July 21, 1827, at Torrecilla de Cameros. He studied physics and mathematics, and in 1843 entered the school of engineering at Madrid. After he had practised engineering in the provinces he was elected in 1854 to the Constituent Córtes by the provinces of Zamora. After taking part in the Madrid insurrection of July, 1856, he had to flee to France. He was amnestied and became professor in the school of engineering. As a member of the Córtes he belonged to the progressive minority and edited their organ, " La Imperia." After the unsuccessful insurrection of July 22, 1866, he again fled to France, but at the beginning of the revolution of 1868 he returned to Spain and became minister of the interior in the provisional government. He was a zealous supporter of General Prim and a decided opponent of Zorilla. On October 3, 1871, he was elected president of the Córtes, in December he became minister of the interior, and on February 18, 1872, was entrusted with the formation of the cabinet. Under Serrano, in January, 1874, he became minister of the exterior, in May of the interior, and in August president of the ministry, resigning in December in consequence of the enthronement of Alphonso XII. He was later elected to the Córtes and joined the Liberals. Thenceforward he was head of the Constitutional party opposed to the Conservative party led by Cánovas, whom he succeeded as minister-president when his party came into power. Just after the death of Alphonso XII, November 25, 1885, he again succeeded Cánovas as prime minister. In December, 1885, he sought to reconcile all parties by a general amnesty and to restore tranquillity by means of vigorous military regulations. He was successful in resisting the republican element after the introduction of universal suffrage. His ministry was condemned in consequence of the military conspiracies in Madrid in 1886, but he organized a new cabinet which was pledged to various important reforms. In 1887 he put down a minor conspiracy among the Republicans and in 1890 he introduced the universal suffrage to a certain extent in order to meet the rivalry of Cánovas. In the same year he had to deal with the insubordination of certain generals and in consequence retired from the primacy. He again came into power in December, 1892, and in consequence of similar disturbances retired in March, 1895. After the death of Cánovas his party was entrusted with power and had to face the serious situation presented by the Cuban insurrection and the consequent war with the United States.

(8969)

IN DEFENCE OF THE UNITY OF ITALY

DELIVERED IN THE SESSION OF THE CORTES ON MARCH 6, 1861

WHAT are, in effect, the treaties of 1815? The treaties of 1815 are no more than the superb pretension of those who believed themselves omnipotent, seeking to establish the equilibrium of Europe like a mere piece of mechanism and to organize Europe as they would install a machine whose wheels revolved at the impulse of a motor; they are nothing more than the covenant of the nations of the north to destroy the nations of the south; they are nothing more than the pact of absolutism against liberty; the understanding among various races to put an end to our Latin race; they are nothing more than an act of vengeance against a powerful enemy that years before had humiliated them; they are, finally, nothing more than a parade of power and insolence that dismembered Italy and humiliated Spain. And Spain, nation of the south; and Spain, nation of Latin race, has to support treaties that do not exist; that could not be kept alive by the very nations interested; that were broken with the separation of Belgium and Holland, and which, at last, disappeared with the smoke of powder at Magenta and Solferino! Spain defending those treaties that offended her dignity!

And what signified those treaties in relation to the law? What difference is there between the geography that Napoleon I in the midst of great battles, in the midst of great combats, traced with the point of his sword and the geography which, in complete silence and in all security and without any risk whatever, was traced by those powers with the point of the pencil or the pen? What right had the authors of those treaties to dispose of and parcel out according to their whim peoples, nationalities and citizens as if they were flocks of sheep? With what satisfaction were they complying, to what vow were they responding, to what rule were they conforming?

If the signatories of the treaty of 1815, instead of contenting themselves with the subjection of Spain, with her humiliation, had dismembered her as they did Italy, would Spain have rested content therewith? No, a thousand times no! She would have suffered it as a burden until she had acquired the strength to hurl it back upon those that unjustly laid it upon her.

But the government of the Liberal Union, for which, as it would appear, there is no right above the right of kings, for which, as it would appear, there are families chosen by Providence that they may reign forever; for which there is no other sovereignty and no other origin of power than that of divine right; the government of the Liberal Union believed that Spain should remain very well satisfied with certain treaties because they favored the interests of certain families; believed that Spain should resign herself to the humiliation that came from those treaties solely because in their redistribution of territory a portion of that territory concerned the Bourbon family. The government of the Liberal Union believed that Spain would behold with pleasure the reduction of her interests and the lowering of her dignity in consequence of the growth of a certain family's interests, forgetting that the dignity of Spain is very much above a name, a family, however important and traditional it may be.

But not even this personal politics, not even this disastrous policy, has been conducted with the dignity and decorum that belongs to the government of a state.

It is necessary for me to reproduce part of one of the notes that I have already read. I will repeat what the government said lest the honorable deputies may have forgotten it. In the first despatch from the minister of state to our representative at Turin it said the following among other things: "If, contrary to our expectations, the revolt of Sicily should triumph and it should be decided to concede to the King of Sardinia or to any of the princes of the family, the sovereignty of said island, it will be the duty of your Excellency to manifest verbally to the honorable Count Cavour that her Majesty's government would be obliged to sustain, with suitable firmness, the rights that appertain to her Majesty the Queen," etc.

This is what the government said in its first note when it learned of the invasion of Sicily by Garibaldi. Very well! Not only has that occurred which the government did not even venture to fear, not only has Victor Emmanuel been offered the sovereignty of one of the Sicilies, but the insurrection has extended to the two Sicilies and he has been offered the sovereignty of both; and at last the crown has even been torn from the brow of Francisco II and placed upon Victor Emmanuel's. And what did the government of Spain do after the consequences exceeded its extraordinary previsions, after having sent that strong note, for it was a strong note to send to a friendly government when there was no reason to expect that Piedmont had any influence whatever in the invasion of Sicily? What did the government do after all this? The following: In another note, dated October 24, the minister of state said to our representative at Turin: "After the protest presented by your Excellency, her Majesty's government does not judge convenient your presence at that court. Thus your Excellency may signify the same in appropriate terms to the minister of foreign affairs, retiring from Turin when you have accredited the secretary of legation as *chargé d'affaires.*

That is to say, in the second note, in the last note, after the consequences had gone much beyond the expectations of the government, it contented itself with saying: "Come back to Madrid; but before you leave put the secretary in charge that your absence from the embassy may not be noted and come exactly as you have come at other times to take part in the debates of the Córtes."

Does this last note respond to that which the government promised in the first? Is there harmony between the strength of the first and the tolerance and suavity of the second? One of the two: either the government exceeded itself in the first and failed in the second, or it promised much and performed little. If in the first event the government was short-sighted, in the second it was weak; the lack of foresight might have brought upon us grave conflicts, disasters uncounted; the weakness might have brought upon us humiliation and ridicule, and humiliation and ridicule in the presence of other nations is our death. And is that the way to conduct the high interests of State? Is that the way to regard the dignity of the Spanish nation? Is that the way to secure the aggrandizement of our position abroad? Unhappy government, which, wherever it has gone with its sympathies, as for example, at Naples or at Rome, has encountered catastrophe; and at the same time, wherever it has gone with its threats and its opposition, fortune has come to favor the menaced with victory! Thus is it in consequence: Piedmont, which was a corner of Europe almost hidden by the folds spread from the Alps, is to-day a nation of the first rank.

But if from notes and documents we pass to deeds, if leaving the diplomatic documents out of account we take into consideration the practical conduct of the government and of its agents in regard to this question, what do we see? We see, or we have seen, a Spanish ambassador, a representative of this nation, choose to act like a faithful and compliant subject of an unfortunate monarch. We see, or we have seen, his pertinacity in keeping at the side of him who seemed to be his lord; with pains that distinguished him from the diplomatic agents of the other nations that were not satellites of Austria he has let it be said that our ships signalled the besieged to let them know the positions occupied by the besiegers; has given occasion to have it said in a circular of the last minister of state of Francisco II that, having counselled the ambassadors of all the powers to stay away from him that they might escape the horrors of the siege, all did so excepting the Spanish minister, who declared that he would remain at the side of Francisco II, whatever might be his fate; and that he gave ground upon which he might be officially accused before Europe that his counsels had probably contributed to the resistance of Francisco II at Gaeta. That is to say, our representative with Francisco II had decided, undoubtedly on his own account, that whatever might be the fate of him who was King of Naples — and I do not believe he will ever be so again — he would continue near his person; that is to say, that he intervened all he actively could in a struggle in which the Spanish government, in the face of Europe, had declared itself completely neutral. If the Spanish agent with that monarch had debts of affection to pay, or extraordinary recompenses

to satisfy, he might have done so without in any way compromising the interests of the Spanish nation. If he had
desired to act the part of an attached man he might have
done so by disinvesting himself and taking sword or gun
in hand, had he been so disposed, to defend in the breach the
honor of his lord.

All the rest of it has been venturesome, has been without
foresight, has had the possibility of bringing very grave consequences for us, in a way compromising us for the worst of
causes, or exposing us to suffer a ridiculous humiliation
before the powers that had promised one another not to
intervene in the struggle, or to permit anybody to intervene.
We have also seen that our agents abroad have acted in a
way to convert Spain into an officious mail-bearer for other
powers; it has been seen that our war-ships were apparently
destined to act the contraband with diplomatic documents,
until it was said that nothing but the envelopes were for the
Spanish ambassador, and the result was that it looked as if
we sought to cause to enter furtively into a blockaded city
the correspondence of other powers, thus occasioning our
maritime dignity to suffer shameful humiliation and exposing Spain to grave and terrible conflicts.

Lastly we see that our representative has disappeared from
the territory of Naples, that we do not know where he is, nor
who is to defend the interests of our citizens there. The
ambassador at Naples should be present only in the territory
of Naples, and it is not to be conceived that, having abandoned the interests confided to him, he can be anywhere
else than in Spain, if he has been given license to come
back.

But, however this may be, I ask the government: Has
he representative of Spain at Naples worked in conformity

with the instructions of the government, or not? Has he worked in conformity with the instructions of the government? Then the Congress may see what has become of neutrality. Has he not worked in conformity with those instructions? Then that diplomatic agent has committed grave faults, the responsibility for which can never disappear from the government, because it sent him thither, because it keeps him there, because it has not removed him, because thus it gives it to be understood that it approves the policy he has followed. Certainly no other than the government can be charged with this responsibility (and if there were other, so much the worse), for the times have gone by in which the ambassadors represented solely and exclusively the persons of the monarchs from whom they were sent.

To-day they do not represent, to-day they must not represent, to-day they cannot represent more than the policy and the interests of the governments that sent them. Lastly — in order that in everything, down to the smallest details, there may be seen the position of the government and the hostility which it shows towards that grand idea, towards that grand movement of Italy — when the vacancy occurred in the embassy at Rome, where is manifest the struggle between the principle of liberty and the principle of absolutism, where is manifest the struggle between the liberal principle and the reactionary principle, it sends to occupy that post as representative of Spain a man of eminently reactionary ideas in politics. And as if it were not sufficient to send a man known for his reactionary ideas it is necessary that the hostility that he bears towards that grand movement be manifest even in the nomination.

When in Italy there is hostility to the temporal power of the Pope, who is nominated? A political person who has

ventured to show the bad taste of designating as loathsome
the principle of national sovereignty, one of the two principles which are at issue in that country. Gentlemen, what
foresight, what prudence, and above all what neutrality!

The Congress, gentlemen, has already seen the reasons that
the government had, which were the considerations upon
which it founded absolutely its policy relative to the question
of Italy, to settle one of the most important of the questions
under debate. Therefore I will now leave to the consideration of the Congress, and later to the consideration of the
country, the disastrous consequences, the melancholy results,
which such a policy may bear. When the question that to-day
is debated in Europe absorbs the attention of almost all the
powers on earth, when to settle them appeal is made to the
highest regions of politics, when from its results is made t
depend, and with right, the stable peace of the nations, when
everywhere this great movement of public opinion is
respected, when for such elevated considerations the family
compact is prescinded that has already on the other part been
broken and completely destroyed, when for such elevated
considerations certain surnames are prescinded and those who
up to now have been sovereigns in Italy are abandoned to
their fate, can there be anything more inappropriate, anything more dangerous, than to oppose a policy so elevated
with a family policy, a personal policy, a mean policy.

Can there be anything more prejudicial than the invoca-
tion of antiquated law, than to talk the language of antiquated times? Can there be anything more disastrous than to
establish a species of hand community between the fate of the
Bourbons there and the fate of the Bourbons here? What is
to become of a discredited and selfish government with no
incentive other than its own interest, with no other idea, with

no other dogma, with no other system than that of governing one day longer? What is to become of a ministry that keeps its gaze constantly fixed on the governmental bench when it should keep it directed toward the future? What is to become of a ministry that is as changeable as a weathercock? that chooses all forms, that assumes all colors, in order to keep itself in power one day more? What is to become of a ministry, parasitic plant of the throne, upon whose substance it aims to feed itself and from whose life it seeks to live like the clinging plant that feeds itself upon the substance and the life of the tree, without considering that if the clinging plant lives longer the tree lives less and that there will come a day when both the plant and the tree may fall from the same stroke of the axe? What is to become of a ministry that takes no account whatever of the lessons of history?

There will happen that which has always happened, the inevitable will happen.

Not long ago, gentlemen, a powerful dynasty existed in a neighboring nation. At the head of this dynasty stood a monarch endowed with the greatest qualities. Ministers of this monarch, either as a stimulus to conserve power or as a means for not losing it, counselled or consented to a political course which, even though developed by the most elevated means, resembled the political course which the Liberal Union government has adopted for international questions since its advent to power. That monarch and his ministers believed that family interests were the interests of the country and followed an external family policy, a personal policy, a policy that constantly tended to advance the interests of the family. That dynasty, that powerful monarch, disappeared, gentlemen, as phantasms disappear; and at the same time as the splintered throne was pitched from the balconies of the

Tuileries the monarch fled to seek shelter on foreign soil, and Europe, which one day had seen him great and powerful, had not a friendly hand to reach him when the political convulsions of his kingdom drove him from his throne. A person who had figured so highly, a king who had grown to be so beloved, so respected and so great spent his last days, gentlemen, in the silence of indifference, died in the solitude of oblivion.

Unfortunate are the governments for whom these eloquent lessons of history pass unheeded! Time will soon charge itself with the repetition of like terrible lessons for their benefit.

The government of the Liberal Union, therefore, the government of national sovereignty, the government of liberty, the government of modern law, presents itself in opposition to representative institutions in Italy; presents itself not like any ordinary reactionist, but like the chief, like the Quixote, of the reaction; it invokes the antiquated law founded upon the treaties 1758 and 1815 and modified in 1817, under which, should they exist, we should have in Spain neither the shadow of constitutional government that we now have, neither would the ministers be able to seat themselves upon those benches, neither would the minister of state be able to write his notes, neither would I censure, as I am doing, the conduct of the government, neither could you, gentlemen, be here as representatives of the Spanish nation to approve or disapprove that conduct.

This government defends a dynasty that has always been our constant enemy, that has fomented our civil discords, that has procured our misfortune by all possible means, guided ever by its blind despotism; and invoking all this as law and as right — how absurd! — the same as would be the condemnation of our existence, forgetting our history, running contrary to our institutions, protesting against our future.

Hence let Spain know, let Europe know, let all the world know, that a government that thus forgets the highest interests of the nation does not represent, nor can it represent, the will, the aspirations, the desires, of the Spanish people; the Spanish people can by no means make itself responsible for the gross mistakes committed by this government contrary to its opinion; for the gross mistakes which it has committed upon this great question of the unity of Italy. For if you protest against the nationality of Italy you protest against our history, which from Sagunto to Saragossa represents the cause of the nationality and of the independence of peoples. To be recreant to the action of the Italians is to be recreant to the action of our fathers; you will be recreant to the blood that has flowed since from Cavadonga to Granada we saved our independence from the African yoke.

In condemning the sentiment of Italy you will condemn the sentiment of Daoiz and Velarde; you will condemn the sentiment that animated the Spanish people with a heroism unequalled in history, that it might recover its independence. If you condemn that which the Italian people does, you will condemn those who with their heroism raised the altar of country and nourished with their blood the tree of liberty. Then you may efface from those marbles the names of Padilla, of Daoiz, of Torrijos, to replace them with those of the Flemings of Carlos V, those of Napoleon's generals, those of Torquemada and Calomarde.

In this epoch, in which opinion has for some time been falsifying itself; in this epoch, in which, thanks to moral influence, popular assemblies cannot, according to my conception, faithfully represent the desires and opinions of the people, and in which for this reason these bodies are losing much of their importance even to the point that the governments in power may not be their legitimate expression, I do not know what will happen; but happen whatever may, I conclude these words satisfied in having spoken the truth, in having spoken it with loyalty, with noble intent, even though this truth may be heard with scorn on one hand and with displeasure on the other; on one hand and on the other there will come an occasion when this same truth will accredit itself; and come what will, I sit down, but partially satisfied, because while I firmly believe that I have complied with my duty, I cannot persuade myself that I have performed it with the effectiveness demanded by a matter so important.

VOORHEES

DANIEL WOLSEY VOORHEES, an American politician, was born at Liberty, Ohio, September 26, 1827, and educated at Indiana Asbury (now De Pauw) University. He studied law and after his admittance to the bar in 1851 began practice in Covington, Indiana. In 1856 he was an unsuccessful Democratic candidate for Congress, and in the following year removed to Terre Haute in the same State. From 1858 to 1861 he was United States district attorney, within that period defending John E. Cook, one of the associates of John Brown at Harper's Ferry, indicted for treason, murder, and inciting slaves to rebel, his address to the court on that occasion giving him a wide reputation as an orator. He was a Democratic representative in Congress, 1861-65, and again, 1869-71. In 1877 he entered the national Senate and was re-elected in 1885 and 1891. Very soon after his appearance in the Senate he made there an eloquent plea for the free coinage of silver and for the acceptance of greenbacks as full legal tender money. In 1893 however he voted for the repeal of the silver purchase clause of "The Sherman Act." From 1880 to 1897 he was chairman of the joint select committee to provide additional accommodation for the library of Congress, and to his continued efforts is due in great measure the erection of the present congressional library building. Voorhees failed of re-election to the Senate in January, 1897, and died in Washington city on the 10th of the following April. He was a strong partisan in his political views, and in allusion to his stature was sometimes styled "The Tall Sycamore of the Wabash." His "Speeches" were issued in 1875; and "Forty Years of Oratory," published in 1898, contains his "Lectures, Addresses and Speeches," with a brief biography.

DEFENCE OF JOHN E. COOK

DELIVERED AT CHARLESTOWN, VIRGINIA, NOVEMBER 8, 1859

WHO is John E. Cook?

He has the right himself to be heard before you; but I will answer for him. Sprung from an ancestry of loyal attachment to the American government, he inherits no blood of tainted impurity. His grandfather an officer of the Revolution, by which your liberty, as well as mine was achieved, and his gray-haired father, who lived to

(8982)

weep over him, a soldier of the war of 1812, he brings no dishonored lineage into your presence. If the blood which flows in his veins has been offered against your peace, the same blood in the veins of those from whose loins he sprang has been offered in fierce shock of battle and foreign invasion in behalf of the people of Virginia and the Union. Born of a parent stock occupying the middle walks of life, and possessed of all those tender and domestic virtues which escape the contamination of those vices that dwell on the frozen peaks, or in the dark and deep caverns of society, he would not have been here had precept and example been remembered in the prodigal wanderings of his short and checkered life.

Poor deluded boy! wayward, misled child! An evil star presided over thy natal hour and smote it with gloom. The hour in which thy mother bore thee and blessed thee as her blue-eyed babe upon her knee is to her now one of bitterness as she stands near the bank of the chill river of death and looks back on a name hitherto as unspotted and as pure as the unstained snow. May God stand by and sustain her, and preserve the mothers of Virginia from the waves of sorrow that now roll over her! . . .

In an evil hour — and may it be forever accursed!— John E. Cook met John Brown on the prostituted plains of Kansas. On that field of fanaticism, three years ago, this fair and gentle youth was thrown into contact with the pirate and robber of civil warfare.

To others whose sympathies he has enlisted I will leave the task of transmitting John Brown as a martyr and hero to posterity. In my eyes he stands the chief of criminals, the thief of property stolen — horses and slaves — from the citizens of Missouri, a falsifier here in this court, as I shall yet show, and a murderer not only of your citizens, but of the young men who have already lost their lives in his bloody foray of your border. This is not pleasant to say, but it is the truth, and, as such, ought to be and shall be said. You have seen John Brown, the leader.

Now look on John Cook, the follower. He is in evidence before you. Never did I plead for a face that I was more willing to show. If evil is there, I have not seen it. If murder is there, I am to learn to mark the lines of the murderer anew. If the assassin is in that young face, then commend me to the look of an assassin. No, gentlemen, it is a face for a mother to love, and a sister to idolize, and in which the natural goodness of his heart pleads trumpet-tongued against the deep damnation that estranged him from home and its principles.

Let us look at the meeting of these two men. Place them side by side. Put the young face by the old face; the young head by the old head. We have seen somewhat of the history of the young man. Look now for a moment at the history of the old man.

He did not go to Kansas as a peaceable settler with his interests linked to the legitimate growth and prosperity of that ill-fated Territory. He went there in the language of one who has spoken for him since his confinement here, as the Moses of the slaves' deliverance. He went there to fulfil a dream, which had tortured his brain for thirty years, that he was to be the leader of a second exodus from bondage. He went there for war and not for peace. He went there to call around him the wayward and unstable elements of a society in which the bonds of order, law, and religion were loosened, and the angry demon of discord was unchained. Storm was his element by his own showing. He courted the fierce tempest. He sowed the wind that he might reap the whirlwind. He invoked the lightning and gloried in its devastation. Sixty summers and winters had passed over his head, and planted the seeds of spring and gathered the harvests of autumn in the fields of his experience. He was the hero, too, of battles there. If laurels could be gained in such a fratricidal war as raged in Kansas, he had them on his brow.

Ossawatomie was given to him, and added to his name by the insanity of the crazy crew of the North as Napoleon conferred the names of battlefields on his favorite marshals. The action of Black Jack, too, gave him consideration, circumstance, and condition with philanthropists of bastard quality, carpet knight heroes in Boston, and servile followers of fanaticism throughout the country. His courage is now lauded to the skies by men who have none of it themselves. This virtue, I admit, he has — linked, however, with a thousand crimes. An iron will, with which to accomplish evil under the skilful guise of good, I also admit to be in his possession — rendering his influence over the young all the more despotic and dangerous.

Imagine, if you please, the bark on which this young man at the bar, and all his hopes were freighted, laid alongside of the old weather-beaten and murderous man-of-war whose character I have placed before you. The one was stern and bent upon a fatal voyage. Grim-visaged war, civil commotion, pillage and death, disunion and universal desolation thronged through the mind of John Brown. To him law was nothing, the Union was nothing, the peace and welfare of the country were nothing, the lives of the citizens of Virginia were nothing.

Though a red sea of blood rolled before him, yet he lifted

up his hand and cried Forward. Shall he now shrink from
his prominence, and attempt to shrivel back to the grade of
his recruits and subalterns? Shall he deny his bad pre-eminence, and say that he did not incite the revolt which has
involved his followers in ruin? Shall he stand before this
court and before the country, and deny that he was the master-spirit, and gathered together the young men who followed him to the death in this mad expedition?

No! his own hand signs himself " Commander-in-chief,"
and shows the proper distinction which should be made
between himself and the men who, in an evil moment,
obeyed his orders. Now turn to the contrast again and
behold the prisoner. Young and new to the rough ways of
life, his unsandalled foot, tender and unused to the journey
before him, a waif on the ocean, at the mercy of the current
which might assail him, and unfortunately endowed with
that fearful gift which causes one to walk as in a dream
through all the vicissitudes of a lifetime; severed and wan-
dering from the sustaining and protecting ties of kindred, he
gave, without knowing his destination or purpose, a pledge
of military obedience to John Brown, " Commander-in-
chief." . . .

John Brown was the despotic leader and John E. Cook
was an ill-fated follower of an enterprise whose horror he
now realizes and deplores. I defy the man, here or elsewhere, who has ever known John E. Cook, who has ever
looked once fully into his face, and learned anything of his
history, to lay his hand on his heart and say that he believes
him guilty of the origin or the results of the outbreak at
Harper's Ferry.

Here, then, are the two characters whom you are thinking
to punish alike. Can it be that a jury of Christian men will

find no discrimination should be made between them? Are the tempter and the tempted the same in your eyes? Is the beguiled youth to die the same as the old offender who has pondered his crimes for thirty years? Are there no grades in your estimation of guilt? Is each one, without respect to age or circumstances, to be beaten with the same number of stripes?

Such is not the law, human or divine. We are all to be rewarded according to our works, whether in punishment for evil, or blessings for good that we have done. You are here to do justice, and if justice requires the same fate to befall Cook that befalls Brown, I know nothing of her rules, and do not care to learn. They are as widely asunder, in all that constitutes guilt, as the poles of the earth, and should be dealt with accordingly. It is in your power to do so, and by the principles by which you yourselves are willing to be judged hereafter, I implore you to do it!

Come with me, however, gentlemen, and let us approach the spot where the tragedy of the 17th of October occurred, and analyze the conduct of the prisoner there. It is not true that he came as a citizen to your State and gained a home in your midst to betray you. He was ordered to take his position at Harper's Ferry in advance of his party for the sole purpose of ascertaining whether Colonel Forbes, of New York, had divulged the plan. This order came from John Brown, the "Commander-in-chief," and was doubtless a matter of as much interest to others of prominent station as to himself.

Cook simply obeyed — no more. There is not a particle of evidence that he tampered with your slaves during his temporary residence. On the contrary, it is admitted on all hands that he did not. His position there is well defined.

Nor was he from under the cold, stern eye of his leader. From the top of the mountain his chief looked down upon him, and held him as within a charmed circle. Would Cook have lived a day had he tried to break the meshes which environed him?

Happy the hour in which he had made the attempt even had he perished, but in fixing the measure of his guilt, the circumstances by which he was surrounded must all be weighed. At every step we see him as the instrument in the hands of other men, and not as originating or advising anything. . . .

But it has been said that Cook left the scene at Harper's Ferry at an early hour to avoid the danger of the occasion, and thus broke faith with his comrades in wrong. Even this is wholly untrue. Again we find the faithful, obedient subaltern carrying out the orders of his chief, and when he had crossed the river and fulfilled the commands of Brown, he did what Brown's own son would not do — by returning and exposing himself to the fire of the soldiers and citizens for the relief of Brown and his party. We see much, alas! too much, to condemn in his conduct, but nothing to despise; we look in vain for an act that belongs to a base or malignant nature. Let the hand of chastisement fall gently on the errors of such as him, and reserve your heavy blows for such as commit crime from motives of depravity.

Up to this point I have followed the prisoner, and traced his immediate connection with this sad affair. You have everything before you. You have heard his own account of his strange and infatuated wanderings up and down the earth with John Brown and his coadjutors; how like a fiction it all seems, and yet how lamentably true; how unreal to minds like ours; how like the fever dream of a mind warped and disordered to the borders of insanity does the part which the prisoner has played seem to every practical judgment!

Is there nothing in it all that affords you the dearest privilege which man has on earth — the privilege of being merciful? Why, the very thief on the cross, for a single moment's repentance over his crimes, received absolute forgiveness, and was rewarded with paradise.

But, gentlemen, in estimating the magnitude of this young man's guilt, there is one fact which is proven in his behalf by the current history of the day which you cannot fail to consider. Shall John E. Cook perish, and the real criminals who for twenty years have taught the principles on which he acted, hear no voice from this spot? Shall no mark be placed on them? Shall this occasion pass away, and the prime felons who attacked your soil and murdered your citizens at Harper's Ferry escape? The indictment before us says that the prisoner was "seduced by the false and malignant counsels of other traitorous persons."

Never was a sentence written more just and true. "False and malignant counsels" have been dropping for years, as deadly and blighting as the poison of the Bohun upas tree, from the tongues of evil and traitorous persons in that section of the Union to which the prisoner belongs. They have seduced not only his mind, but many others, honest and misguided like him, to regard the crime at Harper's Ferry as no crime, your rights as unmitigated wrongs, and the constitution of the country as a league with hell and a covenant with death. On the skirts of the leaders of abolition fanaticism in the North is every drop of blood shed in the conflict at Harper's Ferry; on their souls rests the crime of murder for every life there lost; and all the waters of the ocean could not wash

the stains of slaughter from their treacherous and guilty
hands.

A noted Boston abolitionist [Wendell Phillips], a few
days ago, at Brooklyn, New York, in the presence of thousands, speaking of this tragic occurrence, says: "It is the
natural result of anti-slavery teaching. For one, I accept it.
I expected it." I, too, accept it in the same light, and so
will the country. Those who taught, and not those who
believed and acted, are the men of crime in the sight of God.
And to guard other young men, so far as in my power, from
the fatal snare which has been tightened around the hopes
and destiny of John E. Cook, and to show who are fully
responsible for his conduct, I intend to link with this trial
the names of wiser and older men than he; and, if he is to be
punished and consigned to a wretched doom, they shall stand
beside him in the public stocks; they shall be pilloried forever in public shame as "the evil and traitorous persons who
seduced him to his ruin by their false and malignant counsels."

The chief of these men, the leader of a great party, a senator of long standing, has announced to the country that there
is a higher law than the constitution, which guarantees to each
man the full exercise of his own inclination. The prisoner
before you has simply acted on the law of Wm. H. Seward,
and not the law of his fathers. He has followed the Mahomet
of an incendiary faith.

Come forth, ye sages of abolitionism, who now cower and
skulk under hasty denials of your complicity with the bloody
result of your wicked and unholy doctrines, and take your
places on the witness stand. Tell the world why this thing
has happened. Tell this jury why they are trying John E.
Cook for his life. You advised his conduct and taught him
that he was doing right. You taught him a higher law and

then pointed out to him the field of action. Let facts be submitted. Mr. Seward, in speaking of slavery, says: "It can and must be abolished, and you and I must do it."

What worse did the prisoner attempt? Again, he said, upon this same subject, "Circumstances determine possibilities;" and doubtless the circumstance with which John Brown had connected his plans made them possible in his estimation, for it is in evidence before the country, unimpeached and uncontradicted, that the great senator of New York had the whole matter submitted to him, and only whispered back, in response, that he had better not have been told. He has boldly announced an irrepressible conflict between the free and slave States of this Union.

These seditious phrases, "higher law" and "irrepressible conflict," warrant and invite the construction which the prisoner and his young deluded companions placed upon them. Yet they are either in chains, with the frightful gibbet in full view, or sleep in dishonored graves, while the apostle and master-spirit of insurrection is loaded with honors, and fares sumptuously every day. Such is poor, short-handed justice in this world.

An old man, and for long years a member of the national Congress from Ohio, next shall testify here before you that he taught the prisoner the terrible error which now involves his life. Servile insurrection have forever been on the tongue and lips of Joshua R. Giddings. He says " that when the contest shall come, when the thunder shall roll and the lightning flash, and when the slaves shall rise in the South, in imitation of the horrid scenes of the West Indies, when the Southern man shall turn pale and tremble, when your dwellings shall smoke with the torch of the incendiary, and dismay sit on each countenance, he will hail it as the approaching dawn of that political and moral millennium which he is well assured will come upon the world."

The atrocity of these sentiments chills the blood of honest patriots, and no part of the prisoner's conduct equals their bloody import. Shall the old leader escape and the young follower die? Shall the teacher, whose doctrines told the prisoner that what he did was right, go unscathed of the lightning which he has unchained? If so, Justice has fled from her temples on earth, and awaits us only on high to measure out what is right between man and man.

The men who have misled this boy to his ruin shall here receive my maledictions. They shrink back from him now in the hour of his calamity. They lift up their hands and say, Avaunt! to the bloody spectre which their infernal orgies have summoned up. You hear them all over the land ejaculating through false, pale, coward lips, "Thou canst not say I did it," when their hands are reeking with all the blood that has been shed and which yet awaits the extreme penalty of the law. False, fleeting, perjured traitors, false to friends as well as country, and perjured before the constitution of the Republic — ministers who profess to be of God who told this boy here to carry a Sharpe's rifle to Kansas instead of his mother's Bible — shall this jury, this court, and this country forget their guilt and their infamy because a victim to their precepts is yielding up his life before you?

May God forget me if I here, in the presence of this pale face, forget to denounce with the withering, blighting, blasting power of majestic truth, the tall and stately criminals of the Northern States of this Union.

The visionary mind of the prisoner heard from a member of congress from Massachusetts that a new constitution, a new Bible, and a new God were to be inaugurated and to

possess the country. They were to be new, because they
were to be anti-slavery, for the old constitution, and the old
Bible, and the God of our fathers, the ancient Lord God of
Israel, the same yesterday, to-day, and forever, were not on
the side of abolitionism.

Is there no mitigation for his doom in the fact that he took
his life in his hand, and aimed at that which a coward taught
him, but dared not himself attempt? Base, pusillanimous
demagogues have led the prisoner to the bar, but while he
suffers — if suffer he must — they, too, shall have their
recreant limbs broken on the wheel.

I will not leave the soil of Virginia, I will not let this
awful occasion pass into history, without giving a voice and
an utterance to its true purport and meaning, without heap-
ing upon its authors the load of execration which they are
to bear henceforth and forever. Day after day and year
after year has the baleful simoon of revolution, anarchy, discord, hostility to the South and her institutions, swept over
that section of the country in which the lot of the prisoner
has been cast. That he has been poisoned by its breath
should not cut him off from human sympathy; rather should
it render every heart-element toward him.

He never sought place or station, but sought merely to
develop those doctrines which evil and traitorous persons have
caused him to believe were true. Ministers, editors, and
politicians — Beecher, Parker, Seward, Giddings, Sumner,
Hale, and a host of lesser lights of each class — who in this
court-room, who in this vast country, who in the wide world
who shall read this trial believes them not guilty as charged
in the indictment in all the counts to a deeper and far more
fearful extent than John E. Cook. Midnight gloom is not
more somber in contrast with the blazing light of the merid-

ian sun than is the guilt of such men in comparison with
that which overwhelms the prisoner. They put in motion
the maelstrom which has engulfed him. They started the
torrent which has borne him over the precipice. They called
forth from the caverns the tempest which wrecked him on a
sunken reef.

Before God, and in the light of eternal truth, the disaster
at Harper's Ferry is their act, and not his. May the ghost
of each victim to their doctrines of disunion and abomination
sit heavy on their guilty souls! May the fate of the
prisoner, whatever it may be, disturb their slumbers and
paralyze their arms when they are again raised against the
peace of the country and the lives of its citizens!

I know by the gleam of each eye into which I look in this
jury-box, that if these men could change places with young
Cook, you would gladly say to him, " Go, erring and repentant youth, our vengeance shall fall on those who paid their
money, urged on the attack, and guided the blow." Let me
appeal to you, gentlemen of the jury, in the name of eternal
truth and everlasting right, is nothing to be forgiven to
youth, to inexperience, to a gentle, kind heart, to a wayward
and peculiar though not vicious character, strangely apt to be
led by present influences?

I have shown you what those influences, generally and
specially, have been over the mind of the prisoner. I have
shown you the malign influence of his direct leader. I have
shown you, also, the " false and malignant counsels " in
behalf of this sad enterprise, emanating from those in place,
power, and position. It might have been your prodigal son
borne away and seduced by such counsels, as well as my
young client. Do with him as you would have your own
child dealt by under like circumstances. He has been stolen

from the principles of his ancestors and betrayed from the teachings of his kindred. If he was your own handsome child, repentant and confessing his wrong to his country, what would you wish a jury of strangers to do? That do yourselves.

By that rule guide your verdict; and the poor boon of mercy will not be cut off from him. He thought the country was about to be convulsed; that the slave was pining for an opportunity to rise against his master; that two thirds of the laboring population of the country, north and south, would flock to the standard of revolt; that a single day would bring ten, fifty — yea, a hundred thousand men — to arms in behalf of the insurrection of the slaves. This is in evidence.

Who are responsible for such terribly false views? and what kind of a visionary and dreaming mind is that which has so fatally entertained them? That the prisoner's mind is pliant to the impressions, whether for good or for evil, by which it is surrounded, let his first interview in his prison with Governor Willard, in the presence of your senator, Colonel Mason, bear witness. His error was placed before him. His wrong to his family and his country was drawn by a patriotic, and, at the same time, an affectionate hand. His natural being at once asserted its sway. The influence of good, and not of evil, once more controlled him as in the days of his childhood; and now here before you he has the merit at least of a loyal citizen, making all the atonement in his power for the wrong which he has committed. That he has told strictly the truth in his statement is proven by every word of evidence in this cause.

Gentlemen, you have this case. I surrender into your hands the issues of life and death. As long as you live, a more important case than this you will never be called to try.

Consider it, therefore, well in all its bearings. I have tried to show you those facts which go to palliate the conduct of the prisoner. Shall I go home and say that in justice you remembered not mercy to him? Leave the door of clemency open; do not shut it by a wholesale conviction. Remember that life is an awful and a sacred thing; remember that death is terrible — terrible at any time, and in any form.

> " Come to the bridal chamber, Death!
>   Come when the mother feels
> For the first time, her first-born's breath;
>   Come when the blessed seals
> That close the pestilence are broke,
> And crowded cities wail its stroke;
> Come in consumption's ghastly form,
> The earthquake's shock, the ocean's storm;
> Come when the heart beats high and warm
>   With banquet song, and dance, and wine,
> And thou art terrible. The groan,
> The knell, the pall, the bier,
> And all we know, or dream, or fear
>   Of agony, are thine."

But when to the frightful mien of the grim monster, when to the chill visage of the spirit of the glass and scythe, is added the hated, dreaded spectre of the gibbet, we turn shuddering from the accumulated horror. God spare this boy, and those who love him, from such a scene of woe.

I part from you now, and most likely forever. When we next meet — when I next look upon your faces and you on mine — it will be in that land and before that Tribunal where the only plea that will save you or me from a worse fate than awaits the prisoner, will be mercy. Charity is the paramount virtue; all else is as sounding brass and a tinkling cymbal. Charity suffereth long, and is kind. Forbid it not to come into your deliberation; and, when your last hour comes, the memory that you allowed it to plead for your erring brother, John E. Cook, will brighten your passage over the dark river, and rise by your side as an interceding angel in that day when your trial as well as his shall be determined by a just but merciful God.

I thank the court and you, gentlemen, for your patient kindness, and I am done.

ON THE WELFARE OF THE NATION

DELIVERED IN THE HOUSE OF REPRESENTATIVES, MARCH 9, 1864

MR. CHAIRMAN,—I arise to address the House to-day with feelings of profound depression and gloom. It is a melancholy spectacle to behold a free government die. The world it is true is filled with the evidences of decay. All nature speaks the voice of dissolution, and the highway of history and of life is strewn with the wrecks which time, the great despoiler, has made.

But hope of the future, bright visions of reviving glory are nowhere denied to the heart of man save as he gazes upon the downfall of legal liberty. He listens sorrowfully to the autumn winds as they sigh through dismantled forests, but he knows that their breath will be soft and vernal in the spring, and that the dead flowers and the withered foliage will blossom and bloom again. He sees the sky overcast with the angry frown of the tempest, but he knows that the sun will reappear, and the stars, the bright emblazonry of God, cannot perish.

Man himself, this strange connecting link between dust and deity, totters wearily onward under the weight of years and pain toward the gaping tomb, but now briefly his mind lingers around that dismal spot. It is filled with tears and grief, and the willow and the cypress gather around it with their loving, but mournful embrace.

And is this all? Not so. If a man die shall he not live again? Beyond the grave, in the distant Aiden, hope provides an elysium of the soul where the mortal assumes immortality and life becomes an endless splendor.

But where, sir, in all the dreary regions of the past, filled with convulsions, wars, and crimes, can you point your finger to the tomb of a free commonwealth on which the angel of resurrection has ever descended or from whose mouth the stone of despotism has ever been rolled away? Where, in what age and in what clime, have the ruins of constitutional freedom renewed their youth and regained their lost estate? By whose strong grip has the dead corpse of a republic once fallen ever been raised?

The merciful master who walked upon the waters and bade the winds be still left no ordained apostles with power to wrench apart the jaws of national death and release the victims of despotism. The wail of the heart-broken over the dead is not so sad to me as the realization of this fact.

But all history, with a loud unbroken voice, proclaims it, and the evidence of what the past has been is conclusive to my mind of what the future will be. Wherever in the wide domain of human conduct a people once possessed of liberty, with all power in their own hands, have surrendered these great gifts of God at the command of the usurper they have never afterwards proven themselves worthy to regain their forfeited treasures.

Sir, let history speak on this point. Bend your ear, and listen to the solemn warnings which distant ages perpetually utter in their uneasy slumbers. Four thousand years of human experience are open and present for the study of the American people. Standing as we do the last and greatest republic in the midst of the earth, it becomes us most deeply in this crisis of our destiny to examine well the career and the final fate of kindred governments in the past.

The principles of self-government are of ancient origin. They were not created by the authors of the American constitution. They were adopted by those wise and gifted minds from the models of former times and applied to the wants of the American people.

Far back in the gray, uncertain dawn of history, in the land of mystery and of miracles, the hand of Almighty benevolence planted the seeds of constitutional government by which life, liberty and property were made secure. Abraham and Lot each governed his household and his herdmen by law; and although they became offended at each other, yet under the divine sanction they refrained from the pleasures of conquest, subjugation, confiscation. They divided the country before them by a primitive treaty, and the grass continued to grow for their flocks unstained by fraternal blood and uncrushed by the hoof of war.

And in long after years, when the descendants of the patriarchs broke their prison doors in Egypt and lay encamped in the wilderness, the ominscient presence came down and gave them a framework of fundamental law in which the popular will was largely recognized. A system of jurisprudence was devised for the people of Israel which protected liberty and administered justice. Under its influence the feeble fugitives and homeless wanderers without bread and without water in the desert became an empire of wisdom, of wealth, and of power.

The liberal institutions of the Jewish theocracy produced statesmen, poets, historians, and warriors, who will continue to challenge the admiration of posterity by the splendor of their achievements as long as generations come and go on the waves of time. They lived within the immediate jurisdiction of Jehovah. They possessed the ark of the covenant and took counsel with ministering angels directly from the portals of Paradise.

With all these evidences of celestial favor in their behalf, it is not to be wondered that they claimed an exemption from the changes and mutations of human affairs, and boasted that the seal of perpetuity had been impressed by the divine hand on the pillars of their government.

But public virtue became debauched; the popular heart corroded with the lust of conquest and of gain; primitive purity faded away under the baleful breath of embittered factions; the fires of patriotism were smothered by rankling hate and the thirst for revenge; and all these evil passions broke forth in the voice of a malignant majority clamoring for a king. In that hour of disastrous eclipse, the spirit of liberty took her flight forever from the hills of Judea. Thousands of years have rolled away since then. The Holy Land has been the theatre of conflicts which rocked the world as the throes of an earthquake. Genius and heroism have there blazed as stars in the eastern skies. There, too, was enacted the sublime tragedy of redemption — that tragedy which summoned the inhabitants of all worlds as its witnesses, and filled nature with agony in all her parts. The eyes of mankind have been turned back and fixed upon those scenes of immortal interest for more than thirty centuries. But who has lifted up and restored her fallen system of liberal institutions? The people surrendered their rights, their franchises, their self-control, and welcomed the power of one man. The base act has never been reversed. As the tree fell so it lies. It died at the root. Despotism reigns undisturbed and unbroken, in darkness and in silence, where once the light

and music of freedom gladdened the souls of the stately sons
and dark-eyed daughters of Israel.

And leaving the land of sacred history, what similar scenes
of human weakness and human folly meet us at every step
in the onward pathway of time. Where now are those splendid structures which once adorned the shores of the Ægean,
the Euxine, and the Mediterranean? Athens, the eye of
Greece, the school of the world — has her dismal fate
impressed no lesson on the thoughts of mankind? Fifteen
hundred years before the birth of our Saviour, the light of
civil order and civil freedom arose in the Island of Crete, and
sent its rays through the vale of Tempe, the rich plains of
Thessaly, over the fruitful fields of Attica and Bœotia, and
hovered with an everlasting and imperishable radiance around
the heads of Olympus, Helicon, and Parnassus. It is true
that kings governed in those early days, but absolute power
in one man was unknown. Laws made by the people chained
the licentious hand of oppression. The proudest monarchs
of those warlike ages governed in obedience to the will of the
legislative departments. They enacted no laws; they executed them as they found them. A house of peers and an
assembly of the people shared the supreme authority and
ensured safety and liberty to the citizen. Ulysses speaks of
one chief "to whom Jupiter hath intrusted the sceptre and
the laws, that by them he may govern." But he recognizes
that these instruments of government are bestowed by the
popular favor, for, when shipwrecked upon a strange coast and
addressing himself as a supplicant to its queen, he says: "May
the gods grant you and your guests to live happily; and may
you all transmit to your children your possessions in your
houses and whatsoever honors the people hath given you."
But even this limited and constitutional system of monarchy

was not long borne by that proud race which drank in the love
of liberty from the free air of the mountains over their heads,
and the breath of the restless and stormy ocean at their feet.
" Those vigorous principles of democracy which had always
existed in the Grecian governments began to ferment; and,
in the course of a few ages monarchy was everywhere abolished; the very name of king was very generally proscribed;
a commonwealth was thought the only government to which
it became men to submit; and the term tyrant was introduced
to denote those who, in opposition to these new political principles, acquired monarchical sway." Then sprang into existence that wonderful cluster of republics whose memory yet
fills the earth with its fragrance of noble deeds and exalted
genius.   Liberty hovered over that classic peninsula of
southern Europe like the angel of creation hovering over
night and chaos, and from the fostering warmth of her
embrace came forth an immortal world of letters, of art, of
science, and of law.   The Macedonian, the Spartan, the
Athenian, and all lifted their heads among the stars, and
barely condescended to pity and despise neighboring nations
who were less free than themselves.   They pointed to Marathon and Salamis, Thermopylæ and Platæa, as the American
points to Saratoga and Bunker Hill, Yorktown and New
Orleans.   They kept their festive days of national deliverance and joy as the fourth day of July and the eighth day
of January have been commemorated and hallowed by us.
They sounded all the depths and shoals of honor; drank deep
draughts from the very fountains of freedom; achieved
immortality in every department of human thought and
action.   And yet, with their cup full of glory for more than
a thousand years, sparkling to the brim with rights and privileges more sweet to their taste than the honey of Hymettus,

they dashed it to the earth, and its shattered fragments remain as they fell. The lust of power on the part of public rulers, and the luxury, sloth, and indifference of the people, nursed so long in the lap of prosperity that they allowed the usurper to march on in his lawless career unchallenged and unquestioned, worked the overthrow of the republics of Greece. And what traveller, standing upon those blighted and withered plains, has beheld a sign of resurrection for more than two thousand years? Now and then, it is true, a murmur or a groan has disturbed the deadly sleep in which that land is embraced, but it only shows that she dreams of the past, not that she will awake to the future. Her birthright was abandoned by her own sordid hand, and it cannot be reclaimed. A petty power of northern Europe now gives a king to the countrymen of Homer, Themistocles, and Solon.

But, sir, another name more prominent than all others, presents itself to the student of antiquity in this connection. Roman history stands out upon the canvas of time as plainly marked as the events of modern ages. We see Tarquin the Proud expelled from his throne, and the foundations of the commonwealth laid five hundred years before the Christian era. For the next five centuries we behold a race of men who "would have brooked the eternal devil to keep his state in Rome, as easily as a king."

How fondly the devotee of liberty dwells upon that period! With what grandeur the names of the mighty dead, and the sublime creations of their genius, arise to our view! In what does the boasted civilization of the present surpass the achievements of a race and an age to whom the revelations of God were unknown? Who has spoken as Cicero spoke? What historian has guided a pen so full of majesty and of beauty

as that which inscribed the annals of Tacitus? Whose muse
has winged a loftier flight or sung a nobler strain than Vir-
gil's? In arms, too, what warriors have improved upon the
skill and magnificence of Scipio and Cæsar? But it was still
more in the dignity and freedom of her private citizens that
Rome was great than in the renown of her most illustrious
leaders, statesmen, and orators. Kings of powerful nations
bowed their uncovered heads before the Roman people. The
magistrates, consuls, and military commanders paid homage
and obedience directly to the public will. The sovereignty
of the people was absolute. The principles of self-government were never in the history of nations more fully or clearly
displayed. Jurisprudence became an enlightened science,
from whose pages a light extends to the present hour, and
under whose guardian protection the humblest citizen of
Rome was secure in every right declared inalienable by the
Declaration of American Independence. But why linger
upon the well-known story of Roman liberty and Roman
greatness. I use it but to illustrate. The melancholy conclusion came. As the son of the morning fell from heaven,
so Rome fell from the luminous sphere of liberty never to
hope again. The world grew dark as her light faded away,
and ten centuries of gloom succeeded her downfall. And
why perished this mistress of the earth? Not because the
vandal ravaged her borders; not because the Gaul burned to
avenge the victims of Cæsar; not because the Goth beat her
gates to pieces; but because her people submitted to the
encroachments of executive authority, lulled by the syren
voice of a false security, until at last they awakened to find
their chains and manacles forged and fastened. Their links
yet fester in the flesh of the descendants of Brutus, and their
clankings may yet be heard in the forum where Cato warned

his countrymen against the approach of despotic power. No deliverer has ever arisen. Liberty has never been wooed to return. Once abandoned and surrendered by those whom she has crowned with honor and greatness, in the midst of the earth she goes forth with the air and feelings of insulted majesty to seek more worthy objects of her love and care.

Sir, modern history contains no exception to the rule which the fate of ancient republics has established. Aspirations for freedom have at different periods ascended from almost every portion of the map of modern Europe. A system of confederated states built up and nurtured the free institutions of Holland for more than three hundred years, while the night of despotism lay thick and heavy on all the surrounding horizon. As revolted colonies, as states in rebellion, the Dutch republic maintained a defensive war for thirty years against the whole power of Spain when Philip II controlled the councils and commanded the wealth of the civilized world. Their proudest cities were besieged and fell a prey to pillage and murder. In pitched battles they seldom triumphed over the superior numbers and equipments of the powerful Spaniard. Their country was trodden under foot; their houses plundered; their fields laid waste; and the wild boar and the wolf roamed unmolested through the streets of once populous towns. But the endurance and patriotism of a people to whom no terms were offered except abject, unconditional submission, outlived and broke the rage of their oppressors. A free commonwealth, the United States of Holland, arose and extended the spirit of enterprise, commerce, and refinement into all the four quarters of the earth. She conquered the sea and subdued distance. The peaceful victories of her trade were celebrated at the Cape of Good Hope, and in the harbor of New York, in the Indies of the east, and in every latitude of the western hemisphere. Nor was she less renowned in war. The broom at the masthead swept the ocean of her enemies, and the only guns of a foreign power whose hostile roar ever penetrated the Tower of London, were the guns of the Free States of Holland. Louis XIV, the grand monarch of imperial France, when Turenne and Luxemburg and Condé led his armies, poured the torrents of his power against her for conquest and subjugation; but they were poured in vain. She fought with the inspiration of freedom, and made her history secure and illustrious as long as a generous heart shall be found to throb in sympathy with the welfare and happiness of a heroic people. But where now is that noble prodigy of liberal institutions? Why does she lift her beautiful head to the heavens no longer? Her glories declined under the burthen of unbounded wealth and overflowing prosperity. Her people relaxed the vigilance of their guard over the citadel of their liberties, and slumbered at their posts while unlawful power fortified itself beyond successful attack. Thus she perished ignobly by her own hand, having throughout her whole career defied and held at bay a world in arms. And how still and heavy has been her long repose? No awakening convulsions shake her rigid limbs, or disturb her frozen arteries. Once fallen, and forever lost is the mournful epic of her fate. She takes her place in the dreary catalogue furnished by antiquity.

But cross the Channel and take your stand on the soil of England. She too has furnished mankind with a short-lived experiment of republican government. Wrongs and outrages inflicted on the English people, similar in kind, but far less enormous than those which now oppress the citizen of the United States of America, wrought the volcanic eruption of 1640. The best blood of England perished in the conflict between Magna Charta on one side and absolutism on the other. John Hampden bled on the plains of Chalgrave, but the royal Stuart bled on the scaffold. When the strife died away, the British constitution was found to be possessed and upheld by those who partook of the sacrament of the Lord's supper with bloody hands, and who enforced the Sermon on the Mount with fire and sword. They were the ancestors of those who to-day in this land are crucifying liberty afresh, and putting her to open shame. God does not allow himself to be mocked, and Cromwell and the Commonwealth of England went out together, while a wrathful tempest raged around the dying bed of the great, but bloody and tyrannical Protector. The incoming wave, the reaction in the tide of human affairs, bore back the dissolute and worthless Charles II to the home of his ancestors, and Englishmen have never from that time to this lifted their hands or their voices in behalf of a republic.

France points to the revolting blotch, the stain of mingled blood and tears, which her wild and mad attempts at freedom have left upon the page of history. We gaze at it but for an instant, and turn away with horror. At the very moment almost that the President of the French Directory declared "that monarchy would never more show its frightful head in France," Bonaparte with his grenadiers entered the palace of St. Cloud, and dispersing with the bayonet the deputies of the people deliberating on the affairs of state, laid the foundation of that vast fabric of despotism which overshadowed all Europe.

Sir, I pause in this train of sorrowful illustrations. I tremble at their contemplation when my mind is brought to embrace the conclusions which flow from them. But shall we shrink back affrighted and appalled because the great les-

sons of uniform history come to us with a voice of solemn
and prophetic warning? Shall the universal experience of
the human race bring us no wisdom? Shall we wrap ourselves in a sweet delusion and lie down to pleasant dreams
when we know by every chart of navigation that the fatal
maelstrom is just at hand? Will the proud and daring people
of America close their eyes and ears against the teaching of
ages, and wait for fetters and gyves to convince them that
their liberties are in danger? Are they to be chained like
Prometheus to the rock, while the vulture of despotism preys
forever upon their bleeding vitals? Sir, in my hours of
seclusion and study I have to the best of my humble capacity
held up the lamp of the past to the face of the future, and I
call God to witness that I would be recreant and faithless to
my own conscience if I did not proclaim, as far as my voice
will reach, that a danger is this hour upon the American people more deadly than the juices of the hemlock or the bite
of the asp. This government is dying; dying, sir, dying.
We are standing around its bed of death, and will soon be
wretched mourners at its tomb, unless the sovereign and
heroic remedy is speedily applied. I will submit the facts in
condensed array on which I make this assertion, that a candid
public may judge between me and that pestilent class who,
failing to answer, resort to slander.

The American republic was established in order to accomplish avowed and specified purposes. The objects of its
creation were left in no uncertainty. Its mission was clear
and distinct by the terms of the constitution. It came into
existence "in order to form a more perfect union, establish
justice, ensure domestic tranquillity, provide for the common
defence, promote the general welfare, and secure the blessings
of liberty" to that and all succeeding generations of Ameri-

can citizens. Who will dare to rise in his place and say that this government has been administered during the last three years in a mode even tending toward the accomplishment of these grand results? Has the establishment of justice been maintained? The sword has been thrown into the scales of justice, and there is not this hour a court between the two oceans left free to decide the laws as they have uniformly been decided in England and America for the last two hundred years. The very foundations of civilized jurisprudence have been torn away, and the whole edifice is in ruins. The Magna Charta is erased; the habeas corpus is dead; the very soul and spirit of liberty is extinguished in the forum of the judiciary. To this sacred sanctuary, more than to any other department of the government, the blessings of liberty were entrusted. But has the present administration made them secure? It is required to do so by the terms of the constitution. Let each mind give its own answer. Not one right which constitutes the freedom and safety of the citizen but what has been wickedly and wantonly violated. Prisons filled without indictment and without warrant; long and bitter punishment inflicted without trial or conviction; the whole jury system abolished by a stroke of the pen in the hand of the Executive, or his subordinates in crime; no witnesses brought to the face of the accused; no counsel permitted to appear in his behalf; his house broken open and his papers searched in the midst of his pallid and terrified wife and children; such are some of the evidences which exist on every hand that our free institutions are hastening to their overthrow. And not content with breaking down all the ancient safeguards of liberty, new and malignant measures of legislation have been continually devised by a slavish Congress by which to more effectually reach, and torture, and grind the citizen. The most innocent conduct, a harmless word, a simple look has been enacted into guilt. The hired hounds of arbitrary power find conspiracy and crime in the friendly greetings of neighbors on their farms. Speaking of the period of 1795 in England, that great modern philosopher, Henry Thomas Buckle, in his " History of Civilization," uses the following language, which I adopt as faithfully descriptive of the conduct of the party now in power, and of the times in which we live.

" Nothing, however, could stop the government in its headlong career. The ministers, secure of a majority in both Houses of Parliament, were able to carry their measures in defiance of the people, who opposed them by every mode short of actual violence. And as the object of these new laws was to check the spirit of inquiry and prevent reforms which the progress of society rendered indispensable, there were also brought into play other means subservient to the same end. It is no exaggeration to say that for some years England was ruled by a system of absolute terror. The ministers of the day, turning a struggle of party into a war of proscription, filled the prisons with their political opponents, and allowed them when in confinement to be treated with shameful severity. If a man was known to be a reformer he was constantly in danger of being arrested; and if he escaped that, he was watched at every turn, and his private letters were opened as they passed through the postoffice. In such cases no scruples were allowed. Even the confidence of domestic life was violated. No opponent of government was safe under his own roof against the tales of eavesdroppers and the gossip of servants. Discord was introduced into the bosom of families, and schisms caused between parents and their children. Not only were the most strenuous attempts made to silence the press, but the booksellers were so constantly prosecuted that they did not dare to publish a work if its author were obnoxious to the court. Indeed, whoever opposed the government was proclaimed an enemy to his country. Political associations and public meetings were strictly forbidden.   Every popular leader was in personal danger, and every popular assemblage was dispersed. either by threats or by military execution.   That hateful machinery familiar to the worst days of the seventeenth century, was put into motion.   Spies were paid; witnesses were suborned; juries were packed.   The coffee-houses, the inns, and the clubs were filled with emissaries of the government, who reported the most hasty expressions of common conversation. If by these means no sort of evidence could be collected, there was another resource which was unsparingly used.   For, the habeas corpus act being constantly suspended, the Crown had the power of imprisoning without inquiry and without limitation any person offensive to the ministry, but of whose crime no proof was attempted to be brought."

Sir, why are you, why am I out of the vaults of a dungeon, and standing on this floor to-day?   Not because we are guilty of no offence; not because the broad shield of the law interposes its protection, but simply because the Executive has not yet seen fit and proper in the exercise of his absolute and unrestrained will to lay us in irons.   This is the ultimate climax of despotic power.   Each one of the twenty millions of people within the control of the United States holds his or her tenure to personal liberty — the right to walk the green earth, to breathe the air, and look at the sun — not by virtue of a free constitution, but dependent upon the clemency and pleasure of one man.   May I not be arrested to-night?   May not you or any one else to-morrow?   Has it not been done in more than a thousand instances, and have not the courts, and the laws been powerless to save?   While I am now speaking, may not some minion who licks the hand of power, and whom it would honor to call a slave, be preparing notes from which to testify against me before a military commission?   Have we in the West forgotten Burnside, and the infamy of his reign in our midst?   Will the inhabitants of the western circuit in England ever forget the monster Jeffries and the murder of Alice Lisle? Will some poor, crawling, despised sycophant and tool of executive despotism dare to say that I shall not pronounce the name of Vallandigham? The scandal and stigma of his condemnation and banishment have filled the civilized world; and the Lethean and oblivious waves of a thousand years will not wash away the shame and reproach of that miserable scene from the American name. Some members on the other side of this chamber have attacked with fierce clamor the great American statesman and the Christian gentleman who suffers his exile in the cause of liberty on a foreign soil. So the basest cur that ever kennelled may bay, at the bidding of his master, the caged lion in the distance. Protract this iniquity, this crime, as long as you will, however, the judgment of history will at last overwhelm you with an insufferable odium, as certainly as the streams of truth emanate from beneath the great white throne of God. "Establish justice!" "Secure the blessings of liberty!" Oh! bitter mockery. Justice has been dethroned and the blessings of liberty annihilated. There is not one square mile of free soil in the American Republic. It is slave territory from the Aroostook to the Columbia. Every man in all that vast expanse may be reduced in an instant to hopeless bondage, every home may be broken open and pillaged, every dollar's worth of property may be swept into that yawning and bottomless gulf — the national treasury; and all under the sanction of the principles and practices daily exemplified by the administration which now hurls us on to ruin.

But the "domestic tranquillity," has it been insured? When the present party came into power the road to an honorable peace on the basis of the Union was still open. Before the inauguration of Mr. Lincoln his friends and supporters held the issues of life and death, peace and war in their hands in this capitol. The records of the last session of the 36th Congress are immortal. They cannot perish; and as the woes and calamities of the people thicken and magnify by the frightful war in which we are engaged, they increase in value to posterity more rapidly than the leaves of the Sybilline book. The baleful brood of political destructionists who now unhappily possess the high seats of national authority did not then want public tranquillity. They invoked the storm which has since rained blood upon the land. They courted the whirlwind which has prostrated the progress of a century in ruins. They danced with a hellish glee around the bubbling cauldron of civil war and welcomed with ferocious joy every hurtful mischief which flickered in its lurid and infernal flames. Compromise, which has its origin in the love and mercy of God; which made peace and ratified the treaty on Calvary between heaven and the revolted and rebellious earth; which is the fundamental basis of all human association, and by which all governments the world ever knew have been created and upheld; compromise, which fools pronounce a treasonable word, and skillful knaves cover with reproach, because they are enriching themselves at the expense of the national sorrow and blood, was discarded by the North and accepted by the South when offered by Mr. Crittenden. By it domestic tranquillity could have been ensured. But an ulterior and destructive spirit ruled the hour and flooded the nation with misery. And since the breaking up of the fountains of the great deep who of this party have labored to tranquillize our disordered affairs? Who has endeavored, in the name of Christ and by the omnipotent power of the principles which he left his Father's throne to proclaim and for which he drank the wormwood and the gall on the cross, to expel the cruel and ferocious demon of civil war that has howled so fiercely for the last three years among the tombs of our young and heroic dead? Not one, sir; not one. Wise and Christian measures, looking to reconciliation and peace and union, have been repeatedly spurned by the Executive and this legislative department which he holds in duress. At no distant day, when the horror of this war can no longer be borne, the various propositions which have been made and rejected in behalf of enlightened negotiation and a constitutional restoration will be gathered up and hurled at those in power as an accusation more appalling, an indictment more damning, than was ever levelled against a murderer upon his trial. Nor can they, in that hour of their fear and calamity at which the righteous world will laugh and mock, hide their guilty heads under the assertion that the South will not treat for peace; yes, peace which shall restore the Union under the constitution as it was written by the fathers, and as it has been interpreted by the supreme judicial tribunals. Why came that wasted figure, that gifted child of genius, the pure and elevated Stephens, of Georgia, from Richmond on his way to this capitol in the midsummer of 1863? Was it a trifling cause that moved him? All the world knows that his judgment and his heart clung fondly and to the last to the old government, in whose councils he had won so much honor. It is equally well known that he has never embraced the suicidal doctrine of State secession. The right of revolution is the ground upon which he stands. The malignant portion of the Southern press, too, such mischievous and damaging prints as the "Examiner and Inquirer" at Richmond, and the "Register" at Mobile, who continually cripple the interests and friends of humanity in this baleful contest, assailed Mr. Stephens for his attempt at negotiation, which they averred would lead to reunion. Yet, with these things well known, and perhaps much more, which now slumbers in the secret drawers of the Executive, this great messenger of peace, this most acceptable mediator between an estranged and misled people, was denied a hearing — turned back in silence; and the festival of death commanded to proceed. The book of time in all its ample folds contains no more inhuman or revolting spectacle. Those who love war for the mere sake of war, when the same objects can be better attained by the gentle and holy influences of peace, are monsters of such frightful depravity that the blackest of those murdering ministers, "who in their sightless substance wait on nature's mischief," appear as angels of light and benevolence in the comparison.

Sir, I will not here pause to dwell in detail on the usages of civilized nations in conducting civilized warfare. But I challenge history, that "reverend chronicler of the grave," whether in its sacred or profane records, to produce a parallel to the spirit and temper with which the party now in power has conducted the awful struggle in which we are engaged. Commence at the early daybreak of the world, traverse all time, and explore all space, grope your way among the vast hecatombs of all former wars, examine the gory stains of every battle plain, ransack the archives of kings, cabinets, and councils, and no instance, not one, can be found where a people claiming Christian civilization has waged a war of any kind against any foe in dumb, ferocious silence, without a word, a sign, or a look in behalf of a peaceful solution as long as we have now been engaged in this cruel conflict. " Blessed are the peace-makers," was not spoken for the present administrators of American affairs. They spurn the examples and teachings of all Christian ages and enlightened people. They drink not from the benevolent fountains whose waters were unsealed to gladden and refresh the earth by the divine Nazarene on the Mount of Olives. They lave their lips, rather, in a stream whose waves, more putrid than the river of Egypt when smitten by the rod of Moses, taint the air with pestilence and calamity. Nor are they wholly without models in the past. The boundaries of civilization, it is true, as I have stated, are barren of any precedents for their conduct, but the dark regions of barbarism furnish here and there a ghastly and horrible example of fury, hate, and revenge, which is now followed by the Executive and his partisan supporters. Demons have occasionally, in the mysterious providence of God, visited the earth in the guise of men, to prey upon the human species from the mere love of slaughter and misery. Alaric, the Gothic monster, never treated with his enemies, never negotiated for a peace. The dying groan of the soldier on the field, the bitter wail of the widow and the choking sob of the orphan at home were equally music in his ear. Attila, the fierce Hun, known to history as "the scourge of God," neither sent or received commissioners to discuss and allay the causes of war. He painted upon his banners the sword, and the sword alone, and proclaimed that by that sign, and by it alone, he would conquer. Genghis Khan and Tamerlane, preserved by the pen of the historian for universal execration, found no pursuit so pleasant as calling for more men, more men, more men for the harvest of death, and, like our present Executive, snuffing with jests and ribaldry the warm taint of blood on every gale. The patriots who surrounded these barbarian chiefs spurned with eager indignation all proffers of mediation, all efforts at compromise, all talk of negotiation, just as do now the patriots who are seated on the west side of this chamber, and who pay court for contracts at the west end of the avenue. Nor did Hyder Ali, that more modern incarnation of unconditional exterminating war, regard with favor the suggestions of peace, when pausing for a moment like a cloud of wrath on the brow of the mountain he swept down over the plains of the Carnatic, and smote them with blasts of fire, with indiscriminate woe. Sir, these are your examples. These are they who never said conciliate, but always said crush; who never said harmonize, but who always said destroy; who denounced fraternal affection and embraced the doctrine of subjugation; who never sought to restore peaceful relations with their neighbors, but who always sought to ruin them by confiscation and plunder, whose voice was forever like the voice of Moloch in hell, and the voice of those who now rule this nation, for war, for mere war, and war alone, as a cure for every evil, a remedy for every grievance fancied or real. With what loathing and abhorrence does a Christian world now regard these destroyers of their kind! All countries and every people utter a cry of horror at the mention of their names. No pillar, no monument, no fountain, no grove perpetuates their place in the respect of a single human being that ever lived or died. And yet who will compare the ages in which they enacted their various tragedies to the one in which we live, and call them to such an account as awaits those who in this period of gospel light have fashioned the administration of the American Republic on the principles and practices of unenlightened barbarians?

But I will cease to reason on this point by comparison. I will grasp the naked question which the supporters of this administration have so persistently clamored into the public ear for the last three wretched years. Is it right in itself

to treat with those who are in rebellion, with a view to a
restoration of their allegiance, and thus to ensure the domestic
tranquillity? If we draw an answer from the conduct of this
government in former instances of treasonable resistance to
law that answer is all in favor of negotiation and compromise.
Washington set the example in the case of Pennsylvania, and
Jackson followed it in the more celebrated case of South
Carolina in 1832. In our wars with foreign powers the
same course has uniformly been pursued. And we ourselves were the objects of similar treatment even from the
tyrannical ministry of George III in the days of the Revolution. Commissioners from the Court of England came to our
shores more than once a year during that struggle to treat
for a return of the rebellious colonies to the union of the
British Empire. But I shall not content myself with the
enlightened precedents furnished by the history of our own
and other countries. Is there no higher standard of moral
right to which to appeal? Is the voice of him who spake
as never man spake hushed and stifled by the hoarse cry of
passion and rage? Have those pages which blaze with inspiration and which contain all the principles of national as well
as individual morality and justice lost their light and power
in this unhappy land? Can a government long survive or
hope to escape retributive punishment which blots out the
doctrines of Christ in the regulation of its affairs? Shall a
sneer, the sneer of the Jacobin and the Atheist deter me from
seeking the path of public as well as private duty in the
declared record of the Great Father of us all? Have Robe-
spierre and Marat come from their dishonored graves to
dethrone God and to give us the hideous infidelity of the
French Revolution? Sir, I ask you to go with me to the
unsullied fountain of eternal truth:

"Moreover if thy brother shall trespass against thee, go
and tell him his fault between thee and him alone; if he shall
hear thee, thou hast gained thy brother.

"But if he will not hear thee, then take with thee one or
two more, that in the mouth of two or three witnesses every
word may be established.

"And if he shall neglect to hear them, tell it unto the
church; but if he neglect to hear the church, let him be unto
thee as an heathen man and a publican."

In these brief but comprehensive sentences are embraced
the great principles of social harmony, individual charity, and
national fraternity. They were written by divinity to convey a lesson of humane philosophy into every department of
life and to every succeeding age. They furnish the text for
every treaty of peace which nations ever framed to prevent
the effusion of blood. They inculcate the duty of not one
only, but repeated attempts at reconciliation; and those
attempts, too, upon the part of those who have suffered the
injury. Under the malignant auspices, however, of the present hour in this afflicted country, what a contrast is presented
to these sacred passages! Not only do we refuse to go to our
brother who has committed the trespass, but we reject him
when he offers to come to us.

Sir, I take my stand on these immortal maxims and appeal
to the native justice of the human heart. I appeal to those
instincts of charity and benevolence by which it is allied to
the attributes of deity. The plain people of America, those
who with honest hands earn their daily bread, whose wearing apparel is not purple and fine linen, flashing with dia-
monds and pearls purchased by the blood and tears of millions — to them, in their humble homes, darkened perhaps
by the death of the first-born, I make this solemn invoca-
tion. Before that pure and unselfish tribunal I lodge my

cause in behalf of domestic tranquillity, and tender the Bibl
as authority for the principles which I declare. By the voic
of my own heart, unseduced by gain and unawed by terror
I know what will be the verdict of an incorruptible and fre
people. But there is another class who preside over the min
istrations of this inspired book, and who mingle with thei
offerings to God the poison of political prejudices, befor
whom the cause of humanity, union, and peace need not b
presented. That large portion of the clergy of the land who
claiming to be the chosen agents of the merciful Redeemer,
fill the cup of his sacrament with rancor and vengeance, hear
none of the sweet, angelic tones which plead from every page
of his gospels in favor of that individual and national charity which suffereth long and is kind. They teach their flocks
no longer to hunger and thirst after righteousness, but to hunger and thirst for the blood of their enemies. They ascend
the sacred desk no more to pray that gentle peace like the
dews of heaven may descend upon our wounded and dis-
tracted country, but to declaim in warlike strains in the face
of the Almighty upon the delight which they feel in the
infliction of human agony. They have reversed the order of
the millennium which the Christian world has looked forward
to since the days of the prophets. The one which they hail
in fond anticipation is that in which every ploughshare shall
become a sword, and every pruning-hook a spear; in which
conscription, slaughter, and taxation shall go hand in hand;
"when the keepers of the house shall tremble, and the strong
men shall bow themselves, and the grinders cease because
they are few, and those that look out of the windows be
darkened, and the doors shall be shut in the streets when the
sound of the grinding is low: . . . because man goeth to his
long home, and the mourners go about the streets."

To these men much of the sorrow which now overshadows our homes is properly attributable. They have ever been, and are to-day, the foremost enemies of domestic tranquillity. Agitation on matters pertaining to civil government has been their element. Sedition against laws which conflict with their ignorant and selfish bigotry has been their favorite calling in all countries and in every age. They have a higher law than the Sermon on the Mount; and the word of God is made to fit the Procustean bed of their blind and furious prejudices, which they mistake for conscience. Sir, I here proclaim as a fact to which all history attests, that wherever in the tide of time the ministry of the Most High have assumed as a part of their duties the control of affairs of state and the policy of nations, they have appeared as the advocates of despotism, the friends of high prerogative, the defenders of oppression, the allies of tyranny — obstacles in the pathway of progress, enemies to popular rights, and extortioners of the poor and laboring masses. I might dwell long on the evidence which the old and the new world furnish on this point. That great author and majestic thinker, Buckle, whom I have already quoted, in speaking of the conduct of the political clergy in the reign of James II, says:

"They looked on in silence while the King was amassing the materials with which he hoped to turn a free government into an absolute monarchy. They saw Jeffreys and Kirke torturing their fellow subjects. They saw the jails crowded with prisoners, and the scaffolds streaming with blood. They were well pleased that some of the best and ablest men in the kingdom should be barbarously persecuted; that Baxter should be thrown into prison, and that Howe should be forced into exile."

I pause but for a moment to point to the history of Puritan Massachusetts as a confirmation of my statement on this side

of the ocean. What oppression did a political priesthood fai
to approve? What cruelty did they not instigate and sanc
tion in the early days of that famous colony? They scourged,
seared, cropped, burned, and gibbetted the bodies of those
who were unable to conform their views in all matters, civil
and religious, to the reigning fanaticisms; and then consigned
their souls to the regions of the lost. Carpenter, in his standard history of Massachusetts, a work warmly partial to that
State, says:

"In July, 1656, several Quakers arrived in Massachusetts
from Barbadoes, two of whom were women. Fully aware
of the contemptuous disregard for existing ordinances
indulged in by the more zealous of the sect in England, the
magistrates in Boston brought the law against heresy to bear
upon the intruders and ordered their immediate arrest.
After their persons had been examined for those marks
which were supposed at that period to indicate such as dealt
in witchcraft, no satanic signs being discovered, their trunks
were rifled, and the books found therein ordered to be publicly burned. A brief imprisonment was imposed upon
them, but they were finally released and banished the
colony. Several others who arrived subsequently were sent
back to England by the vessels in which they came. About
the same time a law was passed to prevent their introduction
into the colony, and imposing the penalty of stripes and coer-
cive labor upon all Quakers that should infringe it. . . .
Some of the women were whipped, and several men condemned to lose an ear. . . . When seized they offered no
resistance. Sentenced to be flogged, they yielded with entire
satisfaction their backs to the executioner."

Finding that these atrocious measures were not sufficient
to crush out the liberty of thought, a law was passed, says
the same historian, in 1658, banishing the Quakers from the
United Colonies of New England, and forbidding their
return under pain of death:

"This sanguinary and unjustifiable enactment was carried by one vote only. Various staunch friends of the government strongly protested against it, not only as cruel, but as liable to invite the persecution it sought to avoid. The result soon proved how well grounded was the fear. Marmaduke Stephenson, William Robinson and Mary Dyer courted the danger to which they were exposed and quietly awaited the operation of the law. In September, 1658, they were seized, and, after trial, condemned to be hanged. The sentence was carried into effect upon Robinson and Stephenson, but Mary Dyer was reprieved upon the scaffold, and again thrust from the colony. Resolute in seeking a martyr's death, she returned soon after and was publicly executed on Boston Common."

"Oh! the rarity of Christian charity." Will not some New England clergyman of modern orthodoxy shed at least one tear over the scarlet sins of his own ancestors who assisted in the murder of this poor woman on Boston Common, while he is weeping as if his head was a fountain of waters over the landing of the Dutch ship with slaves at Jamestown?

But again, says the same friendly historian:

"It was at the beginning of this year that many persons of piety and good understanding were again led to believe in the great prevalence of witchcraft in the province. Prominent among the most credulous of these was Cotton Mather, son to the Reverend Increase Mather, for some time past the agent of Massachusetts in England, and himself a clergyman. . . . The alarm of witchcraft was again sounded. The ministers feasted and prayed with the distressed father. The villagers of Salem also fasted and prayed; and the fear of demoniacal influences becoming general, a day of fasting and prayer was specially set apart to be kept by the whole colony. The belief in witchcraft being thus solemnly recognized and fostered, it was not long before the delusion spread across the whole breadth of the province. The number of victims so rapidly increased that many of the colonists, perfectly panic-stricken, became the accusers of others, lest they should be brought under suspicion themselves. The execution at Salem village of Mr. Burroughs, a minister of blameless life, was a terrible instance of the power which the delusion exercised over the strongest minds in the community. For fifteen months this strange belief held full possession of the popular faith. During this period, out of twenty-eight persons capitally convicted of witchcraft, nineteen had been hanged and one pressed to death."

Sir, let not these remarks and records of faithful history be construed into an attack upon the ministers of our divine religion. I have endeavored rather to portray the evil results which flow from a desecration of that high calling. To my mind there is no vocation on this side of the mysterious river which divides time from eternity so lofty, no career of life so serenely beautiful and bordering so closely upon heaven as the benevolent pursuits of him who tenders the cup of salvation to the lips of a fallen world. A halo hovers around his head which tells that he walks in the footsteps of his blessed Master. In the presence of such a man I would stand uncovered and do him reverent homage. And there are many such whose pure and noiseless lives pass almost unheeded by the busy, striving world, but around whom the comforting angels of the Lord encamp by night and by day. In their keeping are all the future hopes of the church — the Christian welfare of mankind. The youth of the land should sit at their feet and learn wisdom, and both young and old should rise up and call them blessed. But in this bright category of human excellence — this high galaxy of stars shining with an unearthly splendor — there is no place for such as take charge of churches by order of the war department, and preach the gospel as commanded by the President of the United States. The vineyards where they labor will never bear the fruits of peace — never smile with domestic tranquillity. Before them I do not plead my cause. From them I expect to hear no voice save the continued and protracted cry of havoc.

But, sir, I will be told by the advocates of force and violence as a remedy, and the sole remedy, for our troubles, that although the South might send commissioners to treat for peace, yet they would accede to no terms save recognition and separation. In support of this view, certain propositions recently offered in the Congress at Richmond are cited. To my mind they indicate a far different conclusion. It is true they do not signify to me that the power of the Southern people is exhausted; that the rebellion is crushed; that a panic of fear prevails in the Southern mind; that a government, whether *de facto* or *de jure,* which can maintain an army of half a million of well-armed men in the field is conquered. I do not see the evidence of all this as some have professed to do every sixty days since the war began; but I do see in these propositions an earnest desire upon the part of the South to conform to the usages of the civilized world, and to bring this unhappy and disastrous conflict to a close by the power of reason. It is true that certain objects are declared for which they desire to negotiate; but does that fact include final results which may grow out of negotiation when once commenced? What nation at war with another ever opened communication for a treaty of peace by proclaiming in advance the precise terms on which it was to be concluded? Such a course peremptorily excludes the very idea of negotiation. Commissioners would have no discretion, and reason and argument would have no room to act. Such is not, in my judgment, the meaning of this movement in the Confederate Congress. Sir, what is this contest? What interests does it involve? They are very distinct and simple when divorced from fanaticism. On the part of those who have kept their allegiance, it is a struggle to maintain the boundaries of the Republic, and thus defeat the ruinous doctrine that a State has a right to secede. On the part of those in rebellion, it is an effort, in their estimation, to preserve the integrity of their local laws, their social institutions, the right to control their domestic affairs free from federal interference. With some, this attempt is made under a claim of the right of secession; others proclaim a revolution, which is the right of all people if grievances sufficient exist as a justification. But the people of the South are united in the objects at which they aim, and if they could be attained in the Union, and without war, would they not gladly embrace and accept them rather than continue in a state of endless hostility, which is destroying the very interests they seek to protect? Why, the gentleman from Ohio [Mr. Garfield] declared a few days ago on this floor, that if the privates of the opposing armies in the field were permitted to come together in peace, they would speedily remove all our troubles; and yet he spoke and voted in favor of taking from even the wives and children of the Southern masses, who he asserts, are thus willing to return to the Union, the last foot of soil, and the last crust of bread by which life is sustained. With such evidence then as this can we justify ourselves before God or man if we fail to respond to the action of the South in favor of negotiation, which promises in advance such happy results? Let all grievances, whether fancied or real, be considered by candid statesmanship. Let there be safe and unrepealable guarantees adopted against those that are found to be real; and those that are fancied will be easily explained away. Five enlightened commissioners from each section, imbued with the spirit of

Christian benevolence, animated by an unselfish love of country and of their fellow men, meeting by the consent and encouragement of their respective authorities, could, and in my solemn and deliberate judgment would, in ninety days agree upon terms which would be acceptable to a large majority of the American people, and by which the Union of these States would be more firmly established than ever before — the lives of millions spared, the hard earnings of the laborer left for him to enjoy, peace and domestic tranquillity restored. I would improve the armistice which winter declares to achieve many bloodless and permanent victories in favor of the Union and the constitution. I would not stop there. I would extend the armistice as long as there was hope of inducing the return of a single State. But suppose negotiation should fail. Then, indeed, would this administration be armed with an argument in favor of war which it has never yet possessed. This fact is well understood by the Executive and his advisers, but they refuse to negotiate because they have reason to believe that the Union would thus be restored and the war ended. But slavery would not thereby be abolished, and the scheme of building up a despotic, centralized federal government would be defeated. The war, therefore, goes on; the young men of the nation are swept into their graves upon the plain of battle, and the old men become slaves to the tax gatherer, not to restore the Union, but to give a worthless liberty to the black man, and to strike down the legal rights and privileges of the white man.

Sir, upon this question of negotiation, concession, compromise and union, I appeal for approval to my own conscience. It sustains me with all the force of a burning conviction of duty. By it I am lifted beyond the reach of partisan malice. I appeal to the people! The voice and humane instincts of honest nature will plead my cause in their hearts. At their hands I fear no evil for the country. They are just and will appreciate a plain and inherent element of right. I appeal to future years. When candor, reason and Christianity sit in judgment on this struggle, every line which records the history of war or peace in all former ages, tells me that their verdict will be in favor of the principles which I advocate. I seize this hour of future triumph by anticipation. That it will come I entertain no more doubt than I do that I breathe the air of life this moment. I appeal, finally, to God before whom I stand, and into whose presence we all hasten to answer for our conduct and our motives. In that awful hour I humbly trust and believe that my feeble efforts to turn aside the devouring edge of the sword; to stay the hand of the great reaper, death; to pause in the horrid work of sending souls to their eternal account without repentance or pardon; to stop bereavement, woe, and tears around every fireside; to brighten the mournful face of the land with the radiance of peace; to reconstruct and restore a fraternal and harmonious Union will meet with the approval of the Father and go far toward relieving the newly liberated and trembling spirit of the terrors which surround it.

But, Mr. Chairman, what other declared purposes of the constitution for the accomplishment of which this government was established have been carried out by the policy and administration of the party now in power? Do they " promote the general welfare ? " With the principles of justice everywhere suppressed, the blessing of liberty annihilated throughout all our borders, and the domestic tranquillity utterly destroyed, it is almost needless to inquire what is left to constitute the general welfare. But it is my painful duty on this occasion not only to show that the principles of free government are dying, rapidly dying before our faces, but that the material prosperity, the absolute physical resources of the country are perishing also. The welfare, the strength, and glory of a nation are dependent in a vast measure upon the extent of its population and the amount of its wealth. Next to the virtue and intelligence of the people their numbers constitute the power and dignity of a State. The ancient commandment and the blessing delivered to the original founders of the human race was to be fruitful, multiply, and replenish the earth. And one of the richest promises to the Patriarchs of old was that their tribes and their descendants should increase until they became as the leaves of the forest and the sands of the seashore. Every public ruler who by wise political and social economy has rapidly swelled the population of his country, holds a place in history as a benefactor of his kind. Every human being is a machine of labor. Each head and each hand is a producer. The busy brain and the active muscle are perpetually adding to the storehouses, the granaries, and the merchant-ships of the world. It was a blessing and not a curse; it was in mercy and not in wrath that man was commanded to eat his bread in the sweat of his face. By obedience to this command the glory of civilization adorns the earth, and commerce penetrates the most distant seas. The fulfilment of this decree redeems the savage face of nature, builds up the great marts of trade, patronizes sciences and letters, erects temples to art and progress, and is a forerunner of the Christian faith. Labor is the fountain of all wealth, and of all happiness. Nations and individuals are alike utterly and entirely dependent upon it for their prosperity. And national pros-

perity is simply the result of individual labor. The humble
and obscure toil of the honest ploughman, who,

> " Homeward plods his weary way "

at nightfall, is the source of all the nation's greatness, the
foundation of all its vast enterprises, the support of all its
boasted revenues; it is the small spring breaking into a
rivulet from the hill side, which flowing on and mingling
with the other waters of its kindred at last swells into an
ocean on whose bosom the destinies of the world are
determined. . . .

Sir, I take leave of the question of the " general welfare."
The bitter hour of a people's bloody sweat and agonizing
tears will soon be here. The mournful shadows of its
funeral pall are already penetrating the once bright and
abundant homes of virtuous labor. The spirit of oppression
is omnipresent in the land, and, like death and famine, none
will escape the pangs which it inflicts. Let each eye which
now beholds the sun take its last look at scenes of plenty and
prosperity. Our fall from bounding wealth and unlimited
resources to pinched and shrunken poverty and cowering
bankruptcy, is as certain and as fatal under our present
policy as the fall of Lucifer, the morning star, from heaven.
And the exclamation of the laborer as he toils in a hopeless
bondage to the public debt may well be as despairing as the
anguish of the lost angel:

> " Farewell happy fields,—
> Where joy forever dwells. Hail horrors, hail
> Infernal world, and thou, profoundest Hell,
> Receive thy new possessor."

And, now, Mr. Chairman, what else remains? What portion of the constitution can yet be found alive? What principle has been spared, preserved, or protected by the

destroyers who rule the nation? Have they provided for the common defence against foreign powers? The Emperor of France tramples the Monroe doctrine disdainfully under his feet. He overthrows the Republic of Mexico, and on its ruins erects an imperial despotism in immediate contact with our borders. A prince of the house of Hapsburg, trained in the courts of Austrian oppression, becomes our closest neighbor. Perhaps it is needless to complain of this near example of one-man power — this European head wearing a crown on North American soil. It will not be long if our present career is unchecked until the terms dictator, king and emperor will be as familiar in Washington as in the palace of St. Cloud.

But, sir, the saddest question embraced within the scope of my remarks, remains to be answered as I draw them to a close. Has the policy pursued for the last three years resulted in the formation of " a more perfect Union ? "

No language that the tongue of man can utter would form so expressive an answer to such a question as a silent survey of the dreadful scene which lies before us. A gulf of blood and tears and all of human agony which the afflicted race of man can know this side of the dread abodes of the damned, divides the suffering and miserable sections of a once fraternal and contented people. Statesmen of Christian faith, imbued with the lofty spirit of him who gave his blessing to the merciful, could again span this horrid chasm and bind together the torn and bleeding ligaments of the Union. But an evil star is raging in our sky, and under its malign power the legislation of the land appears as the frenzied, murderous, disjointed dreams of a madman in his cell. Such a penal code as now stands in the way of the return of the men, women and children of the South to their allegiance, has no

parallel in the annals of the human race. A thousand miles
of gibbets with the dangling halter and the ready executioner; universal confiscation of property to the remotest
period of an innocent posterity; the absolute extermination
of a whole people and the appropriation of the depopulated
country to the unsparing demands of a more than Norman
conquest; the utter extinction of every vestige of our present
form of government by States, all this and infinitely more is
contained in the enactments which already stain the records
of American legislation. But why need I dwell upon these
evidences of disunion? The great leader of the administration on this floor, the gentleman from Pennsylvania
[Mr. Stevens] has deliberately here announced after all our
sacrifices, sorrows, and loss, that the Union of our fathers
is dead, and that he who attempts its resurrection is a criminal instead of a patriot. He goes further and admits all the
seceded States have ever claimed — their nationality. They
have sought in vain in all the four quarters of the earth for
recognition. They find it at last at the hands of those who
speak for the administration on this floor.

Sir, I deny this doctrine. I plant myself on the constitution which recognizes an unbroken Union. I shall stand
there in every vicissitude of fortune, and if I fall it will be
when the people themselves abandon their own constitution.
By the principles of this mighty instrument I expect finally
a restoration of the Union of the States. Every hour which
the party of power prolongs its control of affairs, postpones
the auspicious day, but as I behold the future, it will
assuredly come. Material and indestructible interests unite
every section, except that which prospers on fanaticism.
And I here to-day, in the spirit of one who expects and
desires his posterity and theirs to live together in the ancient

nd honorable friendship of their fathers, warn the Southern
people not to look forward to separation and independence,
ut to embrace every opportunity for co-operation with the
onservative men of the North, who will aid with their lives,
f need be, to secure them all their rights and institutions as
ree and equal citizens of the United States. If this be
done, the approaching presidential election will bring peace,
union and liberty. But if the peaceful popular revolution
f the ballot-box fails to produce these results, then darkness
will settle upon the face of the deep, and the free institutions
f America will exist only on the page of the future historian.
Four years more of our present policy will leave the Repub-
ic an unshapen mass of ruins — a wreck more melancholy
and hopeless than any that strew the pathway of ages. And
here, in this fair young western world, as in all former times,
a despotism will arise from the shattered fragments of self-
government, to which each succeeding generation shall pay
the extorted tribute of its blood and toil.

HARCOURT

SIR WILLIAM GEORGE GRANVILLE VENABLES VERNON HAR
COURT, a distinguished English statesman, the grandson of a former
archbishop of York, was born October 14, 1827, and educated at Trinity
College, Cambridge University, where he won high honors. Called to the
bar at the Inner Temple in 1854, he became queen's counsel in 1866, pro
fessor of international law at Cambridge University in 1869, and wa.
solicitor-general, 1873-74. He entered Parliament as Liberal member for
Oxford in 1868 and was secretary of state for the home department in
1880. On the fall of the Liberal party in 1885 he went out of office, but
on their return to power in January, 1886, he was made chancellor of the
exchequer, to which post he was again appointed in 1892. From 1880 to
1895 he represented Derby in the House of Commons, but has since sat
for West Monmouthshire. He is among the most prominent debaters in
the House and an impressive orator, his oration upon Gladstone before
the Commons being especially memorable. His budget of 1894, which
created a great sensation on its appearance, is usually accounted his
greatest achievement. In 1899 he retired from the Liberal leadership and
now sits in the House as a private member. He was one of the original
contributors to the "Saturday Review," and his "Historicus" letters
on international law to the "Review" and the "Times" were collected
in a volume in 1883.

GOOD WILL TO AMERICA

SPEECH AT BREAKFAST HELD IN LONDON IN HONOR OF
MR. GARRISON, JUNE 29, 1867

SMALL as are the pretensions which, on any account, I
can have to present myself to the attention of this
remarkable assemblage, I have had no hesitation in
answering the call which has just been made upon me by discharging a duty which is no less gratifying to me than I know
it will be agreeable to you — that of proposing that the thanks
of this meeting be offered to the chairman for his presidence
over us to-day Every one who admires Mr. Garrison for the
qualities on account of which we have met to do him honor
on this occasion, must feel that there is a singular appropriate-

ness in the selection of the person [1] who has presided here to-day. No one can fail to perceive a striking similarity — I might almost say a real parallelism of greatness — in the careers of these two eminent persons. Both are men who, by the great qualities of their minds, and the uncompromising spirit of justice which has animated them, have signally advanced the cause of truth and vindicated the rights of humanity. Both have been fortunate enough in the span of their own lifetime to have seen their efforts in the promotion of great ends crowned by triumphs as great as they could have desired, and far greater than they could have hoped. There is no cause with which the name of Mr. Bright has been associated which has not sooner or later won its way to victory.

I shall not go over the ground which has been so well dealt with by those who have preceded me. But though there have been many abler interpreters of your wishes and aspirations to-day than I can hope to be, may I be permitted to join my voice to those which have been raised up in favor of the perpetual amity of England and America. It seems to me that with nations, as well as with individuals, greatness of character depends chiefly on the degree in which they are capable of rising above the low, narrow, paltry interests of the present, and of looking forward with hope and with faith into the distance of a great futurity. And where, I will ask, is the future of our race to be found? I may extend the question — where is to be found the future of mankind? Who that can forecast the fortunes of the ages to come will not answer — it is in that great nation which has sprung from our loins, which is flesh of our flesh and bone of our bone. The stratifications of history are full of the skeletons of ruined kingdoms and of races that are no more. Where

---

[1] John Bright.

are Assyria and Egypt, the civilization of Greece, the universal dominion of Rome? They founded empires of conquest, which have perished by the sword by which they rose. Is it to be with us as with them? I hope not — I think not. But if the day of our decline should arise, we shall at least have the consolation of knowing that we have left behind us a race which shall perpetuate our name and reproduce our greatness. Was there ever parent who had juster reason to be proud of its offspring? Was there ever child that had more cause for gratitude to its progenitor? From whom but us did America derive those institutions of liberty, those instincts of government, that capacity of greatness, which has made her what she is, and which will yet make her that which she is destined to become? These are things which it becomes us both to remember and to think upon. And, therefore, it is that, as our distinguished guest, with innate modesty, has already said, this is not a mere personal festivity — this is no occasional compliment. We see in it a deeper and wider significance. We celebrate in it the union of two nations. While I ask you to return your thanks to our chairman, I think I may venture also to ask of our guest a boon which he will not refuse us. We have a great message to send, and we have here a messenger worthy to bear it. I will ask Mr. Garrison to carry back to his home the prayer of this assembly and of this nation that there may be forever and forever peace and good will between England and America. For the good will of America and England is nothing less than the evangel of liberty and of peace. And who more worthy to preside over such a gospel than the chairman to whom I ask you to return your thanks to-day? I beg to propose that the thanks of the meeting be given to Mr. Bright.

BAYARD

THOMAS FRANCIS BAYARD, a noted American statesman, whose father, grandfather, and great-grandfather had represented Delaware in the national Senate, was born in Wilmington, Delaware, October 29, 1828. He was educated at a private school in Flushing, Long Island, and after studying law with his father was admitted to the bar in 1851 and began the practice of his profession in his native city. He entered Congress in 1869 as successor in the Senate to his father, James A. Bayard, and served there continuously until 1885, leading the Democratic minority for much of that period. He served on many congressional committees, and was a member of the electoral commission in 1876-77. During the four years of President Cleveland's first administration Bayard was secretary of state, and after four more years passed in the exercise of his profession at Wilmington was appointed the first ambassador to Great Britain in 1893. His social tact and his eloquence made him popular in England. He returned to the United States on the expiration of his term of office in March, 1897, and died at Dedham, Massachusetts, September 28, 1898. Bayard was a man of the most scrupulous integrity, who commanded the respect of all parties. A number of his speeches were issued singly, but no collection has been made.

ON THE UNITED STATES ARMY

[From an address on "Unwritten Law," delivered before the Phi Beta Kappa Society of Harvard University, June 28, 1877.]

THE army of the United States, like the militia of the several States, is the creation of their respective legislation; like the " princes and lords " of Goldsmith's verse,—

"A breath can make them, as a breath hath made."

" He has kept among us, in times of peace, standing armies, without the consent of the legislature," was one of the facts justifying revolution, " submitted to a candid world," by the founders of this government. So long as human nature remains unchanged, the final argument of force cannot be disregarded; but, outside and beyond the will of the people expressed by law, an American army cannot exist; it is but their instrument for their own service. It is wholly dependent upon them; and they are never dependent upon it, and never will be while civil liberty exists in substance among us.

When called into existence, the army represents the military spirit of the whole nation, and is supported by the enthusiasm and pride of all. It is composed of American valor, skill, and energy, and is dedicated to the glory of our common country, whose history contains no brighter pages than those which record the naval and military achievements of her sons; but neither army nor navy stands now, nor ever did, nor ever will, toward the American people in the relation of policemen to a turbulent crowd. And those who would wish to see it placed in such an attitude, and employed in such work, are short-sighted indeed, and little regard the true dignity of the American soldier, or the real security of the American citizen.

The army of the United States is born of the martial spirit of a brave people, and is the product of national courage. This hall is hallowed as a memorial of the valor and devotion of those gallant youths who made themselves part of the army, at a time when they felt their country needed their service, and who freely offered up their lives upon the altar of patriotism.

" O, those who live are heroes now, and martyrs those who sleep."

Their surviving companions have returned to the paths of civil life, and the community is gladdened by their presence and strengthened by their example. If, to-morrow, the individuals who compose the army of the United States should return to the occupations of civil life, they would be quietly engulfed in the great wave of humanity which rolls around them, and the true forces of the government would move on in their proper orbits as quietly and securely as before the event.

Louis XIV of France, " Le grand Monarque,"— of whom it was truly said, " his highest praise was that he supported the stage-trick of royalty with effect,"— caused his cannon to be cast with the words, " *Ultima ratio regum;* " and his apothegm has so far advanced that in our day cannon seem, not the last, but the first and only, argument of royal government in Europe.

In the maze of strife, armed diplomacy, and exhausting warfare, in which all Europe now seems about to be involved, how just the picture drawn by Montesquieu nearly a century and a half ago!

" A new distemper has spread itself in Europe, infecting our princes, and inducing them to keep up an exorbitant number of troops. It has its redoublings, and of necessity becomes contagious; for as soon as one prince augments his forces the rest, of course, do the same, so that nothing is gained thereby but public ruin. Each monarch keeps as many armies on foot as if his people were in danger of being exterminated, and they give the name of peace to this effort against all."

But a few weeks ago at Berlin, during a debate in the Imperial Parliament in relation to an increased grant of new captaincies of their army, a remarkable speech was made by General Von Moltke, the venerable master of the science of warfare. The telegram says:

" He insisted on the necessity of the grant. He said he wished for long peace, but the times did not permit such hope. On the contrary, the time was not far distant when

every government would be compelled to strain all it
strength for securing its existence. The reason for this wa
the regretable distrust of governments toward each other
France had made great strides in her defences. Uncom
monly large masses of troops were at present between Pari
and the German frontier. Everything France did for he
army received the undivided approval of her people. Sh
was decidedly in advance of Germany in having her *cadre*
for war ready in times of peace. Germany could not avoic
a measure destined to compensate for it."

Will it not be well for Americans to comprehend full
the importance of the confession contained in this speech

To-day the consolidated Empire of Germany is confessedly
the best organized and equipped military power on the globe

To reach this end every nerve has been strained, every
resource of that people freely applied. The idea of military
excellence, like the rod of Aaron, has swallowed up all others
all others have bent to its service, until upon the shoulder
of every man within her borders capable of bearing arms, the
hand of the drill-sergeant has been laid, and from centre
to circumference of the empire centralized military power
reigns supreme.

Whatever of unqualified success a victory of arms can
yield, surely it was achieved by Germany in her last memorable campaign against France. And history nowhere else
exhibits in such completeness and precision the mathematical
demonstration of successful scientific warfare.

With a rapidity and fulness scarcely credible, the student
of history saw the "whirligig of time bring in his revenges,"
whilst the disciples of military art witnessed demonstrations
of the problems of war executed upon a scale and with a
steady and intelligible certainty that approached the
marvellous.

Never was a military campaign more completely and at
l points successful,— even to the conquest and dismember-
ent of the hostile territory as a safeguard for the future,
d the exaction of enormous tribute by way of pecuniary
imbursement from the vanquished. Let us note well the
uit of it all, and learn, so far as we may by the costly
perience of others, what are the consequences of such a
stem and policy. Does it secure peace, prosperity, and
anquil happiness? Let the victor answer.

It is Von Moltke, one of the chief architects of the system,
mself who confesses,— even whilst the garlands of his
eat triumph are yet unfaded on his brow,— that he "longs
r peace, but the times do not permit such hope. That
ery government is soon to be compelled to strain all its
rength for securing its existence."

To the worshippers of military power and the believers
armed force as the chief instrumentality of human govern-
ent I commend Von Moltke's speech.

If perfected military rule brings a people to such a pass,
ay Heaven preserve our country from it.

Well may we exclaim with the sightless apostle of English
erty,—

"What can war, but endless war still breed."

Even victory must have a future and the only victories
iich can have permanence, and the fruits of which grow
ore secure with time, are those of justice and reason; those
mere force are almost certain to contain self-generated
eds for their own subsequent reversal.

The safety and strength of our American government con-
sts in the self-reliant and self-controlling spirit of its
ople.

It was their courage, their intelligence, their virtues, th
enabled our forefathers to build it up; and the same qualiti
and our sense of its value will inspire their descendants wi
love and courage to defend it.

> "Full flashing on our dormant souls the firm conviction comes
> That what our fathers did for theirs—we would for our homes."

In 1789, no sooner was the original constitution of o
government adopted than the several States and their peop
hastened unanimously to declare in a second article of amen
ment that,

" A well-regulated militia being necessary to the securi
of a free state, the right of the people to keep and bear ar
shall not be infringed."

And by article third,

" No soldier shall, in time of peace, be quartered in a
house without the consent of the owner; nor in time of wa
but in a manner to be prescribed by law."

The right of the people to bear arms was thus sedulous
guarded, and the necessary security of a free state w
declared to be a " well-regulated militia." By the fi
article of the original constitution, power was given
Congress to raise and support armies, but coupled with t
express condition that no appropriation of money to that p
pose should be made for a longer period than two yea
When delegating power to Congress to call forth the mili
to execute the laws of the Union, and suppress insurrecti
and invasion, the power was expressly reserved to the Stat
respectively, to appoint their own officers, and to train t
militia according to the discipline prescribed by Congre
Thus it will be seen that in the martial spirit of a fr

eople, and in their right to bear arms, the founders of our
overnment reposed their trust, and experience has proved
ow wisely.

The army of the United States is our honorable instrument of self-defence, and its organization, its numbers, its
mployment, are to be regulated wholly by law. The mili-
ry is at all times to be subordinate to the civil authority,
nd dependent upon law for its powers, and the prescription
of its duties.

The existence or non-existence of an army makes no change
in the character or methods of our government. It would
be difficult to imagine a more unwarranted, and, to our
American ear, more offensive statement than that "without
the army the American people would be a mob."

The army and navy of the United States will be maintained in such strength as convenience, or the necessity of
the government, shall dictate; and they will be held in the
respect and honor due to valiant and faithful public servants,
but there must be no confusion in the public mind as to the
nature and proper theatre of their duties, and their true
relation to their fellow citizens.

If erroneous ideas on this subject are beginning to take
shape and find expression among us, let them be quietly
but effectually discouraged.

Military force is always to be regarded with jealousy by
people who would be free.

It is only by military force that usurped power can have
its pretensions enforced.

All history tells us that those who aspire to extraordinary
power and dominion seldom trouble themselves about anything other than armies to enforce their pretensions, always
aided by the possession of the longest sword.

BAYARD

And here, almost in the shadow of Bunker Hill, wh
words so befitting this grave topic, and the words of wh
man so proper to be recalled and heeded, as those of th
patriot Webster, uttered four-and-thirty years ago, upon th
completion of the monument there erected to the valor
the citizen-soldiers of America?

" Quite too frequent resort is made to military force; an
quite too much of the substance of the people is consume
in maintaining armies, not for defence against foreig
aggression, but for enforcing obedience to domestic autho
ity. Standing armies are the oppressive instruments f
governing the people in the ranks of hereditary and arbitrar
monarchs.

"A military republic, a government founded on moc
elections, and supported only by the sword, is a movemen
indeed, but a retrograde and disastrous movement, from th
regular and old-fashioned monarchical systems.

"If men would enjoy the blessings of the republica
government, they must govern themselves by reason,
mutual counsel and consultation, by a sense and feeling
general interest, and by an acquiescence of the minority
the will of the majority properly expressed; and above a
the military must be kept, according to our bill of rights,
strict subordination to the civil authority.

" Wherever this lesson is not both learned and practise
there can be no political freedom. Absurd and preposterov
is it, a scoff and satire on free forms of constitutional libert
for frames of government to be prescribed by military lea
ers, and the right of suffrage to be exercised at the poi
of the sword."

The grandeur and glory of our Republic must have its ba
in the interests and affections of our whole people; th
must not be oppressed by its weight, but must see in it t
work of their own hands, which they can recognize a
uphold with an honest pride, and which every emotion th
influences men will induce them to maintain and defend.

They must feel in their hearts "the ever-growing and
eternal debt which is due to generous government from
protected freedom."

Silently and almost imperceptibly the generations succeed
each other, and at the close of every third lustrum it is
startling to mark what a new body of men have come into
the rank of leadership in our public affairs.

How few of those who to-day guide and influence public
measures did so fifteen years ago.

While it may not be in the power of leading men to control the decision of issues, it is in a great degree within their
ability to create issues, by pressing forward subjects for
public consideration; and herein lies much of the power of
the demagogue, that pest of popular government, who, seeking only his own advancement, adroitly presents topics to the
public calculated only to arouse their passions and prejudices,
to the neglect of matters really vital.

Despite the almost perfect religious liberty in this country, the passions of sectarianism and the prejudices insepa-
rable from such a subject are always to be discovered floating
on the surface of society, ready to be seized upon by the
shallow and unscrupulous.

The embers of such differences among mankind are never
old, and the breath of the demagogue can always fan them
into flame, until the placid warmth of religion, instead of
gently thawing the ice around human hearts, and imparting
a glow of comfort to the homes of a happy community,
becomes a raging conflagration in which the peace and good
will of society are consumed.

In a country so vast in its area, and differing so widely
in all the aspects of life and occupation of its inhabitants,
antagonism of interest, rivalry in business, and misunder-

standings are frequently and inevitably to be expected; and
the constant exercise of conciliation and harmony is called
for to accommodate differences and soothe exasperation.

It is in the power of unscrupulous self-seekers to raise such
issues as shall involve, not the real interest and welfare of
their countrymen, but their passions only, which are easily
kindled, and can leave nothing but the ashes of disappoint
ment and bitterness as the residuum.

The war between the good and evil influences in human
society will never cease, and the champions of the former
can never afford to lean idly on their swords, or slumber in
their tents.

All around us we see successful men, vigorous and able,
but unscrupulous and base, who have engraved success alone
upon their banners, and as a consequence do not hesitate
to trail them in the dust of low action, and stain them with
disrepute, in pursuit of their object.

They keep within the pale of the written law, having its
words on their lips, but none of its spirit in their hearts.
Audacity and a self-trumpeting assurance are their characteristics. They reach a bad eminence, and contrive to
maintain it, by all manner of self-advertisement; utterly
immodest and indelicate, but successful in keeping them
selves in the public eye. To them, politics is a mere game
in which stratagem and finesse are the means, and self
interest and personal advancement the end. Great aid is
given to such characters by the public press, whose columns
too often laud their tricky, shifty action, or at least give it
the publicity it desires, without accompanying it with the
condemnation it deserves.

How shall such influences be overcome? How shall we
purge places of public station of men whose open boast i

that they may be proven to be knaves, but cannot be called
" fools ? "

Nothing can effect this but the unwritten law, which
shall create a tone on national honesty, truthfulness and
honor, to which the people will respond, and which will compel at least an outward imitation of the virtues upon which
it is founded.

The armor of the Roman soldier covered only the front of
his body. The cuirass shielded his breast, but his back was
left unprotected. Each man felt himself to be the representative of the valor and good fame of his legion and his
country.

The unwritten law of honor forbade him to turn his back
upon danger, and thus became his impenetrable shield.

Such is the spirit and such are the laws that constitute
the true safeguards of a nation against dangers from within
and without.

SCHURZ

CARL SCHURZ, a distinguished American statesman and orator, was born at Liblar, near Cologne, Prussia, March 2, 1829. His parents were Catholics and peasants, but he received an excellent education at Bonn University. After a romantic career as a revolutionist, he was exiled from his native country. He came to the United States in 1852 and settled in Watertown, Wisconsin. He was studious and ambitious and in 1858 was nominated for the second place on the State ticket of Wisconsin, but was defeated. He was a delegate to the Republican national convention at Chicago in 1860, and, on the election of President Lincoln, was given the mission to Spain. At the outbreak of the Civil War he entered the Union army as a brigadier-general. In 1865-66 he was Washington correspondent of the New York "Tribune." In 1866 he founded the "Post" at Detroit, Michigan, and the following year became an editor of the "Westliche Post" of St. Louis. He was chairman of the Republican convention of 1868, which nominated Grant, and in 1869 was elected United States senator from Missouri. He became a leader in the Republican party and started the "Liberal Republican" movement in 1871. In 1877 President Hayes appointed him secretary of the interior. He was an active opponent of James G. Blaine and supported Grover Cleveland in the presidential campaigns of 1884, 1888, and 1892. In 1881 he was made editor-in-chief of the New York "Evening Post," but resigned in 1883 to become the New York agent for a German steamship line. In 1892 he began his contributions to the editorial page of "Harper's Weekly." He was president of the National Civil Service Reform League and a profound student of public affairs. Among his most famous speeches are "The Irrepressible Conflict" (1858); "The Doom of Slavery" (1860); "The Abolition of Slavery as a War Measure" (1862). His publications include a volume of speeches and a "Life of Henry Clay."

ARRAIGNMENT OF STEPHEN A. DOUGLAS

DELIVERED IN SPRINGFIELD, MASSACHUSETTS, JANUARY 4, 1860

WHEN great political or social problems, difficult to solve and impossible to put aside, are pressing upon the popular mind, it is a common thing to see a variety of theories springing up, which purport to be unfailing remedies, and to effect a speedy cure. Men, who look only at the surface of things, will, like bad physicians,

(9048)

pretend to remove the disease itself by palliating its most violent symptoms, and will astonish the world by their inventive ingenuity, no less than by their amusing assurance. But a close scrutiny will in most cases show that the remedies offered are but new forms of old mistakes.

Of all the expedients which have been invented for the settlement of the slavery question, Mr. Douglas's doctrine of popular sovereignty is certainly the most remarkable, not only by the apparent novelty of the thing, but by the pompous assurance with which it was offered to the nation as a perfect and radical cure.

Formerly, compromises were made between the two conflicting systems of labor, by separating them by geographical lines. These compromises did, indeed, produce intervals of comparative repose, but the war commenced again, with renewed acrimony, as soon as a new bone of contention presented itself. The system of compromises as a whole proved a failure.

Mr. Douglas's doctrine of popular sovereignty proposed to bring the two antagonistic elements into immediate contact, and to let them struggle hand to hand for the supremacy on the same ground. In this manner, he predicted the slavery question would settle itself in the smooth way of ordinary business. He seemed to be confident of success; but hardly is his doctrine, in the shape of a law for the organization of Territories, put upon the statute book, when the struggle grows fiercer than ever, and the difficulties ripen into a crisis.

This does not disturb him. He sends forth manifesto upon manifesto, and even during the State campaign of last fall, he mounts the rostrum in Ohio, in order to show what he can do; and, like a second Constantine, he points his finger

at the great principle of popular sovereignty, and says to his
followers: "In this sign you will conquer."

But the tendency of events appeared unwilling to yield to
his prophecy. There seemed to be no charm in his command; there was certainly no victory in his sign. He had
hardly defined his doctrine more elaborately than ever before,
when his friends were routed everywhere, and even his great
party is on the point of falling to pieces. The failure is
magnificently complete.

There certainly was something in his theories that capti-
vated the masses. I do not speak of those who joined their
political fortunes to his, because they saw in him a man who
some day might be able to scatter favors and plunder around
him. But there were a great many, who, seduced by the
plausible sound of the words "popular sovereignty," meant
to have found there some middle ground, on which the rights
of free labor might be protected and secured, without exasper-
ating those interested in slave labor.

They really did think that two conflicting organizations of
society, which are incompatible by the nature of things,
might be made compatible by legislative enactments. But
this delusion vanished. No sooner was the theory put to a
practical test, when the construction of the Nebraska bill
became no less a matter of fierce dispute than the construction of the constitution had been before.

Is this pro-slavery, or is it anti-slavery? it was asked.
The South found in it the right to plant slave labor in the
Territories unconditionally, and the North found in it the
right to drive slavery out of them. Each section of the country endeavored to appropriate the results of the Nebraska
bill to itself, and the same measure, which was to transfer
the struggle from the halls of Congress into the Territories,

transferred it from the Territories back into Congress; and there the Northern and the Southern versions of the Nebraska bill fight each other with the same fury with which the Southern and Northern versions of the constitution have fought each other before. What does the constitution mean in regard to slavery? That question remains to be settled. What does the Nebraska bill mean? This question depends upon the settlement of the former.

Of all men, Mr. Douglas ought to be the first to know what the true intent and meaning of the Nebraska bill and the principle of popular sovereignty is. He is said to be a states-man, and it must be presumed that his measure rests upon a positive idea; for all true statesmanship is founded upon positive ideas.

In order to find out Mr. Douglas's own definition of his own "great principle," we are obliged to pick up the most lucid of his statements as we find them scattered about in numerous speeches and manifestoes. After multifarious cruisings upon the sea of platforms and arguments, Mr. Douglas has at last landed at the following point:

"A slave," says he, in his famous "Harper's Magazine" article, "a slave, within the meaning of the constitution, is a person held to service or labor in one State, ' under the laws thereof '— not under the constitution of the United States, or under the laws thereof, nor by virtue of any Federal authority whatever, but under the laws of the particular State where such service or labor may be due."

This is clear; and with his eyes firmly fixed upon the people of the North, he goes on:

"If, as Mr. Buchanan asserts, slavery exists in the Terri-tories by virtue of the constitution of the United States, then it becomes the imperative duty of Congress, to the perform-ance of which every member is bound by his conscience and

his oath, and from which no consideration of policy or expe
diency can release him, to provide by law such adequate and
complete protection as is essential to the enjoyment of an
important right secured by the constitution — in one word
to enact a general slave code for the Territories."

But Mr. Douglas is not satisfied with this. In order to
strengthen his assumption, and to annihilate Mr. Buchanan's
construction of the Nebraska bill still more, he proceeds:

" The constitution being uniform everywhere within the
dominions of the United States, being the supreme law of
the land, anything in the constitutions or laws of any of the
States to the contrary notwithstanding, why does not slavery
exist in Pennsylvania, just as well as in Kansas or in South
Carolina, by virtue of the same constitution, since Pennsylvania is subordinate to the constitution in the same manner
and to the same extent as South Carolina and Kansas ? "

Just so. Mr. Douglas having been so positive, he cannot
deny us the privilege of making a few logical deductions
from his own premises. We expect him to proceed in the
following manner:

" Since a slave is held under the laws of a State, and not
under the constitution or the laws of the United States,
slavery exists only by virtue of local law."

Or, as the Court of Appeals of Kentucky expressed it,

" The right to hold a slave exists only by positive law of
a municipal character, and has no foundation in the law of
nature, or the unwritten and common law."

If slavery cannot exist except by virtue of local law of a
municipal character, it follows, as an irresistible consequence, that a slaveholder cannot hold a slave as property
in a Territory where there is no local law of a municipal
character establishing that right of property. And, further,

ıe right to hold a slave having no foundation in the law of
ature, or the unwritten and common law, we are forced to
ıe conclusion that a slave, brought by his owner upon the
ɔil of a Territory before the Territorial legislature have
ɹacted laws establishing slavery, becomes of necessity free,
ɔr there is no local law of a municipal character under which
e might be held as a slave. This principle is recognized by
ɹe decisions of several Southern courts. Having gone so
ar (and, indeed, I cannot see how a logical mind can escape
ıese conclusions from Mr. Douglas's own premises),
Ir. Douglas would be obliged to define his popular sov-
reignty to be the right of the people of a Territory, repre-
ɛnted in the Territorial legislature, to admit slavery by
ositive enactment, if they see fit, but it being well under-
tood that a slaveholder has not the least shadow of a right
ɔ take his slave property into the Territory before such
ositive legislation has been had. This definition would
ave at least the merit of logical consistency.

But what does Mr. Douglas say? " Slavery," so he tells
s in his " Harper's Magazine " article, " slavery being the
reature of local legislation, and not of the constitution of the
Jnited States, it follows that the constitution does not estab-
ish slavery in the Territories beyond the power of the people
ɔ control it by law."

What? The constitution does not establish slavery in the
'erritories beyond a certain something! What does that
ıean? If slavery is the creature of local law, how can the
onstitution, by its own force, permit slavery to go into a
'erritory at all?

Here is a dark mystery — a pitfall; and we may well
ake care not to fall into the trap of some sophistry. Why
ɔes he not speak of the admission of slavery by positive

enactments? Why not even of the power of the people to exclude it by law? We look in vain for light in "Harper's Magazine" (and is it, indeed, true, what Judge Black intimates, that that article is one of the obscurest documents by which ever a politician attempted to befog his followers?) but we may gather Mr. Douglas's real opinion from another manifesto preceding this. In his New Orleans speech, delivered after his recent success in Illinois, he defined his position, in substance, as follows:

"The Democracy of Illinois hold that a slaveholder has the same right to take his slave property into a Territory as any other man has to take his horse or his merchandise."

What? Slavery is the creature of local law, and yet a slaveholder has the right to take his slave property into a Territory before any local law has given him that right? A slave does not become free when voluntarily brought by his owner upon the soil of a Territory where no positive local law establishing slavery exists. How is this possible? How can even the elastic mind of a Democratic candidate for the Presidency unite these contradictory assumptions?

And yet there it stands, and nothing that Mr. Douglas ever said can be more unequivocal in its meaning. And here again we may claim the privilege of drawing a few logical deductions from Mr. Douglas's own premises. If, as Mr. Douglas distinctly and emphatically tells us, a slaveholder has a right to take his slave, as property, into a Territory, and to hold him there as property, before any legislation on that point is had, from what source does that right arise?

Not from the law of nature, for the right to hold a slave is " unfounded in the law of nature, and in the unwritten and common law; " and even Mr. Douglas, little as he may care about nature and her laws, will hardly dare to assert that the system of slave labor is the natural and normal condition of society. It must then spring from positive law. But from what kind of positive law? Not from any positive law of a local and municipal character, for there is none such in the Territory so far. Where is its source, then? There is but one kind of positive law to which the Territories are subject before any local legislation has been had, and that is the constitution of the United States.

If, therefore, Mr. Douglas asserts, as he does, that a slaveholder has a right to take his slave as property into a Territory, he must, at the same time, admit that, in the absence of local legislation positively establishing slavery, the constitution of the United States, the only valid law existing there, must be the source of that right. What else does Mr. Buchanan assert, but that slavery exists in the Territories by virtue of the Federal constitution? Where is, then, the point of difference between Mr. Buchanan and Mr. Douglas? Why all this pomp and circumstance of glorious war? Whence these fierce battles between the Montechi and Capuletti of the Democratic camp? Are ye not brothers?

But Mr. Douglas is a statesman (so they are all, all statesmen), and pretends that the constitution does not establish slavery in the Territories, " beyond the power of the people to control it by law."

What does that mean? It means that the people of a Territory shall have the power to embarrass the slaveholder in the enjoyment of his right by " unfriendly legislation."

" The right to hold slaves," says he in another place, " is a worthless right, unless protected by appropriate police regulations. If the people of a Territory do not want slavery, they have but to withhold all protection and all friendly legislation."

Indeed, a most ingenious expedient. But, alas! Here is one of those cases where the abstract admission of a right is of decisive importance. Suppose, for argument's sake, a slave might escape from his owner in a Territory, without being in actual danger of recapture, would that in any way affect the constitutional right of the slaveholder to the possession and enjoyment of his property? I have already quoted Mr. Douglas's own answer to this question.

" If," says he, " slavery exists in the Territories by virtue of the constitution " (that is, if a slaveholder has a right to introduce his " slave property " where there is no other law but the constitution), " then it becomes the imperative duty of Congress, to the performance of which every member is bound by his oath and conscience, and from which no consideration of policy or expediency can release him, to provide by law such adequate and complete protection as is essential to the enjoyment of that important right."

And Mr. Douglas, after having emphatically admitted the right of property in a slave, where that right can spring from no other law but the constitution, then dares to speak of unfriendly legislation. Where is his conscience? Where is his oath? Where is his honor?

But Mr. Douglas says more:

" The constitution being the supreme law of the land, in the States as well as in the Territories, then slavery exists in Pennsylvania just as well as in Kansas and in South Carolina, and the irrepressible conflict is there!"

Ay, the irrepressible conflict is there, not only between the two antagonistic systems of labor, but between Mr. Douglas's own theories; not only in the States and Territories, but in Mr. Douglas's own head.

Whatever ambiguous expressions Mr. Douglas may invent, the dilemma stares him in the face (and here I put myself on his own ground), either slavery is excluded from the Territories so long as it is not admitted by a special act of Territorial legislation, or, if a slaveholder has the right to introduce his slave property there before such legislation is had, he can possess that right by virtue of no other but the only law existing there, the constitution of the United States.

Either slavery has no rights in the Territories, except those springing from positive law of a local or municipal character, or, according to Judge Douglas's own admission, the Southern construction of the constitution and of the principle of popular sovereignty is the only legitimate one, that the constitution, by its own force, carries slavery wherever it is the supreme law of the land, that Congress is obliged to enact a slave code for its protection, and that popular sovereignty means the power of the people to vote for slavery, but by no means against it. There is no escape from this dilemma.

Which side will Mr. Douglas take? Will he be bold enough to say that slavery, being the creature of local law only, is excluded from the Territories in the absence of positive law establishing it; or will he be honest enough to concede that, according to his own proposition in his New Orleans speech, slavery exists in the Territories by virtue of the Federal constitution? He will neither be bold enough to do the first, nor honest enough to do the second; he will be cowardly enough to do neither. He is in the position of that Democratic candidate for Congress in the West, who, when asked: "Are you a Buchanan or a Douglas man?" answered, "I am."

If you ask Mr. Douglas, "Do you hold that slavery is the creature of local law, or that a slaveholder has the right to introduce his slave property where there is no local law?" he will answer, "I do."

Such is Mr. Douglas's doctrine of popular sovereignty. But after having given you Mr. Douglas's own definitions in his own words, I see you puzzled all the more, and you ask me again: "What is it?"

I will tell you what judgment will be passed upon it by future historians, who may find it worth while to describe this impotent attempt to dally and trifle with the logic of things. They will say:

"It was the dodge of a man who was well aware that, in order to be elected President of the United States, the vote of a few northern States must be added to the united vote of the South. Knowing by experience that the Democratic road to the White House leads through the slaveholding States, he broke down the last geographical barrier to the extension of slavery.

"So he meant to secure the South. But in conceding undisputed sway to the slaveholding interests, he saw that he was losing his foothold in the northern States necessary to his election; he availed himself of the irresistible pressure of the Free-State movement in Kansas, and opposed the Lecompton constitution. So he saved his senatorship in Illinois, as the champion of free labor.

"But the South frowned, and immediately after his victory he went into the slaveholding States, and admitted in his speeches that slavery may go into the Territories without a special act of Territorial legislation.

"Believing the South satisfied, and seeing his chances in the North endangered, he wrote his 'Harper's Magazine' essay, assuming that slavery can exist only by virtue of local law. The South frowning again, he endeavored to make his peace with the slaveholders by declaring that he would submit to the Charleston convention, and instructing his nearest friends in the House to vote for the administration candidate for the speakership.

"So he endeavored to catch both sections of the Union successively in the trap of a double-faced sophistry. He tried to please them both in trying to cheat them both. But he placed himself between the logic of liberty on one and the logic of slavery on the other side. He put the sword of logic into the hands of his opponents, and tried to defend himself with the empty scabbard of ' unfriendly legislation.'

"Unfriendly legislation, which in one case would have been unnecessary, in the other unconstituional — the inventi n of a mind without logic, and of a heart without sympathies; recognized on all sides as a mere subterfuge, behind which the moral cowardice of a presidential candidate entrenched itself."

Such will be the verdict of future historians. They will indulge in curious speculations about the times when such doctrines could be passed off as sound statesmanship — a statesmanship, indeed, the prototype of which may be found, not in Plutarch, but in Aristophanes — but they will be slow to believe that there were people dull enough to be deceived by it.

Leaving aside the stern repudiation which Mr. Douglas's popular sovereignty has received at the hands of the people at the last State elections all over the Union, it is a characteristic sign of the times, that even one of his political friends, an anti-Lecompton Democrat, recently went so far as to declare, on the floor of Congress, that he would not vote for Mr. Douglas, if nominated by the Charleston convention, unless a clear and unequivocal construction were affixed to the reaffirmation of the Cincinnati platform. A wise precaution, indeed!

But whatever construction might be given to the Cincinnati platform, what will that gentleman do with the double-faced platform which Mr. Douglas has laid down for himself? What will the abstract pledge of a convention be worth to him, if Mr. Douglas's principles pledge him to nothing? What will he do with a man who, when pressed to take an unequivocal position, is always ready to sneak behind a superior authority, declaring that " these are questions to be settled by the courts? "

Mr. Douglas's situation is certainly a very perplexing one. On one side, he is ostracised by the administration Democracy for his illogical and unconstitutional doctrine, that the legislature of a Territory has control over slavery; and, on the other hand, one of his nearest friends, Mr. Morris, of Illinois, in his recent speech on the President's message, denounces the doctrine that slave property may be carried into the Territories just like other property, as an atrocious " abomination."

Was Mr. Morris not aware that this " abomination " is the identical doctrine advocated by Mr. Douglas in his New Orleans speech? Let Mr. Morris examine the record of Judge Douglas, and he will find out that whatever abominations Mr. Buchanan brings forward in his message, he advocates none that is not a direct logical consequence of Mr. Douglas's own admissions.

I see the time coming when those who rallied around Douglas's colors, because they believed in his principles, will, from his most devoted friends become his most indignant accusers. They are already, unwittingly, denouncing his doctrines, when they intend to defend him; they will not be sparing in direct denunciations as soon as they discover how badly they had been deceived, and how ignominiously they were to be sold. We might, indeed, feel tempted to pity him, if we had not to reserve that generous emotion of our hearts for those who are wrong by mistake and unfortunate without guilt.

Mr. Douglas's ambiguous position, which makes it possible for him to cheat either the North or the South, without adding a new inconsistency to those already committed, makes it at the same time necessary for him to put his double-faced theories upon an historical basis, which relieves him of the necessity of expressing a moral conviction on the matter of slavery either way.

To say that slavery is right would certainly displease the North; to say that slavery is wrong would inevitably destroy him at the South. In order to dodge this dangerous dilemma, he finds it expedient to construe the history of this country so as to show that this question of right or wrong in regard to slavery had nothing whatever to do with the fundamental principles upon which the American Republic was founded.

Dealing with slavery only as a matter of fact, and treating the natural rights of man and the relation between slavery and republican institutions as a matter of complete indifference, he is bound to demonstrate that slavery never was seriously deemed inconsistent with liberty, and that the black never was seriously supposed to possess any rights which the white man was bound to respect.

But here he encounters the Declaration of Independence, laying down the fundamental principles upon which the Republic was to develop itself; he encounters the ordinance of 1787, the practical application of those principles; both historical facts, as stern and stubborn as they are sublime. But as Mr. Douglas had no logic to guide him in his theories, so he had no conscience to restrain him in his historical constructions. To interpret the Declaration of Independence

according to the evident meaning of its words would certainly displease the South; to call it a self-evident lie would
certainly shock the moral sensibilities of the North. So he
recognizes it as a venerable document, but makes the language, which is so dear to the hearts of the North, express
a meaning which coincides with the ideas of the South.

We have appreciated his exploits as a logician; let us follow him in his historical discoveries.

Let your imagination carry you back to the year 1776.
You stand in the hall of the old colonial court house of Philadelphia. Through the open door you see the Continental
Congress assembled; the moment of a great decision is drawing near. Look at the earnest faces of the men assembled
there, and consider what you may expect of them. The
philosophy of the eighteenth century counts many of them
among its truest adepts. They welcomed heartily in their
scattered towns and plantations the new ideas brought forth
by that sudden progress of humanity, and, meditating them
in the dreamy solitude of virgin nature, they had enlarged
the compass of their thoughts, and peopled their imaginations
with lofty ideals. A classical education (for most of them
are by no means illiterate men) has put all the treasures of
historical knowledge at their disposal, and enabled them to
apply the experience of past centuries to the new problem
they attempt to solve.

See others there of a simple but strong cast of mind, whom
common sense would call its truest representatives. Wont to
grapple with the dangers and difficulties of an early settler's
life, or, if inhabitants of young uprising cities, wont to carry
quick projects into speedy execution, they have become
regardless of obstacles and used to strenuous activity. The
constant necessity to help themselves has developed their

mental independence; and, inured to political strife by the continual defence of their colonial self-government, they have at last become familiar with the idea, to introduce into practical existence the principles which their vigorous minds have quietly built up into a theory.

The first little impulses to the general upheaving of the popular spirit — the tea tax, the stamp act — drop into insignificance; they are almost forgotten; the revolutionary spirit has risen far above them. It disdains to justify itself with petty pleadings; it spurns diplomatic equivocation; it places the claim to independence upon the broad basis of eternal rights, as self-evident as the sun, as broad as the world, as common as the air of heaven.

The struggle of the colonies against the usurping government of Great Britain has risen to the proud dimensions of a struggle of man for liberty and equality. Behold, five men are advancing towards the table of the president. First, Thomas Jefferson, whose philosophical spirit grasps the generality of things and events; then Benjamin Franklin, the great apostle of common sense, the clear wisdom of real life beaming in his serene eye; then the undaunted John Adams, and two others. Now Jefferson reads the Declaration of Independence, and loudly proclaims the fundamental principle upon which it rests: "All men are created free and equal!"

It is said; history tells you what it meant. The sceptre of royalty is flung back across the ocean; the prerogatives of nobility are trodden into the dust; every man a king, every man a baron; in seven of the original colonies the shackles of the black man struck off; almost everywhere the way prepared for gradual emancipation. "No recognition of the right of property in man!" says Madison. "Let slavery be abolished by law!" says Washington. Not only the suprem-

acy of Old England is to be shaken off, but a new organizatio
of society is to be built up on the basis of liberty and equality
That is the Declaration of Independence! That is the Amer
can Revolution. All men free and equal! Not even th
broad desert of the Atlantic ocean stops the triumphant shout
Behold, the nations of the Old World are rushing to arms
Bastiles are blown into the dust as by the trumpets of Jerichd
and like a pillar of fire by night and a pillar of cloud by day
the great watchword of the American Revolution shows fo
ever the way to struggling humanity. All men are create
free and equal! Whence the supernatural power in thes
seven words?

Turn your eyes away from the sublime spectacle of 1776
from that glorious galaxy of men whose hearts were larg
enough for all mankind, and let me recall you to the sobe
year of 1857. There is Springfield, the capital of Illinois, on
of those States which owe their greatness to an ordinanc
originally framed by the same man whose hand wrote th
Declaration of Independence. In the Hall of the Assembly
there stands Mr. Douglas, who initiates an eager crowd int
the mysteries of "popular sovereignty." He will tell yo
what it meant, when the men of 1776 said that "all men ar
created free and equal." He says:

"No man can vindicate the character, the motives, an
the conduct of the signers of the Declaration of Independence
except upon the hypothesis that they referred to the whit
race alone, and not to the African, when they declared al
men to have been created free and equal — that they wer
speaking of British subjects on this continent being equal t
British subjects born and residing in Great Britain — tha
they were entitled to the same inalienable rights, and among
them were enumerated life, liberty, and the pursuit of happi
ness. The Declaration of Independence was adopted merel
for the purpose of justifying the colonists in the eyes of th

civilized world in withdrawing their allegiance from the British Crown, and dissolving their connection with the mother country."

What? Is that all? Is that little heap of quicksand the whole substructure on which a new organization of society was to be built? The whole foundation upon which the proud and ponderous edifice of the United States rests? They did, then, not mean all men, when they said all men. They intended, perhaps, even to disfranchise those free blacks who in five of the original thirteen colonies enjoyed the right of voting? They meant but the white race. Oh, no, by no means, the whole white race; not the Germans, not the French, not the Scandinavians; they meant but British subjects. "British subjects on this continent being equal to British subjects born and residing on the other side of the great water!"

There is your Declaration of Independence, a diplomatic dodge, adopted merely for the purpose of excusing the rebellious colonies in the eyes of civilized mankind. There is your Declaration of Independence, no longer the sacred code of the rights of man, but an hypocritical piece of special pleading, drawn up by a batch of artful pettifoggers, who, when speaking of the rights of man, meant but the privileges of a set of aristocratic slaveholders, but styled it "the rights of man," in order to throw dust into the eyes of the world, and to inveigle noble-hearted fools into lending them aid and assistance.

These are your boasted Revolutionary sires, no longer heroes and sages, but accomplished humbuggers and hypocrites, who said one thing and meant another; who passed counterfeit sentiments as genuine, and obtained arms and money and assistance and sympathy on false pretences!

There is your great American Revolution, no longer the great
champion of universal principles, but a mean Yankee trick —
a wooden nutmeg — the most impudent imposition ever prac-
ticed upon the whole world!

That is the way Mr. Douglas wants you to read and to
understand the proudest pages of American history! That is
the kind of history with which he finds it necessary to prop
his mongrel doctrine of popular sovereignty! That is what
he calls vindicating the character and the motives and the
conduct of the signers of the Declaration of Independence.

Thus he did not blush to slander Jefferson, who, when
speaking of his country, meant the world and, when speaking
of his fellow citizens, meant mankind; and Franklin, in whose
clear head theory and practice were the same, and who, having
declared "all men to be created free and equal," became the
first president of the first great Abolition Society; and John
Adams, the representative of that State which abolished
slavery within its limits with one great stroke of legislation;
and Washington, who declared it to be "his fondest wish to
see slavery abolished by law," and affixed to the Declaration
of Independence the broad signature of his heroic sword; and
Madison, who deemed it "absurd to admit the idea of property in man;" and of the framers of the constitution, who
took care not to disgrace that instrument with the word
"slavery," and, before adopting it finally, blotted out from
the extradition clause the word "servitude," avowedly because
it signified the condition of a slave, and substituted the word
"service," avowedly because it signified the condition of a
freeman.

Thus Mr. Douglas dares to speak of all those true men,
who, after having proclaimed their principles in the Declaration, endeavored to introduce them into practical life in

almost every State, in the way of gradual emancipation! That they have failed in this, is it a fault of theirs? It shows not that they were less great and sincere, but that subsequent generations were hardly worthy of so noble an ancestry!

There is Mr. Douglas's version of your history. He despairs of converting you without slandering your fathers. His present doctrines cannot thrive, unless planted in a calumny on the past. He vindicates the signers of the Declaration of Independence! Indeed, they need it sadly. I see the illustrious committee of five rise from their graves, at their head Thomas Jefferson, his lips curled with the smile of contempt, and I hear him say to Mr. Douglas:

"Sir, you may abuse us as much as you please, but have the goodness to spare us with your vindications of our character and motives."

It is a common thing that men of a coarse cast of mind so lose themselves in the mean pursuit of selfish ends as to become insensible to the grand and sublime. Measuring every character and every event in history by the low standard of their own individualities, applying to everything the narrow rule of their own motives, incapable of grasping broad and generous ideas, they will belittle every great thing they cannot deny, and drag down every struggle of principles to the sordid arena of aspiring selfishness, or of small competing interests.

Eighteen hundred years ago, there were men who saw nothing in incipient Christianity but a mere wrangle between Jewish theologians, got up by a carpenter's boy, and carried on by a few crazy fishermen.

Three hundred years ago, there were men who saw in the great reformatory movement of the sixteenth century, not the emancipation of the individual conscience, but a mere fuss kicked up by a German monk who wanted to get married.

Two hundred years ago, there were men who saw in Hampden's refusal to pay the ship money, not a bold vindication of constitutional liberty, but the crazy antics of a man who was mean enough to quarrel about a few shillings.

And now there are men who see in the Declaration of Independence and the American Revolution, not the reorganization of human society upon the basis of liberty and equality, but a dodge of some English colonists who were unwilling to pay their taxes.

But the dignity of great characters and the glory of great events find their vindication in the consciences of the people. It is in vain for demagogism to raise its short arms against the truth of history. The Declaration of Independence stands there. No candid man ever read it without seeing and feeling that every word of it was dictated by deep and earnest thought, and that every sentence of it bears the stamp of philosophical generality.

It is the summing up of the results of the philosophical development of the age; it is the practical embodiment of the progressive ideas, which, very far from being confined to the narrow limits of the English colonies, pervaded the very atmosphere of all civilized countries. That code of human rights has grown on the very summit of civilization, not in the miry soil of a South Carolina cottonfield. He must have a dull mind or a disordered brain, who misunderstands its principles; but he must have the heart of a villain, who knowingly misrepresents them.

Mr. Douglas's ambition might have been satisfied with this ignominious exploit. But the necessities of the popular sovereignty doctrine do not stop there. After having tried to explain away the fundamental principles underlying this Republic, which are hostile to slavery and its extension, Mr. Douglas finds it exceedingly inconvenient to encounter facts which prove, beyond doubt, that these principles, from a mere theoretical existence, rose to practical realization. Popular sovereignty, which is at war with the doctrines of the Declaration of Independence, demands the slaughter of the ordinance of 1787, and Mr. Douglas is up to the task. He does not stop at trifles.

And here we must return to the "Harper's Magazine" manifesto. He leads us through a century of colonial history, in order to show that the people of the colonies claimed the right to legislate on the subject of slavery. And, remarkably enough, all the instances quoted show a uniform tendency adverse to the peculiar institution.

Mr. Douglas then proceeds to discover the germs of his popular sovereignty doctrine in the first congressional legislation concerning the Territories. I will not undertake to criticise that singular historical essay, although some of its statements are such as to make the freshmen of our colleges smile. The "statesman" Douglas does not seem to be aware that the ability to read history ought to precede the attempt to write it.

He leads us back to the Congress of 1784. Mr. Jefferson and his colleagues have just executed the deed of cession of the Northwestern Territory, and the same Mr. Jefferson, as chairman of a committee, then submits "a plan for the temporary government of the Territories ceded or to be ceded by the individual States to the United States."

Mr. Douglas proceeds to describe how the Territorial governments were to be organized, what rights and powers were put into the hands of the people, and how they were to be exercised; and, after having demonstrated that the term "new States" meant the same thing which is now designated by "Territories," he comes to the conclusion that the spirit pervading that plan was in exact consonance with his doctrine of "popular sovereignty."

Mr. Douglas ostentatiously calls this "the Jeffersonian plan." "It was," says he, "the first plan of government for the Territories ever adopted in the United States. It was drawn by the author of the Declaration of Independence, and revised and adopted by those who shaped the issues which produced the Revolution, and formed the foundations upon which our whole system of American government rests."

But Mr. Douglas skips rather nimbly over the significant fact that the same "author of the Declaration of Independence" put into that plan a proviso, excluding slavery from the Territories. Was that a mere accident? Mr. Jefferson showed thereby, conclusively, that, in his opinion, the exclusion of slavery by congressional legislation was by no means inconsistent with the spirit of "popular sovereignty" which Mr. Douglas discovers in the plan of 1784; but this does not disturb Mr. Douglas.

"The fifth article," says he, "relating to the prohibition of slavery, having been rejected by Congress, never became a part of the Jeffersonian plan of government for the Territories, as adopted April 23, 1784."

Although with a large numerical majority in its favor (sixteen to seven), this article did indeed fail to obtain a constitutional majority, the vote of New Jersey not being counted, in consequence of there being but one delegate from that State present; yet it had been drawn up by Mr. Jefferson, introduced by Mr. Jefferson, and sustained by Mr. Jefferson's vote. Nevertheless, Mr. Douglas persists in calling a plan, from which the peculiar Jeffersonian feature had been struck out, the "Jeffersonian plan." This is the play of Hamlet with the character of Hamlet omitted.

"This charter of compact," proceeds Mr. Douglas, "with its fundamental conditions, which were unalterable without the joint consent of the people interested in them, as well as of the United States, then stood upon the statute book unrepealed and irrepealable, when, on the 14th day of May, 1787, the federal convention met at Philadelphia."

Does Mr. Douglas not know that on the 16th of March, 1785, a proposition was introduced in Congress by Rufus King, to exclude slavery from the States described in the resolve of April 23, 1784, and to make this provision part of the compact established by that resolve? Does he not know that this provision, restoring the Jeffersonian feature to the "Jeffersonian plan," was committed, by the vote of eight States against four?

Does he not know that the plan of 1784 never went into practical operation, but was expressly set aside by Congress in 1787? Does he not know that the ordinance of 1787 was the first legislative act ever practically organizing a Territory of the United States, and that one of its most prominent features was the proviso excluding slavery from all the Territories then in possession of the United States?

Mr. Douglas's historical recollections of the ordinance of 1787 seem to be very indistinct. Indeed, he deems it only worthy of an occasional, passing, almost contemptuous notice. He speaks of it as "the ordinance of the 12th of July, 1787, which was passed by the remnant of the Congress of the Confederation, sitting in New York, while its most eminent members were at Philadelphia, as delegates to the federal convention."

For three quarters of a century, people were in the habit of thinking that the ordinance of 1787 was an act of the highest order of importance, but we now learn that it was a rather indifferent affair, passed on an indifferent occasion, by an exceedingly indifferent set of fellows, while the plan of 1784, a mere abstract program, completely overruled by subsequent legislation, is represented as the true glory of the age. How is this?

The reason is obvious. Mr. Douglas belongs to that class of historians who dwell upon those facts which suit their convenience, and unceremoniously drop the rest. I once heard of a Jesuit college where they used a text book of history, in which the French Revolution was never mentioned, while the Emperor Napoleon figured there only as a modest Marquis Bonaparte, who held a commission under Louis XVII, and fought great battles for the glory of the Catholic Church.

So it is with Mr. Douglas and the history of this country. He ignores the universal principles of the Declaration of Independence, and represents the great founders of the Republic as merely paving the way for his "great principles," while a few village politicians get up an obscure ordinance, adverse to the general tendency of things.

But as those Jesuits never could prevent their students from peeping out of their college windows into the wide world, where they perceived a very different state of things, so Mr. Douglas cannot prevent us from travelling out of the yellow covers of "Harper's Magazine," into the open records of history, where we find Mr. Jefferson's anti-slavery clause, although accidentally lost in 1784, strenuously insisted upon by the leading spirits of the Republic, incorporated in the great act of 1787, solemnly reaffirmed by the first Congress under the constitution, and firmly maintained even against the petition of the people of one of the Territories.

This is the true "Jeffersonian plan," the plan which Jefferson framed, voted for, and which was carried out in his spirit; not that mangled report of 1784, which Mr. Douglas wants us to take as the foundation of all Territorial government, because an historical accident happens to coincide with his schemes.

That true Jeffersonian plan rested, indeed, on the principle of popular sovereignty, but it will be conceded that Mr. Jefferson's great principle was as widely different from that of Mr. Douglas as the ordinance of 1787 is different from the Nebraska bill. While Mr. Jefferson's notion of popular sovereignty sprung from the idea that man has certain inalienable rights which the majority shall not encroach upon, Mr. Douglas's doctrine rests upon the idea that the highest development of liberty consists in the right of one class of men to hold another class of men as slaves, if they see fit to do so.

While Mr. Jefferson excluded slavery from the Territories, in order to make room for true popular sovereignty, Mr. Douglas invents his false popular sovereignty in order to make room for slavery. The ordinance of 1787, the true "Jeffersonian plan," was indeed no mere accident, no mere occasional act of legislation. It sprang from the idea, as Madison expressed it, "that republican institutions would become a fallacy where slavery existed;" and in order to guarantee republican institutions to the Territories they excluded slavery.

The ordinance of 1787 was the logical offspring of the principles upon which your independence and your constitution are founded; it is the practical application of the Declaration of Independence on the government of the Territories.

Its very existence sets completely at nought Mr. Douglas's doctrine and historical construction, and the dwarfish hand of the demagogue tries in vain to tear this bright page out of your annals.

The ordinance of 1787 stands written on the very gate-posts of the Northwestern States; written on every grain-field that waves in the breeze, on every factory that dots the course of their rushing waters, on every cottage that harbors thrifty freemen; written in every heart that rejoices over the blessings of liberty.

There it stands, in characters of light. Only a blind man cannot see it; only a fool can misunderstand it; only a knave can wilfully misinterpret it.

Such is Mr. Douglas's principle of popular sovereignty in its logical and historical aspect; apparently adopting the doctrine that slavery is the creature of local law only, and fighting against a congressional slave code, but, on the other hand, admitting the very principle on which protection to slave property becomes a logical necessity; and again assuming the ground that slave property may be introduced where there is no local law, but explaining away the logical consequences of that doctrine by the transparent sophistry of unfriendly legislation; dragging the proudest exploits of American statesmanship into the dust; emasculating the Declaration of Independence, because incompatible with its principles; setting aside the ordinance of 1787, because that stern fact is a conclusive historical argument against it; a jesuitical piece of equivocation and double dealing, unable to stand before the criticism of a logical mind, because it is a mixture of glaring contradictions; unable to stop the war of principles and interests, because it is at war with itself.

It is true, its principal champion worked hard to cover

with bullying boisterousness the moral cowardice from which it sprang; but in vain. He mistakes the motive power which shapes the actions of free nations. Having no moral convictions of his own to stand upon, he could never address himself to the moral sense of the people.

Having no moral convictions of his own! This is a grave charge, but I know what I say. I respect true convictions wherever I find them. Among the fire-eaters of the South, there are men who speak of the moral basis of slavery and believe in it; who speak of the blessings of servitude and believe in it; who assert that slavery is right and believe it.

Atrocious as their errors may be, and deeply as I deplore them, yet I respect their convictions as soon as I find them out. But look into the record of the champion of " popular sovereignty; " scan it from syllable to syllable; and then tell me, you Douglasites of the South, do you find one word there indicating a moral conviction that slavery is right? And you Douglasites of the North, who are in the habit of telling us that you are the true anti-slavery men, and that popular sovereignty will surely work the overthrow of the institution, did your master ever utter a similar sentiment? Do you find in his record one word of sympathy with the down-trodden and degraded? One spark of the humane philosophy of our age? One syllable in vindication of the outraged dignity of human nature? One word which might indicate a moral conviction that slavery is wrong? Not one!

But one thing he does tell you: "I do not care whether slavery be voted up or down!" There is then a human heart that does not care! Sir, look over this broad land, where the struggle has raged for years and years; and across the two oceans, around the globe, to the point where the far

West meets the far East; over the teeming countries where the cradle of mankind stood; and over the workshops of civilization in Europe, and over those mysterious regions under the tropical sun, which have not emerged yet from the night of barbarism to the daylight of civilized life — and then tell me, how many hearts do you find that do not tremble with mortal anguish or exultant joy as the scales of human freedom or human bondage go up or down?

Look over the history of the world from the time when infant mankind felt in its heart the first throbbings of aspiring dignity down to our days when the rights of man have at last found a bold and powerful champion in a great and mighty Republic; where is the page that is not spotted with blood and tears shed in that all-absorbing struggle; where a chapter which does not tell the tale of jubilant triumph or heart-breaking distress as the scales of freedom or slavery went up or down?

But to-day, in the midst of the nineteenth century, in a Republic whose program was laid down in the Declaration of Independence, there comes a man to you and tells you with cynical coolness that he does not care! And because he does not care, he claims the confidence of his countrymen and the highest honors of the Republic! Because he does not care, he pretends to be the representative statesman of this age!

Sir, I always thought that he can be no true statesman whose ideas and conceptions are not founded upon profound moral convictions of right and wrong. What, then, shall we say of him who boastingly parades his indifference as a virtue? May we not drop the discussion about his statesmanship and ask, What is he worth as a man?

Yes; he mistakes the motive power which shapes the events

of history. I find that in the life of free nations mere legal disquisitions never turned the tide of events, and mere constitutional constructions never determined the tendency of an age. The logic of things goes its steady way, immovable to eloquence and deaf to argument. It shapes and changes laws and constitutions according to its immutable rules, and those adverse to it will prove no effectual obstruction to its onward march. In times of great conflicts the promptings and dictates of the human conscience are more potent than all the inventive ingenuity of the human brain.

The conscience of a free people, when once fairly ruling the action of the masses, will never fail to make new laws, when those existing are contrary to its tendency, or it will put its own construction upon those that are there. Your disquisitions and plausibilities may be used as weapons and stratagems in a fencing-match of controversing parties; but, powerless as they are before the conscience of man, posterity will remember them only as mere secondary incidents of a battle of great principles in which the strongest motive powers of human nature were the true combatants.

There is the slavery question; not a mere occasional quarrel between two sections of country divided by a geographical line, not a mere contest between two economical interests for the preponderance, not a mere wrangle between two political parties for power and spoils; but the great struggle between the human conscience and a burning wrong, between advancing civilization and retreating barbarism, between two antagonistic systems of social organization.

In vain will our impotent mock giants endeavor to make the test question of our age turn on a ridiculous logical quibble, or a paltry legal technicality; in vain will they invent small dodges and call them " great principles;" in vain will they attempt to drag down the all-absorbing contest to the level of a mere pot-house quarrel between two rival candidates for a presidential nomination.

The wheel of progressing events will crush them to atoms, as it has crushed so many abnormities, and a future generation will perhaps read on Mr. Douglas's tombstone the inscription:

" Here lies the queer sort of a statesman, who, when the great battle of slavery was fought, pretended to say that he did not care whether slavery be voted up or voted down."

But as long as the moral vitality of this nation is not entirely exhausted, Mr. Douglas, and men like him, will in vain endeavor to reduce the people to that disgusting state of moral indifference which he himself is not ashamed to boast of. I solemnly protest that the American people are not to be measured by Mr. Douglas's low moral standard. However degraded some of our politicians may be, the progress of the struggle will show that the popular conscience is still alive, and that the people do care!

THE POLICY OF IMPERIALISM

ADDRESS AT THE ANTI-IMPERIALISTIC CONFERENCE IN CHICAGO, OCTOBER 17, 1899

MORE than eight months ago I had the honor of addressing the citizens of Chicago on the subject of American imperialism, meaning the policy of annexing to this Republic distant countries and alien populations that will not fit into our democratic system of government. I discussed at that time mainly the baneful effect the pursuit of an imperialistic policy would produce upon our political institutions.

After long silence, during which I have carefully reviewed my own opinions as well as those of others in the light of the best information I could obtain, I shall now approach the same subject from another point of view.

We all know that the popular mind is much disturbed by the Philippine war, and that, however highly we admire the bravery of our soldiers, nobody professes to be proud of the war itself. There are few Americans who do not frankly admit their regret that this war should ever have happened.

In April, 1898, we went to war with Spain for the avowed purpose of liberating the people of Cuba, who had long been struggling for freedom and independence. Our object in that war was clearly and emphatically proclaimed by a solemn resolution of Congress repudiating all intention of annexation on our part and declaring that the Cuban people "are, and of right ought to be, free and independent." This solemn declaration was made to do justice to the spirit of the American people, who were indeed willing to wage a war of liberation, but would not have consented to a war of conquest. It was also to propitiate the opinion of mankind for our action. President McKinley also declared with equal solemnity that annexation by force could not be thought of, because, according to our code of morals, it would be "criminal aggression."

Can it justly be pretended that these declarations referred only to the island of Cuba? What would the American people, what would the world have said, if Congress had resolved that the Cuban people were indeed rightfully entitled to freedom and independence, but that as to the people of other Spanish colonies we recognized no such right; and if President McKinley had declared that the forcible annexation of Cuba would be criminal, but that the forcible annexation of other Spanish colonies would be a righteous act? A general outburst of protest from our own people, and of derision and contempt from the whole world, would have been the answer. No; there can be no cavil. That war was proclaimed to all mankind to be a war of liberation, and not of conquest, and even now our very imperialists are still boasting that the war was prompted by the most unselfish and generous purposes, and that those insult us who do not believe it.

In the course of that war Commodore Dewey, by a brilliant feat of arms, destroyed the Spanish fleet in the harbor of Manila. This did not change the heralded character of the war — certainly not in Dewey's own opinion. The Filipinos, constituting the strongest and foremost tribe of the population of the archipelago, had long been fighting for freedom and independence, just as the Cubans had. The great mass of the other islanders sympathized with them. They fought for the same cause as the Cubans, and they fought against the same enemy — the same enemy against whom we were waging our war of humanity and liberation. They had the same title to freedom and independence which we recognized as "of right" in the Cubans — nay, more, for, as Admiral Dewey telegraphed to our government, "They are far superior in their intelligence, and more capable of self-government than the natives of Cuba." The Admiral adds: "I am familiar with both races, and further intercourse with them has confirmed me in this opinion."

Indeed, the mendacious stories spread by our imperialists which represent those people as barbarians, their doings as mere "savagery," and their chiefs as no better than "cut-throats," have been refuted by such a mass of authoritative testimony, coming in part from men who are themselves imperialists, that their authors should hide their heads in shame; for surely it is not the part of really brave men to calumniate their victims before sacrificing them. We need not praise the Filipinos as in every way the equals of the " embattled farmers " of Lexington and Concord, and Aguinaldo as the peer of Washington; but there is an overwhelming abundance of testimony, some of it unwilling, that the Filipinos are fully the equals, and even the superiors, of the Cubans and the Mexicans. As to Aguinaldo, Admiral Dewey is credited with saying that he is controlled by men abler than himself. The same could be said of more than one of our Presidents. Moreover, it would prove that those are greatly mistaken who predict that the Filipino uprising would collapse were Aguinaldo captured or killed. The old slander that Aguinaldo had sold out the revolutionary movement for a bribe of $400,000 has been so thoroughly exploded by the best authority that it required uncommon audacity to repeat it.

Now let us see what has happened. Two months before the beginning of our Spanish war our consul at Manila reported to the State Department: " Conditions here and in Cuba are practically alike. War exists, battles are almost of daily occurrence. The crown forces (Spanish) have not been able to dislodge a rebel army within ten miles of Manila. A republic is organized here as in Cuba." When two months later our war of liberation and humanity began, Commodore Dewey was at Hongkong with his ships. He received orders to attack and destroy the Spanish fleet in those waters. It was then that our consul-general at Singapore informed our State Department that he had conferred with General Aguinaldo, then at Singapore, as to the co-operation of the Philippine insurgents, and that he had telegraphed to Commodore Dewey that Aguinaldo was willing to come to Hongkong to arrange with Dewey for " general co-operation, if desired;" whereupon Dewey promptly answered: " Tell Aguinaldo come oon as possible." The meeting was had. Dewey sailed o Manila to destroy the Spanish fleet, and Aguinaldo vas taken to the seat of war on a vessel of the United States. His forces received a supply of arms through Commodore Dewey, and did faithfully and effectively co-operate with our forces against the Spaniards, so effectively, indeed, that soon afterward by their efforts the Spaniards had lost the whole country except a few garrisons in which they were practically blockaded.

Now, what were the relations between the Philippine insurgents and this Republic? There is some dispute as to certain agreements, including a promise of Philippine independence, said to have been made between Aguinaldo and our consulgeneral at Singapore, before Aguinaldo proceeded to co-operate with Dewey. But I lay no stress upon this point. I will let only the record of facts speak. Of these facts the first, of highest importance, is that Aguinaldo was " desired "— that is, invited — by officers of the United States to co-operate with our forces. The second is that the Filipino junta in Hongkong immediately after these conferences appealed to their countrymen to receive the American fleet about to sail for Manila as friends, by a proclamation which had these words:

" Compatriots, divine Providence is about to place independence within our reach. The Americans, not from any mercenary motives, but for the sake of humanity, have considered it opportune to extend their protecting mantle to our beloved country. Where you see the American flag flying assemble in mass. They are our redeemers."

With this faith his followers gave Aguinaldo a rapturous greeting upon his arrival at Cavité, where he proclaimed his government and organized his army under Dewey's eyes.

The arrival of our land forces did not at first change these relations. Brig.-Gen. Thomas M. Anderson, commanding, wrote to Aguinaldo, July 4, as follows: "General, I have the honor to inform you that the United States of America, whose land forces I have the honor to command in this vicinity, being at war with the kingdom of Spain, has entire sympathy and most friendly sentiments for the native people of the Philippine Islands. For these reasons I desire to have the most amicable relations with you, and to have you and your people co-operate with us in military operations against the Spanish forces," etc. Aguinaldo responded cordially, and an extended correspondence followed, special services being asked for by the party of the first part, being rendered by the second, and duly acknowledged by the first. All this went on pleasantly until the capture of Manila, in which Aguinaldo effectively co-operated by fighting the Spaniards outside, taking many prisoners from them, and hemming them in. The services they rendered by taking thousands of Spanish prisoners, by harassing the Spaniards in the trenches, and by completely blockading Manila on the land side, were amply testified to by our own officers. Aguinaldo was also active on the sea. He had ships, which our commanders permitted to pass in and out of Manila Bay, under the flag of the Philippine republic, on their expeditions against other provinces.

Now, whether there was or not any formal compact of alliance signed and sealed, no candid man who has studied the official documents will deny that in point of fact the Filipinos, having been desired and invited to do so, were, before the capture of Manila, acting, and were practically recognized as our allies, and that as such they did effective service, which we accepted and profited by. This is an indisputable fact, proved by the record.

It is an equally indisputable fact that during that period the Filipino government constantly and publicly, so that nobody could plead ignorance of it or misunderstand it, informed the world that their object was the achievement of national independence, and that they believed the Americans had come in good faith to help them accomplish that end, as in the case of Cuba. It was weeks after various proclamations and other public utterances of Aguinaldo to that effect that the correspondence between him and General Anderson, which I have quoted, took place, and that the useful services of the Filipinos as our practical allies were accepted. It is, further, an indisputable fact that during this period our government did not inform the Filipinos that their fond expectations as to our recognition of their independence were mistaken.

Our secretary of state did, indeed, on June 16 write to Mr. Pratt, our consul-general at Singapore, that our government knew the Philippine insurgents, not indeed as patriots struggling for liberty, and who, like the Cubans, "are and of right ought to be free and independent," but merely as "discontented and rebellious subjects of Spain," who, if we occupied their country in consequence of the war, would have to yield us due "obedience." And other officers of our government were instructed not to make any promises to the Filipinos as to the future. But the Filipinos themselves were not so informed. They were left to believe that, while fighting in co-operation with the American forces, they were fighting for their own independence. They could not imagine that the government of the great American Republic, while boasting of having gone to war with Spain under the banner of liberation and humanity in behalf of Cuba, was capable of secretly plotting to turn that war into one for the conquest and subjugation of the Philippines.

Thus the Filipinos went faithfully and bravely on doing for us the service of allies, of brothers-in-arms, far from dreaming that the same troops with whom they had been asked to co-operate would soon be employed by the great apostle of liberation and humanity to slaughter them for no other reason than that they, the Filipinos, continued to stand up for their own freedom and independence.

But just that was to happen. As soon as Manila was taken and we had no further use for our Filipino allies, they were ordered to fall back and back from the city and its suburbs. Our military commanders treated the Filipinos' country as if it were our own. When Aguinaldo sent one of his aides-de-camp to General Merritt with a request for an interview, General Merritt was "too busy." When our peace negotiations with Spain began, and representatives of the Filipinos asked for audience to solicit consideration of the rights and wishes of their people, the doors were slammed in their faces, in Washington as well as in Paris.

And behind those doors the scheme was hatched to deprive the Philippine Islanders of independence from foreign rule and to make them the subjects of another foreign ruler, and that foreign ruler their late ally, this great Republic which had grandly proclaimed to the world that its war against Spain was not a war of conquest, but a war of liberation and humanity.

Behind those doors which were tightly closed to the people of the Philippines a treaty was made with Spain, by the direction of President McKinley, which provided for the cession of the Philippine Islands by Spain to the United States for a consideration of $20,000,000. It has been said that this sum was not purchase money, but a compensation for improvements made by Spain, or a *solatium* to sweeten the pill of cession, or what not; but, stripped of all cloudy verbiage, it was really purchase money, the sale being made by Spain under duress. Thus Spain sold, and the United States bought, what was called the sovereignty of Spain over the Philippine Islands and their people.

Now look at the circumstances under which that "cession" was made. Spain had lost the possession of the country, except a few isolated and helpless little garrisons, most of which were effectively blockaded by the Filipinos. The American forces occupied Cavité and the harbor and city of Manila, and nothing more. The bulk of the country was occupied and possessed by the people thereof, over whom Spain had, in point of fact, ceased to exercise any sovereignty, the Spanish power having been driven out or destroyed by the Filipino insurrection, while the United States had not acquired, beyond Cavité and Manila, any authority of whatever name by military occupation, nor by recognition on the part of the people. Aguinaldo's army surrounded Manila on the land side, and his government claimed organized control over fifteen provinces. That government was established at Malolos, not far from Manila; and a very respectable government it was. According to Mr. Barrett, our late minister in Siam, himself an ardent imperialist, who had seen it, it had a well-organized executive, divided into several departments, ably conducted, and a popular assembly, a congress, which would favorably compare with the Parliament of Japan — an infinitely better government than the insurrectionary government of Cuba ever was.

It is said that Aguinaldo's government was in operation among only a part of the people of the islands. This is true. But it is also certain that it was recognized and supported by an immeasurably larger part of the people than Spanish sovereignty, which had practically ceased to exist, and than American rule, which was confined to a harbor and a city and which was carried on by the exercise of military force under what was substantially martial law over a people that constituted about one twentieth of the whole population of the islands. Thus, having brought but a very small fraction of the country and its people under our military control, we bought by that treaty the sovereignty over the whole from a power which had practically lost that sovereignty and therefore did no longer possess it; and we contemptuously disdained to consult the existing native government, which actually did control a large part of the country and the people, and which had been our ally in the war with Spain. The sovereignty we thus acquired may well be defined as Abraham Lincoln once defined the "popular sovereignty" of Senator Douglas's doctrine — as being like a soup made by boiling the shadow of the breastbone of a pigeon that had been starved to death.

No wonder that treaty found opposition in the Senate. Virulent abuse was heaped upon the "statesman who would oppose the ratification of a peace treaty." A peace treaty? This was no peace treaty at all. It was a treaty with half a dozen bloody wars in its belly. It was, in the first place, an open and brutal declaration of war against our allies, the Filipinos, who struggled for freedom and independence from foreign rule. Every man not totally blind could see that. For such a treaty the true friends of peace could, of course, not vote.

But more. Even before that treaty had been assented to by the Senate — that is, even before that ghastly shadow of our Philippine sovereignty had obtained any legal sanction — President McKinley assumed of his own motion the sovereignty of the Philippine Islands by his famous " benevolent-assimilation " order of December 21, 1898, through which our military commander at Manila was directed forthwith to extend the military government of the United States over the whole archipelago, and by which the Filipinos were notified that if they refused to submit, they would be compelled by force of arms. Having bravely fought for their freedom and independence from one foreign rule, they did refuse to submit to another foreign rule, and then the slaughter of our late allies began — the slaughter by American arms of a once friendly and confiding people. And this slaughter has been going on ever since.

This is a grim story. Two years ago the prediction of such a possibility would have been regarded as a hideous nightmare, as the offspring of a diseased imagination. But to-day it is a true tale — a plain recital of facts taken from the official records. These things have actually been done in these last two years by and under the administration of William McKinley. This is our Philippine war as it stands. Is it a wonder that the American people should be troubled in their consciences? . . .

I am not here as a partisan, but as an American citizen anxious for the future of the Republic. And I cannot too earnestly admonish the American people, if they value the fundamental principles of their government and their own security and that of their children, for a moment to throw aside all partisan bias and soberly to consider what kind of a precedent they would set if they consented to, and by consenting approved, the President's management of the Philippine business merely " because we are in it."

We cannot expect all our future Presidents to be models of public virtue and wisdom, as George Washington was. Imagine now in the presidential office a man well-meaning, but, it may be, short-sighted and pliable, and under the influence of so-called " friends " who are greedy and reckless speculators, and who would not scruple to push him into warlike complications in order to get great opportunities for profit; or a man of that inordinate ambition which intoxicates the mind and befogs the conscience; or a man of extreme partisan spirit, who honestly believes the victory of his party to be necessary for the salvation of the universe, and may think that a foreign broil would serve the chances of his party; or a man of an uncontrollable combativeness of temperament which might run away with his sense of responsibility — and that we shall have such men in the presidential chair is by no means unlikely with our loose way of selecting candidates for the presidency.

Imagine, then, a future President belonging to either of these classes to have before him the precedent of Mr. McKinley's management of the Philippine business, sanctioned by the approval or only the acquiescence of the people, and to feel himself permitted — nay, even encouraged — to say to himself that, as this precedent shows, he may plunge the country into warlike conflicts of his own motion, without asking leave of Congress, with only some legal technicalities to cover his usurpation, or even without such, and that he may, by a machinery of deception called a war censorship, keep the people in the dark about what is going on; and that, into however bad a mess he may have got the country, he may count upon the people, as soon as a drop of blood has been shed, to uphold the usurpation and to cry down everybody who opposes it as a "traitor," and all this because "we are in it!" Can you conceive a more baneful precedent, a more prolific source of danger to the peace and security of the country? Can any sane man deny that it will be all the more prolific of evil if in this way we drift into a foreign policy full of temptation for dangerous adventure?

I say, therefore, that if we have the future of the Republic at heart we must not only not uphold the administration in its course because "we are in it," but just because we are in it, have been got into it in such a way, the American people should stamp the administration's proceedings with a verdict of disapproval so clear and emphatic and "get out of it" in such a fashion that this will be a solemn warning to future Presidents instead of a seductive precedent.

What, then, to accomplish this end is to be done? Of course we, as we are here, can only advise. But by calling forth expressions of the popular will by various means of public demonstration and, if need be, at the polls, we can make that advice so strong that those in power will hardly disregard it. We have often been taunted with having no positive policy to propose. But such a policy has more than once been proposed and I can only repeat it.

In the first place, let it be well understood that those are egregiously mistaken who think that if by a strong military effort the Philippine war be stopped everything will be right and no more question about it. No; the American trouble of conscience will not be appeased, and the question will be as big and virulent as ever, unless the close of the war be promptly followed by an assurance to the islanders of their freedom and independence, which assurance, if given now, would surely end the war without more fighting.

We propose, therefore, that it be given now. Let the Philippine islanders at the same time he told that the American people will be glad to see them establish an independent government, and to aid them in that task as far as may be necessary, and even, if required, lend our good offices to bring it about; and that meanwhile we shall deem it our duty to protect them against interference from other foreign powers — in other words, that with regard to them we mean honestly to live up to the righteous principles with the profession of which we commended to the world our Spanish war.

And then let us have in the Philippines, to carry out this program, not a small politician, nor a meddlesome martinet, but a statesman of large mind and genuine sympathy, who will not merely deal in sanctimonious cant and oily promises with a string to them, but who will prove by his acts that he and we are honest; who will keep in mind that their government is not merely to suit us, but to suit them; that it should not be measured by standards which we ourselves have not been able to reach, but be a government of their own, adapted to their own conditions and notions — whether it be a true republic, like ours, or a dictatorship like that of Porfirio Diaz, in Mexico, or an oligarchy like the one maintained by us in Hawaii, or even something like the boss rule we are tolerating in New York and Pennsylvania.

Those who talk so much about " fitting a people for self-government " often forget that no people were ever made " fit " for self-government by being kept in the leading strings of a foreign power. You learn to walk by doing your own crawling and stumbling. Self-government is learned only by exercising it upon one's own responsibility. Of course there will be mistakes and troubles and disorders. We have had and now have these, too — at the beginning our persecution of the Tories, our flounderings before the constitution was formed, our Shay's rebellion, our whisky war, and various failures and disturbances, among them a civil war that cost us a loss of life and treasure horrible to think of, and the murder of two Presidents. But who will say that on account of these things some foreign power should have kept the American people in leading strings to teach them to govern themselves? If the Philippine islanders do as well as the Mexicans, who have worked their way, since we let them alone after our war of 1847, through many disorders, to an orderly government, who will have a right to find fault with the result? Those who seek to impose upon them an unreasonable standard of excellence in self-government do not seriously wish to let them govern themselves at all. You may take it as a general rule that he who wants to reign over others is solemnly convinced that they are quite unable to govern themselves.

Now, what objection is there to the policy dictated by our fundamental principles and our good faith? I hear the angry cry: "What? Surrender to Aguinaldo? Will not the world ridicule and despise us for such a confession of our incompetency to deal with so feeble a foe? What will become of our prestige?" No, we shall not surrender to Aguinaldo. In giving up a criminal aggression we shall surrender only to our own consciences, to our own sense of right and justice, to our own understanding of our own true interests, and to the vital principles of our own Republic. Nobody will laugh at us whose good opinion we have reason to cherish. There will of course be an outcry of disappointment in England. But from whom will it come? From such men as James Bryce or John Morley or any one of those true friends of this Republic who understand and admire and wish to per-

petuate and spread the fundamental principles of its vitality?
No, not from them.

But the outcry will come from those in England who long
to see us entangled in complications apt to make this American Republic dependent upon British aid and thus subservient to British interests. They, indeed, will be quite angry.
But the less we mind their displeasure as well as their flat-
tery the better for the safety as well as the honor of our
country.

The true friends of this Republic in England, and, indeed,
all over the world, who are now grieving to see us go astray,
will rejoice and their hearts will be uplifted with new confidence in our honesty, in our wisdom, and in the virtue of
democratic institutions when they behold the American people throwing aside all the puerilities of false pride and
returning to the path of their true duty. . . .

Who are the true patriots in America to-day — those who
drag our Republic, once so proud of its high principles and
ideals, through the mire of broken pledges, vulgar ambitions
and vanities and criminal aggressions; those who do violence to their own moral sense by insisting that, like the
Dreyfus iniquity, a criminal course once begun must be per-
sisted in, or those who, fearless of the demagogue clamor,
strive to make the flag of the Republic once more what it
was once — the flag of justice, liberty, and true civilization
— and to lift up the American people among the nations of
the earth to the proud position of the people that have a
conscience and obey it.

The country has these days highly and deservedly honored
Admiral Dewey as a national hero. Who are his true friends
— those who would desecrate Dewey's splendid achievement
at Manila by making it the starting point of criminal aggres-

sion, and thus the opening of a most disgraceful and inevitably disastrous chapter of American history, to be remembered with sorrow, or those who strive so to shape the results of that brilliant feat of arms that it may stand in history not as a part of a treacherous conquest, but as a true victory of American good faith in an honest war of liberation and humanity — to be proud of for all time, as Dewey himself no doubt meant it to be.

I know the imperialists will say that I have been pleading here for Aguinaldo and his Filipinos against our Republic. No, not for the Filipinos merely, although, as one of those who have grown gray in the struggle for free and honest government, I would never be ashamed to plead for the cause of freedom and independence, even when its banner is carried by dusky and feeble hands. But I am pleading for more. I am pleading for the cause of American honor and self-respect, American interests, American democracy; aye, for the cause of the American people against an administration of our public affairs which has wantonly plunged this country into an iniquitous war; which has disgraced the Republic by a scandalous breach of faith to a people struggling for their freedom whom we had used as allies; which has been systematically seeking to deceive and mislead the public mind by the manufacture of false news; which has struck at the very foundation of our constitutional government by an Executive usurpation of the war power; which makes sport of the great principles and high ideals that have been and should ever remain the guiding star of our course, and which, unless stopped in time, will transform this government of the people, for the people, and by the people into an imperial government cynically calling itself republican — a government in which the noisy worship of arrogant might will drown the voice of right; which will impose upon the people a burdensome and demoralizing militarism, and which will be driven into a policy of wild and rapacious adventure by the unscrupulous greed of the exploiter — a policy always fatal to democracy.

I plead the cause of the American people against all this, and I here declare my profound conviction that if this administration of our affairs were submitted for judgment to a popular vote on a clear issue it would be condemned by an overwhelming majority.

I confidently trust that the American people will prove themselves too clear-headed not to appreciate the vital difference between the expansion of the Republic and its free institutions over contiguous territory and kindred populations, which we all gladly welcome if accomplished peaceably or honorably, and imperialism which reaches out for distant lands to be ruled as subject provinces; too intelligent not to perceive that our very first step on the road of imperialism has been a betrayal of the fundamental principles of democracy, followed by disaster and disgrace; too enlightened not to understand that a monarchy may do such things and still remain a strong monarchy, while a democracy cannot do them and still remain a democracy; too wise not to detect the false pride, or the dangerous ambitions, or the selfish schemes which so often hide themselves under that deceptive cry of mock patriotism: "Our country, right or wrong!" They will not fail to recognize that our dignity, our free institutions, and the peace and welfare of this and coming generations of Americans will be secure only as we cling to the watchword of true patriotism: "Our country — when right to be kept right; when wrong to be put right."

LIDDON

HENRY PARRY LIDDON, a distinguished English preacher and theologian, the son of a naval officer, was born at North Stoneham, Hampshire, August 20, 1829. He was educated at King's College School, London, and Christ Church College, Oxford, and took orders in the Anglican church in 1850. After several years' experience as a curate in Wantage, in which period his extraordinary talent for preaching began to manifest itself, he became in 1854 vice-principal of Cuddesdon Theological College. In 1859 he accepted the vice-principalship of St. Edward's Hall at Oxford; and four years later was appointed select preacher to Oxford University and was reappointed in 1870, 1877, and 1884, and was twice select preacher to Cambridge University also. In 1864 he was made one of the examining chaplains to the Bishop of Salisbury and given a prebend's stall in Salisbury Cathedral. In 1870 his lectures at St. James's Church, Piccadilly, attracted wide attention and brought him the offer of a canonry at St. Paul's Cathedral which he accepted. For the next twenty years his sermons at St. Paul's were one of the factors of London life, attracting thither men of all nations, ranks, and creeds. Liddon had formed his style on a careful study of such great French preachers as Massillon, Bourdaloue, and Lacordaire, and owed to this study the completeness of the construction of his sermons. His discourses were masterly and impassioned efforts to prove and persuade, and to the attainment of his purpose, his enthusiasm, perfect intonation, gestures, learning, and argumentative skill all contributed. In spite of the inelastic temper of his mind in theological matters he was a liberal in general politics, ardently supporting Gladstone in the anti-Turkish movement in 1876-78. In 1886 he declined the bishopric of Edinburgh, at other times also declining any suggestion of episcopal honors. He died at Weston-super-Mare, September 9, 1890. His published works comprise "Some Words for God" (1865); republished as "Sermons Preached at Oxford;" "Some Elements of Religion" (1886); "Advent in St. Paul's" (1888); "The Magnificat" (1889); "Christmastide in St. Paul's" (1890); "Passiontide Series" (1891); "Sermons on Old Testament Subjects" (1891); "Sermons on Some Words of Christ" (1892); "Essays and Addresses" (1892). He left a "Life of Pusey" unfinished, which has since been completed by other hands.

SERMON: THE ADEQUACY OF PRESENT OPPORTUNITIES

" And he said unto him, If they hear not Moses and the prophets, neither will they be persuaded, though one rose from the dead."—Luke xvi, 31.

ON this the first of the long line of Sundays after Trinity, the parable of the rich man and Lazarus opens the lessons on Christian duty, which are set before us in the successive gospels, with a force and a pathos which we feel from our early childhood — at least, if I may trust my own experience. The three vivid contrasts of this parable are among the very first features in the gospel to take possession of the imagination and the heart.

First there is the contrast between the rich and the poor — that great contrast which is apparently rooted in the nature of things, which reappears in all ages and countries wherever there is a settled order of human society. Dives, with his outer robe of purple wool and with his under tunic of fine linen — Dives, with his table furnished day after day with every delicacy that money can buy — he is always here. And Lazarus, thrown down — such is the original expression—thrown down, to lie at the gate of the outer court of the rich man's mansion — Lazarus who feeds upon the crumbs which the slaves of Dives, half contemptuously, throw to him — Lazarus so unclothed that his very wounds are without bandages, and the dogs that roam through the streets of the eastern city stop for a moment as they pass to lick his sores — he, too, is always here; a contrast, I say, as old and as lasting as society, a contrast which met the eye centuries ago in Rome and in Jerusalem, just as it meets it when we walk from the east to the west end of London; a contrast, it must be added, which social science and wise legislation and above all the divine charities of Jesus Christ our Lord filling the regenerated hearts of men, makes less harsh, less shocking, but the cause of which they cannot really remove.

And there is a second contrast — that of the living and the dead. The parable places us face to face with Dives and Lazarus, first in life and then in the world which follows. This is a more solemn contrast than that between the rich and the poor. It is a contrast between that which passes and that which lasts — between appearance and reality.

Lazarus — so we are told — dies in time, worn out, no doubt, by want and sickness. Nothing is said of his burial: perhaps he was not buried at all. And after a while Dives dies too, and of course is buried — buried with all due respect and ceremony. And after the brief sleep of death they wake, as we shall all one day wake, in a new world. The life of that world is a continuation of the life of this. Circumstances are altered; characters remain. Enough now to repeat that what we see here is the apparent: what we shall see there is the real. And this contrast between the living and the dead is much more rooted in the nature of things than that between the rich and the poor. It is as old, it is as wide, it is as enduring, as the human race. Day by day men and women around us are exploring it: day by day they are passing the line which separates the living and the dead, and sounding the heights and depths of its stern, of its blessed, significance.

And the parable brings before us a third contrast, differing from the two former in this,— that whereas they belong, the first wholly, and the second in part, to this present world, this third is altogether concerned with the next. In the next

EMILIO CASTELAR

Orations—Volume twenty-one

world there are two companies of beings, the miserable and
the blessed. All are not blessed: numbers, thank God, are
certainly not miserable. There Lazarus rests in the bosom
of Abraham: there Dives lifts up his eyes being in torment.
And between the two there is a great gulf fixed, " so that," in
Abraham's words, " they which would pass from hence to
you cannot; neither can they pass to us, that would come
from thence."

A contrast, my brethren, yet more solemn than that
between the living and the dead — a contrast which will
still endure when all that now meets the eye of sense shall
have passed away.

As we dwell on our Saviour's words we are, perhaps,
tempted to say to ourselves, " After all, it is only a parable."

Well brethren, it is a parable, although it is possibly also
a history. There is something, at any rate, to be said for
the opinion that Dives and Lazarus were real persons with
whose earthly circumstances our Lord's hearers were
acquainted, and whose destiny after death he authoritatively
proclaims.

But, however this may be, a parable, though it be a purely
fictitious narrative, teaches something when it comes from
the mouth of the Master of Eternal Truth. Its imagery, its
rabbinical phraseology, its incidents — these all, each of
them, do mean something. They may be translated into corresponding realities. And this parable, I submit, if it
teaches anything at all, can certainly teach nothing less than
these three contrasts — the contrasts between the rich — the
selfish rich — and the poor, the suffering poor; the contrast
between the living and the dead; the contrast between the
happy and the miserable in another world.

Now is it to the last of these three contrasts that our text belongs? Dives and Lazarus are now among the dead, not yet separated, as they will be after the final judgment, but separated, we are told, by an impassable gulf. They are in that sphere of being into one district of which our Lord descended after his death, and which we call "hell" in the creed,— which contains, on the one hand, paradise and Abraham's bosom — anticipations, these, of a perfect happiness to come; and which also contains that which is already the portion of Dives while he awaits the final judgment. Yet between Dives and Abraham, it would seem, some sort of communication is still possible; and in this report or representation of the divine Teacher we have put before us two separate conversations.

First of all Dives petitions Abraham, as the father of all faithful Israelites, that a drop of water may be sent him by the hand of Lazarus; and Abraham tells his son — (mark the tragic irony of the expression) — that this cannot be, partly because an absolute justice is redressing the inequalities of that life on earth, and partly because there is a great gulf fixed: the divine reward is irreversible.

Then, since nothing can be done among the dead, Dives thinks of the living. Dives is ruined, as he now knows, not because he was rich, but because he abused his wealth. He has five brethren who are living as he once lived on earth. He thinks that if Lazarus could visit them, speaking of what happens beyond the grave with the authority of experience, they would be changed men. Abraham answers, "They have Moses and the prophets; let them hear them." Dives remembers that he in his earthly days had Moses and the prophets too, close at hand, and yet that he had died as he had lived; and so he pleads with Abraham that, if only a visitor from the realms of death should see them, these five brethren would really repent. And to this Abraham answers again that, "if they hear not Moses and the prophets, neither will they be persuaded, though one rose from the dead."

Now perhaps if we were to say out what we really think — some of us — we should say that it seems to us, at first sight, almost hard in Abraham to answer Dives as he does answer him; for, after all, Dives was doing all that it was still possible for him to do. For himself, he was ruined — ruined irretrievably; but these five brethren — could nothing be done for them? If Lazarus might not cross the great gulf fixed, with a drop of water for the tongue of Dives, might he not visit the world of living men to speak a word of warning to the rich man's five surviving brethren?

No, Abraham will not allow that this demand is justified; for, if we translate the parable into the meaning which the divine Speaker and his hearers would alike put on it, what is this demand of Dives, virtually, but an indictment against God for not having furnished the rich Israelites of that day with sufficiently strong motives to holiness and amendment of life?

The Jewish opponents of Jesus Christ our Lord were continually asking in this way for signs and wonders, and our Lord was constantly replying that there were proofs enough and to spare, of his mission, in the law, in the prophets, in his own works, in his own words — proofs enough to dispense with anything of the kind.

Dives talks still like the ordinary Pharisees of the day. When he asks that Lazarus may be sent to his brethren, he implies, you observe, that if he himself had been visited by one who had seen the realities of the other life he would have lived and died quite differently. As it was, he had only had the old Book to fall back upon — only Moses and the prophets. There was something, he tacitly suggests, there was something to be said for him, after all; and therefore when Abraham refers to the five brethren he means Dives himself as well. If Dives had not heard Moses and the prophets, neither would he have been persuaded, though one had risen from the dead to warn him.

Now this answer to Dives is undoubtedly meant to represent the mind and judgment of our Lord himself. Abraham in the parable declares the will of God, just as Dives puts into words the thoughts of the Pharisees of the day. Let us, then, consider this reply of Abraham somewhat more at length. What does it teach us?

It teaches us, first of all, how far the actual sight of a miracle would be likely to produce real faith in the unseen world. Dives let Lazarus lie at his gate. Why? Because he had no true belief in the unseen. The brethren of Dives would do their duty by such as Lazarus if they only could see, in all his perfections, him who is invisible — their present Master — their future Judge. Hundreds of men in our day, who have lost living faith in the religion of Jesus Christ our Lord, think that if they could only witness a miracle they could not help believing again — believing at once.

"It is all very well," they say, "to read in the gospels about the stilling the tempest, about feeding the five thousand, about the raising three persons from the dead, about the resurrection of the Lord himself. More than eighteen centuries have passed since those events, and there are no miracles, it seems, now. Let us see a miracle," they say; "let us have it examined and approved by competent persons, and, depend upon it, it will not fail in its effect. People will then believe, because they will not be able to help believing in the truth of the creed which the miracle is intended to attest."

This, you observe, is exactly what Dives thought and said about the five brethren, if Lazarus were allowed to appear before them. The apparition, he thought, must make them live for another life — that is to say, live by faith. Moses and the prophets, he implied, had lost their power: they were old books dealing with matters which had been said and done hundreds of years ago. They were books which Dives and his brethren had known from childhood, and familiarity had bred indifference, or something worse.

And men ask now, in the heart of Christendom, " Is there not something in this?" Is not that which appeals to sense more powerful with most of us than that which appeals to thought? Is not the present more moving than the past — a witnessed action than a written testimony or an abstract argument? Would not a dead man standing before our eyes, telling us that he had revived to come from the regions of the dead, with an appearance and other evidences that justified his assertion, have, of necessity, an influence upon us which a Bible read quietly in our church, or in our bedroom, or a Christian teacher listened to under accustomed circumstances, could never command? Would not a preternatural apparition exert over us a sway, immediate, resistless, making us believers — earnest, clear-sighted, impartial believers — in spite of our very selves?

All these questions our Lord answers now, and for this answer the reasons are not hard to find. Miracles are called in the Bible, with reference to their effect upon the human mind, " signs and wonders." They excite astonishment: they call attention to the mission or message of the worker. A miracle is intended, first of all, to startle the beholder: it is a wonder; and it is intended, next, to point toward the unseen and the eternal: it is a sign.

But even if the sight of a miracle produces these effects,— if it first startles the man, and next suggests that there is something which he does not see and which is worth his attention and belief — this does not amount to actual faith. It is one thing to be convinced of the truth of the unseen; it is another thing to be startled. At some time in our lives we must all of us have been startled by occurrences which, although unaccustomed, at least to us, could not be deemed miracles. A friend has died without any sort of warning. We have been in a railway accident in which several persons have lost their lives, and we have escaped — we know not how — through a series of unforeseen contingencies. Or some historical catastrophe, like the surrender of Sedan, or like the recent tragedies at Constantinople, has happened, and for the moment the world holds its breath, and seems to feel that God is passing along the corridors of human history. And events like these, on a small scale or a great, are intended to remind us that what we see and are is very insignificant indeed, compared with what we do not see and what we shall be. Events like these, though occurring in a strictly natural way, do, up to a certain point, the very proper work of miracles. They flash upon our minds for a moment the truth that God is not now only but always near, with his eye upon us, guarding us, judging us in his perfect truth, his perfect love, his perfect justice.

Ah, these occurrences startle us, but what does it amount to? A momentary sensation; a mental, a moral spasm, which comes and goes and leaves us as we were, or perhaps, religiously speaking, if it goes, not quite so well off as we were. Of course a shock of this kind, like St. Paul's great experience on the road to Damascus, may be our very door of entrance into the life of faith; but the shock of itself does not insure these consequences. Utter astonishment and bewilderment is one thing; faith in the unseen is another. A swift succession of several new phases of thought and feeling, produced by a grand catastrophe and compressed into a single minute, may be the turning point of an existence, or only a strange experience.

No doubt the five brethren and Dives too in his earthly lifetime would have been startled by the appearance of Lazarus, fresh from the scenes beyond the grave; but this does not at all prove that they would have been endued with that new and vivid perception of unseen things which we call faith.

For, secondly, a miracle is only likely to have real and lasting effect when it is addressed to a particular set of men. A sonata of Beethoven means nothing for a man who has no ear for music. A picture of Raphael is lost upon the observer who has no sense of color, of proportion, of artistic beauty. And, in the same way, the mind of the man who witnesses a miracle must be predisposed in a certain way, or the miracle will altogether fail of its intended effect.

The observer must, in the psalmist's words, have an eye to God, if he is to be enlightened by the miracle. He must be already looking out for God — looking out for some token of the will of God. He believes, we will suppose, in a vague way, that there is a Maker and Ruler of the world. He believes that there is an Author of the law of right and wrong which he recognizes within himself. Now, depend upon it, the more he makes of this law of right and wrong, the more disposed he will be to make the most of what will be told him on authority about the Being who gave the law.

In this state of mind he will watch anxiously for any sign that the Lord of nature may deign or seem to deign to make on the surface of nature, with a view to showing that he is also the Lord of conscience and the Lord of revelation. But if the man has no such interests, no such anticipations, to begin with, then the miracle says nothing to him; for him the miracle is a mere curious irregularity observable upon the surface of nature. It arrests his attention; perhaps it excites his apprehension for a moment; but that is all. And if he has already made up his mind against the truth of which the miracle is the divine certificate, then the miracle must be powerless to move him.

"If they hear not Moses and the prophets, neither will they be persuaded, though one rose from the dead."

This was actually the case with those Jews, to whom our Lord was speaking, not long after. Moses and the prophets had foretold him — the true Messiah. "Search the Scriptures — your own Scriptures," he had said — "for in them ye think ye have eternal life: and they are they which testify of me."

But Moses and the prophets had written in vain, as far as that generation of Israelites was concerned. "Their table" — as prophet and apostle had said — "their table was made a snare to take themselves withal; and the things which should have been for their wealth were unto them an occasion of falling."

Scripture had failed. Could miracle succeed? Jesus Christ died in public; he was buried; on the third day he rose from the dead. His resurrection was a well-attested fact. Those who had known him best saw him singly — saw him with others. He was seen again and again during the period of forty days. On one occasion he was seen by five hundred persons, half of whom were living some twenty-five years afterward. But were the Jews as a people convinced?

On the contrary, they set themselves at once to get rid of this stupendous miracle, intended though it was to convince them that he to whom their whole history pointed had really come, by every explanation they could devise. The disciples, they said, had stolen the body. The disciples had conspired to palm off an imposture on the world. Our Lord might as well have remained in his grave, as far as the great men in Jerusalem were concerned. They began, you see, by refusing to hear Moses and the prophets; they were not persuaded, though he, their true King, had risen from the dead.

Remember this, brethren, when you are tempted to think that faith would have been easier in the days of the apostles than it is now. "If a miracle could only be worked before my eyes," it is sometimes said, "I should have believed without difficulty."

Would you? The probability is that the very temper of mind which makes you ask for the miracle would kill belief in the presence of the miracle. Miracles are intended to assist those who are already seeking God. They are not intended to inflict the sense of God's power and presence and truth on those who do not wish to know more about him. A miracle cannot force a soul to believe: it does not act like a machine or like a chemical solvent, producing the specific effect whether men will or not.

There are many ways of neutralizing this proper effect; and if we have heard Moses and the prophets,— if we have listened to evangelists and apostles, and to the Lord of life himself, to no real or lasting purpose — we should not, of necessity, be persuaded, though the floor of this abbey were this evening to break up beneath our feet, and the buried dead were to come forth to tell us that the world to come is an awful and overwhelming reality.

And next, Abraham's reply to Dives teaches us how far circumstances can be presumed to determine conduct. What a miracle is to faith, that favorable circumstances are to duty. As a miracle makes faith easy, so favorable circumstances, good examples, encouraging friends, the urgency of great opportunities, the inheritance of a noble name — these make duty easy. But duty is no more necessarily forced upon us by circumstances than faith is forced upon us by miracle.

Yet if there are hundreds who say, " I should be a sincere believer in Christianity if I could only see a person who had come from the dead," there are thousands who say, " I should be a better woman or man than I am if only I were differently circumstanced — if I were not tempted by poverty or tempted by wealth,— if I had religious and high-minded friends about me,— if I lived near a church, or knew a good clergyman,— if I had lived in other ages, the ages of faith, as they are called, when all the controversies that fill the air in modern times were quite unknown, and everybody was of one mind as to the best way of getting to heaven."

My brethren, it is not the same thing to any one of us whether we have good friends or bad — whether we have religious privileges at hand or are quite without them,— whether we can resort at will for counsel or comfort to the servants of Christ, or are debarred from doing so,— whether we are exposed to the temptations of luxury or to the temptations of want, or are blessed with that amount of competency which saves us from these temptations.

Circumstances are judgments, or they are blessings, from God; and when he surrounds us with such circumstances as to make it easier for us to live for him and to attain the true end of our existence, we have, indeed, great reason to bless him for the blessings of this life, since, like all other good things, they come from him, the Fountain of all goodness.

But these blessings do not of themselves make a moral, religious, beneficent, Christian life necessary. They do not act upon us as the rain or the sunshine or the atmosphere act upon plants. Under favorable circumstances a plant cannot help growing. It obeys the law of its kind by an inevitable necessity. But under favorable circumstances,— nay, under the most favorable that we can possibly conceive — a human soul can refuse to grow — can remain resolutely stunted, dwarfed, misshapen — can resist triumphantly, aye, to its final ruin, all the blessed influences that might draw it upward and onward,— all that might purify, invigorate, transfigure, save it.

Felix was not compelled to be a Christian by the Apostle's burning words about righteousness, temperance, and judgment to come, though he felt their awful force. Demas was not cured of his love of this present world by the sight and friendship of Christ's aged servant Paul, now in chains at Rome, and on the eve of his martyrdom. Nay, if circumstances were ever favorable — so we may well think — to the well-being and growth of any human soul, they were the circumstances of the unhappy Judas, blessed as he was with the daily visible divine companionship of the Saviour of the world. They did not arrest the commission of two tremendous crimes,— first, that of betraying the Most Holy into the hands of his enemies, and next of rushing by his own act, impenitent, into the presence of his Judge.

Certainly let us admit that if favorable circumstances do not force holiness upon us, they may and do often protect us against monstrous vice — against the outcome of passions and dispositions which, it may be, are still unsubdued within us, though kept more or less in check. When we read of a great crime how rarely does it occur to us to ask ourselves, with Augustine, whether, but for God's protection and grace, we too might not have been the criminal.

We read in boyhood the histories, no doubt, of the early Roman Emperors — of Caligula, of Nero, of Domitian, of Commodus; and we said to ourselves that it was wonderful that men so lost to the better instincts of our common nature should have been permitted to cumber the high places of the earth.

But should we have been better in their circumstances? With unlimited power of gratifying our own selfish instincts, and of making all others with whom we came into contact the slaves of our will,— without the fear of another world before our eyes, the fear of judgment, the fear of God,— without the light which streams — more or less of it — upon the most benighted consciences in Christendom from the radiant Figure of our Lord Jesus Christ, should we have been better than they? Should we have been capable of unselfishness, or disinterestedness, or largeness of heart, or self-discipline, in that place of dizzy, awful elevation, with all the world at our feet,— with every incentive to indulge the whims and passions of self at the cost of others? Should we have been capable of the splendid natural virtues — I will not say of Antoninus or of Marcus Aurelius, but even of Trajan — even of Hadrian?

In our Lord's day the Jews of Palestine used to compare themselves with their forefathers who had a hand in murdering the prophets. They said that had they been there they would not have killed the prophets. But he who knew what was in man saw them through and through. He knew that they would have done just what their fathers had done before them. He looked onwards a few months into the future; he knew what was coming; he saw the Jewish mob which would arrest him in the garden; he heard the insults in the house of Caiaphas; he witnessed the long tragedy of the Way of Sorrows — the hours which he would spend on the cross of shame.

"Fill ye up, therefore, the measure of your fathers. Do not criticise men whose conduct would have been — whose temper and principles were — exactly your own."

Yes, circumstances have an immense restraining power, but they have of themselves no active power to change the heart. Dives and his brethren knew that divine code, the tenderness and mercy of which for the suffering and the poor had been so fully drawn out by the great Jewish teacher Nimonides. They were flooded with the light of God's moral law. Israel was the very home of the traditions of compassion and mercy that were to be found in the ancient world. Its higher conscience — this, as always, was on the side of the suffering and the poor.

"Be merciful after thy power. If thou hast much, give plenteously; if thou hast little, do thy diligence gladly to give of that little." "Give alms of thy goods, and never turn thy face from any poor man; and then the face of the Lord shall not be turned away from thee."

These were among its later utterances. The synagogue could name teachers famous for their tenderness, famous for their generosity and compassion; but Dives thought that these examples and motives were quite insufficient. We marvel at Dives; but, brethren, is it otherwise with ourselves? Do we not dwell on the difficulties of serving God in this as in other matters, and forget the grace, the light, the strength, the examples, the encouragements, which he has given us in the kingdom of his Son?

What might not heathens have done with our measure of opportunity — with our measure of light? There were towns in Israel of old the streets of which were trodden by the feet of the Saviour of the world, and he pronounced with his own blessed lips their condemnation on this very ground: because pagan cities with their advantages would have been very much more responsive to his presence and his words.

"Woe unto thee Chorazin! woe unto thee Bethsaida! for if the mighty works, which were done in you, had been done in Tyre and Sidon, they would have repented long ago in sackcloth and ashes."

No, it is something else than circumstances which makes us do God's will, just as it is something else than miracle which makes us believe his word. Miracle and circumstances do their part. They assist the heart; they make the task of the will easier; they do not compel obedience. He who has made us free respects our freedom even when we use it against himself — even when we resist his own most gracious and gentle pressure and choose to disbelieve or to disobey him. If Moses and the prophets are to persuade us — if we are not to be beyond persuasion, though one rose from the dead — there must be that inward seeking, yearning after God, that wholeness of heart, that tender and affectionate disposition towards him who is the end as he is the source of our existence, of which the Bible is so full from first to last — which is the very essence of religion — which he, its object and its author, gives most assuredly to all who ask him.

My brethren, few of us, it may be, are exactly in the case of Dives. Probably at least nine tenths of those who hear me have something to give, if they will make an effort at self-denial, in order to meet the claims of Lazarus. And to-day is a great occasion for discovering how far we are capable of persuasion by the love of God, by the chains of humanity, by the example and precepts of our divine Lord and Saviour, to say nothing of Moses and the prophets.

We have many of us, it may be, in our time, had before our minds visions of doing splendid deeds of benevolence — visions which belonged not to our actual means or circumstances, but to those of others, or to a fancy world. We have said to ourselves, "If I had the fortune of such and such a nobleman at my command, and if such and such a catastrophe were only to occur, how I should delight at laying out a hundred thousand pounds or half a million of money for the relief, the pure relief, of human suffering."

Oh, admirable aspiration! But the worst of it is that the occasion and the means of meeting it are alike hypothetical; and this purely hypothetical benevolence is like a certain sort of novel: it taxes our sympathy without resulting in any real good either to our own characters or to other people.

Do not let us wait to do what good we can till some one comes from the dead: do not let us wait till our circumstances change. Ere they change all may have ended with us, in this life of probation. "Though one rose from the dead."

A Lazarus has risen before now in history, not to persuade the selfish possessors of property to recognize their responsibilities towards human want and pain around them, but to judge. He has risen from the oppressions, from the neglect of a thousand years; he has risen, it may be, more than once in history amid scenes of blasphemy and violence and blood, but he has risen in the name of a forgotten justice to plead the cause which has been pleaded in vain by his open sore for ages, lying as he was at the gate of Dives.

The spectre of a social revolution has been happily unknown in England — unknown for this among other reasons — that the duties of the wealthy towards the suffering classes have been — I dare not say adequately, but largely — recognized among us for a great number of years. But the immense disparities of our society — its masses, its increasing masses, of poverty — its vast accumulations of wealth — present a contrast which year by year may well cause, as it does cause, increasing anxiety; and this anxiety can only be lessened, if those to whom God has given wealth and influence lose no opportunity at their disposal of supplying the wants and bettering the position of their poorer fellow countrymen.

Here is Hospital Sunday upon us,— a great, a blessed occasion for the fruitful exercise of pure benevolence. All the common objections to charitable effort are silent here. The social and political economists do not warn us to-day that we demoralize the poor when we bring them the highest medical skill and knowledge as they lie on their bed of pain. The financiers do not suggest that our alms are spent partly or wholly on the way to the object for which we give them. And at the gates of the hospitals, those true temples of compassion, our controversies are silent. Those who know most of our Lord and Saviour — those who know less or least about him — those even who do not own the empire of his ever blessed name — agree as to the urgency of his precept and his blessing, "Blessed are the merciful, for they shall obtain mercy." Lazarus is close to us. Hundreds of thousands in this vast city have succeeded to his inheritance; and if we, the servants of Christ, would not be as was Dives here and hereafter, we must not wait for larger means, for more striking occasions, for more commanding motives to self-sacrifice than we have.

We must enter now the secret chambers of our own hearts We must listen to all that God has taught us individually of his own astonishing mercy to us in Jesus Christ — of our utter need of it. For us Christians, Christ is Lazarus to the end of time, coming to us from the dead to warn us of our duty, receiving in the persons of his poor what we give as given to himself. Surely no social catastrophe, no unforeseen providence, no palpable miracle, could restrain us more effectually than his boundless, his patient, his unmerited love — than those divine words of his which faith, it seems to me, must trace over the door of every hospital: "Inasmuch as ye have done it unto one of the least of these my brethren, ye have done it unto me."

CONKLING

ROSCOE CONKLING, a noted American politician, was born at Albany, New York, October 30, 1829. He was educated at Mount Washington Collegiate Institute in New York city, and after pursuing the study of law at Utica, New York, was admitted to the Oneida County bar in 1850. Here he soon became conspicuous for his abilities, and was especially noted for his successful management of criminal cases. He took an active interest in politics and was mayor of Utica in 1858. In the year following he was sent to Congress as a Republican representative and after the outbreak of the Civil War stoutly upheld the Union cause. He failed of re-election in 1862 and practised his profession in Utica until in 1864 he was again returned to Congress. In 1867 he was elected to the national Senate. He took a leading part in the debate on reconstruction measures, opposing the policy of President Johnson with great vigor, and heartily deploring the failure of the impeachment proceedings against him. He was a zealous supporter of the administrations of President Grant, over which he exerted almost a controlling influence in certain directions, and in 1880 ardently championed the nomination of Grant for a third term, but was finally persuaded to acquiesce in the nomination of Garfield. Soon after Garfield's inauguration Conkling and his colleague Platt withdrew from the Senate on account of the President's assumption of the control of official appointments in New York, which the Senate confirmed. The remainder of Conkling's career was spent in New York city in the exercise of his profession. In 1882 he declined the offer of a seat on the Supreme Bench of the United States as associate-justice, tendered him by President Arthur, and refusing all inducements to return to public life remained unreconciled till his death, which occurred in New York city, April 18, 1888. Among his most noted speeches are the oration in the Senate in 1867 on the proposed impeachment of Henry Smythe, and a brief speech on the Cincinnati convention of 1880 nominating Grant for a third term in the presidency. Conkling was a man of fine powers but imperious and self-willed.

SUMMING-UP IN THE HADDOCK COURT-MARTIAL [1]

DELIVERED AUGUST, 1865

MAY IT PLEASE THE COURT,— Happily for the honor of the military profession, and for the fair fame of our land, prosecutions such as this have, until of late, been unknown in our history. In olden time, and

---

[1] Used by permission of A. R. Conkling.

(9116)

in later time, a commission in the army was a certificate of character and a passport everywhere. But the Rebellion, now ended, seems to have been appointed to illustrate, in manifold ways, the shame not less than the glory of humanity. A vessel tossed and groaning in a gale, a crew heroically manful, and a myriad of sharks following the ship — such is a faithful emblem of our condition during the mighty convulsion which has just subsided.

The nation was in the last peril of existence. The continent quaked under the tramp of an uncounted host, eager, from general to private, to suffer all, and dare all, for the salvation of the government of their fathers. But with them came knaves, titled and even shoulder-strapped, a darkening cloud of vampires, gorging themselves upon the heart's blood of their country. Shoddy contractors, bounty gamblers and base adventurers found their way even into the army, in order that they might the better, under patriotic pretensions, make to themselves gain of the woes of the community.

And accordingly spectacles like this trial have come to be familiar to the public eye. Officers are put to the bar of justice for crimes deserving rank among the baser felonies. Whether such instances shall continue, depends largely upon the result of exposures of which this trial is a somewhat conspicuous one. It is the peculiar privilege of the army that its honor is confided to its own keeping solely.

Infractions of its integrity are triable before soldiers alone, and thus the officers of the army become the guardians and avengers of its purity and honor. Such a prerogative is the property of no other profession, and it imposes responsibilities in the ratio of its exclusiveness. In one sense, this trial relates to the *morale* of the army. In another and a broader sense, it relates to the universal interest of the whole public. The war has ushered in an epoch of heroes and thieves. A carnival of venality has raged, until business connected with the government has become one grand masquerade of fraud.

Courts of every grade are kept open. The national jurisprudence, civil and military, is administered in splendid expense and with superfluous appointment. Petty offenders and common culprits are the vermin destroyed by the great machinery of justice, while right is humbled and baffled, if not abashed, in the presence of criminals too great to be punished.

A prolific cause of this is the free-masonry of profitable crime. Accusations, such as you sit to try, usually involve, as they do in this case, the impunity of many men. The prosecution must encounter, as it has done here, classes and combinations; and the result of pursuing offenders of such a grade, with the shrewdness, the money, the facilities they possess, is certain to be abortive unless special and exceptional effort is employed. Therefore, special and exceptional effort should be made. Whenever an instance occurs of guilt, traceable to one in an official station of power and sacredness, its exposure and punishment is a triumph of right, which should be emphasized by every salutary lesson which the fact can be made to enforce.

Such is, fortunately, the opinion of the government. Such is the undoubting faith of him selected to conduct this prosecution.

The arraignment of the accused proceeds upon the distinct avowal that it is not only justifiable and right, but the solemn duty of the government to ferret out those iniquities which have marred the sublimest moral spectacle of all time. The prosecution illustrates the principle that no partisanship of the criminal toward the administration, that no chagrin which may be felt by the government at the exposure of the fact that unfit men have been selected for high places, that nothing whatever shall stand in the way of the detection and punishment of crime.

But because vigilance has been employed in uncovering fraud and wrong, the managers of the defence have seen fit to decorate me, and even the government, with their censure. A labored effort is made to confound vigilance with persecution and injustice, and the resort which has been had to the evidence of a person involved in the misconduct of the accused is made this occasion of censorious complaint. The counsel forget that this trial will stand alone among military trials in the liberties and advantages accorded to the defence. A court composed of those who could have no bias against the accused was appointed at a place selected from regard to his interest, and thronged with the creatures of his official favor; three counsel were admitted, and have been allowed to argue, to examine, and to manage with unrestrained freedom; the chief witness for the defence has been suffered, before being called himself to hear all the testimony of opposing witnesses upon the very points upon which a witness should most be tested; a copy of the record has been furnished the accused from day to day; an extraordinary number of witnesses have been asked for, and not a witness, however obvious his uselessness, has been refused; and at length, having assented to reading the record from the shorthand notes, until three weeks of extended record had accumulated, the accused was indulged in an objection, the effect of which was, after the case for the prosecution was fully disclosed, to give to the defence six weeks to prepare to meet it; and during this long interval, the accused has had the range of the country.

In all this lenity of the court the judge-advocate has fully concurred, but he protests against the attempt now to manufacture anything from the case with which to deck, in specious disguises, the plea of "malice" and "persecution," that oldest and most threadbare resort of guilt. The true and only question is, What is established by the evidence? and to that inquiry immediate attention is invited. . . .

The case is one requiring of the prosecution the clearest and most convincing evidence. Proof should always be strong and satisfactory in the same degree in which the guilt it indicates is enormous. The accused is peculiarly entitled to the benefit of this principle of reason and of law. The crimes imputed to him are both atrocious and detestable, and a great presumption of innocence belongs to him as an officer and a man.

If guilty, his offence is nothing less than basely intriguing against the army, in the most critical period of its fate, and wielding the powers of a great official station against the life of the Republic itself. Is the accusation less heinous than this?

It is charged that when the army, thinned by battles and hardships, stood waiting for re-enforcements before closing with the enemy in the last grapple for the mastery; when exhaustion and divided sentiment in the loyal States told but too plainly that victory lost for a season would be lost forever; when a call for three hundred thousand more men had been made, and the destiny of the cause hung upon the response — that then, while standing in double trust as a soldier and as a high civil officer, the accused, for a consideration, thwarted the efforts to succor his comrades in the field, first by conniving at worthless enlistments, and second, by allowing recruits to be robbed, knowing that desertions and demoralization must follow.

But yet more sinister acts are laid at his door. It is alleged against him that he conspired to take to himself the moneys by which the army and the government subsisted, and to add exactions to taxes, making them too grievous to be borne, and this at a time when pecuniary disorders were about to solve disastrously the whole problem of the war. The range of such perfidy is bounded only by its power of mischief, and perhaps no man in the nation, save only the provost-marshal-general himself, held greater sway for good or evil in the special field of alleged malfeasance than he who presided with autocratic discretion over one third of the State of New York. . . .

This trial and its result may be looked at by those who come after us as a straw denoting currents in the decadence or the regeneration of public morals. Should it be ever so recurred to, each one who has acted his part in it decently and in order may rest assured that it will be well with him. One humble part has been, we are told, acted zealously — that part is mine. Is it true that I have been diligent in laying bare these iniquities? Give me a certificate of my zeal, that I may leave it as a legacy to my children; and bid them say of me, " He did his utmost to gibbet at the cross-roads of public justice all those who, when war had drenched the land with blood and covered it with mourning, parted the garment of their country among them, and cast lots upon the vesture of the government, even while they held positions of emolument and trust."

SPEECH NOMINATING GRANT[1]

DELIVERED JUNE 5, 1880

IN obedience to instructions I should never dare to disregard — expressing, also, my own firm convictions — I rise to propose a nomination with which the country and the Republican party can grandly win. The election before us is to be the Austerlitz of American politics. It will decide, for many years, whether the country shall be Republican or Cossack. The supreme need of the hour is not a candidate who can carry Michigan. All Republican candidates can do that. The need is not of a candidate who is popular in the Territories, because they have no vote. The need is of a candidate who can carry doubtful States. Not the doubtful States of the north alone, but doubtful States of the South, which we have heard, if I understand it aright, ought to take little or no part here, because the South has nothing to give, but everything to receive.

No, gentlemen, the need that presses upon the conscience of this convention is of a candidate who can carry doubtful States both north and south. And believing that he, more surely than any other man, can carry New York against any opponent, and can carry not only the North, but several States of the South, New York is for Ulysses S. Grant. Never defeated in peace or in war, his name is the most illustrious borne by living man.

His services attest his greatness, and the country — nay, the world — knows them by heart. His fame was earned

[1] Used by permission of A. R. Conkling.

'not alone in things written and said, but by the arduous greatness of things done. And perils and emergencies will search in vain in the future, as they have searched in vain in the past, for any other on whom the nation leans with such confidence and trust. Never having had a policy to enforce against the will of the people, he never betrayed a cause or a friend, and the people will never desert nor betray him.

Standing on the highest eminence of human distinction, modest, firm, simple, and self-poised, having filled all lands with his renown, he has seen not only the high-born and the titled, but the poor and the lowly in the uttermost ends of the earth rise and uncover before him. He has studied the needs and the defects of many systems of government, and he has returned a better American than ever, with a wealth of knowledge and experience added to the hard common sense which shone so conspicuously in all the fierce light that beat upon him during sixteen years, the most trying, the most portentous, the most perilous in the nation's history.

Vilified and reviled, ruthlessly aspersed by unnumbered presses, not in other lands but in his own, assaults upon him have seasoned and strengthened his hold on the public heart. Calumny's ammunition has all been exploded; the powder has all been burned once; its force is spent; and the name of Grant will glitter a bright and imperishable star in the diadem of the Republic when those who have tried to tarnish that name have moldered in forgotten graves, and when their memories and their epitaphs have vanished utterly.

Never elated by success, never depressed by adversity, he has ever, in peace as in war, shown the genius of common sense. The terms he prescribed for Lee's surrender foreshadowed the wisest prophecies and principles of true reconstruction. Victor in the greatest war of modern times, he quickly signalized his aversion to war and his love of peace by an arbitration of internal disputes, which stands as the wisest, the most majestic example of its kind in the world's diplomacy. When inflation, at the height of its popularity and frenzy, had swept both Houses of Congress, it was the veto of Grant which, single and alone, overthrew expansion and cleared the way for specie resumption. To him, immeasurably more than to any other man, is due the fact that every paper dollar is at last as good as gold.

With him as our leader we shall have no defensive campaign. No! We shall have nothing to explain away. We shall have no apologies to make. The shafts and the arrows have all been aimed at him, and they lie broken and harmless at his feet.

Life, liberty and property will find a safeguard in him. When he said of the colored men in Florida, "Wherever I am, they may come also" — when he so said, he meant that, had he the power, the poor dwellers in the cabins of the South should no longer be driven in terror from the homes of their childhood and the graves of their murdered dead. When he refused to see Dennis Kearney in California, he meant that communism, lawlessness, and disorder, although it might stalk high-headed and dictate law to a whole city, would always find a foe in him. He meant that, popular or unpopular, he would hew to the line of right, let the chips fly where they may.

His integrity, his common sense, his courage, his unequalled experience, are the qualities offered to his country. The only argument, the only one that the wit of man or the stress of politics has devised is one which would dumfounder Solomon, because he thought there was nothing new under the sun. Having tried Grant twice and found him faithful, we are told that we must not, even after an interval of years, trust him again.

My countrymen! my countrymen! what stultification does not such a fallacy involve! The American people exclude Jefferson Davis from public trust! Why? why? Because he was the arch-traitor and would-be destroyer; and now the same people are asked to ostracize Grant and not to trust him. Why? why? I repeat: because he was the arch-preserver of his country, and because, not only in war, but twice as civil magistrate, he gave his highest, noblest efforts to the republic. Is this an electioneering juggle, or is it hypocrisy's masquerade?

There is no field of human activity, responsibility, or reason in which rational beings object to an agent because he has been weighed in the balance and not found wanting. There is, I say, no department of human reason in which sane men reject an agent because he has had experience, making him exceptionally competent and fit.

From the man who shoes your horse to the lawyer who tries your cause, the officer who manages your railway or your mill, the doctor into whose hands you give your life, or the minister who seeks to save your soul, what man do you reject because by his works you have known him and found him faithful and fit? What makes the presidential office an exception to all things else in the common sense to be applied to selecting its incumbent? Who dares — who dares to put fetters on that free choice and judgment which is the birthright of the American people? Can it be said that Grant has used official power and place to perpetuate his term?

He has no place, and official power has not been used for him. Without patronage and without emissaries, without committees, without bureaus, without telegraph wires running from his house to this convention, or running from his house anywhere else, this man is the candidate whose friends have never threatened to bolt unless this convention did as they said. He is a Republican who never wavers. He and his friends stand by the creed and the candidates of the Republican party. They hold the rightful rule of the majority as the very essence of their faith, and they mean to uphold that faith against not only the common enemy, but against the charlatans, jayhawkers, tramps and guerrillas — the men who deploy between the lines, and forage now on one side and then on the other. This convention is master of a supreme opportunity. It can name the next President. It can make sure of his election. It can make sure not only of his election, but of his certain and peaceful inauguration. More than all, it can break that power which dominates and mildews the South. It can overthrow an organization whose very existence is a standing protest against progress.

The purpose of the Democratic party is spoils. Its very hope of existence is a Solid South. Its success is a menace to order and prosperity. I say this convention can overthrow that power. It can dissolve and emancipate a Solid South. It can speed the nation in a career of grandeur eclipsing all past achievements.

Gentlemen, we have only to listen above the din and look beyond the dust of an hour to behold the Republican party advancing with its ensigns resplendent with illustrious achievements, marching to certain and lasting victory with its greatest marshal at its head.

ISSUES OF THE CAMPAIGN

FROM SPEECH DELIVERED AT THE ACADEMY OF MUSIC, NEW YORK
SEPTEMBER 17, 1880

WHOEVER is given greeting and audience in such a presence ought indeed to have something worthy — something fit and wise to say. Inadequate in all, save only grateful and respectful appreciation, must be my return. We are citizens of a republic. We govern ourselves. Here no pomp of eager array in chambers of royalty awaits the birth of boy or girl to wield an hereditary sceptre whenever death or revolution pours on the oil of coronation. We know no sceptre save a majority's constitutional will. To wield that sceptre in equal share is the duty and the right, nay, the birthright, of every citizen. The supreme, the final, the only peaceful arbiter here, is the ballot-box: and in that urn should be gathered and from it should be sacredly recorded the conscience, the judgment, the intelligence of all. The right of free self-government has been in all ages the bright dream of oppressed humanity — the sighed-for privilege to which thrones, dynasties, and power have so long blocked the way. France seeks it by forced marches and daring strides. Mr. Forster, secretary for Ireland, tells the peerage of England it must take heed lest it fall; and Westminster and England ring with dread echoes of applause. But in the fulness of freedom the Republic of America is alone in the earth; alone in its grandeur; alone in its blessings; alone in its promises and possibilities, and therefore alone in the devotion due from its citizens. The time has come when law, duty, and interest require the nation to determine for at least four years its policy in many things. Two parties exist; parties should always exist in a government of majorities, and to support and strengthen the party which most nearly holds his views is among the most laudable, meritorious acts of an American citizen; and this whether he be in official or in private station. Two parties contend for the management of national affairs. The question is, Which of the two is it safer and wiser to trust? It is not a question of candidates. A candidate, if he be an honest, genuine man, will not seek and accept a party nomination to the presidency, vice-presidency, or Congress, and after he is elected become a law unto himself. The higher obligations among men are not set down in writing and signed or sealed — they reside in honor and good faith. The fidelity of a nominee belongs to this exalted class, and therefore a candidate of a party is but the exponent of a party. The object of political discussion and action is to settle principles, policies, and issues. It is a paltry incident of an election affecting fifty million people that it decides for an occasion the aspirations of individual men. The Democratic party is the Democratic candidate, and I am against the ticket and all its works.

The general issue confronting us is in itself and in its bearings sectional. I would, and you would, it were not so, but it is so. If in one portion of the country one party outnumbers the other even by overwhelming odds the fact need not be blamable, nor proof of sectional aggression. But if in any section a party gains and keeps control, not by numbers, not by honesty and law, and then, stifling free discussion and action, attempts to grasp the government of the whole country, the proceeding is sectional, guilty, and monstrous. In twelve States of the Union the approaching election is to be no more than a farce, unless, as has sometimes happened, it be turned into a tragedy. There is to be no free debate, no equal rights, no true expression in these States; and in several States the clear majority is to have no deciding power — not even a chance in a raffle such as that in which lots were cast and the booty divided the other day between Tammany Hall and the upper-air and solar-walk reform Democracy. Senator Hampton largely promises forty thousand Democratic majority in South Carolina, where the actual majority is forty thousand the other way. In several Southern States there is a large, well-known, often-ascertained Republican majority, but all Southern States alike, without exception or doubt, are relied upon to count on the Democratic side, and to score one hundred and thirty-eight electoral votes,— lacking but forty-seven of a majority of all. The causes of such a condition, and the consequences if it succeeds, are matters which no sane, intelligent man can put out of view, and yet he who discusses them must be told in the coarse parlance of the day that he waves "the bloody shirt." It is a relief to remember that this phrase and the thing it means is no invention of our politics. It dates back to Scotland three centuries ago. After a massacre in Glenfruin not so savage as has stained our annals, two hundred and twenty widows rode on white palfreys to Sterling towers bearing each on a spear her husband's bloody shirt. The appeal waked Scotland's slumbering sword, and outlawry and the block made the name of Glenfruin terrible to victorious Clan Alpine even to the third and fourth generation. I am not going to recite horrors, nor to allude to them, nor to the chapter of cruelty they fill; nor to retry the issues of the war. My purpose is quite different. It is to show, if I can, what is actually at stake now, who and what the contending forces are, how much the result may mean, and which way prudence and wisdom point.

You have listened to a letter from one to whom at least as much as to any other man the nation owes its preservation, prosperity, and primacy. This letter, instinct with common sense, hits the nail on the head. Its writer generally does hit nails, rebellions, and pretenders on the head. He says:—

This meeting should awaken the people to the importance of keeping control of the government in the hands of the Republican party until we can have two national parties, every member of which can cast his ballot as judgment dictates, without fear of molestation or ostracism, and have it honestly counted; parties not differing in opinion as to whether we are a nation, but as to the policy to secure the greatest good to the greatest number of its citizens. Sincerely believing that the Democratic party, as now constituted and controlled, is not a fit party to trust with the control of the general government, I believe it to the best interest of all sections, South as well as North, that the Republican party should succeed in November.

> Yours very truly,
> U. S. GRANT.

Lord Chesterfield said that a letter shows the man it is written to as well as the man it is written by. This letter bears Lord Chesterfield out. It is written to General Arthur, and it reveals the confidence and esteem in which the writer holds him. Informed by many years of intimate acquaintance, General Grant knew and felt as we know and feel, that he was writing not only to a friend, but to one of the most genuine, patriotic, and honorable of men.

This letter furnishes a text for many sermons. "The Democratic party as now constituted and controlled." How is it constituted, how controlled? There is a vast number of upright, patriotic men in it,— a vast number of men who gave all and did all they should have given and done to uphold their government and their flag in the supreme and dire hour of trial. A vast number who imperilled their lives, as other Democrats laid down their lives for their country. Many Northern Democrats who cast all their weight and sympathy on the nation's side, after the war was over returned to their former party associations; many others never did so return. Were such Democrats to guide and influence a Democratic Congress and a Democratic administration, their party would not be "constituted and controlled" as it is. As the Democratic party is constituted, not the men of the North, not the men who were for the Union and the constitution, but the men of the South who were against the Union and the constitution, men whose policy and purposes are still hurtful to the country, are bound and predestined to control a Democratic administration and a Democratic Congress. In the Senate and in the House the South has an overwhelming majority of the Democratic members, and most of them are men who led in the rebellion. Every party measure in Congress is settled in party caucus by a party majority; thus the southern members hold absolute sway. In possession of the law-making power, of the purse, and of the power to confirm or reject treaties and appointments, the South is also to furnish all the votes to elect the Democratic candidates, save only the forty-seven votes which must be raffled, or certified, or produced from the northern States, particularly not excepting Oregon. Should the election be close, there is no knowing but the two Democratic Houses may find ground on which to throw out a part or all of any State's electors. With much unemployed leisure on their hands, with the danger which the electoral commission of 1877 alone overpassed, for that time, staring the country in the face, these Democratic Houses have adopted no measure to ensure order and right in ascertaining the result of the presidential election. Should the controversy arise and the election be thrown into the House, there, the vote being taken by States, the South would cast nearly all the Democratic votes, and in the Senate the vote for vice-president would come from the same source. In every event of Democratic success the southern end of the Democratic party must be to the northern end as the locomotive is to the tender, as the horse is to the cart. This is as plain as any truth in gravitation or arithmetic. . . .

The resolution admitting Texas to the Union in 1845 provided for erecting out of Texas four additional States. The area and population are both sufficient. Such a proceeding would add eight to the number of southern senators, and add to Southern power in the electoral college. From New Mexico and other Territories, whose traditions and prejudices have descended from slaveholding influences, several new States may also be made. Schemes exist, not in embryo, but far advanced, to obtain "a slice of Mexico." Cattle stealing on the Rio Grande has been, and is, a fruitful occasion for incursions into Mexico. Special cavalry regiments of unusual size have been raised and stationed on the Texan frontier. It is an open secret that not long ago much exertion and alertness were needed to keep us out of another Mexican war. Without violating the constitution, or transcending the usages of the Republic, at least seven new States could be brought in, and in the case of some of them a very plausible case could be made. The project would become a high party measure. Its success would assure complete Democratic ascendency in the nation for a generation at least. It would put the government not merely in the hands of the Democratic party, but of the southern Democratic party. Why should not this be done? Who and what is to prevent it if the Democratic party is elected? The northern wing could never resist the southern wing in Congress were these new States brought forward for admission. The northern wing never could, never will, and never can withstand the pressure of the far stronger south wing. The past is pitiful in its warnings in this behalf. Despite pledges and northern indignation, northern Democrats in Congress united in voting down the Wilmot proviso in order to make California a slave State; united in voting for the Fugitive Slave Law; united in the mighty perfidy which overthrew the Missouri Compromise in order to fasten slavery on Kansas and other States, and united in defeating the Homestead Law — all at the behest of the southern majority. Mr. Van Buren at last, like Macbeth, would " go no further in this bloody business," and political destruction was his reward. Mr. Douglas at last made a brave stand against sectional aggression, and he was hunted to his grave. Caucus is king, and the avenging angel is hardly more inexorable in decree, or more unerring in retribution.

One of the main bulwarks of the Republic is the judiciary. The courts of justice are umpire, conservator, citadel. The Supreme Court is the final arbiter of many momentous controversies. This great tribunal is very obnoxious to Southern leaders in Congress and out. Mutterings deep and loud, breathings of dire longings to " go for " the court, have for years been gathering in volume. In the House of Representatives for two or three years this feeling has now and again found harsh voice in unseemly sinister words. Not only Kentucky, through the chairman of the judiciary committee, Mr. Knott, but Missouri, North Carolina, and other

States, assisted, I regret to say, by a representative from this city, have uttered language gross and calumnious of the court, aspersing its integrity and its decisions. "Mere drivel," "plausible sophistry," "packed, partisan, and demoralized," "packed tribunal," "decisions to be observed *pro tempore* only," "dirty work of its masters," "made a political decision to order," "fiery indignation of an inflamed people"—these are some of the buffetings to be found in the "Congressional Record," delivered sometimes from carefully written speeches, and sometimes received, the "Record" says, with "loud applause!" To what does all this pave the way? The "Congressional Record" will inform you. On the 26th of January, 1880, Mr. Manning of Mississippi — a State well known to be jealously sensitive to the pure administration of justice and the rigorous punishment of crimes, especially hideous, cowardly murder and massacre — introduced a bill to place twelve new additional judges on the Supreme Bench. What an easy, effectual, and withal plausible, disposition this would make of the court! Increased business would be such an innocent excuse — the court could sit by sevens for some purposes, and meet *in banque* for all large purposes when State sovereignty and State rights amendments to the constitution, and cotton taxes and the like are at stake. The circuit and district courts are obnoxious also. They are still more easy to deal with. . . . With courts revolutionized to conform to reactionary notions and dogmas, prejudices and interests, what may be the fate of questions affecting "commerce among the several States," revenue, bank and legal-tender currency, the taxation of government bonds, the currency in which these bonds are payable, civil rights acts, election laws, claims growing out of the war, claims for refunding the war tax on cotton, the late amendments, and many other grave matters, no man can predict. . . .

The army, too, is envied — its "offence is rank." It has been reduced to a skeleton, and whenever a scare, a pretence, a speck of war on the Mexican border or elsewhere can be discovered, the army must be increased and filled up. Filled up by whom? That depends on the approaching election. If Garfield and Arthur are chosen, by Union men always for the Union to the core. If Hancock and English and the Democratic party get in, by men who "went with their States." Confederate soldiers would flock to the standard of military as well as of civil service reform, and flock in a fervor of magnanimity and devotion, ready to let by-gones be by-gones, and to forgive the "usurpations of Lincoln" and the "unconstitutional coercion of sovereign States." Why shouldn't they? Who would be warranted to assert that a Confederate soldier was false or immodest in professing patriotic intentions while seeking rank in the army of the Republic. No man ought to assert it, and yet all fair men would agree that, other things being equal, preferments in the army should be given to those who fought in that army, rather than to those who assailed it in the dread extremity of the nation's life.

The recent amendments to the constitution and the laws made in pursuance of them are objects of unabated Democratic wrath — a wrath going to such excess as to compel the belief that free fraud in elections is deemed the only adequate means to party success. These amendments of freedom, especially the thirteenth and fourteenth, are constantly and flagrantly defied in more than half the Democratic States, and have been for years. The laws enacted under them have been denounced in every form, and denounced as null and void, even since the Supreme Court has solemnly decided otherwise. It was to get rid of these laws that the revolutionary plot was laid last year to stop the wheels of government, to close the courts and post-offices, and put out the beacon lights on the sea and on the lakes unless a repeal was yielded. With a thoroughbred Democratic President, whatever may happen in form to the amendments, they will become more a dead letter than a quickening spirit, and the laws made to enforce them will be swept like leaves before a gale. Should these laws be swept away, and should the spirit which assails them in the South, and which called them into being, continue to rage, mildew will follow in the wake. When Lincoln issued his proclamation of emancipation, men and women in this city were maddened by being made to believe that the slaves set free would swarm to the North, crowd out white labor, and cut down its wages. The draft riots were largely incited by this wicked, insane pretence. Throughout the North this was the appeal to the laboring-man, and many members of Congress who had supported Lincoln were defeated at the ensuing election. Vainly we pleaded for reason. We said no; men do not fly from liberty; they fly from slavery and wrong. Events have vindicated the logic of freedom. Once more I repeat the argument and the warning. The black man wants to remain by the graves of his fathers, but let persecutions go on, and the story of Pharaoh and of Egypt will be repeated. An exodus, not of a few despairing souls, but a real exodus will begin, depriving Southern fields of the hands that should and would till them, and bringing to the North and West a population not inured to Northern climes, and not adapted to usefulness and advantage here which fairly treated would come from them in the South.

The national banking system is another eyesore to the opposition. Their national conventions have denied all power of Congress to authorize banks. By votes and speeches in Congress, by declarations of conventions and leaders, by studied amendments offered to the bills, under which the national debt has been refunded, the national banking system has been struck wherever a blow could be put in. This fabric of banking is now inwrought not only with the business of the country, but with the maintenance of specie payments,— it stands a lion in the path of fiat money, inflation, and all the long train of financial heresies which possess the Democratic mind, especially in the South. In unnumbered ways, direct and indirect, this vast interest is constantly exposed to the action of Congress. The Cincinnati convention seems to have felt the need of a little caution on this point when it nominated Mr. English for Vice-President. He is president of a national bank. They nominated a Union general as a blind to the soldiers, and a bank officer as a blind to the bankers. Evidently it is thought the Northern Democratic team drives better with blinders. But even blinders do not always answer. In 1864, after solemnly asserting, just when the rebellion was gasping its last, that the war for the Union was a failure, the Democratic convention, at instigation coming then from the sheltering refuge of the Canadian shore, the same instigation which prompted a like expedient now, put up a Union general. That general did not issue order No. 40 in the midst of lawlessness and butchery, which civil authority could not arrest. No, he issued orders arresting the legislature of Maryland, a State which had not seceded, and he issued orders proclaiming martial law and suspending the habeas corpus at election time, and placed soldiers as supervisors of the polls. But

even with such a Union general the disguise was too
thin. . . .

War claims upon the treasury have been and will be a
subject fruitful of much agitation. I am moved to refer to
it by the wholly groundless assertion in regard to it now
going the rounds of party journals. The fashion of this
assertion seems to have been set by Mr. Randall, the speaker
of the House of Representatives. Mr. Randall is one of the
ablest and most intelligent, as he is one of the most courage-
ous men of his party, and I speak of him with much respect.
In several speeches he has taken up the matter of southern
claims, always to say that they are barred by the fourteenth
amendment of the constitution. It puzzles me to see how
so discerning a man can have fallen into such an error. The
proceedings over which he presides constantly refutes the
assertion. In the fourteenth amendment stand these words:
"Neither the United States nor any State shall assume or
pay any debt or obligation incurred in aid of insurrection or
rebellion against the United States, or any claim for the loss
or emancipation of any slave; but all such debts, obligations,
and claims shall be held illegal and void." The claims which
stand in staggering totals in bills already before Congress,
and in other bills said to be waiting, are not touched by this
section of the constitution. For example, it is insisted that
the direct tax imposed by the nation on all States in 1861
should as to the seceded States be refunded. The amount
claimed is $2,492,110. Again, it is said the war tax laid on
cotton should be refunded. The argument is that cotton,
like wheat and corn, is a product of the earth, and that wheat
and corn were not taxed, and, therefore, cotton should not
have been taxed. There is plausibility in this; but petro-
leum is a product of the earth also, and that was heavily

taxed, not only during the war, but afterward, and yet Pennsylvania has never claimed that the money should be refunded. The amount of cotton tax claimed is $170,180,220. Again, buildings were occupied, crops were trampled, fences and woods were burned, provisions were consumed, edifices were demolished, and regions were laid waste by the armies of the Union. The total of such claims dizzies arithmetic. These are not " debt or obligations incurred in aid of insurrection or rebellion," — decidedly not in aid of rebellion. They are claims because of the acts done to crush rebellion. The constitutional amendment does not come within gunshot of them. The error of the distinguished speaker is the more puzzling because, as reported, he said in another part of his address recently that the Republican majority in Congress had paid $100,000,000 of such claims. This I presume is true if he means that Republicans have voted to pay Union men whose property was taken for public use the value of the property so taken. But, whether correct in the amount or not, he is certainly correct in saying that a vast sum has been so paid. Does not this fact clearly show that such claims are not extinguished by the constitution? If they were so extinguished, surely the law-making power would not have been so stupid or wicked as to pay them year after year, and this without any member of either House ever suggesting that the constitution stood in the way. These appropriations for southern claims also throw light on the question whether Republican action in Congress has been hostile and cruel to the South. The statutes on the subject enacted by Republicans have made the loyalty of the claimant a *sine qua non*, and the Democrats have repeatedly voted to repeal the loyalty test, and bills for this purpose are now pending. There can be no doubt that the way is wide open to all the southern claims which a majority can be found to vote for and a President to sign. . . .

In the face of the facts, bald and arrant as the claim is, the country is gravely told of wondrous Democratic economies, and it now begins to be stated that the resumption of specie payments was really brought about by the frugality of a Democratic Congress. If a race was to be sailed on the sea of fiction, the inventor of this statement would surely take the cup. The resumption of specie payments was a transcendent achievement. The credit of it belongs to some party, and to that party future generations will look back with grateful admiration. Whoever would know the truth about it can easily do so. After the war we had afloat well toward a thousand millions of paper currency. It fluctuated in value from thirty-eight to seventy cents in the dollar. The public debt was more than twenty-eight hundred millions, and more than twenty-three hundred millions of it bore interest. The annual interest charge was a hundred and fifty millions. The first presidential election afterward was in 1868. The two parties, of course, arrayed themselves on the greatest financial issue which has ever arisen in this country, or perhaps in any country. The question was, what should be done with the colossal debt inflicted by the rebellion, and with the sea of paper promises we had been compelled to put out. The Democratic party pronounced for repudiation. The declaration was covert and indirect, but it meant repudiation. They resolved that all debts should be paid in paper promises unless the obligation expressly on its face said otherwise, or unless the law mentioned that coin should be paid. They resolved that " government bonds and all other securities " should all be taxed. They resolved that " every species of property " should be taxed, and taxed at its " real value." They resolved that there should be but one currency for the government and the " bondholder." Taken together, these declarations were plain repudiation.

The Republicans in their national convention declared two things: First, that repudiation is a national crime; and that every debt must be paid to the uttermost, not according to the letter but the spirit of the law. Second, that the wise course was to improve our credit so as to refund our bonded debt at lower interest, and that this could not be done if repudiation, open or covert, partial or total, was threatened or suspected. On this platform General Grant was elected. His first presidential syllable was spoken on the portico of the Capitol to assembled thousands, and spoken with lips which only an instant before had touched the Bible to solemnize an oath of faithfulness in office. In his inaugural address, then delivered, stand these words: —

" A great debt has been contracted in securing to us and our posterity the Union; the payment of this debt, principal and interest, as well as the return to a specie basis as soon as it can be accomplished without material detriment to the debtor class or to the country at large, must be provided for. To protect the national honor, every dollar of government indebtedness should be paid in gold, unless otherwise expressly stipulated in the contract. Let it be understood that no repudiator of one farthing of our public debt will be trusted in public place, and it will go far toward strengthening a credit which ought to be the best in the world, and will ultimately enable us to replace the debt with bonds bearing less interest than we now pay."

This significant declaration produced a deep sensation. Both Houses of Congress were Republican. Immediately a bill was introduced in each House " to strengthen the public credit." In less than a fortnight it had passed both Houses and was approved by President Grant March 18, 1869. It was the first act he ever signed. It declared that "the faith of the United States is solemnly pledged to the payment in coin or its equivalent of all the obligations of the United States not bearing interest, known as United States notes, and of all the interest-bearing obligations of the United States, except in cases where the law authorizing the issue of any such obligations had expressly provided that the same may be paid in lawful money, or other currency than gold and silver. . . . And the United States also solemnly pledges its faith to make provision at the earliest practicable period for the redemption of the United States notes in coin."

This bill was resisted by the solid Democracy in both Houses. They voted against it, they voted against considering it, they voted for amendments to pervert and reverse its meaning. Senator Thurman of Ohio moved to add to it: "Provided that nothing herein contained shall apply to obligations called 5-20 bonds." Every Democratic senator present voted for this, every Republican voted against it. The 5-20 bonds then constituted the great bulk of the public debt, and this proviso would have frustrated and vitiated the whole act. Senator Davis of Kentucky moved to amend so as to scale down the bonds to the coin value at the time of the currency received for them. This was supported by the Democrats, Senator Bayard of Delaware among others speaking in its favor. Senator Vickers of Maryland moved to amend so as to prevent coin ever being purchased to be used to pay bonds. Senator Bayard denounced the bill as wrong, unwise, and as a "stock-jobbing operation." After all this the bill passed, and not one Democrat voted for it in either House. The next step in this progress was the funding act of July, 1870,— the act authorizing the redemption of the 5-20 or 6 per cent. bonds by negotiating bonds bearing lower interest. All the Democrats resisted this bill also, and voted against it. Exempting the new bonds from taxation was opposed. In the Senate, Mr. Bayard moved to strike out the provision and to subject the bonds to taxation; all the Democrats voted for it. Again, Mr. Bayard moved an amendment to bring back the State banking system, and all the Democrats voted for that also. The bill was at length carried by Republican votes. By this time our currency had much appreciated, and funding at lower interest began.

In 1874, by a vote not Democratic alone, an inflation bill made its way through both Houses. The pressure upon President Grant to induce him to sign it exceeded anything of the kind I have ever witnessed. Men who should have upheld his hands not only threw their weight upon him, but industriously criticised and even ridiculed his venturing to set up his opinion against a majority in such a crisis. He vetoed the bill, however. In his message, returning it unsigned, he referred to the declaration of the Republican party, to his inaugural, to the act of 1869 already cited, and he said the proposed act would violate faith, and he was against it. This happened on the 22d of April, 1874. About a month later a conversation occurred one evening between the President and his chief adviser, Secretary Fish, and others about the wise course out of the increased difficulties which had come from the disasters of the year before. One of those present at this conversation was Senator Jones of Nevada. So struck was he with the views expressed by President Grant, that the next day (June 4, 1874) he by letter requested that the substance of them should be put in writing and a copy sent him. This was done, and the memorandum made by the President was handed about among members of the two Houses and afterward found its way into print.

Here it is. It is the foreshadow of the Resumption Act, to which the veto had paved the way. I read two passages:

"I believe it a high and plain duty to return to a specie basis at the earliest practical day, not only in compliance with legislative and party pledges, but as a step indispensable to lasting national prosperity. I believe further that the time has come when this can be done, or at least begun with less embarrassment to every branch of industry than at any future time after resort has been had to unstable and temporary expedients to stimulate unreal prosperity and speculation on a basis other than coin, the recognized medium of exchange throughout the commercial world. The particular mode selected to bring about a restoration of the specie standard is not of so much consequence as that some plan be devised, the time fixed when currency shall be exchangeable for coin at par, and the plan adopted rigidly adhered to. . . . I would like to see a provision that at a fixed day, say July 1, 1876, the currency issued by the United States should be redeemed in coin on presentation to any assistant treasurer, and that all the currency so redeemed should be cancelled and never reissued. To effect this, it would be necessary to authorize the issue of bonds payable in gold, bearing such interest as would command par in gold, to be put out by the treasury only in such sums as should from time to time be needed for the purpose of redemption."

It was not long before this advice found the form of law. A committee composed wholly of Republican senators, of whom I was myself one, prepared the bill now known as the resumption act. It was not the work of any one senator, nor did it express literally and in full, perhaps, the views of any single member of the committee. It was a compromise of somewhat conflicting opinions. It was submitted to every Republican member of the Senate, and every one, after consideration, determined to vote for it. It was brought forward in the Senate, and every Republican senator did vote for it. Every Democratic senator present voted against it. It went to the House, and there encountered a solid Democratic opposition, but it was carried by Republican votes. President Grant promptly signed it. It fixed the 1st of January, 1879, for the resumption of specie payments, and when the day came, as noiselessly and naturally as night melts into day, specie payments were resumed.

A triumphant nationality — a regenerated constitution — a free Republic — an unbroken country — untarnished credit — solvent finances — unparalleled prosperity — all these are ours despite the policy and the efforts of the Democratic party. Along with the amazing improvement in national finances, we have amazing individual thrift on every side. In every walk of life new activity is felt. Labor, agriculture, manufactures, commerce, enterprises, and investments, all are flourishing, content and hopeful. But in the midst of this harmony and encouragement comes a harsh discord crying, "Give us a change — anything for a change." This is not a bearing year for "a change." Every other crop is good, but not the crop of "change"— that crop is good only when the rest are bad. The country does not need or wish the change proposed, and the pressing invitation of our Democratic friends is much like "Will you walk into my parlor, said the spider to the fly." A good-natured but firm "No, I thank you," will be the response at the polls. . . .

Upon its record and its candidates the Republican party asks the country's approval, and stands ready to avow its purposes for the future. It proposes to rebuild our commercial marine, driven from the sea by Confederate cruisers, aided and abetted by foreign hostility. It proposes to foster labor, industry, and enterprise. It proposes to stand for education, humanity, and progress. It proposes to administer the government honestly, to preserve amity with all the world, observing our own obligations with others and seeing that others observe theirs with us, to protect every citizen of whatever birth or color in his rights and equality before the law, including his right to vote and to be counted, to uphold the public credit and the sanctity of engagements; and by doing these things the Republican party proposes to assure to industry, humanity, and civilization in America the amplest welcome and the safest home.

BLAINE

JAMES G. BLAINE was born in Washington County, Pennsylvania, in 1830, and, having graduated at Washington College in that State, emigrated to Maine, where he became editor of the Portland "Advertiser" and the Kennebec "Journal." He was a member of the popular branch of the Maine Legislature from 1859 to 1862, and in the last named year was chosen Speaker of that body. He was sent to Congress in 1862, and served continuously in the House of Representatives until 1876, when he was appointed United States Senator from Maine. For three successive terms, that is to say during the period from 1869 to 1875 inclusive, he had been chosen Speaker of the House of Representatives. Upon the whole, he must be regarded as having been the Republican leader in that assembly after the death of Thaddeus Stevens. He was a conspicuous candidate for the Republican nomination for the Presidency in 1876; in 1880 he was Secretary of State under President Garfield, and was himself nominated for the Presidency in 1884. In 1888 he declined a renomination for that office, but he had many supporters in the Republican Convention in 1892. He died in January, 1893.

ORATION ON GARFIELD

IN THE HALL OF THE HOUSE OF REPRESENTATIVES, FEBRUARY 27, 1882

Mr. President:

FOR the second time in this generation the great departments of the government of the United States are assembled in the Hall of Representatives, to do honor to the memory of a murdered President. Lincoln fell at the close of a mighty struggle, in which the passions of men had been deeply stirred. The tragical termination of his great life added but another to the lengthened succession of horrors which had marked so many lintels with the blood of the firstborn. Garfield was slain in a day of peace, when brother had been reconciled to brother, and when anger and hate had been banished from the land.

"Whoever shall hereafter draw a portrait of murder, if he will show it as it has been exhibited where such example was last to have been looked for, let him not give it the grim visage of Moloch, the brow knitted by revenge, the face black with settled hate. Let him draw, rather, a decorous, smooth-faced, bloodless demon; not so much an example of human nature in its depravity and in its parroxysms of crime, as an infernal being, a fiend in the ordinary display and development of his character."

From the landing of the Pilgrims at Plymouth till the uprising against Charles I., about twenty thousand emigrants came from old England to New England. As they came in pursuit of intellectual freedom and ecclesiastical independence, rather than for worldly honor and profit, the emigration naturally ceased when the contest for religious liberty began in earnest at home. The man who struck his most effective blow for freedom of conscience, by sailing for the Colonies in 1620, would have been accounted a deserter to leave after 1640. The opportunity had then come on the soil of England for that great contest which established the authority of Parliament, gave religious freedom to the people, sent Charles to the block, and committed to the hands of Oliver Cromwell the supreme executive authority of England. The English emigration was never renewed, and from these twenty thousand men, with a small emigration from Scotland and from France, are descended the vast numbers who have New England blood in their veins.

In 1685 the revocation of the Edict of Nantes by Louis XIV., scattered to other countries four hundred thousand

Protestants, who were among the most intelligent and enterprising of French subjects—merchants of capital, skilled manufacturers, and handicraftsmen superior at the time to all others in Europe. A considerable number of these Huguenot French came to America; a few landed in New England and became honorably prominent in its history. Their names have in large part become Anglicized, or have disappeared, but their blood is traceable in many of the most reputable families and their fame is perpetuated in honorable memorials and useful institutions.

From these two sources, the English-Puritan and the French-Huguenot, came the late President—his father, Abram Garfield, descended from the one, and his mother, Eliza Ballou, from the other.

It was good stock on both sides—none better, none braver, none truer. There was in it an inheritance of courage, of manliness, of imperishable love of liberty, of undying adherence to principle. Garfield was proud of his blood; and, with as much satisfaction as if he were a British nobleman reading his stately ancestral record in Burke's "Peerage," he spoke of himself as ninth in descent from those who would not endure the oppression of the Stuarts, and seventh in descent from the brave French Protestants who refused to submit to tyranny even from the Grand Monarque.

General Garfield delighted to dwell on these traits, and during his only visit to England he busied himself in discovering every trace of his forefathers in parish registers and on ancient army rolls. Sitting with a friend in the gallery of the House of Commons one night after a long day's labor in this field of research, he said with evident elation that in every war in which for three centuries patriots of **English blood** had struck sturdy blows for constitutional government and human liberty, his family had been represented. They were at Marston Moor, at Naseby, and at Preston; they were at Bunker Hill, at Saratoga, and at Monmouth, and in his own person had battled for the same great cause in the war which preserved the Union of the States.

Losing his father before he was two years old, the early life of Garfield was one of privation, but its poverty has been made indelicately and unjustly prominent. Thousands of readers have imagined him as the ragged, starving child, whose reality too often greets the eye in the squalid sections of our large cities. General Garfield's infancy and youth had none of their destitution, none of their pitiful features appealing to the tender heart and to the open hand of charity. He was a poor boy in the same sense in which Henry Clay was a poor boy; in which Andrew Jackson was a poor boy; in which Daniel Webster was a poor boy; in the sense in which the large majority of the eminent men of America in all generations have been poor boys. Before a great multitude of men, in a public speech, Mr. Webster bore this testimony:

"It did not happen to me to be born in a log-cabin, but my elder brothers and sisters were born in a log-cabin raised amid the snowdrifts of New Hampshire, at a period so early that when the smoke rose first from its rude chimney and curled over the frozen hills, there was no similar evidence of a white man's habitation between it and the settlements on the rivers of Canada. Its remains still exist. I make to it an annual visit. I carry my children to it to teach them the hardships endured by the generations which have gone before them. I love to dwell on the tender recollections, the kindred ties, the early affections, and the touch-

The subsequent military career of Garfield fully sustained its brilliant beginning. With his new commission he was assigned to the command of a brigade in the Army of the Ohio, and took part in the second decisive day's fight in the great battle of Shiloh. The remainder of the year 1862 was not especially eventful to Garfield, as it was not to the armies with which he was serving. His practical sense was called into exercise in completing the task assigned him by General Buell, of reconstructing bridges and re-establishing lines of railway communication for the army. His occupation in this useful but not brilliant field was varied by service on courts-martial of importance, in which department of duty he won a valuable reputation, attracting the notice and securing the approval of the able and eminent judge-advocate-general of the army. That of itself was a warrant to honorable fame; for among the great men who in those trying days gave themselves, with entire devotion, to the service of their country, one who brought to that service the ripest learning, the most fervid eloquence, the most varied attainments, who labored with modesty and shunned applause, who in the day of triumph sat reserved and silent and grateful—as Francis Deak in the hour of Hungary's deliverance—was Joseph Holt, of Kentucky, who in his honorable retirement enjoys the respect and veneration of all who love the Union of the States.

Early in 1863 Garfield was assigned to the highly important and responsible post of chief of staff to General Rosecrans, then at the head of the Army of the Cumberland. Perhaps in a great military campaign no subordinate officer requires sounder judgment and quicker knowledge of men than the chief of staff to the commanding general. An indiscreet man in such a position can sow more discord, breed more jealousy, and disseminate more strife than any other officer in the entire organization. When General Garfield assumed his new duties he found various troubles already well developed and seriously affecting the value and efficiency of the Army of the Cumberland. The energy, the impartiality, and the tact with which he sought to allay these dissensions, and to discharge the duties of his new and trying position, will always remain one of the most striking proofs of his great versatility. His military duties closed on the memorable field of Chickamauga, a field which, however disastrous to the Union arms, gave to him the occasion of winning imperishable laurels. The very rare distinction was accorded him of great promotion for his bravery on a field that was lost. President Lincoln appointed him a major-general in the army of the United States for gallant and meritorious conduct in the battle of Chickamauga.

The Army of the Cumberland was reorganized under the command of General Thomas, who promptly offered Garfield one of its divisions. He was extremely desirous to accept the position, but was embarrassed by the fact that he had, a year before, been elected to Congress, and the time when he must take his seat was drawing near. He preferred to remain in the military service, and had within his own breast the largest confidence of success in the wider field which his new rank opened to him. Balancing the arguments on the one side and the other, anxious to determine what was for the best, desirous, above all things, to do his patriotic duty, he was decisively influenced by the advice of President Lincoln and Secretary Stanton, both of whom assured him that he could, at that time, be of especial value in the House of Representatives. He resigned his commission of major-general on the fifth day of December, 1863, and took his seat in the House of Representatives on the seventh. He had served two years and four months in the army, and had just completed his thirty-second year.

The Thirty-eighth Congress is pre-eminently entitled in history to the designation of the War Congress. It was elected while the war was flagrant, and every member was chosen upon the issues involved in the continuance of the struggle. The Thirty-seventh Congress had, indeed, legislated to a large extent on war measures, but it was chosen before any one believed that secession of the States would be actually attempted. The magnitude of the work which fell upon its successor was unprecedented, both in respect to the vast sums of money raised for the support of the army and navy, and of the new and extraordinary powers of legislation which it was forced to exercise. Only twenty-four States were represented, and one hundred and eighty-two members were upon its roll. Among these were many distinguished party leaders on both sides, veterans in the public service with established reputations for ability and with that skill which comes only from parliamentary experience. Into this assemblage of men Garfield entered without special preparation, and it might almost be said unexpectedly. The question of taking command of a division of troops under General Thomas, or taking his seat in Congress, was kept open till the last moment; so late, indeed, that the resignation of his military commission and his appearance in the House were almost contemporaneous. He wore the uniform of a major-general of the United States army on Saturday, and on Monday, in civilian's dress, he answered to the roll call as a Representative in Congress from the State of Ohio.

He was especially fortunate in the constituency which

elected him. Descended almost entirely from New England stock, the men of the Ashtabula district were intensely radical on all questions relating to human rights. Well educated, thrifty, thoroughly intelligent in affairs, acutely discerning of character, not quick to bestow confidence, and slow to withdraw it, they were at once the most helpful and most exacting of supporters. Their tenacious trust in men in whom they have once confided is illustrated by the unparalleled fact that Elisha Whittlesey, Joshua R. Giddings, and James A. Garfield represented the district for fifty-four years.

There is no test of man's ability in any department of public life more severe than service in the House of Representatives; there is no place where so little deference is paid to reputation previously acquired or to eminence won outside; no place where so little consideration is shown for the feelings or failures of beginners. What a man gains in the House he gains by sheer force of his own character, and if he loses and falls back he must expect no mercy and will receive no sympathy. It is a field in which the survival of the strongest is the recognized rule and where no pretence can deceive and no glamour can mislead. The real man is discovered, his worth is impartially weighed, his rank is irreversibly decreed.

With possibly a single exception, Garfield was the youngest member in the House when he entered, and was but seven years from his college graduation. But he had not been in his seat sixty days before his ability was recognized and his place conceded. He stepped to the front with the confidence of one who belonged there. The House was crowded with strong men of both parties; nineteen of them have since been transferred to the Senate, and many of them have served with distinction in the gubernatorial chairs of their respective States and on foreign missions of great consequence; but among them all none grew so rapidly, none so firmly, as Garfield. As is said by Trevelyan of his parliamentary hero, Garfield succeeded "because all the world in concert could not have kept him in the background, and because when once in the front he played his part with a prompt intrepidity and a commanding ease that were but the outward symptoms of the immense reserves of energy on which it was in his power to draw." Indeed, the apparently reserved force which Garfield possessed was one of his great characteristics. He never did so well but that it seemed he could easily have done better. He never expended so much strength but that he seemed to be holding additional power to call. This is one of the happiest and rarest distinctions of an effective debater, and often counts for as much in persuading an assembly as the eloquent and elaborate argument.

The great measure of Garfield's fame was filled by his service in the House of Representatives. His military life, illustrated by honorable performance, and rich in promise, was, as he himself felt, prematurely terminated and necessarily incomplete. Speculation as to what he might have done in the field, where the great prizes are so few, cannot be profitable. It is sufficient to say that as a soldier he did his duty bravely; he did it intelligently; he won an enviable fame, and he retired from the service without blot or breath against him. As a lawyer, though admirably equipped for the profession, he can scarcely be said to have entered on its practice. The few efforts that he made at the bar were distinguished by the same high order of talent which he exhibited on every field where he was put to test, and if a man may be accepted as a competent judge of his own capacities and adaptation, the law was the profession to which Garfield should have devoted himself. But fate ordained it otherwise, and his reputation in history will rest largely upon .his service in the House of Representatives. That service was exceptionally long. He was nine times consecutively chosen to the House, an honor enjoyed by not more than six other Representatives of the more than five thousand who have been elected from the organization of the government to this hour.

As a parliamentary orator, as a debater on an issue squarely joined, where the position had been chosen and the ground laid out, Garfield must be assigned a very high rank. More, perhaps, than any man with whom he was associated in public life he gave careful and systematic study to public questions, and he came to every discussion in which he took part with elaborate and complete preparation. He was a steady and indefatigable worker. Those who imagine that talent or genius can supply the place or achieve the results of labor will find no encouragement in Garfield's life. In preliminary work he was apt, rapid, and skilful. He possessed in a high degree the power of readily absorbing ideas and facts, and, like Dr. Johnson, had the art of getting from a book all that was of value in it by a reading apparently so quick and cursory that it seemed like a mere glance at the table of contents. He was a preeminently fair and candid man in debate, took no petty advantage, stooped to no unworthy methods, avoided personal allusions, rarely appealed to prejudice, did not seek to inflame passion. He had a quicker eye for the strong point of his adversary than for his weak point, and on his own side he so marshalled his weighty arguments as to make his hearers forget any possible lack in the complete strength of his position. He had a habit of stating his opponent's side with such amplitude of fairness and such liberality of concession that his followers often complained that he was giving his case away. But never in his prolonged participation in the proceedings of the House did he give his case away, or fail in the judgment of competent and impartial listeners to gain the mastery.

These characteristics, which marked Garfield as a great debater, did not, however, make him a great parliamentary leader. A parliamentary leader, as that term is understood wherever free representative government exists, is necessarily and very strictly the organ of his party. An ardent American defined the instinctive warmth of patriotism when he offered the toast, "Our country always right; but, right or wrong, our country." The parliamentary leader who has a body of followers that will do and dare and die for the cause is one who believes his party always right, but, right or wrong, is for his party. No more important or exacting duty devolves upon him than the selection of the field and the time of the contest. He must know not merely how to strike, but where to strike and when to strike. He often skilfully avoids the strength of his opponent's position and scatters confusion in his ranks by attacking an exposed point, when really the righteousness of the cause and the strength of logical intrenchment are against him. He conquers often both against the right and the heavy battalions; as when young Charles Fox, in the days of his Toryism, carried the House of Commons against justice, against immemorial rights, against his own convictions—if, indeed, at that period Fox had convictions—and in the interest of a corrupt administration, in obedience to a tyrannical sovereign, drove Wilkes from the seat to which the electors of Middlesex had chosen him and installed Luttrell, in defiance, not merely of law, but of public decency. For an achievement of that kind Garfield was disqualified—disqualified by the texture of his mind, by the honesty of his heart, by his conscience, and by every instinct and aspiration of his nature.

The three most distinguished parliamentary leaders hitherto developed in this country are Mr. Clay, Mr. Douglas, and Mr. Thaddeus Stevens. Each was a man of consummate ability, of great earnestness, of intense personality, differing widely each from the others, and yet with a signal trait in common—the power to command. In the "give and take" of daily discussion; in the art of controlling and consolidating reluctant and refractory followers; in the skill to overcome all forms of opposition, and to meet with competency and courage the varying phases of unlooked-for assault or unsuspected defection, it would be difficult to rank with these a fourth name in all our Congressional history. But of these Mr. Clay was the greatest. It would, perhaps, be impossible to find in the parliamentary annals of the world a parallel to Mr. Clay, in 1841, when at sixty-four years of age he took the control of the Whig party from the President who had received their suffrages, against the power of Webster in the Cabinet, against the eloquence of Choate in the Senate, against the herculean efforts of Caleb Cushing and Henry A. Wise in the House. In unshared leadership, in the pride and plenitude of power he hurled against John Tyler with deepest scorn the mass of that conquering column which had swept over the land in 1840, and drove his administration to seek shelter behind the lines of his political foes. Mr. Douglas

JAMES G. BLAINE

achieved a victory scarcely less wonderful when, in 1854, against the secret desires of a strong administration, against the wise counsel of the older chiefs, against the conservative instincts and even the moral sense of the country, he forced a reluctant Congress into a repeal of the Missouri Compromise. Mr. Thaddeus Stevens, in his contests from 1865 to 1868, actually advanced his parliamentary leadership until Congress tied the hands of the President and governed the country by its own will, leaving only perfunctory duties to be discharged by the Executive. With two hundred millions of patronage in his hands at the opening of the contest, aided by the active force of Seward in the Cabinet, and the moral power of Chase on the Bench, Andrew Johnson could not command the support of one-third in either House against the parliamentary uprising of which Thaddeus Stevens was the animating spirit and the unquestioned leader.

From these three great men Garfield differed radically; differed in the quality of his mind, in temperament, in the form and phase of ambition. He could not do what they did, but he could do what they could not, and in the breadth of his Congressional work he left that which will longer exert a potential influence among men, and which, measured by the severe test of posthumous criticism, will secure a more enduring and more enviable fame.

Those unfamiliar with Garfield's industry, and ignorant of the details of his work, may in some degree measure them by the annals of Congress. No one of the generation of public men to which he belonged has contributed so much that will be valuable for future reference. His speeches are numerous, many of them brilliant, all of them well studied, carefully phrased, and exhaustive of the subject under consideration. Collected from the scattered pages of ninety royal octavo volumes of the Congressional Record, they would present an invaluable compendium of the political history of the most important era through which the national government has ever passed. When the history of this period shall be impartially written, when war legislation, measures of reconstruction, protection of human rights, amendments to the Constitution, maintenance of public credit, steps toward specie resumption, true theories of revenue may be reviewed, unsurrounded by prejudice and disconnected from partisanism, the speeches of Garfield will be estimated at their true value and will be found to comprise a vast magazine of fact and argument, of clear analysis and sound conclusion. Indeed, if no other authority were accessible, his speeches in the House of Representatives from December, 1863, to June, 1880, would give a well connected history and complete defence of the important legislation of the seventeen eventful years that constitute his parliamentary life. Far beyond that, his speeches would be found to forecast many great measures yet to be completed—measures which he knew were beyond the public opinion of the hour, but which he confidently believed would secure popular approval within the period of his own lifetime, and by the aid of his own efforts.

Differing, as Garfield does, from the brilliant parliamentary leaders, it is not easy to find his counterpart anywhere in the record of American public life. He perhaps more nearly resembles Mr. Seward in his supreme faith in the all-conquering power of a principle. He had the love of learning and the patient industry of investigation to which John Quincy Adams owes his prominence and his Presidency. He had some of those ponderous elements of mind which distinguished Mr. Webster, and which indeed, in all our public life, have left the great Massachusetts Senator without an intellectual peer.

In English parliamentary history, as in our own, the leaders in the House of Commons present points of essential difference from Garfield. But some of his methods recall the best features in the strong, independent course of Sir Robert Peel, and striking resemblances are discernible in that most promising of modern Conservatives, who died too early for his country and his fame, Lord George Bentinck. He had all of Burke's love for the sublime and the beautiful, with, possibly, something of his superabundance, and in his faith and his magnanimity, in his power of statement, in his subtle analysis, in his faultless logic, in his love of literature, in his wealth and world of illustration, one is reminded of that great English statesman of to-day, who, confronted with obstacles that would daunt any but the dauntless, reviled by those whom he would relieve as bitterly as by those whose supposed rights he is forced to invade, still labors with serene courage for the amelioration of Ireland and for the honor of the English name.

Garfield's nomination to the Presidency, while not predicted or anticipated, was not a surprise to the country. His prominence in Congress, his solid qualities, his wide reputation, strengthened by his then recent election as Senator from Ohio, kept him in the public eye as a man occupying the very highest rank among those entitled to be called statesmen. It was not mere chance that brought him this high honor. "We must," says Mr. Emerson, "reckon success a constitutional trait. If Eric is in robust health, and has slept well and is at the top of his condition, and thirty years old at his departure from Greenland, he

will steer west and his ships will reach Newfoundland.
But take Eric out and put in a stronger and bolder man
and the ships will sail six hundred, one thousand, fifteen
hundred miles further and reach Labrador and New England. There is no chance in results.''

As a candidate Garfield steadily grew in public favor.
He was met with a storm of detraction at the very hour of
his nomination, and it continued with increasing volume
and momentum until the close of his victorious campaign:

> "No might nor greatness in mortality
> Can censure 'scape; backwounding calumny
> The whitest virtue strikes. What king so strong
> Can tie the gall up in the slanderous tongue?"

Under it all he was calm, strong, and confident; never
lost his self-possession, did no unwise act, spoke no hasty
or ill-considered word. Indeed, nothing in his whole life
is more remarkable or more creditable than his bearing
through those five full months of vituperation—a prolonged
agony of trial to a sensitive man, a constant and cruel draft
upon the powers of moral endurance. The great mass of
these unjust imputations passed unnoticed, and, with the
general *debris* of the campaign, fell into oblivion. But in
a few instances the iron entered his soul and he dies with
the injury unforgotten if not unforgiven.

One aspect of Garfield's candidacy was unprecedented.
Never before in the history of partisan contests in this
country had a successful Presidential candidate spoken
freely on passing events and current issues. To attempt
anything of the kind seemed novel, rash, and even desperate. The older class of voters recalled the unfortunate
Alabama letter, in which Mr. Clay was supposed to have
signed his political death-warrant. They remembered also

the hot-tempered effusion by which General Scott lost a large share of his popularity before his nomination, and the unfortunate speeches which readily consumed the remainder. The younger voters had seen Mr. Greeley in a series of vigorous and original addresses preparing the pathway for his own defeat. Unmindful of these warnings, unheeding the advice of friends, Garfield spoke to large crowds as he journeyed to and from New York in August, to a great multitude in that city, to delegations and to deputations of every kind that called at Mentor during the summer and autumn. With innumerable critics, watchful and eager to catch a phrase that might be turned into odium or ridicule, or a sentence that might be distorted to his own or his party's injury, Garfield did not trip or halt in any one of his seventy speeches. This seems all the more remarkable when it is remembered that he did not write what he said, and yet spoke with such logical consecutiveness of thought and such admirable precision of phrase as to defy the accident of misreport and the malignity of misrepresentation.

In the beginning of his Presidential life Garfield's experience did not yield him pleasure or satisfaction. The duties that engross so large a portion of the President's time were distasteful to him, and were unfavorably contrasted with his legislative work. "I have been dealing all these years with ideas," he impatiently exclaimed one day, "and here I am dealing only with persons. I have been heretofore treating of the fundamental principles of government, and here I am considering all day whether A or B shall be appointed to this or that office." He was earnestly seeking some practical way of correcting the evils arising from the distribution of overgrown and unwieldy patronage—evils always appreciated and often discussed by him, but whose magnitude had been more deeply impressed upon his mind since his accession to the Presidency. Had he lived, a comprehensive improvement in the mode of appointment and in the tenure of office would have been proposed by him, and, with the aid of Congress, no doubt perfected.

But, while many of the executive duties were not grateful to him, he was assiduous and conscientious in their discharge. From the very outset he exhibited administrative talent of a high order. He grasped the helm of office with the hand of a master. In this respect, indeed, he constantly surprised many who were most intimately associated with him in the government, and especially those who had feared that he might be lacking in the executive faculty. His disposition of business was orderly and rapid. His power of analysis and his skill in classification enabled him to despatch a vast mass of detail with singular promptness and ease. His cabinet meetings were admirably conducted. His clear presentation of official subjects, his well-considered suggestion of topics on which discussion was invited, his quick decision when all had been heard, combined to show a thoroughness of mental training as rare as his natural ability and his facile adaptation to a new and enlarged field of labor.

With perfect comprehension of all the inheritances of the war, with a cool calculation of the obstacles in his way, impelled always by a generous enthusiasm, Garfield conceived that much might be done by his administration toward restoring harmony between the different sections of the Union. He was anxious to go South and speak to the people. As early as April he had ineffectually endeavored to arrange for a trip to Nashville, whither he had been cordially invited, and he was again disappointed a few weeks later to find that he could not go to South Carolina to attend the centennial celebration of the victory of the Cowpens. But for the autumn he definitely counted on being present at the three memorable assemblies in the South, the celebration at Yorktown, the opening of the Cotton Exposition at Atlanta, and the meeting of the Army of the Cumberland at Chattanooga. He was already turning over in his mind his address for each occasion, and the three taken together, he said to a friend, gave him the exact scope and verge which he needed. At Yorktown he would have before him the association of a hundred years that bound the South and the North in the sacred memory of a common danger and a common victory. At Atlanta he would present the material interests and the industrial development which appealed to the thrift and independence of every household, and which should unite the two sections by the instinct of self-interest and self-defence. At Chattanooga he would revive memories of the war only to show that after all its disaster and all its suffering the country was stronger and greater, the Union rendered indissoluble, and the future, through the agony and blood of one generation, made brighter and better for all.

Garfield's ambition for the success of his administration was high. With strong caution and conservatism in his nature, he was in no danger of attempting rash experiments or of resorting to the empiricism of statesmanship. But he believed that renewed and closer attention should be given to questions affecting the material interests and commercial prospects of fifty millions of people. He believed that our continental relations, extensive and undeveloped as they are, involved responsibility and could be cultivated into profitable friendship or be abandoned to harmful **indifference or** lasting enmity. He believed with equal confidence that an essential forerunner to a new era of national progress must be a feeling of contentment in every section of the Union and a generous belief that the benefits and burdens of government would be common to all. Himself a conspicuous illustration of what ability and ambition may do under republican institutions, he loved his country with a passion of patriotic devotion, and every waking thought was given to her advancement. He was an American in all his aspirations, and he looked to the destiny and influence of the United States with the philosophic composure of Jefferson and the demonstrative confidence of John Adams.

The political events which disturbed the President's serenity for many weeks before that fatal day in July, form an important chapter in his career, and, in his own judgment, involved questions of principle and right which are vitally essential to the constitutional administration of the Federal Government. It would be out of place here and now to speak the language of controversy, but the events referred to, however they may continue to be a source of contention with others, have become, as far as Garfield is concerned, as much a matter of history as his heroism at Chickamauga or his illustrious service in the House. Detail is not needful, and personal antagonism shall not be rekindled by any word uttered to-day. The motives of those opposing him are not to be here adversely interpreted nor their course harshly characterized. But of the dead President this is to be said, and said because his own speech is forever silenced and he can be no more heard except through the fidelity and the love of surviving friends: From the beginning to the end of the controversy he so much deplored, the President was never for one moment actuated by any motive of gain to himself or of loss to others. Least of all men did he harbor revenge, rarely did he even show resentment, and malice was not in his nature. He was congenially employed only in the exchange of good offices and the doing of kindly deeds.

There was not an hour, from the beginning of the trouble till the fatal shot entered his body, when the President would not gladly, for the sake of restoring harmony, have retracted any step he had taken if such retracting had merely involved consequences personal to himself. The pride of consistency, or any supposed sense of humiliation that might result from surrendering his position, had not a feather's weight with him. No man was ever less subject to such influences from within or from without. But after the most anxious deliberation and the coolest survey of all the circumstances, he solemnly believed that the true prerogatives of the Executive were involved in the issue which had been raised and that he would be unfaithful to his supreme obligation if he failed to maintain, in all their vigor, the constitutional rights and dignities of his great office. He believed this in all the convictions of conscience when in sound and vigorous health, and he believed it in his suffering and prostration in the last conscious thought which his wearied mind bestowed on the transitory struggles of life.

More than this need not be said. Less than this could not be said. Justice to the dead, the highest obligation that devolves upon the living, demands the declaration that in all the bearings of the subject, actual or possible, the President was content in his mind, justified in his conscience, immovable in his conclusions.

The religious element in Garfield's character was dee[
and earnest. In his early youth he espoused the faith o
the Disciples, a sect of that great Baptist Communion
which in different ecclesiastical establishments is so numer
ous and so influential throughout all parts of the Unite
States. But the broadening tendency of his mind and hi
active spirit of inquiry were early apparent, and carrie
him beyond the dogmas of sect and the restraints of asso
ciation. In selecting a college in which to continue hi
education he rejected Bethany, though presided over b
Alexander Campbell, the greatest preacher of his Church
His reasons were characteristic: First, that Bethany leane
too heavily toward slavery; and, second, that being himsel
a Disciple, and the son of Disciple parents, he had littl
acquaintance with people of other beliefs, and he though
it would make him more liberal, quoting his own words
both in his religious and general views, to go into a ne
circle and be under new influences.

The liberal tendency which he had anticipated as th
result of wider culture was fully realized. He was eman
cipated from mere sectarian belief, and with eager interes
pushed his investigations in the direction of modern pro
gressive thought. He followed with quickening steps i
the paths of exploration and speculation so fearlessly trod
den by Darwin, by Huxley, by Tyndall, and by othe
living scientists of the radical and advanced type. Hi
own Church, binding its disciples by no formulated creed
but accepting the Old and New Testaments as the wor
of God, with unbiased liberality of private interpretation
favored, if it did not stimulate, the spirit of investigation
Its members profess with sincerity, and profess only, to b
of one mind and one faith with those who immediatel

followed the Master and who were first called Christians
at Antioch.

But however high Garfield reasoned of "fixed fate, free-
will, foreknowledge absolute," he was never separated from
the Church of the Disciples in his affections and in his associations. For him it held the Ark of the Covenant. To
him it was the gate of heaven. The world of religious belief is full of solecisms and contradictions. A philosophic
observer declares that men by the thousand will die in defence of a creed whose doctrines they do not comprehend
and whose tenets they habitually violate. It is equally true
that men by the thousand will cling to church organizations
with instinctive and undenying fidelity when their belief in
maturer years is radically different from that which inspired
them as neophytes.

But after this range of speculation and this latitude of
doubt, Garfield came back always with freshness and delight
to the simpler instincts of religious faith, which, earliest im-
planted, longest survive. Not many weeks before his as-
sassination, walking on the banks of the Potomac with a
friend, and conversing on those topics of personal religion
concerning which noble natures have unconquerable reserve, he said that he found the Lord's Prayer and the
simple petitions learned in infancy infinitely restful to him,
not merely in their stated repetition, but in their casual and
frequent recall as he went about the daily duties of life.
Certain texts of Scripture had a very strong hold on his
memory and his heart. He heard, while in Edinburgh
some years ago, an eminent Scotch preacher, who prefaced
his sermon with reading the eighth chapter of the Epistle
to the Romans, which book had been the subject of careful study with Garfield during his religious life. He was

greatly impressed by the elocution of the preacher and declared that it had imparted a new and deeper meaning to the majestic utterances of Saint Paul. He referred often in after years to that memorable service, and dwelt with exaltation of feeling upon the radiant promise and the assured hope with which the great Apostle of the Gentiles was "persuaded that neither death, nor life, nor principalities, nor powers, nor things present, nor things to come, nor height, nor depth, nor any other creature, shall be able to separate us from the love of God, which is in Christ Jesus our Lord."

The crowning characteristic of Garfield's religious opinions, as, indeed, of all his opinions, was his liberality. In all things he had charity. Tolerance was of his nature. He respected in others the qualities which he possessed himself—sincerity of conviction and frankness of expression. With him inquiry was not so much what a man believes, but Does he believe it? The lines of his friendship and his confidence encircled men of every creed and men of no creed, and, to the end of his life, on his ever lengthening list of friends were to be found the names of a pious Catholic priest and of an honest-minded and generous-hearted freethinker.

On the morning of Saturday, July 2d, the President was a contented and happy man—not in an ordinary degree, but joyfully, almost boyishly, happy. On his way to the railroad station, to which he drove slowly, in conscious enjoyment of the beautiful morning, with an unwonted sense of leisure and a keen anticipation of pleasure, his talk was all in the grateful and gratulatory vein. He felt that, after four months of trial, his administration was strong in its grasp of affairs, strong in popular favor, and destined to grow stronger; that grave difficulties confronting him at his inauguration had been safely passed; that troubles lay behind him, and not before him; that he was soon to meet the wife whom he loved, now recovering from an illness which had but lately disquieted and at times almost unnerved him; that he was going to his Alma Mater to renew the most cherished associations of his young manhood, and to exchange greetings with those whose deepening interest had followed every step of his upward progress, from the day he entered upon his college course until he had attained the loftiest elevation in the gift of his countrymen.

Surely, if happiness can ever come from the honors or triumphs of this world, on that quiet July morning James A. Garfield may well have been a happy man. No foreboding of evil haunted him; no slightest premonition of danger clouded his sky. His terrible fate was upon him in an instant. One moment he stood erect, strong, confident in the years stretching peacefully out before him. The next he lay wounded, bleeding, helpless, doomed to weary weeks of torture, to silence and the grave.

Great in life, he was surpassingly great in death. For no cause, in the very frenzy of wantonness and wickedness, by the red hand of murder, he was thrust from the full tide of this world's interest, from its hopes, its aspirations, its victories, into the visible presence of death—and he did not quail. Not alone for one short moment in which, stunned and dazed, he could give up life, hardly aware of its relinquishment, but through days of deadly languor, through weeks of agony, that was not less agony because silently borne, with clear sight and calm courage he looked into his open grave. What blight and ruin met his anguished eyes, whose lips may tell—what brilliant, broken plans, what baffled, high ambitions, what sundering of strong, warm, manhood's friendship, what bitter rending of sweet household ties! Behind him a proud, expectant nation, a great host of sustaining friends, a cherished and happy mother, wearing the full, rich honors of her early toil and tears; the wife of his youth, whose whole life lay in his; the little boys not yet emerged from childhood's day of frolic; the fair, young daughter; the sturdy sons just springing into closest companionship, claiming every day and every day rewarding a father's love and care; and in his heart the eager, rejoicing power to meet all demands. And his soul was not shaken. His countrymen were thrilled with instant, profound, and universal sympathy. Masterful in his mortal weakness, he became the centre of a nation's love, enshrined in the prayers of a world. But all the love and all the sympathy could not share with him his suffering. He trod the wine-press alone. With unfaltering front he faced death. With unfailing tenderness he took leave of life. Above the demoniac hiss of the assassin's bullet he heard the voice of God. With simple resignation he bowed to the Divine decree.

As the end drew near his early craving for the sea returned. The stately mansion of power had been to him the wearisome hospital of pain, and he begged to be taken from his prison walls, from its oppressive, stifling air, from its homelessness and its hopelessness. Gently, silently, the love of a great people bore the pale sufferer to the longed-for healing of the sea, to live or to die, as God should will, within sight of the heaving billows, within sound of its manifold voices. With a wan, fevered face, tenderly lifted to the cooling breeze, he looked out wistfully upon the ocean's changing wonders; on its far sails; on its restless

waves, rolling shoreward to break and die beneath the noonday sun; on the red clouds of evening, arching low to the
horizon; on the serene and shining pathway of the stars.
Let us think that his dying eyes read a mystic meaning
which only the rapt and parting soul may know. Let us
believe that in the silence of the receding world he heard
the great waves breaking on a further shore and felt already
upon his wasted brow the breath of the eternal morning.

ON THE REMONETIZATION OF SILVER

UNITED STATES SENATE, FEBRUARY 7, 1878

THE discussion on the question of remonetizing silver,
Mr. President, has been prolonged, able, and exhaustive. I may not expect to add much to its
value, but I promise not to add much to its length. I
shall endeavor to consider facts rather than theories, to
state conclusions rather than arguments:

First. I believe gold and silver coin to be the money
of the Constitution—indeed, the money of the American
people anterior to the Constitution, which that great organic
law recognized as quite independent of its own existence.
No power was conferred on Congress to declare that either
metal should not be money. Congress has therefore, in my
judgment, no power to demonetize silver any more than to
demonetize gold; no power to demonetize either any more
than to demonetize both. In this statement I am but repeating the weighty dictum of the first of constitutional
lawyers. "I am certainly of opinion," said Mr. Webster,

"that gold and silver, at rates fixed by Congress, constitute the legal standard of value in this country, and that neither Congress nor any State has authority to establish any other standard or to displace this standard." Few persons can be found, I apprehend, who will maintain that Congress possesses the power to demonetize both gold and silver, or that Congress could be justified in prohibiting the coinage of both; and yet in logic and legal construction it would be difficult to show where and why the power of Congress over silver is greater than over gold—greater over either than over the two. If, therefore, silver has been demonetized, I am in favor of remonetizing it. If its coinage has been prohibited, I am in favor of ordering it to be resumed. If it has been restricted, I am in favor of having it enlarged.

Second. What power, then, has Congress over gold and silver? It has the exclusive power to coin them; the exclusive power to regulate their value; very great, very wise, very necessary powers, for the discreet exercise of which a critical occasion has now arisen. However men may differ about causes and processes, all will admit that within a few years a great disturbance has taken place in the relative values of gold and silver, and that silver is worth less or gold is worth more in the money markets of the world in 1878 than in 1873, when the further coinage of silver dollars was prohibited in this country. To remonetize it now as though the facts and circumstances of that day were surrounding us, is to wilfully and blindly deceive ourselves. If our demonetization were the only cause for the decline in the value of silver, then remonetization would be its proper and effectual cure. But other causes, quite beyond our control, have been far more potentially operative than the simple fact of Congress prohibiting its further coinage;

and as legislators we are bound to take cognizance of these causes. The demonetization of silver in the great German Empire and the consequent partial, or wellnigh complete, suspension of coinage in the governments of the Latin Union, have been the leading dominant causes for the rapid decline in the value of silver. I do not think the over-supply of silver has had, in comparison with these other causes, an appreciable influence in the decline of its value, because its over-supply with respect to gold in these later years has not been nearly so great as was the over-supply of gold with respect to silver for many years after the mines of California and Australia were opened; and the over-supply of gold from those rich sources did not effect the relative positions and uses of the two metals in any European country.

I believe then if Germany were to remonetize silver and the kingdoms and states of the Latin Union were to reopen their mints, silver would at once resume its former relation with gold. The European countries when driven to remonetization, as I believe they will be, must of necessity adopt their old ratio of fifteen and a half of silver to one of gold, and we shall then be compelled to adopt the same ratio instead of our former sixteen to one. For if we fail to do this we shall, as before, lose our silver, which like all things else seeks the highest market; and if fifteen and a half pounds of silver will buy as much gold in Europe as sixteen pounds will buy in America, the silver, of course, will go to Europe. But our line of policy in a joint movement with other nations to remonetize is very simple and very direct. The difficult problem is what we shall do when we aim to re-establish silver without the co-operation of European powers, and really as an advance movement to coerce them

there into the same policy. Evidently the first dictate of
prudence is to coin such a dollar as will not only do justice
among our citizens at home, but will prove a protection—
an absolute barricade—against the gold monometallists of
Europe, who, whenever the opportunity offers, will quickly
draw from us the one hundred and sixty millions of gold
coin still in our midst. And if we coin a silver dollar of
full legal tender, obviously below the current value of the
gold dollar, we are opening wide our doors and inviting
Europe to take our gold. And with our gold flowing out
from us we are forced to the single silver standard and
our relations with the leading commercial countries of the
world are at once embarrassed and crippled.

Third. The question before Congress then—sharply
defined in the pending House bill—is, whether it is now
safe and expedient to offer free coinage to the silver dollar
of 412½ grains, with the mints of the Latin Union closed
and Germany not permitting silver to be coined as money.
At current rates of silver, the free coinage of a dollar con-
taining 412½ grains, worth in gold about ninety-two cents,
gives an illegitimate profit to the owner of the bullion,
enabling him to take ninety-two cents' worth of it to the
mint and get it stamped as coin and force his neighbor to
take it for a full dollar. This is an undue and unfair advantage which the government has no right to give to the
owner of silver bullion, and which defrauds the man who
is forced to take the dollar. And it assuredly follows that
if we give free coinage to this dollar of inferior value and
put it in circulation, we do so at the expense of our better
coinage in gold; and unless we expect the uniform and
invariable experience of other nations to be in some mysterious way suspended for our peculiar benefit, we inevi-

tably lose our gold coin. It will flow out from us with the certainty and resistless force of the tides. Gold has indeed remained with us in considerable amount during the circulation of the inferior currency of the legal tender; but that was because there were two great uses reserved by law for gold: the collection of customs and the payment of interest on the public debt. But if the inferior silver coin is also to be used for these two reserved purposes, then gold has no tie to bind it to us. What gain, therefore, would we make for the circulating medium, if on opening the gate for silver to flow in, we open a still wider gate for gold to flow out? If I were to venture upon a dictum on the silver question, I would declare that until Europe remonetizes we cannot afford to coin a dollar as low as 412½ grains. After Europe remonetizes on the old standard, we cannot afford to coin a dollar above 400 grains. If we coin too low a dollar before general remonetization our gold will flow out from us. If we coin too high a dollar after general remonetization our silver will leave us. It is only an equated value both before and after general remonetization that will preserve both gold and silver to us. . . .

Fifth. The responsibility of re-establishing silver in its ancient and honorable place as money in Europe and America, devolves really on the Congress of the United States. If we act here with prudence, wisdom, and firmness, we shall not only successfully remonetize silver and bring it into general use as money in our own country, but the influence of our example will be potential among all European nations, with the possible exception of England. Indeed, our annual indebtment to Europe is so great that if we have the right to pay it in silver we necessarily coerce those nations by the strongest of all forces, self-interest, to aid us in upholding the value of silver as money. But if we attempt the remonetization on a basis which is obviously and notoriously below the fair standard of value as it now exists, we incur all the evil consequences of failure at home and the positive certainty of successful opposition abroad. We are and shall be the greatest producers of silver in the world, and we have a larger stake in its complete monetization than any other country. The difference to the United States between the general acceptance of silver as money in the commercial world and its destruction as money, will possibly equal within the next half century the entire bonded debt of the nation. But to gain this advantage we must make it actual money—the accepted equal of gold in the markets of the world. Remonetization here followed by general remonetization in Europe will secure to the United States the most stable basis for its currency that we have ever enjoyed, and will effectually aid in solving all the problems by which our financial situation is surrounded.

Sixth. On the much-vexed and long-mooted question of a bimetallic or monometallic standard my own views are sufficiently indicated in the remarks I have made. I believe the struggle now going on in this country and in other countries for a single gold standard would, if successful, produce widespread disaster in the end throughout the commercial world. The destruction of silver as money and establishing gold as the sole unit of value must have a ruinous effect on all forms of property except those investments which yield a fixed return in money. These would be enormously enhanced in value, and would gain a disproportionate and unfair advantage over every other species of property. If, as the most reliable statistics affirm, there are nearly seven thousand millions of coin or bullion in the world, not very unequally divided between gold and silver, it is impossible to strike silver out of existence as money without results which will prove distressing to millions and utterly disastrous to tens of thousands.   Alexander Hamilton, in his able and invaluable report in 1791 on the establishment of a mint, declared that "to annul the use of either gold or silver as money is to abridge the quantity of circulating medium, and is liable to all the objections which arise from a comparison of the benefits of a full circulation with the evils of a scanty circulation."   I take no risk in saying that the benefits of a full circulation and the evils of a scanty circulation are both immeasurably greater to-day than they were when Mr. Hamilton uttered these weighty words, always provided that the circulation is one of actual money, and not of depreciated promises to pay.

In the report from which I have already quoted, Mr. Hamilton argues at length in favor of a double standard, and all the subsequent experience of wellnigh ninety years has brought out no clearer statement of the whole case nor developed a more complete comprehension of this subtle and difficult subject.   "On the whole," says Mr. Hamilton, "it seems most advisable not to attach the unit exclusively to either of the metals, because this cannot be done effectually without destroying the office and character of one of them as money and reducing it to the situation of mere merchandise."   And then Mr. Hamilton wisely concludes that this reduction of either of the metals to mere merchandise (I again quote his exact words) "would probably be a greater evil than occasional variations in the unit from the fluctuations in the relative value of the metals, especially if care be taken to regulate the proportion between them with an eye to their average commercial value."   I do not think that this country, holding so vast a proportion of the world's supply of silver in its mountains and its mines, can afford to reduce the metal to the "situation of mere merchandise." If silver ceases to be used as money in Europe and America, the great mines of the Pacific Slope will be closed and dead. Mining enterprises of the gigantic scale existing in this country cannot be carried on to provide backs for looking-glasses and to manufacture cream-pitchers and sugar-bowls. A vast source of wealth to this entire country is destroyed the moment silver is permanently disused as money. It is for us to check that tendency and bring the continent of Europe back to the full recognition of the value of the metal as a medium of exchange.

Seventh. The question of beginning anew the coinage of silver dollars has aroused much discussion as to its effect on the public credit; and the Senator from Ohio (Mr. Matthews) placed this phase of the subject in the very forefront of the debate—insisting, prematurely and illogically, I think, on a sort of judicial construction in advance, by concurrent resolution, of a certain law in case that law should happen to be passed by Congress. My own view on this question can be stated very briefly. I believe the public creditor can afford to be paid in any silver dollar that the United States can afford to coin and circulate. We have forty thousand millions of property in this country, and a wise self-interest will not permit us to overturn its relations by seeking for an inferior dollar wherewith to settle the dues and demands of any creditor. The question might be different from a merely selfish standpoint if, on paying the dollar to the public creditor, it would disappear after performing that function. But the trouble is that the inferior dollar you pay the public creditor remains in circulation, to the exclusion of the better dollar. That which you pay at home will stay there; that which you send abroad will come back. The interest of the public creditor is indissolubly bound up with the interest of the whole people. Whatever affects him affects us all; and the evil that we might inflict upon him by paying an inferior dollar would recoil upon us with a vengeance as manifold as the aggregate wealth of the Republic transcends the comparatively small limits of our bonded debt. And remember that our aggregate wealth is always increasing, and our bonded debt steadily growing less! If paid in a good silver dollar, the bondholder has nothing to complain of. If paid in an inferior silver dollar, he has the same grievance that will be uttered still more plaintively by the holder of the legal-tender note and of the national-bank bill, by the pensioner, by the day laborer, and by the countless host of the poor, whom we have with us always, and on whom the most distressing effect of inferior money will be ultimately precipitated.

But I must say, Mr. President, that the specific demand for the payment of our bonds in gold coin and in nothing else comes with an ill grace from certain quarters. European criticism is levelled against us and hard names are hurled at us across the ocean, for simply daring to state that the letter of our law declares the bonds to be payable in standard coin of July 14, 1870; expressly and explicitly declared so, and declared so in the interest of the public creditor, and the declaration inserted in the very body of the eight hundred million of bonds that have been issued since that date. Beyond all doubt the silver dollar was included in the standard coins of that public act. Payment at that time would have been as acceptable and as undisputed in silver as in gold dollars, for both were equally valuable in the European as well as in the American market. Seven-eighths of all our bonds, owned out of the country, are held in Germany and in Holland, and Germany has demonetized silver and Holland has been forced thereby to suspend its coinage, since the subjects of both powers purchased our securities. The German empire, the very year after we made our specific declaration for paying our bonds in coin, passed a law destroying so far as lay in their power the value of silver as money. I do not say that it was specially aimed at this country, but it was passed regardless of its effect upon us, and was followed, according to public and undenied statement, by a large investment on the part of the German Government in our bonds, with a view, it was understood, of holding them as a coin reserve for drawing gold from us to aid in establishing their gold standard at home. Thus, by one move the German Government destroyed, so far as lay in its power, the then existing value of silver as money, enhanced consequently the value of gold, and then got into position to draw gold from us at the moment of their need, which would also be the moment of our own sorest distress. I do not say that the German Government in these successive steps did a single thing which it had not a perfect right to do, but I do say that the subjects of that empire have no right to complain of our government for the initial step which has impaired the value of one of our standard coins. And the German Government, by joining with us in the remonetization of silver, can place that standard coin in its old position and make it as easy for this government to pay and as profitable for their subjects to receive the one metal as the other. . . .

The effect of paying the labor of this country in silver coin of full value, as compared with the irredeemable paper or as compared even with silver of inferior value, will make itself felt in a single generation to the extent of tens of millions, perhaps hundreds of millions, in the aggregate savings which represent consolidated capital. It is the instinct of man from the savage to the scholar—developed in childhood and remaining with age—to value the metals which in all tongues are called precious. Excessive paper money leads to extravagance, to waste, and to want, as we painfully witness on all sides to-day. And in the midst of the proof of its demoralizing and destructive effect, we hear it proclaimed in the Halls of Congress that "the people demand cheap money." I deny it. I declare such a phrase to be a total misapprehension, a total misinterpretation of the popular wish. The people do not demand cheap money. They demand an abundance of good money, which is an entirely different thing. They do not want a single gold standard that will exclude silver and benefit those already rich. They do not want an inferior silver standard that will drive out gold and not help those already poor. They want both metals, in full value, in equal honor, in whatever abundance the bountiful earth will yield them to the searching eye of science and to the hard hand of labor.

The two metals have existed side by side in harmonious, honorable companionship as money, ever since intelligent trade was known among men. It is wellnigh forty centuries since "Abraham weighed to Ephron the silver which he had named in the audience of the sons of Heth—four hundred shekels of silver—current money with the merchant." Since that time nations have risen and fallen, races have disappeared, dialects and languages have been forgotten, arts have been lost, treasures have perished, continents have been discovered, islands have been sunk in the sea, and through all these ages, and through all these changes, silver and gold have reigned supreme, as the representatives of value, as the media of exchange. The dethronement of each has been attempted in turn, and sometimes the dethronement of both; but always in vain. And we are here to-day, deliberating anew over the problem which comes down to us from Abraham's time: *the weight of the silver* that shall be "current money with the merchant."

MEANY

STEPHEN JOSEPH MEANY, an Irish journalist and patriot, was born about 1830. He early became interested in national politics and was imprisoned in Carrickfergus Castle in 1848, having been a reporter for a Dublin daily newspaper and a writer for a national journal. He came to America, and, having joined the Fenian movement, was one of the "Senators" in O'Mahony's organization. In December, 1866, he was in England, where he was arrested and taken in custody to Ireland. His trial took place in February, 1867; but as the legality of the mode of his arrest was denied by his counsel it was brought before a court of appeal, which confirmed his conviction.

LEGALITY OF ARREST

SPEECH DELIVERED FROM THE DOCK IN DUBLIN, JUNE 21, 1867

MY LORDS,—There are many reasons I could offer why sentence should not—could not—be pronounced upon me according to law, if seven months of absolute solitary imprisonment, and the almost total disuse of speech during that period, had left me energy enough, or even language sufficient to address the court. But yielding obedience to a suggestion coming from a quarter which I am bound to respect, as well, indeed, as in accordance with my own feelings, I avoid everything like speechmaking for outside effect. Besides, the learned counsel who so ably represented me in the court of appeal, and the eminent judges who in that court gave judgment for me, have exhausted all that could be said on the law of the case. Of their arguments and opinions your lordships have judicial knowledge. I need not say that both in interest as in conviction I am in agreement with the constitutional principles laid down by the minority of the judges in that court, and I have sufficient respect for the dignity of the court, sufficient regard to what is due to myself, to concede fully and frankly to the majority a conscientious view of a novel, and, it may be, a difficult question.

But I do not ask too much in asking that before your lordships proceed to pass any sentence you will consider the manner in which the court was divided on that question—to bear in mind that the minority declaring against the legality and validity of the conviction was composed of some of the ablest and most experienced judges of the Irish bench or any bench—to bear in mind that one of these learned judges who had presided at the Commission Court was one of the most emphatic in the Court of Criminal Appeal in declaring against my liability to be tried; and moreover—and he ought to know—that there was not a particle of evidence to sustain the cause set up at the last moment, and relied upon by the Crown, that I was an accessory before the fact to that famous Dublin overt act for which, as an afterthought of the Crown, I was, in fact, tried.

And I ask you further to bear in mind that the affirmance of the conviction was not had on fixed principles of law—for the question was unprecedented—but on a speculative view of the supposititious case, and I may say a strained application of an already overstrained and dangerous doctrine—the doctrine of constructive criminality—the doctrine of making a man, at a distance of three thousand miles or more, legally responsible for the words and acts of others whom he had never seen, and of whom he had never heard, under the fiction or the " supposition," that he was a co-conspirator. The word " supposition " is not mine, my lords; it is the word put forward descriptive of the point by the learned judges presiding at my trial; for I find in the case prepared by these judges for the Court of Criminal Appeal the following paragraph:

" Sufficient evidence was given on the part of the Crown, of acts of members of the said association in Ireland not named in the indictment, in promotion of the several objects aforesaid, and done within the county of the city of Dublin, to sustain some of the overt acts charged in the indictment, supposing them to be the acts of the defendant himself."

Fortified by such facts—with a court so divided and with opinions so expressed—I submit that neither according to act of Parliament, nor in conformity with the practice at common law, nor in any way in pursuance of the principles of that apocryphal abstraction, that magnificent myth, the British constitution, am I amenable to the sentence of this court—or any court in this country.

True, I am in the toils, and it may be vain to discuss how I was brought into them. True, my long and dreary imprisonment—shut away from all converse or association with humanity, in a cell twelve feet by six—the humiliations of prison discipline—the hardships of prison fare—the handcuffs, and the heart-burnings—this court and its surroundings of power and authority—all these are " hard practical facts " which no amount of indignant protests can negative—no denunciation of the wrong refine away; and it may be, as I have said, worse than useless—vain and absurd—to question the right where might is predominant. But the invitation just extended to me by the officer of the court means, if it means anything—if it be not like the rest, a solemn mockery— that there still is left to me the poor privilege of complaint.

And I do complain. I complain that law and justice have been alike violated in my regard—I complain that the much-

belauded attribute "British fair play" has been for me
a nullity—I complain that the pleasant fiction described in
the books as "personal freedom" has had a most unpleasant
illustration in my person—and I furthermore and particularly complain that by the design and contrivance of what
are called "the authorities" I have been brought to this
country, not for trial, but for condemnation—not for justice,
but for judgment.

I will not tire the patience of the court or exhaust my
own strength by going over the history of this painful case—
the kidnapping in London on the mere belief of a police-
constable that I was a Fenian in New York—the illegal transportation to Ireland—the committal for trial on a specific
charge while a special messenger was despatched to New
York to hunt up informers to justify the illegality and the
outrage, and to get a foundation for any charge.

I will not dwell on the "conspicuous absence" of fair
play in the Crown, at the trial, having closed its cases without any reference to the Dublin transaction, but, as an afterthought, suggested by their discovered failure, giving in
evidence the facts and circumstances of that case, and thus
succeeding in making the jury convict me for an offence for
which, up to that moment, the Crown did not intend to charge
me.

I will not say what I think of the mockery of putting
me on trial in the Commission Court in Dublin for alleged
words and acts in New York, and though the evidence was
without notice, and the alleged overt acts without date,
taunting me with not proving an alibi, and sending
that important ingredient to a jury already ripe for a
conviction.

Prove an alibi to-day in respect of meetings held in Clinton

Hall, New York, the allegations relating to which only came to my knowledge yesterday! I will not refer with any bitter feeling to the fact that while the validity of the conviction so obtained was still pending in the Court of Criminal Appeal, the right honorable and noble the Chief Secretary for Ireland declared in the House of Commons that that conviction was the most important one at the Commission—thus prejudicing my case, I will not say willingly, but the observation was at least inopportune and for me unfortunate.

I will not speak my feeling on the fact that in the arguments in the case in the Court for Reserved Cases, the right honorable the Attorney-General appealed to the passions—if such can exist in judges—and not to the judgment of the court, for I gather from the judgment of Mr. Justice O'Hagan that the right honorable gentleman made an earnest appeal "that such crimes" as mine "should not be allowed to go unpunished"—forgetful, I will not say designedly forgetful, that he was addressing the judges of the land, in the highest court of the land, on matters of law, and not speaking to a pliant Dublin jury on a treason trial in the courthouse of Green street.

Before I proceed further, my lords, there is a matter which, as simply personal to myself, I should not mind, but which, as involving high interests to the community, and serious consequences to individuals, demand a special notice. I allude to the system of manufacturing informers. I want to know, if the court can inform me, by what right a responsible officer of the Crown entered my solitary cell at Kilmainham prison on Monday last—unbidden and unexpected—uninvited and undesired. I want to know what justification there was for his coming to insult me in my solitude and in my sorrow—ostensibly informing me that I was to be brought up for sen-

tence on Thursday, but in the same breath adroitly putting
to me the question if I knew any of the men recently arrested near Dungarvan and now in the prison at Kilmainham.   Coming thus, with a detective dexterity, carrying in
one hand a threat of sentence and punishment; in the other
as a counterpoise, and, I suppose, an alternative, a temptation to treachery.   Did he suppose that seven months of imprisonment had so broken my spirit, as well as my health,
that I would be an easy prey to his blandishments?   Did he
dream that the prospect of liberty which newspaper rumor
and semi-official information held out to me was too dear to
be forfeited for a trifling forfeiture of honor?   Did he believe that by an act of secret turpitude I would open my
prison doors only to close them the faster on others who may
or may not have been my friends—or did he imagine he had
found in me a Massey, to be molded and manipulated into
the service of the Crown; or a Corydon, to have cowardice
and cupidity made the incentives to his baseness?

I only wonder how the interview ended as it did; but I
knew I was a prisoner, and self-respect preserved my patience
and secured his safety.   Great, my lords, as have been my
humiliation in prison, hard and heart-breaking as have been
the ordeals through which I have passed since the first of
December last, there was no incident or event of that period
fraught with more pain on the one hand, or more suggestiveness on the other, than this sly and secret attempt at im-
provising an informer.   I can forget the pain in view of the
suggestiveness; and unpleasant as is my position here to-day,
I am almost glad of an opportunity which may end in putting
some check to the spy systems in prisons.

How many men have been won from honor and honesty
by the stealthy visit to the cell is more, of course, than I can

say; how many have had their weakness acted upon, or their weakness fanned into flame by such means, I have no opportunity of knowing; in how many frailty and folly may have blossomed into falsehood it is for those concerned to estimate. There is one thing, however, certain: operating in this way is more degrading to the tempter than to the tempted, and the government owes it to itself to put an end to a course of tactics pursued in its name, which in the results can only bring its humiliation; the public are bound in self-protection to protect the prisoner from the prowling visits of a too-zealous official.

I pass over all these things, my lords, and I ask your attention to the character of the evidence on which alone my conviction was obtained. The evidence of a special, subsidized spy, an infamous and ingrate informer.

In all ages and among all peoples the spy has been held in marked abhorrence. In the amnesties of war there is for him alone no quarter; in the estimate of social life no toleration; his self-abasement excites contempt, not compassion; his patrons despise while they encourage; and they who stoop to enlist the services shrink with disgust from the moral leprosy covering the servitor. Of such was the witness put forward to corroborate the informer, and still not corroborating him. Of such was that phenomenon, a police spy, who declared himself an unwilling witness for the Crown! There was no reason why, in my regard, he should be unwilling— he knew me not previously. I have no desire to speak harshly of Inspector Doyle; he said in presence of the Crown Solicitor, and was not contradicted, that he was compelled by threats to ascend the witness-table; he may have cogent reasons for his reluctance in his conscience. God will judge him.

But how shall I speak of the informer, Mr. John Devany? What language should be employed in describing the character of one who adds to the guilt of perfidy to his associates the crime of perjury to his God?—the man who, eating of your bread, sharing your confidence, and holding, as it were, your very purse-strings, all the time meditates your overthrow and pursues it to its accomplishment? How paint the wretch who, under pretence of agreement in your opinions, worms himself into your secrets only to betray them; and who, upon the same altar with you, pledges his faith and fealty to the same principles, and then sells faith, and fealty, and principles, and you alike, for the unhallowed Judas guerdon? Of such, on his own confession, was that distinguished upholder of the British Crown and government, Mr. Devany. With an effrontery that did not falter, and knew not how to blush, he detailed his own participation in the acts for which he was prosecuting me as a participator. And is the evidence of a man like that—a conviction obtained upon such evidence—any warrant for a sentence depriving me of all that make life desirable or enjoyable?

He was first spy for the Crown—in the pay of the Crown, under the control of the Crown, and think you he had any other object than to do the behests of the Crown?

He was next the traitor spy who had taken that one fatal step from which in this life there is no retrogression—that one plunge in infamy from which there is no receding—that one treachery for which there is no earthly forgiveness; and think you he hesitated about a perjury more or less to secure present pay and future patronage? Here was one to whom existence offers now no prospect save in making his perfidy a profession, and think you he was deterred by conscience from recommending himself to his patrons? Think you that when at a distance of three thousand miles from the scenes he professed to describe, he could lie with impunity and invent without detection, he was particular to a shade in doing his part of a most filthy bargain? It is needless to describe a wretch of that kind—his own actions speak his character. It were superfluous to curse him; his whole existence will be a living, a continuing curse. No necessity to use the burning words of the poet and say,—

" May life's unblessed cup for him
Be drugged with treacheries to the brim."

Every sentiment in his regard of the country he has dishonored and the people he has humbled will be one of horror and hate. Every sigh sent up from the hearts he has crushed and the homes he has made desolate will be mingled with execration on the name of the informer. Every heart-throb in the prison-cells of this land where his victims count time by corroding his thought—every grief that finds utterance from these victims in the quarries of Portland, will go up to heaven freighted with curses on the Nagles, the Devanys, the Masseys, the Gillespies, the Corydons, and the whole host of mercenary miscreants who, faithless to their friends and recreant to their professions, have, paraphrasing the words of Moore, taken their perfidy to heaven, seeking to make an accomplice of their God—wretches who have embalmed their memories in imperishable infamy and given their accursed names to an inglorious immortality. Nor will I speculate on their career in the future. We have it on the best existing authority that a distinguished informer of antiquity, seized with remorse, threw away his blood-money, " went forth and hanged himself." We know that in times within the memory of living men a government actually set the edifying and praiseworthy example of hanging an informer when they had no further use for his valuable services—thus *dropping* his acquaintance with effect. I have no wish for such a fate to any of the informers who have cropped out so luxuriantly in these latter days: a long life and a troubled conscience would perhaps be their correct punishment—though certainly there would be a consistent compensation, a poetic justice, in a termination so exalted to a career so brilliant.

I leave these fellows and turn for a moment to their victims. And I would here, without any reference to my own case, earnestly implore that sympathy with political sufferers should not be merely telescopic in its character, "distance lending enchantment to the view;" and that when your statesmen sentimentalize upon, and your journalists denounce, far-away tyrannies—the horrors of Neapolitan dungeons—the abridgment of personal freedom in Continental countries—the exercise of arbitrary power by irresponsible authority in other lands—they would turn their eyes homeward and examine the treatment and the sufferings of their own political prisoners. I would in all sincerity suggest that humane and well-meaning men who exert themselves for the remission of the death-penalty as a mercy would rather implore that the doom of solitary and silent captivity should be remitted to the more merciful doom of an immediate relief from suffering by immediate execution—the opportunity of an immediate appeal from man's cruelty to God's justice.

I speak strongly on this point because I feel it deeply. I speak not without example. At the Commission at which I was tried there was tried also, and sentenced, a young man named Stowell. I well remember that raw and dreary morning, the twelfth of March, when, handcuffed to Stowell, I was sent from Kilmainham prison to the county jail of Kildare. I well remember our traversing, so handcuffed, from the town of Sallins to the town of Naas, ankle-deep in snow and mud, and I recall now with pain our sad forebodings of that morning. These in part have been fulfilled. Sunday after Sunday I saw poor Stowell at chapel in Naas jail, drooping and dying. One such Sunday—the thirteenth of May—passed, and I saw him no more. On Wednesday, the fifteenth, he was, as they say, mercifully released from prison, but the fiat of mercy had previously gone forth from a higher Power—the political convict simply reached his own home to die with loving eyes watching by his death-bed. On Sunday, the nineteenth of May, he was consigned to another prison home in Glasnevin cemetery. May God have mercy on his soul—may God forgive his persecutors—may God give peace and patience to those who are doomed to follow.

Pardon this digression, my lords; I could not avoid it. Returning to the question why sentence should not be pronounced upon me, I would ask your lordships' attention to the fact showing, even in the estimate of the Crown, the case is not one for sentence.

On the morning of my trial, and before the trial, terms were offered to me by the Crown. The direct proposition was made through my solicitor, through the learned counsel who so ably defended me, through the governor of Kilmainham prison—by all three—that if I pleaded guilty to the indictment I should get off with six months' imprisonment. Knowing the pliancy of Dublin juries in political cases, the offer was doubtless a tempting one. Valuing liberty, it was almost resistless—in view of a possible penal servitude—but having regard to principle I spurned the compromise. I then gave unhesitatingly, as I would now give, the answer, that not for a reduction of the punishment to six hours would I surrender faith; that I need never look, and could never look, wife or children, friends or family in the face if capable of such a selfish cowardice. I could not, to save myself, imperil the safety of others; I could not plead guilty to an indictment in which six others were distinctly charged by name as co-conspirators with me—one of those six since tried, convicted, and sentenced to death; I could not consent to obtain my own pardon at their expense; furnish the Crown with a case in point for future convictions, and become, even though indirectly, worthy to rank with that brazen battalion of venal vagabonds who have made the holy gospel of God the medium of barter for their unholy gain, and obtained access to the inmost heart of their selected victim only to coin its throbbing into the traitor's gold, and traffic on its very life-blood.

Had I been charged simply with my own words and deeds I would have no hesitation in making acknowledgment. I have nothing to repent and nothing to conceal, nothing to retract and nothing to countermand; but in the language of the learned Lord Chief Baron in this case, I could not admit " the preposterous idea of thinking by deputy " any more than I could plead guilty to an indictment which charged others with crime. Further, my lords, I could not acknowledge culpability for the acts and words of others at a distance of three thousand miles—others whom I had never seen, or of whom I had never heard, and with whom I never had had communication. I could not admit that the demoniac atrocities described as Fenian principles by the constabulary spy Talbot ever had my sanction or approval or the sanction or approval of any man in America.

If, my lords, six months' imprisonment was the admeasurement of the law officers of the Crown as an adequate punishment for my alleged offence,—assuming that the court had jurisdiction to try and punish,—then am I now entitled to my discharge, for I have gone through seven months' imprisonment which could not be excelled by demon ingenuity in horror or in hardship—in solitude, in silence, and in suspense. Your lordships will not only render further litigation necessary by passing sentence for the perhaps high crime—but still the untried crime—of refusing to yield obedience to the Crown's proposition for my self-abasement. You will not, I am sure, visit upon my rejection of Mr. Anderson's delicate overture—you will not surely permit the events occurring, unhappily occurring, since my trial, to influence your judgments. And do not, I implore you, accept as a truth, influencing that judgment, Talbot's definition of the objects of Fenianism.

Hear what Devany, the American informer, describes them to be. "The members," he says, "were pledged by word of honor to promote love and harmony among all classes of Irishmen and to labor for the independence of Ireland." Talbot says that in Ireland "the members are bound by oath to seize the property of the country and murder all opposed to them." Can any two principles be more distinct from each other? Could there be a conspiracy for a common object by such antagonistic means? To murder all opposed to your principles may be an effectual way of producing unanimity, but the quality of love and harmony engendered by such a patent process would be extremely equivocal. Mr. Talbot, for the purpose of his evidence, must have borrowed a leaf from the history of the French Revolution, and adopted as singularly telling and appropriate for effect the saying attributed to Robespiere: "Let us cut everybody's throat but our own, and then we are sure to be masters."

No one in America, I venture to affirm, ever heard of such designs in connection with the Fenian Brotherhood. No one in America would countenance such designs. Revolutionists are not ruffians or rapparees. A judge from the bench at Cork, and a noble lord in his place in Parliament, bore testimony to that fact in reference to the late movement; and I ask you, my lords—I would ask the country from this court—for the sake of the character of your countrymen—to believe Devany's interpretation of Fenianism—tainted traitor though he be—rather than believe that the kindly instincts of Irishmen at home and abroad—their generous impulses—their tender sensibilities—all their human affections, in a word—could degenerate into the attributes of the assassin as stated by that hog-in-armor, that crime-creating constable Talbot.

Taking other ground, my lords, I object to any sentence upon me. I stand at this bar a declared citizen of the United States of America, entitled to the protection of such citizenship; and I protest against the right to pass any sentence in any British court for acts done, or words spoken, or alleged to be done or spoken, on American soil, within the shades of the American flag, and under the sanction of American institutions. I protest against the assumption that would in this country limit the right of thought or control the liberty of speech in an assemblage of American citizens in an American city. The United States will doubtless respect and protect her neutrality laws and observe the comity of nations, whatever they may mean in practice, but I protest against the monstrous fiction—the transparent fraud—that would seek in ninety years after the evacuation of New York by the British to bring the people of New York within the vision and venue of a British jury—that in ninety years after the last British bayonet had glistened in an American sunlight, after the last keel of the last English fleet ploughed its last furrow in the Hudson or the Delaware—after ninety years of republican independence—would seek to restore that city of New York and its institutions to the dominion of the Crown and government of Great Britain.

This is the meaning of it, and, disguise it as you may, so will it be interpreted beyond the Atlantic. Not that the people of America care one jot whether S. J. Meany were hanged, drawn, and quartered to-morrow, but that there is a great principle involved. Personally I am of no consequence; politically I represent in this court the adopted citizen of America—for, as the "New York Herald," referring to this case, observed, if the acts done in my regard are justifiable, there is nothing to prevent the extension of the same justice to any other adopted citizen of the States visiting Great Britain. It is therefore in the injustice of the case that the influence lies, and not in the importance of the individual.

Law is called "the perfection of reason." Is there not danger of its being regarded as the very climax of absurdity if fictions of this kind can be turned into realities on the mere caprice of power? As a distinguished English journalist has suggested in reference to the case, "though the law may doubtless be satisfied by the majority in the court of appeal, yet common sense and common law would be widely antagonistic if sentence were to follow a judgment so obtained."

On all grounds, then, I submit, in conclusion, that this is not a case for sentence. Waiving, for the purpose, the international objection, and appealing to British practice itself, I say it is not a fair case for sentence. The professed policy of that practice has ever been to give the benefit of doubt to the prisoner. Judges in their charges to juries have ever theorized on this principle, and surely judges themselves will not refuse to give practical effect to the theory. If ever there was a case which more than another was suggestive of doubt, it is surely one in which so many judges have pronounced against the legality of the trial and the validity of the conviction on which you are about to pass sentence. Each of these judges, be it remembered, held competent in his individuality to administer the criminal law of the country—each of whom, in fact, in his individuality does so administer it unchallenged and unquestioned.

A sentence under such circumstances, be it for a long period or a short, would be wanting in the element of moral effect—the effect of example—which could alone give it value, and which is professedly the aim of all legal punishment. A sentence under such circumstances would be far from reassuring to the public mind as to the " certainties " of the law, and would fail to commend the approval or win the respect of any man " within the realm or without," while to the prisoner, to the sufferer in chief, it would only bring the bitter, and certainly not the repentant feeling, that he suffered in the wrong—that he was the victim of an injustice based on an inference which not even the tyrant's plea of necessity can sustain—namely, that at a particular time he was at a distance of three thousand miles from the place where he then actually stood in bodily presence, and that at that distance he actually thought the thoughts and acted the acts of men unknown to him even by name. It will bring to the prisoner, I repeat, the feeling—the bitter feeling—that he was condemned on an unindicted charge, pressed suddenly into the service, and for a constructive crime which some of the best authorities in the law have declared not to be a crime cognizable in any of your courts.

Let the Crown put forward any supposition they please— indulge in what special pleadings they will—sugar over the bitter pill of constructive conspiracy as they can—to this complexion must come the triangular injustice of this case— the illegal and unconstitutional kidnapping in England—the unfair and invalid trial and conviction in Ireland for the alleged offence in another hemisphere and under another sovereignty. My lords, I have done.